Westview Special Studies in International Relations

The Third World and U.S. Foreign Policy: Cooperation and Conflict in the 1980s
Robert L. Rothstein

The quest for a viable policy toward the Third World will be a dominant theme in U.S. foreign policy throughout this decade. But before any judgments can be made about the range of choices for U.S. policymakers, it is necessary to understand the pressures that are likely to confront developing nations during the 1980s as well as the efforts of these nations as a group to extract greater resources and attention from the international system.

This book considers policy responses that have been and are likely to be implemented by developing nations as they face increasing pressures in the areas of food, energy, trade, and debt — the main areas of interaction within the international system. The author also presents an analysis of how the North-South Dialogue functions and why it has produced so few genuine settlements, providing an additional perspective on whether the pressures on the developing countries might be diminished by successful global negotiations. The conclusions reached by examining policy responses and the Dialogue itself provide the basis for a number of specific policy prescriptions. They also help to establish a framework within which U.S. policy initiatives toward the Third World must be formed. The two concluding chapters discuss these policy choices in detail, carefully analyzing the advantages and disadvantages of persisting in present policies, attempting a genuine global restructuring, choosing to concentrate attention on a few "new influentials" in the Third World, and trying to construct a new approach out of selected elements of the other policy approaches.

Robert L. Rothstein has taught at Columbia University and Johns Hopkins University and has served as a consultant to the Department of State and other national and international organizations. He has also published four books, including *Global Bargaining* and *The Weak in the World of the Strong*.

The Third World and U.S. Foreign Policy: Cooperation and Conflict in the 1980s

Robert L. Rothstein

Westview Press / Boulder, Colorado

Westview Special Studies in International Relations

Copyright © 1981 by Westview Press, Inc.

Published in 1981 in the United States of America by
  Westview Press, Inc.
  5500 Central Avenue
  Boulder, Colorado 80301
  Frederick A. Praeger, Publisher

Library of Congress Cataloging in Publication Data
Rothstein, Robert L.
    The Third World and U.S. foreign policy.
    (Westview special studies in international relations)
    Includes index.
    1. United States—Foreign relations—1945-   . 2. Underdeveloped areas. I. Title.
II. Title: Cooperation and conflict in the 1980s. III. Series.
E840.R65   327.730172'4   81-4628
ISBN 0-86531-206-0   AACR2
ISBN 0-86531-207-9 (pbk.)

Printed and bound in the United States of America

10   9   8   7   6   5   4   3   2

Contents

List of Tables ix
Preface xi

1. The North-South Arena: Background and Context 1

   A Statement of Intent 1
   Prospects for the International System: The Implications
     of Pessimism 6
   The North-South Dialogue: Conflicts of Vision 10

2. The North-South Dialogue 19

   The Dialogue and the Political Economy of Immobility 20
   Should the United States Take the Dialogue Seriously? 31
   The Dialogue: Criteria of Importance 33

3. Food Policy, Foreign Policy, and the International
   Politics of Food 43

   An Agenda of Questions 43
   The Political Economy of Food 48
   The Foreign Policy of Food 66

4. The Developing Countries and the Energy Crisis 89

   Projections and Prescriptions for Energy in the
     Developing Countries 90
   Choosing by Not Choosing: Policy Dilemmas 97
   Energy Policy: Rising Needs and Insufficient Resources 103
   OPEC, the Nonoil Developing Countries, and the Quest for
     a Global Oil Agreement 114
   The Prospects for a Global Oil Agreement 122
   The International Politics of Energy 130

5. The Developing Countries and the Trading System 143

   Perspectives on Trade 143
   North-South Trade: Problems and Prospects 145
   The Lima Goal and Industrial Redeployment 155
   South-South Trade: Hopes, Realities, and Possibilities 162
   East-South Trade 167
   Conclusions: Are Trade Wars Inevitable? 168
   Postscript: The Debt Problem 171

6. The Search for a Policy Framework for the 1980s 189

   The Context of Decision 189
   Scenarios: A Range of Possibilities 201

7. The United States and the Third World in the 1980s:
   Policy and Choice 215

   Choosing Without Clear Choices 215
   Policy as a Holding Action 222
   Global Restructuring 226
   Selectivity and Differentiation 237
   Policy Options: Problems and Prospects 245
   Eclecticism: Viable Strategy of Change or Euphemism
      for Inaction? 247

Index 265

Tables

3.1 Average Annual Growth Rates of Population and Food
Production in Developing Market Economies, by IFPRI
Category and Region, 1960–1975 and 1975–1990 51

3.2 Import Dependence 52

3.3 Net Cereal Deficits in Less Developed Regions 55

3.4 World Food Council Food Priority Countries 71

4.1 Commercial Primary Energy Balances, 1976 and 1990 93

4.2 Preliminary Projections of Non-OPEC Developing
Countries' (NODCs) Energy Balance, 1975–1985 94

4.3 Oil Production in Non-OPEC Developing Countries,
1972 and 1978 99

4.4 Energy Position of Developing Countries and Territories
by Levels of Energy Consumption, Import Dependence,
and Reserves 106

4.5 Investment in the Energy Sector by the Developing
Countries Not Members of OPEC 110

7.1 1977 Trade Figures: U.S. Trade with Non-OPEC
Developing Countries 241

ix

Preface

In the autumn of 1979 I was invited to participate in what was described as a "high-level" State Department seminar on U.S. policy toward the Third World in the 1980s. The discussion, perhaps inevitably, was very inconclusive and unsatisfying, not least because it seemed to lack any kind of analytic focus. In a concluding comment I argued that although we were all aware of the enormous uncertainties confronting the international system and the consequent dangers of any venture into forecasting, we could certainly do better than we had in the discussion (and indeed in much of the literature attempting to cover the same topic) in providing a framework and some guidelines for the attempt to choose effective policies. We needed also to remember that the choice of present policies already implicitly forecast a particular kind of future and that there might be some virtue in becoming more aware of the potential implications of those — and other — choices. It seemed to me that we could make some start toward providing framework and guidelines if we examined the likely impact of several crucial trends in food, energy, trade, and debt on the range of choices that would confront Third World governments and if we also attempted to understand (or speculate about) whether the adverse impact of those trends might be meliorated through agreements negotiated in the North-South Dialogue. At the very least, one would hope that an understanding of the likely evolution of key trends, the probable domestic responses of developing-country governments, and the likely development of the international policymaking process in the Dialogue would provide some sense of the environment of choice for U.S. policymakers. Only then could we sensibly begin to weigh the pros and cons of particular choices. There were a variety of responses to my comments, but in the present context one was especially crucial: Would I prepare a study (with roughly a one-year deadline) attempting to do what I had argued needed to be done? I agreed to try, even though I was fully and painfully aware that a team of experts might be a more appropriate choice. But I also felt that an integrated approach by one analyst might have some advantages over a corporate approach, and I was intrigued by the notion that I at least would learn a great deal. This book is the outcome.

A number of limitations were imperative to make my task manageable. In the first place, this is obviously meant to be a policy-oriented book, that is, a book written for a loosely defined "foreign policy community" and not primarily for a conventional academic audience or for experts in one or another of the functional areas considered. Needless to say, however, I hope that the latter groups will find something of interest in what follows, perhaps especially in terms of the interconnection between issues and the foreign policy implications that emerge. In the second place, I have provided at best a partial picture of the factors that would need to be considered in the policy process. My analysis is largely (though not exclusively) aggregative, I have concentrated primarily on interactions with the external environment and on the implications of external developments for domestic choices, and I have generally avoided discussion of the political, security, and ideological issues that would require consideration in choosing policies toward particular countries. In short, this is a study of the political economy of U.S. relations with the Third World, and not of the totality of our relationship with either individual developing countries or the Third World as a whole. This seems justified or necessary not only because of limitations on my time, knowledge, and resources, but also because the external economic environment—the international political economy—seems likely to become increasingly crucial, especially if that environment becomes more hostile and less charitable and many developing countries become desperate supplicants for very scarce external resources.

I shall discuss the limitations on forecasting in greater detail later and note here only that I hope to diminish some of the difficulties by concentrating on certain structural developments that seem likely to remain important whatever the unexpected—but inevitable—"shocks" that occur. In addition, as the numbers in many of the forecasts that I shall employ will surely be superseded by more recent estimates by the time this book appears, given the exigencies of publication schedules and the constant appearance of many new studies of the issues, I have relied on estimates that seem to reflect the best expert consensus and that have been salient in conditioning perspectives on a particular problem. In any case, newer estimates are not of great significance in this context unless they change or seem to change our understanding of the basic nature of an issue over the medium and long term. I should also emphasize that my concern is not with forecasts as such, but rather with the policy implications that have been or might be drawn from available estimates.

There are extended analyses in this book of particular issues and the specific policy responses that seem to be entailed. Nevertheless, it became increasingly clear to me as my research proceeded that I could make the most important contribution by analyzing, not so much the details of each issue, but rather their interconnections. I mean this not only in the sense that solutions or improvements of one issue are much more likely to be effective if they are taken in conjunction with actions on other issues, but also in the sense that it was necessary constantly to keep in mind the connections between short-run responses and long-run needs and between external pressures and likely or available domestic responses. The attempt to keep these connections in focus obviously creates great complexities; the tendency to ignore them, which occurs frequently in both the policymaking process and the nonscholarly literature on U.S.-Third World relations, virtually guarantees unpleasant surprises and policy responses that are essentially simplistic. Still, the attempt "to see everything whole" (or, more accurately in the present case, to attempt a better approximation of the whole) has consequences of its own, not least that the inordinate difficulties of devising policies that successfully respond to all the interconnections tend to generate great pessimism about the prospects during this decade (and probably thereafter) and to add another layer of complexity and uncertainty to the policy process.

Pessimism about the prospects for the relationship of the United States with either the Third World or individual developing countries is, of course, very much in fashion. And recent events, such as the continued instability of the world oil market as a result of the Iran-Iraq war and growing fears of an imminent world food crisis, serve merely to reinforce prevailing attitudes. As much as I had hoped initially to discover some grounds for optimism or at least to find some set of policies that I was convinced would lead to better outcomes if accepted and implemented, the fact remains that this book is also generally pessimistic. But it is not pessimistic in the undifferentiated or apocalyptic styles that seem to have become fashionable.

In the first place, the picture that emerges is heavily shaded: Even if the limits of the possible do not extend very far, some countries can still be helped by available means, and there may also be opportunities and policies that offer some hope of gradually increasing the possibilities of doing more (see Chapters 6 and 7). In the second place, there is an obvious need to indicate precisely what the legitimate grounds for pessimism (or optimism) are, as only this understanding permits sensible thinking about policy alternatives. Thus I have throughout emphasized certain factors that seem particularly crucial to me and that have not received enough consideration in the literature. For example, I have stressed less short-run problems than the failure or the inability to make long-term investments that might eventually mitigate existing problems; I have emphasized the costs of failing to make the North-South Dialogue work so that domestic development policies and the international policies of the Dialogue are more closely related; and I have persistently criticized the failure to treat seriously enough the need to rethink development strategies in the emerging international environment.

Moreover, I have also emphasized throughout the impact of external trends on the developing countries as well as the impact of their domestic successes and failures on the viability of different international policies. And in the discussion of U.S. policy options I have suggested some things that might be done about these failures, but I have also discussed the options open to the United States if the failures seem likely to persist (because neither side seems either able or willing to make the necessary, but difficult, changes).

As for the additional difficulties generated for the policy process, a familiar problem — incremental policies are insufficient, but preferred alternatives are infeasible — has been exacerbated by two factors: the compelling need to deal with short-run dangers (energy supply interruptions, monetary instability, domestic stagflation, etc.) and the uncertainty, especially in light of the inadequacy of prevailing theories and assumptions, that policies will produce anticipated consequences. The emphasis on the short run leads easily to the charge that, by a political Gresham's Law, the urgent is driving out the "merely" important or, put differently, that the long-run need to integrate the developing countries more effectively into the international system is being sacrificed to the short-run political and economic needs of the developed countries. Yet if the urgent is ignored, it is improbable that the important will ever be dealt with. I cannot resolve the dilemmas created by this conflict, but I have attempted to suggest policies that provide a consistent direction for incrementalism and that keep open the possibility of wider movement. In addition, in what will be a persistent theme in this book, I have tended to criticize sharply global "solutions" or radical restructuring proposals, not because they are undesirable in the abstract, but because they are too politically ambitious, they require more knowledge than we possess, and they deflect attention from lesser actions that are both necessary and feasible. In short, I have emphasized coping strategies and regional and subregional initiatives that seem immediately workable, but that are also designed to keep the system from slipping backward and that may provide building blocks for global agreements if new opportunities for movement should arise.

This book has been written in the tradition of pragmatic liberalism. What this means will, I hope, emerge from the discussion of specific policies; a more extended treatment has been precluded by limitations of space and time. In any case, points of agreement and disagreement with radicalism and conservatism should be readily apparent, and I shall say no more at this point. But I do want to conclude with a brief comment about some of my disagreements with other liberals, if only to avoid unnecessary misunderstandings.

Articles in recent months by liberal advocates suggest that a few concessions in the North-South Dialogue (and the replacement of a few individuals in the U.S. government) will somehow resolve the extraordinary range of problems that trouble the relationship between rich and poor. Similarly, arguments have appeared suggesting that because North and South share a common interest in avoiding disorderly change or share other common or mutual interests, real progress would be possible if only Northern leaders would exhibit "political will." But such views are simplistic and perhaps deserve the conservative taunt of a former secretary of state that they reflect liberal "sentimentality." The key failure in such views is less in what they include than in what they exclude. There is, for example, insufficient concern with the need for a prior agreement to stabilize the world oil market and indifference to the crucial need to deal with the question of how to negotiate agreements with over 150 countries artificially divided into dysfunctional "groups." There is too little understanding that the kind of agreements that might be possible in the existing system will not eliminate underlying structural problems, will not provide benefits commensurate with rising needs, and will help primarily only a limited number of developing countries. There is also insufficient realization that internal changes in the developing countries are not a separate issue but are closely linked to the viability of different international policy approaches. Finally, there is not enough understanding that in the present international environment the suggested Northern trade-off of short-run sacrifices for hypothetical long-term gains is not politically feasible.

Pragmatic liberalism, by contrast, while fully desiring to provide as much help as possible to the developing countries, while recognizing the long-term U.S. interest in establishing a more stable and more just relationship, and while fully accepting the need to grant most developing countries special dispensations from the rules of the emerging system, is necessarily less normative and more empirical. We shall work "up" from problems to agreements that seem feasible and that reflect mutual interests, not "down" from a synthetic global perspective that bears little relationship to the actual play of forces in the international system. Moreover, this perspective does not automatically attribute all the responsibility for action and for the failure to reach agreement on specific issues to the developed countries; stable agreements, insofar as they are possible, will require domestic and external changes by both sides. Finally, pragmatic liberalism (or at least this advocate of the position) is much more doubtful that we have the knowledge and wisdom to solve all of our problems, especially via one or another grand design, and is much more willing to accept the need, *faute de mieux,* to work with partial solutions and to help those we can help (rather than all who need help) until we are clearer about how to do more. Modest solutions are surely insufficient, but they are not irrelevant and they do not foreclose movement toward less modest outcomes; demanding more may only guarantee less. It is not without interest that even some of the Third World's most fervent exponents of the need for massive and immediate global restructuring have finally and belatedly begun to recognize the virtue or the necessity of moderation.

I want to thank especially Mr. Daniel Fendrick of the Office of External Research of the Department of State, which funded the original research project, for providing a sophisticated understanding of what I was trying to do as well as for helpful comments and suggestions on what I finally accomplished. The State Department, of course, bears not the slightest responsibility for any of the views expressed, nor did anyone in the department make any effort to influence or alter my views. The responsibility for what follows is entirely mine.

Robert L. Rothstein

The North-South Arena: Background and Context

A Statement of Intent

Tension and conflict between North and South in the decades ahead are inescapable. In the worst of circumstances, a massive crisis is far from improbable; even in the best of circumstances, persistent but smaller crises—in part caused by efforts to avoid the larger crises—seem increasingly probable. These are judgments that can and should be challenged, for if they are accurate (or, more properly stated, if they are sufficiently credible to induce new patterns of response), they have severe implications for the policies of the United States, and indeed for the policies of both North and South.

There are so many factors affecting the relationship between North and South and so many uncertainties about how or whether these factors will come into play, that any effort to forecast emerging trends and patterns is likely to seem futile or at least foolhardy. The difficulties involve more than the familiar imperfections of forecasts not based on grounded theories, which must employ data of doubtful validity, and which rest on models that necessarily oversimplify the universe of concern. Additional problems are created by the need to rely on precedents, analogies, or extrapolations from the past, all of which implicitly presume strong elements of continuity, when in fact the systemic framework itself is at issue and new goals seem increasingly imperative. Problems are especially severe in the North-South context because it is very difficult for weak and poor states, exposed to rising internal and external pressures, to respond quickly and consistently to signals for change and because a break in continuity is the primary goal of some important actors in the system.[1]

Forecasting under these circumstances obviously cannot guarantee very precise or very reliable roadmaps of the future. Still, the exercise of forecasting is not without its uses, provided the limitations are kept well in mind. At the very least, we should be able to improve over "muddling through" or ad hoc improvisation, in that all concerned—including analysts and policymakers—may be alerted to the long-run implications of present actions or to the likely development of problems that might be averted or diminished by early responses. Above all, I should like to strongly emphasize that forecasting is not or should not be an academic exercise: The point of attempting to look ahead, particularly when the results are bound to be imperfect and in some cases invalidated by our own actions, is to help us order our current priorities and choose our policies more wisely now.[2]

Forecasts may have implications for policy merely by raising the threshold of concern about the likely outcomes of present actions or by early warning of new problems. But they will have a significant effect on policy only if they go beyond this. They must also refer to a time-period that seems relevant to the policymaker (which clearly may vary for different and differently placed policymakers), and they must suggest responses that fall within the means at the policymaker's disposal. Forecasts about the distant future may be important and interesting, but their validity is too uncertain and their connection to present patterns of concern too obscure or complex to elicit much interest from the policymaking community.[3] Conversely, some immediate forecasts may seem very relevant, but they are hardly likely to induce much response if the means of influence are not in the policymaker's hands. Consequently, in the analyses that follow I have concentrated on the next decade or even on the next five years, and I have attempted throughout to emphasize policy actions that are both practical and feasible. And where I have suggested more long-range actions, I have attempted to indicate the connection between such actions and more immediate patterns of concern.

The broad question that will concern us throughout this study is, What should the policy of the United States be toward the developing countries in the 1980s? But how to answer or even how to provide material that is useful in formulating an answer to such a general question is far from self-evident. In the abstract, with the ground shifting so rapidly that neither past experience nor present "theories" (premises, axioms, aphorisms, dogmas, etc.) seem capable of providing reliable guidance, it might seem sensible to begin by positing the goals that the United States intends to seek. Unfortunately, this is less helpful than it might appear, not only because it seeks so many goals, some of which may be in conflict—rapid growth, the direct reduction of poverty, increased equity, respect for human rights, stability, political and strategic support—but also because priorities among the goals cannot be reasonably posited without prior judgments about the nature of the international system within which they must be sought. Even the rough "rules of thumb" that are occasionally offered as guidance for the practitioner (for example, in a period of vulnerability one should concentrate on avoiding dangers or diminishing risks) may be virtually meaningless, if not actively misleading, when applied to specific cases.

The difficulties of discussing U.S. policy toward a very large group of very different countries during a very unsettled period cannot be eliminated, but they can be diminished by concentrating on certain structural factors in the North-South relationship that are likely to persist and by emphasizing a number of trends that will affect (if differentially) the ability of all the developing countries to cope with their problems. I should emphasize that external factors—structures, trends, patterns, prevailing ideas—tend to exert an exceptional degree of influence or pressure on poor countries that are heavily dependent not only on trade and aid but also on the climate of the international system. This is not to argue, of course, that external factors are entirely determinative—they clearly are not—or that they cannot be resisted, parried, or diminished, but rather that such factors are very powerful, that the means available to deal with them are limited, and that there is no easy and cost-free strategy of turning inward. Concentration on such external factors has costs of its own, as it cannot by its nature provide reliable forecasts of individual decisions. Nevertheless, an analysis of the structure of the North-South Dialogue and of the external trends that are likely to influence the choices of the countries within the Dialogue has virtues of its own: It provides the framework and setting for particular decisions, it may suggest the connections and the means by which long-term goals can be linked to short-term actions, and it should at least demonstrate why certain factors need to be taken into account in choosing policies.

I shall begin in the next chapter with an analysis of how the North-South Dialogue—by which I mean the North-South bargaining relationship within most of the major international institutions—operates and why its results have been so unsatisfactory. The latter issue requires some understanding of the bargaining process itself as well as some sense of how the Dialogue is perceived by developing-country governments "at home," that is, by ministers and officials in the capital, as distinct from representatives in Geneva and New York. Because the Dialogue will surely persist and remain an important part of the North-South relationship, this analysis should provide evidence and insight about one crucial component of the framework of decision. Finally, as I am primarily concerned with U.S. policy, I shall conclude this chapter with a brief discussion of whether and why the state of the Dialogue is a matter of concern to the United States and the other developed countries.

If Chapter 2 is designed to indicate how North and South manage their relationship, Chapters 3, 4, and 5 will attempt to indicate how trends in food, energy, and trade (and, very briefly, debt) may come to affect the choices that the developing countries, individually and jointly, have in the 1980s and the strategies that they may adopt in the Dialogue. The relationship between the material in Chapter 2 and the material in Chapters 3, 4, and 5 could be stated in another fashion: Chapter 2 concentrates on the efforts of the developing countries to establish and maintain a unified international bargaining strategy; the ensuing chapters consider some of the crucial issues that will be included in that strategy, but perhaps more critically the initial impact of trends in food, energy, and trade will fall directly on the governments themselves. Whether a solution to these pressures is sought through unilateral action (for example, special arrangements with a developed country), through unified group pressure, or through some mix of the two (as seems most likely) may determine the substance and significance of the Dialogue in the 1980s and after. At any rate, I shall examine in each chapter what the experts foresee and what they prescribe, but I shall be most concerned with two separate, but connected, policy questions. The first is whether the developing countries are implementing agreed policies and what might be done in the short run to increase the chances that they will do so. The second question, broader in intent, asks what the implications would be for U.S. policy toward the Third World if a significant number of developing countries fail to implement successful policies in food, energy, and trade and become areas of great potential instability. I shall thus move in each chapter from an analysis of the specifics of each issue to an analysis of how the issue might intersect with the more general concerns of foreign policy and international politics.

Taken by themselves, the studies of food, energy, and trade may generate a number of useful, if narrow, policy insights. Taken together, however, they are potentially even more useful for providing a more general perspective on the relationship between the developing countries and the international environment in the 1980s. Common patterns and common deficiencies that cross all of the issues and that are frequently obscured by concentration on a single issue thus help to establish the wider context within which policy choices must be made. These commonalities will be discussed in a number of places, but especially at the end of Chapter 5. As a result, what should emerge from Chapters 2, 3, 4, and 5 is some sense of the structural and intellectual dynamics of the existing Dialogue, some judgments about the stresses and strains that are likely to affect the operation of the North-South system in the 1980s, and some speculations about how effectively the South is likely to respond to these developments. These analyses will provide the essential background for the discussion of the policy choices that confront the government of the United States.

Chapters 6 and 7 will move up one level of analysis. Rather than discussing policy options, in say, food and energy, I shall deal with the broader question of what policy stance the United States should or can adopt toward a very large group of extremely diverse countries in a very difficult environment of decision. Before discussing the range of policy alternatives, Chapter 6 will consider a number of other issues that might affect the process of choice (for example, the significance of declining U.S. power and of changing U.S. goals in the Third World) and it will analyze a few scenarios that suggest possible outcomes of prevailing trends. The material in this chapter consequently will provide further comment on the factors that will affect the setting within which the policy alternatives discussed in Chapter 7 must be assessed and chosen. The analysis of the policy alternatives themselves seems to lead to a particular choice, but it should be emphasized that the discussion of each policy attempts to be even-handed. I discuss advantages and disadvantages of each choice and make a special effort to indicate, within each choice, the policies most likely to keep open the possibility of movement toward a more stable (and thus more equitable) international order.

Implementation will be a concern throughout this study. I shall be interested in what should be done as well as in what is not being done. This is a crucial issue, for while there is wide agreement in some areas on what the developing countries should be doing, there is far less knowledge about what governments are actually doing, because of gaps in the collection of data, serious time lags before the data is available, or an unwillingness to permit the data to be released.[4] The importance of these deficiencies is self-evident, for they have a significant effect on the amounts of resources needed to achieve desired ends, on judgments about the best political and economic strategies to assure effective implementation of policies and on the need to assess the implications for individual countries and the system as a whole of the failure to implement policies successfully.

In addition, there is a persistent tendency in the discussion of issues on the North-South agenda to ignore the problem of implementation. As successful implementation requires effective linkage between three separate and only partially overlapping political "games" (intragroup and intergroup bargaining and bargaining in the context of application), each with different actors, needs, and rules, explicit concern with the issue is imperative. Indeed, understanding why there is so little concern with implementation is illuminating in and of itself and is perhaps a necessary preface to establishing the means by which policies that are made within one political game will be implemented — will achieve their intended effects — in another. Unfortunately, although implementation will surely become an even more crucial issue in a period of slow growth and very scarce resources, I cannot discuss the issue in any detail here; it requires a study of its own. Still, I hope that the comments in Chapters 3 and 4 are at least suggestive. Moreover, it can be useful merely to emphasize how important and how neglected this issue is.

Two other issues require a brief comment in this chapter. The first concerns certain dominant perceptions of the prospects for the international system in this decade. The second concerns the different conceptual frameworks that operate in the North-South arena. Both issues are important, if elusive, because they help to determine the climate of debate — what gets taken for granted or what "stands to reason," even if it should not.

Prospects for the International System: The Implications of Pessimism

Growing interdependence within the world economy, as well as the increasing role of government in the determination of national economic welfare, has generated two widely shared analytic propositions: Nations can no longer choose policies in isolation from the choices made by other nations, and all crises must henceforth be systemic.[5] These propositions seem clearly to imply the need for more central control or management of the international economy. As a result many studies propound the need for new or strengthened international institutions in trade, natural resources, monetary affairs, industrial development, food, energy, the weather, the oceans, and shipping.[6] In the abstract, the case is strong, for economic interdependence *might* well increase in the future, and the existing institutional structure is weak, if not crumbling, and was designed for a different kind of international order. From the perspective of the practitioner, however, a different interpretation of needs and possibilities seems to prevail or at least seems more realistic.

There is a corollary to the theory of the "second-best" that may illuminate the practitioner's dilemma.[7] The corollary states that when market imperfections exist, the elimination or reduction of only one or a few imperfections is not likely to improve welfare as long as the other imperfections or distortions persist; only the removal of all the imperfections guarantees the increased welfare promised by conventional trade theory. Removal of all the imperfections, however, may be too costly in time and resources, not least because the policymaker cannot control the actions of external policymakers. Choice of second-best policies, which may introduce new distortions to counter the old distortions, thus seems imperative. In this sense, the correct second-best response to interdependence is not necessarily to seek optimal solutions to the problems it engenders, which would imply some sacrifices of national control and increased efforts at multilateral cooperation, but rather to increase efforts to limit the effects and growth of interdependence and to increase national control over economic resources and activities.

I should emphasize that second-best policies are likely to seem (relatively) more attractive to powerful and large countries that control enough of their environment to insure continued—if lesser—prosperity. The implications are considerably different for poor and small countries, for whom cooperative solutions may be a sensible choice. Second-best choices by the rich may be disastrous for the poor, unless the poor have been prudent enough to develop some protection against adverse external developments. But it should be noted that the developing countries do not really desire first-best policies (which would imply an open economy in which they might not be able to compete effectively), but second-best policies deliberately biased to protect their interests.

The issue can be restated from a more familiar perspective. Governments have acquired more responsibility for national economic welfare, but their ability to perform effectively has been weakened because of a whole range of relevant external factors they cannot control. In the short run, until the costs of national parochialism become evident to all, they can only respond by seeking control of what is within their means and insulation against external challenges. Increased dependence, implicit in rising levels of interdependence, thus tends primarily to generate insecurity, especially in a context of diminished prosperity, fear for the future, and rising levels of vulnerability. This tendency is exacerbated by the extraordinary uncertainties engendered by the failure of the conventional wisdom to produce anticipated consequences, by the difficulties of the transition to a new energy base, and by the rise and persistence of unprecedented levels of inflation. The danger is not merely the rise of the "new protectionism," a slowing of the pace of adjustment to changes in comparative advantage, or an increased emphasis on some of the more costly forms of self-reliance by both the developed and the developing countries. There is the additional danger that a renewed emphasis on economic security, even at the expense of economic welfare, may not only induce reactions in kind—the familiar perils of a "beggar thy neighbor" world—but may also appear to justify a perception of the future (more closed, more state-centered, less stable, less prosperous) that makes present sacrifices to avert future dangers seem futile or even quixotic.[8]

The obvious limit to increased fragmentation and disorder is self-interest. The dangers of an increasingly closed system are widely recognized, as is well reflected in "standstill" agreements, efforts to control non-tariff barriers, pledges (if not performances) to increase aid to the developing countries, and a nonstop parade of meetings that testifies to the desire to keep the system from premature closure and breakdown—or, more narrowly, efforts to keep from going backwards, if going forward seems too difficult.[9] Perhaps teetering on the brink is all that one can rightfully expect, for even those who want to do more to keep the system open recognize the difficulties and even those who want to retreat into neo-isolationism or a closed system recognize the costs.

What the practitioner thus sees as the limits of the possible in current circumstances—the defense of existing gains, "safety nets" to prevent a systemic disaster, perhaps incremental movements forward—is deemed insufficient by analysts and spokesmen for the South; but what the latter perceive as necessary—global restructuring, massive increases in aid, a system biased toward the needs of the developing countries—seems utopian or unrealistic from the practitioner's perspective. Both are right, given initial premises, but the resulting stalemate helps to generate a great deal of pessimism about the likelihood of significant progress in resolving North-South problems. Pessimism about North-South issues is of course also sharply exacerbated by the more general forecasts of likely trends in this decade: slower growth rates, more inwardness, more concern with short-run questions of economic and military security, an unresolved energy crisis, and persisting problems of effective governance. Indeed, pessimism is so much in fashion that only a very long-range perspective permits a degree of optimism about prospects for the international system.[10] Much of the short-term pessimism seems amply justified, as we shall see in Chapters 3, 4, and 5, but the most interesting question in the present context concerns the impact that pervasive pessimism may have in structuring perceptions of what can or cannot be done.

The most obvious consequence is the tendency to encourage a self-fulfilling prophecy. The defensive and protective measures taken to avert a potential crisis or even to maintain existing gains might "succeed" only at the cost of engendering successive smaller crises that are cumulatively disastrous. This is true for both North and South, as each choice of a more narrow, protective set of policies not only encourages similar action elsewhere but also makes it progressively more difficult to change course. Beyond this, the foreshortening of vision implicit in pessimistic judgments may sharply diminish whatever chance there is to deal with the systemic dimensions of the present crisis. The tendency among politicians to believe, as Sir Harold Wilson once noted, that "a week is a long time in politics," may seem even more justified, thus making North-South settlements more doubtful, as only a long-range view by the North would permit genuine progress.

The solution to these problems cannot be naive optimism or wishful thinking that things cannot be as bad as they seem or that something or other will turn up to facilitate salvation.[11] Pessimism seems too well grounded in prevailing external conditions as well as in the difficult and painful nature of the choices confronting the developing countries in food, energy, trade, and the domestic socioeconomic structure. What seems minimally necessary is a recognition by both sides that we confront a decade of limited, difficult, and uncertain choices and that prevailing conditions make it unlikely that the best way to seek mutually beneficial outcomes is by demanding radical reforms or presumably optimum solutions.[12] In addition, we need to understand that pessimism about future prospects hardly means that better or worse choices cannot be made. All choices may be limited and uncertain, but even within this context some choices seem more sensible than others—less costly, more likely to keep open the possibility of cooperative agreements—and some countries and some areas within both North and South may still do reasonably well and may still be significantly helped by the kind of measures that do seem feasible. In short, although the internal and external problems confronting North and South may provide a strong argument against the quest for the "best" solutions—the best being the enemy of the good in this case—pessimism need not and should not be grounds for immobility or desperation—yet. The next five chapters provide the grounds for these judgments.

One last comment may be appropriate. If conditions continue to deteriorate in the international system, if insecurity, increased conflict, and diminishing resource availabilities become more prevalent, the United States and the other countries in the system will be required to make explicit, but uncertain, choices about proper courses of action in the North-South arena. There will be no possibility of drifting along or "muddling through" in the hope that growth and progress will smooth out the difficulties of integrating the South into the international economic and political systems. This may raise some ideological difficulties for both liberals and conservatives, as both have been implicitly optimistic about future prospects for the South—although of course on the basis of some very different policy premises. But a more important difficulty may be that these choices, both domestic and international, must be made through the political process. The political process at both levels has obviously been significantly weakened by a variety of developments—the energy crisis, slower growth, inflation, the rise of single-issue constituencies, the rapidity and uncertainty of change, and the asymmetry between the demands of interdependence and the response capacity of existing institutions at both national and international levels. I cannot discuss the domestic dimension of these difficulties here, but I shall be very concerned with the international dimension in Chapters 2, 6, and 7. I note this matter only to emphasize from the very beginning the need to keep in mind that there is an underlying question in the North-South arena about how to make international policy or what can be expected from the international policy process that has been neither fully analyzed nor effectively understood.

The North-South Dialogue: Conflicts of Vision

Most of the conflicts within the North-South Dialogue seem to reflect sharp disagreements about specific proposals for change in a variety of areas — trade, commodities, debt, shipping, and so forth. There is also, however, an underlying disagreement about the responsibility for present problems and the kind of policy responses that these problems must or can entail. This additional layer of conflict, which cuts across all the issues, is worth some comment here, not only because it makes the quest for mutually satisfactory agreements more difficult but also because it is frequently obscured by the debate on specific issues. Perhaps the central point is that agreements, should they be achieved, may be intrinsically unstable when each side interprets the meaning of an agreement within a different intellectual framework. Conflicts over the proper framework of interpretation probably cannot be resolved, although they may diminish in force with the passage of time, but it is important to understand what is at issue. Understanding may generate more realism about what can be and has been achieved in specific agreements, and it might even encourage some consideration of how to proceed when there is only agreement to disagree on criteria of interpretation.

Both sides have created considerable confusion about the goals they seek within the Dialogue. The developed countries, particularly the United States, have failed to make clear what relationship they intend between advocacy of a basic human needs strategy and the more conventional trade and aid measures under discussion in the Dialogue. The potential inconsistencies between a basic needs strategy that emphasizes equity, the direct reduction of poverty, agricultural reform, and a "bicycle culture" and a rapid-growth, rapid-industrialization, export-oriented strategy that may increase inequities within developing countries, between developing countries, and between developing and developed countries are readily apparent. The inconsistencies are neither inevitable nor necessarily disabling, provided that careful distinctions are made between different countries and different priorities at various stages of development. But the failure to clarify these issues has allowed suspicions to flourish in the Third World that the basic needs approach is a means of avoiding concessions in the Dialogue and to keep the Third World from industrializing rapidly and thus competing effectively.[13] These suspicions have been exacerbated by the rise in protectionism against Third World exports (via "voluntary export restraints" and the like) and by vacillation and ineptitude in the presentation of the case for basic needs. The result has been great uncertainty about meanings and intentions, increasing mistrust, and an international development strategy that merely adds together all the confusions.

The goals of the developing countries have created both strategic and tactical problems for the developed countries. In general, the developing countries have demanded two kinds of changes in the international system: first, the reduction of various kinds of externally induced instabilities and "shocks" and, second, a number of measures to transfer increased resources quickly and automatically. These are not inherently unreasonable goals, although they raise a number of important questions that have not been adequately analyzed: for example, who will benefit from particular proposals, what should be done about inconsistencies between some goals, and how practical are some of the more extreme proposals?[14]

More serious problems are created by the issue of how (and how quickly) the goals are to be achieved. The developing countries perceive every issue in terms of their own development needs (thus sometimes ignoring short-run systemic needs), they see the international system as primarily responsible for their problems, they perceive an immediate need for massive government intervention to influence or manage (or even control, where possible) the operation of the international economic system for purposes of development, and they seek increased power to implement these purposes quickly.[15] From their perspective, pleas to understand the implications of interdependence seem fraudulent unless they are accompanied by a commitment to global restructuring—the aim of which will be, as noted, to provide protection against external "shocks" and to provide them with a greater share of existing wealth or future gains.[16] The developed countries, conversely, perceive a system that needs to pursue many goals (not only development), they reject the notion that the international system is solely responsible either for creating or removing underdevelopment, they doubt the need for or the effectiveness of global governance in many areas of concern, and they see the current crisis as at least partially cyclical or, if structural, as requiring more moderate kinds of restructuring.[17] There is no obvious meeting ground between such divergent views of the world, which implies pervasive mistrust within the negotiating process and instability for any agreements that it manages to produce.

A practical point about the goals of the developing countries should also be noted. Implementation of these goals would require the developed countries to sacrifice some present benefits, to weigh future benefits more heavily, and to accept some notion of an international community with an explicit principle of distributional justice.[18] By contrast, the developing countries assert their nationalism, their concern for sovereignty, and their desire for increased self-reliance. The need for more independence for the developing countries — before they can begin to worry very much about the requirements of interdependence — and for more commitment to global community goals by the developed countries might be reconciled over time; but in the meantime the inconsistency appears stark and the absence of sufficient emphasis on mutual benefits and systemic stability is at least politically imprudent. And, as I shall argue in Chapter 7, the tendency of the developing countries (and many advocates of one or another "global bargain") to ask the developed countries to exchange short-run sacrifices for hypothetical long-run benefits may be particularly inappropriate or futile in an international system marked by slow growth and rising insecurity.

One might reasonably ask whether the developing countries "really" mean what they say. Perhaps their demands are essentially rhetorical or are merely negotiating tactics. Clearly, their demands are sometimes confused, frequently shifting, and obviously affected by the play of external events. In any case, poor and weak countries, desperately in need of immediate external help, can hardly be expected to follow a "pure" strategy of all or nothing: Commitment to the goals of the New International Economic Order (NIEO) has not implied and cannot imply the rejection of whatever can be gotten at the moment. But in the same sense, the acceptance of today's offer hardly means that the quest for the NIEO has been forsaken. Thus the answer to the question of whether the developing countries really want immediate gains or whether only the achievement of the NIEO (if that) will diminish continually rising demands is that they want both.

This response appears to make genuine negotiations possible, if both sides could agree to disagree about ultimate ends and to concentrate on very critical and perhaps more malleable short-run issues. This is surely unsatisfactory to both sides, but it is likely to yield more than the exchange of manifestos has yet produced, and it is far from clear that this is a necessarily inferior method, practically or intellectually, of achieving wider agreement over time.[19] But here we intersect with the structural and procedural dynamics of the negotiating system itself. What is necessary in an environment of conflict, distrust, uncertainty, and pessimism is a negotiating system that does not transform long-run goals into rigid short-run goals and that provides some resting points that permit adjustment and adaptation before new demands emerge. What we have, however, is a negotiating system that reinforces and exaggerates the immobility generated by intellectual and conceptual conflict and confusion.

I shall analyze this bargaining system in the next chapter. It would be easier to do so if existing concepts provided reliable guidance or explanation, but they do not. As I have noted elsewhere, the precepts of conventional bargaining theory, the ideas that might be extracted from the theory of collective goods, a variety of notions about the role of international organizations in a period of rapid change or about the role of the secretaries-general and the staffs of such organizations, and even the more general framework provided by traditional Realist doctrines or the newer proposals of interdependence have all provided decidedly inadequate explanations of behavior in the North-South arena.[20] It is of course difficult to separate such failures from the more general failure of existing concepts to provide much guidance in understanding any of the major problems within the international system. Still, it would be useful if we could discover a consistent pattern across the conceptual failures in the North-South arena, if only in the hope that the pattern would at least suggest directions for new approaches. Unfortunately, although one might sense that there is something more to the issue, the most obvious patterns are hardly more than commonplaces. It is clear, for example, that the dominant concepts are implicitly conservative and oriented toward stability and gradual change; that they take the existing framework and rules of the game for granted; and that, by extrapolating from Western experience, they may obscure differences in the context of application and imply too much linearity and continuity of experience (thus undervaluing concepts that emphasize less palatable outcomes such as disorder, the absence of inevitable progress for all, and perhaps the need to take some degree of "delinking" more seriously).[21]

Perhaps part of the difficulty in coming to terms conceptually with the North-South arena reflects certain unique elements in the South's challenge. In the first place, a structural challenge to the existing system by a large group of poor and weak states, even if the challenge frequently seems ambivalent because of the very weakness of its proponents, has few precedents. Historically, of course, most such challenges have come from the rise of "new" great powers and have been legitimized and institutionalized only after a major war. In the second place, this challenge *might* have the potential of destabilizing the entire international system, despite the deficiencies of the challengers in terms of conventional indices of power. The potential for instability might emerge from the "OPEC connection," if OPEC (Organization of Petroleum Exporting Countries) became sufficiently radicalized, or perhaps from a genuinely unified assault on the international monetary system (for example, joint defaults), but neither these actions nor more irrational strategies (such as terrorism or nuclear proliferation) seem very probable or, if undertaken, effective. What seems more plausible is a variation on the proposition that a system is as strong as its weakest link or that the most unstable subsystem may come to define systemic stability: As interdependence grows, as the developing countries become more important economically to the developed countries, and as (or if) conditions deteriorate, a marginal power to destabilize may become crucial in a period of precarious stability. In the third place, the challenge to the existing order is obviously concerned with power (who is to decide), but it also has a uniquely moral dimension: Questions of distribution, of fairness, and of equity are perhaps equally significant. And there is no obvious mechanism by which such conflicts can be resolved in an international system dominated by a multiplicity of conflicting values and interests.

This suggests that the best way to proceed is to attempt to work "up" from problems to concepts and theories rather than to try to impose an existing framework on particular problems.[22] The preceding argument also suggests that the North-South Dialogue cannot be adequately understood in its own terms — as could, say, a debate about the Common Fund for buffer stocks or a legally binding code of conduct for the transfer of technology. In this sense the Dialogue might be better understood as part of a field of forces with several levels of interaction and several dimensions of time. At the most basic level, countries obviously determine policies toward the Dialogue in terms of their own interests and their own discount rates on the future. At a second level, these policies are amalgamated into unified group negotiating positions. At another level — the tip of the pyramid — the groups negotiate to establish international policy. But I should emphasize that policy does not always flow upward, as the issues are sometimes defined at the top or at the group level, suggesting a circular flow rather than a pyramid. In addition, bilateral or regional relationships at the first level, and occasionally at the second level, may be more important than anything that happens in the Dialogue itself. This implies that the Dialogue is primarily a residual of what happens at the other levels (or what does not happen when some developing countries simply instruct their delegations to support group policies).

Understanding the forces in play is obviously the first requisite of policy. In this sense, the primary virtue of this picture of the complexities of the Dialogue may well be that it emphasizes the important linkages between what happens in Geneva and New York and what happens in New Delhi and Lagos. The central point that should be kept in mind throughout the ensuing chapters is that the impact of external trends — in food, energy, and trade, but also in inflation, recession, and monetary instability — is felt first and most decisively at the national level. The initial reaction is thus most likely to reflect the coping needs of poor and weak governments. Nevertheless, genuine solutions to these external problems are likely to require concerted international action, which will in turn be more or less successful to the degree that national responses have been timely and effective. The circularity or linkage of this process is crucial but too often forgotten within both the Dialogue and national discussions of development policy, as well as within bilateral North-South negotiations. I have tried to emphasize these linkages throughout and to indicate what they imply for U.S. policy choices.

Notes

1. Daniel Bell has argued that "forecasting is possible only where one can assume a high degree of rationality on the part of men who influence events—the recognition of costs and constraints, the common acceptance or definition of the rules of the game, the agreement to follow the rules, the willingness to be consistent." But rationality in this sense may be unacceptable to countries that want to change the rules and that may feel the need to threaten to act irrationally to call attention to their demands. See Daniel Bell, *The Coming of Post-Industrial Society—A Venture in Social Forecasting* (New York: Basic Books, 1973), p. 4.

2. For a more extensive treatment of this issue, see Robert L. Rothstein, *Planning, Prediction, and Policymaking in Foreign Affairs* (Boston: Little, Brown, 1972).

3. This is not, of course, meant to imply that long-range forecasts are useless. I mean only to suggest that they fall outside the more immediate policy concerns of this study.

4. I should emphasize that the inordinate difficulty of acquiring information on implementation sharply limits the judgments that can be made. I have had to rely, in large part, on interviews and extrapolations from past performance—neither greatly reliable—and on scattered comments in a number of recent studies by international institutions.

5. For one statement of these views, see Daniel Bell, "The Future World Disorder: The Structural Context of Crises," *Foreign Policy*, no. 27 (Summer 1977):109–135.

6. For an extreme statement of the need for new institutions, see Jan Tinbergen, *RIO: Reshaping the International Order* (New York: E.P. Dutton, 1976). The studies prepared for the most recent United Nations Industrial Organization (UNIDO) Conference in New Delhi (January–February 1980) are also instructive, for they demand an extraordinary number of new institutions and funds to facilitate and direct industrial redeployment to the developing countries.

7. On the theory of the second-best, see Ezra J. Mishan, "Second Thoughts on Second Best," *Oxford Economic Papers* (October 1962).

8. For an interesting speculation about a more state-centered and less stable future international system, see Klaus Knorr, "Economic Interdependence and National Security," in Klaus Knorr and Frank Trager, eds., *Economic Issues and National Security* (Lawrence, Kansas: Regents Press of Kansas, 1977), pp. 1–18. I do not mean to suggest that there are no optimists among futurists. For example, Herman Kahn, William Brown, and Leon Martel, in *The Next 200 Years—A Scenario for America and the World* (New York: William Morrow, 1976), are very optimistic, seeing a surplus of energy, resources, and commodities by 1985 and continuing high growth for the LDCs. But their views are so long-range, their understanding of the less developed countries (LDCs) so limited, and their indifference to policy ques-

tions so pervasive that their work is essentially irrelevant — a statement of faith masquerading as serious analysis.

9. From this perspective, the sharp criticism of proposals for "organized free trade" and the like may be overstated. Such proposals might be perceived as efforts to keep from going backward even faster and to do so by multilaterally agreed rather than unilateral restraints. In any case, as some degree of restraint by national means is inevitable in this period, the practical issue centers on whether additional controls and limits can be imposed on unilateral decisions — a point to which I shall return in Chapter 7.

10. Pessimistic forecasts may be overstated because of the policy responses they induce and because of compensating benefits that may occur in some cases (for example, slower growth rates cut energy consumption). It seems generally true that it is more prudent to take seriously pessimistic hypotheses about emerging trends rather than optimistic ones, even if the latter seem equally well (or badly) grounded. We may be able to avert the worst outcomes, or at least diminish their force, if we are more aware of their likelihood and their consequences. (In this sense pessimistic forecasts *might* lead to more beneficial outcomes than optimistic forecasts that generate complacency.) Conversely, if better outcomes do result, we probably can deal with them by conventional responses, and the costs of miscalculating are also probably less. I should also note that optimistic forecasts may be biased because some such forecasts simply assume favorable trends in other areas, because optimism is a political necessity for some institutional forecasters, because some take for granted that governments will respond to trends adequately, and because what seems optimistic to some (a return to growth paths of the 1960s) may seem very insufficient to others — especially those concerned with distributional issues.

11. It might seem unnecessary to make so obvious a point, except that some developing countries seem to act as if wishful thinking (for example, that the developed countries or OPEC will somehow intervene to provide external salvation) will suffice. Of course, the choices confronting most of the nonoil LDCs are so unpalatable that facing reality may be very painful.

12. I say "presumably" optimum because feasibility is not the only criticism that can be made of some of the more radical proposals for change: It is also not clear that some of these proposals would achieve their stated aims or that we know enough to operate effectively the kind of system that is envisaged. I shall discuss this in more detail in Chapter 7.

13. For a recent statement of this view, see Ajit Singh, "The 'Basic Needs' Approach to Development vs. the New International Economic Order: The Significance of Third World Industrialization," *World Development*, Vol. 7, no. 6 (June 1979):587.

14. Equity issues have become increasingly prominent in criticisms of conventional export-oriented development strategies (although there is also some evidence that equity has increased most rapidly in the countries that have chosen an open strategy), but they have also begun to surface in regard to the NIEO itself. I criticized the commodity proposals from this perspective in Robert L. Rothstein, *Global Bargaining: UNCTAD and the Quest for a New International Economic Order* (Princeton, N.J.: Princeton University Press, 1979), and Johan Galtung has recently argued

that the whole NIEO is internally regressive. See his "What Is A Strategy?" *IFDA Dossier*, no. 6 (April 1979):22. However, the equity issue is extremely complex, for it involves judgments about time preferences, about the availability of alternative strategies, and about the commitment and capacity of LDC governments. Moreover, the issue cannot be resolved by simply adding on a basic needs approach to a conventional growth strategy; some difficult choices and trade-offs must be carefully considered.

15. Liberal economists frequently argue that the interventionist policies that the LDCs favor in order to protect themselves against external change and to receive larger transfers of resources will slow the growth rate by increasing inefficiencies, which, in turn, will diminish the opportunity to achieve the initial goals. See, for example, Melvyn B. Krauss, *The New Protectionism: The Welfare State and International Trade* (New York: New York University Press, 1978). But this argument, even if generally true, is also oversimplified, for it ignores the question of who benefits from nonintervention and from increased growth rates — that is, efficiency is not the only value at stake. Moreover, although redistributions (both domestically and internationally) may be initially inefficient, over a longer period they may be both efficient and equitable.

16. This interpretation of developing-country views is drawn from many sources, but the reader interested in a single source reflecting most of these views might read the United Nations Conference on Trade and Development (UNCTAD) position paper for the discussions on a New International Development Strategy. See "The Conceptual Framework for a New International Development Strategy," *Trade and Development*, no. 1 (Spring 1979):83–93.

17. These comments reflect my own judgment about the position of most of the developed countries. They represent not a summary of any particular document, but rather a personal interpretation of how the developed countries — except for the Nordics and the Dutch — have responded to the propositions of the LDCs.

18. Agreeing on a principle of justice is probably impossible, as there is no consensus on what the proper criterion should be. For example, how can there be agreement on what is fair in current circumstances? Even an agreement to facilitate equal opportunity (by preferences and other special treatment) does not help much when the results are inequitable and the losers demand not equal opportunity but equal results. The most that one can expect, at the moment anyway, is agreement on some kind of nominal conception of justice: Outcomes are considered just when they result from a bargaining process into which all enter freely and on which all agree. Beyond this, there has been some progress in explicitly recognizing the need to provide continuing special treatment for the least developed countries.

19. This again raises the question of how policy can or should be made in the international system. Or, put another way, how poor and weak states can or should seek to receive a larger share of the "global product" in a particularly difficult environment and in a struggle with stronger and richer countries that have major problems of their own.

20. See Rothstein, *Global Bargaining*, pp. 242–247. The same point about the failure of prevailing concepts can be made about the dominant doctrines of economic development. For one critique, see Jeffrey B. Nugent and Pan A. Yotopoulos, "What Has Orthodox Development Economics Learned from Recent

Experience?" *World Development,* Vol. 7, no. 6 (June 1979):541–544.

21. I should note also that conceptual analysis from the side of the South does not fare much better. Dependency "theory," which is used by many developing-country elites to explain virtually everything, is hardly satisfactory, if only because those countries that are most dependent are not necessarily worst off (and some states that have few external ties are very badly off) and because the benefits of trade among the developed countries are much greater than the benefits that the latter gain from North-South trade. In addition, attempts to use the NIEO as a conceptual basis for restructuring the international system founder because so many proposals are unworkable, analytically weak, and inequitable to some developing countries.

22. This judgment reflects a bias of my own, as I have previously argued that *both* theory and practice might benefit if the theorist is immersed in practical problems. For example, direct involvement in practical work during World Wars I and II was very fruitful theoretically as well as useful; there is also some evidence that innovative thinking within a discipline may be more likely to emerge from work in a practical setting. For the argument in detail, see Rothstein, *Planning, Prediction, and Policymaking in Foreign Affairs,* pp. 119–122.

2
The North-South Dialogue

The North-South Dialogue is virtually moribund, appearances or rhetoric to the contrary notwithstanding. Immobility and stalemate have become the norm, tempered by occasional counterfeit agreements designed primarily to provide some illusion of progress and to keep the game going.[1] Neither the South's desire to institute and accelerate a major restructuring of the international economic order for its benefit nor the North's desire to justify its preference for moderate case-by-case reforms and to educate the South about the North's political and economic problems have been very persuasive. It has become a classic dialogue of the deaf between speakers with different premises, needs, and goals.

Both sides are extremely unhappy with this state of affairs, although they attribute responsibility differently and disagree about what needs to be done to engender real progress.[2] The unhappiness reflects more than the absence of substantive results and the consequent feeling that scarce resources—especially time and money—have been wasted. There is a feeling on the part of some developed countries that many of the developing nations are using the Dialogue—which incorporates demands for a new international economic order in addition to voicing concerns on the broader question of future North-South relations—to divert attention from their inability or unwillingness to undertake far more crucial, but politically dangerous, domestic change. Inflated expectations of external salvation have taken the place of a realistic sense of what can legitimately be expected from changes in the international system. Conversely, many developing countries argue that this criticism disguises or rationalizes an unwillingness on the part of the developed nations to admit the inequities built into the existing system. These countries also point out that external developments, such as worldwide inflation, for which they bear little responsibility but from which they are disproportionate sufferers, can undermine even wise

Parts of this chapter previously appeared in "The North-South Dialogue: The Political Economy of Immobility," *Journal of International Affairs,* Vol. 34, no. 1 (1980); this material is published here with permission of the *Journal of International Affairs* and the Trustees of Columbia University in the City of New York.

and effective domestic policies. There is much to be said for both arguments, so far as they go, but the inability of both groups to move toward some degree of consensus results only in rhetorical posturing.

The critical question is not whether the Dialogue will "survive," for in some form it will be part of our political universe for generations to come, but whether it will take a form that encourages the negotiation of meaningful agreements or degenerate into a meaningless and cynical charade. To answer this question we need an understanding not only of the political and economic dynamics within the various multilateral settings of the Dialogue but also of the relationship between what happens in, say, Geneva and New York and what happens in, say, New Delhi, Lima, or Abidjan.

The Dialogue and the Political Economy of Immobility

Conflict and confrontation are inevitable in the North-South arena. As Chapter 1 indicated, the participants have different values, different needs and priorities, and different interpretations of past, present, and future. Nevertheless, they have some shared and converging interests. As in the Cold War, sharp conflict need not preclude serious negotiations on mutual interests. Indeed, the very existence of both conflicting and common interests insures that the negotiating system—the means of achieving acceptable compromises—will be critical.

The View from Geneva and New York

One must begin with the Third World's strong belief that unity is its strongest weapon.[3] As President Nyerere of Tanzania declared to the Arusha meeting of the Group of 77, "unity is our instrument—our only instrument—of liberation."[4] Only unity can presumably prevent or at least inhibit successful implementation of "divide and conquer" tactics by the developed countries. In the abstract this is an unassailable argument. In practice, however, the critical question is whether a rather weak form of essentially procedural unity is the best tactic for the developing countries if the most likely outcome is substantive stalemate in negotiations with the developed countries.

As Nyerere himself has emphasized, unity among more than one hundred countries, split every which way in economic, social, and ideological terms, is inherently fragile. It "is basically a unity of opposition. And it is a unity of nationalisms. For it was our separate nationalisms which caused us to come together, not the ideals of human brotherhood, or human equality, or love of each other." The fashionable analogy between the Group of 77 and an "international trade union of the poor" (poor countries, not people) is also suspect, not only because the interests of the members are not always congruent but also because, as Nyerere noted, they lack a strike fund — that is, few can afford the risks implicit in a strike. If Zambia is asked to withhold its copper exports, many Zambians will starve. But the point at which unity is likely to become increasingly weak and rhetorical will probably fall well short of the extreme: Even the offer of a reasonably good deal by the developed countries is bound to be tempting.

How is unity to be achieved and maintained in these circumstances? What has evolved in UNCTAD and other institutional settings is the group system. The primary justification for the group system is that it is the only alternative to chaos — how else could so many developing countries negotiate with so many developed and socialist countries? In any case, in the Group of 77, the regional subgroups caucus on an issue and develop a common position, the leaders of the regional subgroups then caucus with each other and with the leadership of the Group of 77 itself and the leadership of the institution dealing with the issue (if that leadership is considered friendly). What emerges is a common Group of 77 position. This is then presented to the developed countries, who meanwhile have been establishing their own group position in a similar fashion — usually only as a response to expected Group of 77 demands, not as a completely independent position on the issue. Then, either the two positions are compromised during meetings of relatively small "contact groups" or the issue is left in suspension until a later meeting, the bridge usually being an innocuous verbal formula designed to keep lines of communication open.

I should also emphasize that the increasing institutionalization of the Group of 77 plays an important role in keeping pressure on the developed countries and in keeping potential dissidents within the Group itself in line. Very frequent meetings of the Group, the regional groups, various functional committees, and the political and intellectual leaders of the Third World have been deliberately scheduled not only to maintain the common position but also to thwart the tactic of "institutional shopping" by the developing countries. As the secretary-general of UNCTAD once noted, the developed countries can no longer hide from the developing countries by shifting discussions away from an unpopular institution like UNCTAD.

This description is accurate, so far as it goes, but it is decidedly insufficient, for it disguises some of the main characteristics of the bargaining process. For present purposes, it may suffice to note briefly two of these characteristics and their implications for the negotiation of viable substantive agreements:

1. The package proposal that emerges from Group of 77 deliberations is exceedingly complex, as agreement can be achieved only at a very broad level of generality. The issues themselves are, of course, intrinsically com-

plex, but the real difficulty is the operating principle that guides the quest for agreement: As Nyerere noted, successful Group of 77 packages must provide "equal benefit for all the participating Third World countries in each package of cooperation." I need hardly emphasize that this is virtually impossible; interests on many issues are barely compatible, if not overtly conflicting. Consequently, each agreement is burdened, implicitly or explicitly, with promises of side payments or compensation for potential losses, none of which have been, or probably can be, accurately calculated.

More critically, the process of reaching agreement within the Group of 77 is extraordinarily difficult because consensus can be blocked by any country or subgroup. As a result, internal conflicts are not really resolved; each set of particular demands is simply added on to the others. Moreover, negotiations on details with the industrial countries are also very difficult because the package is always threatening to come apart, especially when the discussion moves from the level of grand generalities to the specifics of who gets what and when. The process of reaching agreement within the Group of 77 is so time-consuming that very little time is left over to worry about what the developed countries might see as in their interest; the commitment to Third World unity prevails over the need to achieve agreement by detailed bargaining with the developed countries. Another important byproduct of the process is the inflation of expectations that it creates among many developing countries, which are easily convinced that the international system is solely responsible for all their problems and that external salvation will result if only unity is maintained. But even if all the demands in the New International Economic Order were accepted, the benefits for the developing countries would not be revolutionary, and they would be distributed inequitably.[5]

2. The process of consensus formation within the Group of 77 may appear cumbersome, but nonetheless democratic. There is less here, however, than meets the eye. In fact, the process—setting the agenda, forming proposals, determining tactics—is dominated by a small oligarchy of key Third World delegates and key staff members of a few international institutions. This is hardly surprising if the many are indeed to speak as one, and it is not necessarily improper or malign, but it does create problems that need to be recognized.

The leadership and the staffs of institutions like UNCTAD are critical actors in the North-South arena because they are indispensable. Many Third World countries lack the technical skills necessary to devise policies on complex issues like commodities or the reform of the international monetary system, and they must rely on external expertise. Moreover, the explosion of meetings, conferences, special sessions, and the like overwhelms the capacity of many poor and weak governments to cope; policy must come, virtually by default, from external experts. The staffs are even more critical in putting together a technically acceptable program for the whole Group of 77; they thus play both a technical role in developing proposals and a political role in packaging the elements, in selling them to the various parties (initially within the Group of 77 and, after acceptance, to the developed countries), and in indicating the boundaries of acceptable compromise.

The central point is not that the leadership and the staff *determine* outcomes in the bargaining process — for they can and have been overruled by government officials — but that their influence has not been properly understood. The importance of their role in the early and middle stages of the process needs special emphasis. They are especially critical in deciding what issues will top the agenda and what form the ensuing debate will assume; the political leaders (from both sides) who enter the debate in its late stages (for example, at an UNCTAD conference) are frequently left to haggle over programs that were determined months before. In effect, to get into the bargaining game only at, say, the UNCTAD-V Conference in Manila is to get in too late and to be required to play by someone else's rules.

The specific proposals that emerge from this process tend to have a number of characteristics that make substantive bargaining particularly difficult. They are usually excessively ambitious, perhaps beyond the current state of the art in both politics and economics, for they must promise too much to too many — as with UNCTAD's demand for "global resource management" in commodities, the demand for a legally binding code of conduct for the transfer of technology (which may help the transnational corporations [TNCs] more than the LDCs), or the (original) demands about debt (which might, again, have done the critical debtors more harm than good). The proposals also are frequently badly designed because they seek primarily a single goal — restructuring to facilitate development, usually by a transfer of resources. Not only is this too narrow a goal for developed countries with interests and needs of their own, but it is also excessively simplistic for a world in which each side contains rich and poor (both countries and people) and in which winners and losers are not the same on all issues. Finally, virtually all the proposals would require very large increases in central control or direction of international economic activity, as only centralization can guarantee that benefits will go to enough developing countries — that real benefits and not merely opportunities will be increased. Proposals at the recent UNIDO conference for massive, government-directed, and centrally controlled industrial redeployment to the developing countries are illustrative of the extent of the Group of 77's demands and the problems they raise: A large number of new institutions and funds are advocated to facilitate redeployment, but there is no discussion of whether we can know beforehand which industries to redeploy or of how to determine which developing countries are to receive them.[6]

Beyond the technical problems, it should also be noted that the either/or choice implicit in the North-South confrontation may no longer be the best or the only focus of concern. One of the major consequences of the Dialogue, then, is that it tends to force concentration on one bargaining relationship—a concentration that is appropriate in some cases, but simplistic in others—and, consequently, to ignore other North-South relationships or to force them into the province of "special relationships" or bilateral "deals."

The proposals also usually reflect the interests of the richer developing countries, in part because they are most able to grasp the opportunities created by external changes, and in part because they are more aware of their own interests and more able to influence the process of demand formation.[7] They are also usually able to deflect radical proposals that appear threatening to their own interests into more moderate channels, as with recent compromises on the debt issue.

Finally, the proposals are so difficult to package that movement away from initial "blue sky" demands toward genuine compromise with the developed countries is impeded by fears that the whole package will unravel or that the developed countries will seek to use partial concessions to split the Group of 77. Consequently, even the currently much-vaunted movement away from direct confrontation to detailed negotiation may be more apparent than real. There is still much stonewalling on critical issues by the rich countries, there is much less than meets the eye in some acclaimed "triumphs" (e.g., on the Common Fund), and the developing countries still insist that commitment to broad new principles must precede negotiation of specific issues.[8]

The View from Home

There is persuasive evidence that the Dialogue looks considerably different from Lima, Accra, or New Delhi than it does from Geneva or New York.[9] In the majority of developing countries—for the most part, all but the relatively advanced and ideologically committed—the government elites in the capital seem to know very little about the substance of the Dialogue and in some cases are not even aware of the implications for themselves of the proposals in debate. In part, this reflects technical incapacity, but perhaps in greater part it reflects the feeling of most of the elites that the meaning of the Dialogue is essentially political and symbolic—talking on equal terms with the developed countries symbolizes the new status of the South. For tangible economic returns, virtually all the elites surveyed put primary (and in some cases exclusive) emphasis on bilateral relationships with various developed countries. This is hardly surprising, especially given the minimal benefits produced by the Dialogue, but it has certain implications that should be noted.

The fact that few of the home governments expect major economic benefits from the Dialogue should not be allowed to obscure the fact that there are issues with significant economic costs and benefits under discussion in Geneva and elsewhere. The failure of the home governments to pay early and sufficient attention to these costs and benefits makes it easier to politicize the issues and harder to devise programs that make economic sense to both sides or that stand a good chance of being effectively implemented. Put differently, the elites at home (for example, development planners or treasury officials) and the elites on the development circuit (diplomats or officials of international institutions) have a number of crucial differences in perspective: The former *tend* to be less ideological, more practical, and more concerned with programs that promise real benefits relatively quickly; the latter are more radical, more concerned with global issues, and relatively more willing to let negotiations drag on until some kind of compromise seems possible. Thus, indifference to the practicality or technical quality of many proposals (except, of course, by the minority that expects to benefit or lose) means that a useful constraint on the Dialogue's tendency to degenerate into rhetoric is absent or diminished.

Another implication concerns the role of delegates in Geneva, New York, and elsewhere. The evidence indicates that the lack of technical capacity at home and the assumption that the issues are primarily symbolic, joined to the strong emotional commitment to unity, have tended to generate similar patterns of instructions to the delegates in Geneva and elsewhere: For the most part, they have simply been told to support the Group of 77 position. This is one reason why, in some instances, unanimity has been preserved even though some proposals involved losses for a number of developing countries, and why, as these proposals appeared to move closer to acceptance, the potential losers banded together to block agreement unless they were compensated. But one thing is clear: Blind instructions to support the Group position mean that the power and influence of the staff and the small group of leaders who establish that position is considerably enhanced.

If bilateral relationships seem far more critical from the perspective of the home governments—and few governments in the survey indicated that setbacks in the Dialogue, except for a complete break of some sort, would have major significance in bilateral negotiations—it is reasonable to ask why more of these governments have not actually split with the Group of 77. It is obvious, for example, that many conservative, free-market countries in the Third World are hostile to the NIEO demands on both practical and ideological grounds (and are not averse to currying favor with the developed countries); other countries may find particular proposals directly threatening to their own interests. Nevertheless, the Group of 77 has hung together—and not merely for fear of hanging separately. There are both individual and group explanations for this, which we can see more clearly if we examine the motives of the potential dissenters.

Many of the advanced developing countries have little need to protest because they would be the primary beneficiaries of most of the items on the agenda and they have the capacity and the means to determine and protect their own interests. Conversely, in some cases the poorest developing countries have not been sufficiently aware of the implications for themselves of certain programs, although this is becoming less and less true, especially in the later stages of negotiations when practical concerns begin to become more salient. The advanced developing countries, moreover, have other reasons for their support. Many of them are increasingly concerned about achieving and maintaining access to other developing-country markets, particularly as they fear exclusion from developed-country markets. Thus pro forma adherence to essentially rhetorical principles seems a small price to pay for remaining in the good graces of the majority of the Group of 77.[10] The advanced developing countries want it both ways: preferential advantages from the developed countries as a developing country, and preferential advantages (should a Third World preferential arrangement be negotiated) from the other developing countries. This helps to explain why some of them have been so hostile to the notion of developing a new association with the Organisation for Economic Cooperation and Development (OECD), why they are so fearful of expulsion from the Group of 77, and why they have been among the leading supporters of collective self-reliance.[11]

Some of the "new influentials," like Nigeria, India, Brazil, Mexico, and the "old" Iran, also have leadership aspirations that make it necessary for them to stay in front of their (potential) followers. This is one reason why the Carter administration's effort to concentrate on these countries and to induce them into new forms of cooperation has had so few successes and has been so problematic. The desire of these countries for regional leadership roles means that they must support or appear to support the most radical demands, and the developed countries have offered too little in response—and probably cannot offer enough—to induce movement away from the Group of 77.

Some of the most critical OPEC countries do not fit into the categories noted thus far; they might also be substantial losers from some NIEO programs (e.g., efforts to raise the prices of commodity exports that these countries import). Nevertheless, they maintain the common front primarily because they want to deflect potential verbal attacks from Third World oil importers (and perhaps physical attacks from terrorists) and because they fear developed-country efforts to construct a coalition of the poor against them.[12] These fears are far from illusory; public attacks on OPEC from other developing countries are beginning to surface. At some point the fear of OPEC retaliation or the hope of OPEC charity apparently becomes less compelling than the actuality of OPEC's effects.

The potential for wide fissures within the Group of 77 is thus great. Currently there are three or possibly four primary fault lines—all of which, of course, are imposed over (although they do not supersede) a staggering variety of local fault lines. One major and growing fault line falls between OPEC and the nonoil developing countries (this excludes some non-OPEC oil exporters like Mexico and Egypt). A second fault line separates the newly industrializing countries (NICs) from the rest of the developing world; all of the latter want to become NICs, but may be inhibited from doing so by the early start of present NICs. A third fault line is blurred and shifting, but nonetheless significant: on one side, the NICs, some OPEC countries, and a number of others that are doing reasonably well economically, and on the other side, a majority that is not doing well and that probably will not do well for a very long time.

Perhaps a fourth fault line should be mentioned: the radicals versus the moderates. This split is partially implicit in the others; it is frequently unstable because of regime changes; and it is of uncertain importance because even the radicals are willing to (or must) cross ideological lines to achieve national goals. Thus Algeria, despite strong support for the NIEO and for collective self-reliance, has cooperated with Western companies to exploit its oil and gas resources and has attempted to use the revenues from the sale of its resources to build a modern industrial structure—actions that imply integration with the international economy. Still, the radical-moderate split can assume or has assumed some importance in particular negotiations (for example, the Havana summit of the Nonaligned Movement).

Tactically, each fault line has somewhat different implications and has different effects in different arenas. Strategically, however, an argument might be made that all the fault lines could be collapsed into a single—but not rigid—line of division: those who are coping and think they will be able to continue to cope with the help of special treatment within the prevailing structure versus those who are not coping and who believe that only radical and immediate restructuring of the international system will provide them with the help they need.

The fault lines indicate broad areas of conflict, but they are less useful in indicating exactly where politically and economically effective coalitions are likely to be established. It should be noted that none of the fault lines corresponds very well with the familiar regional splits of the past, especially between the Latin Americans and the Africans (and sometimes the Afro-Asians). Each region has its own oil and nonoil states, its own NICs, its own rich and poor, and its own radicals and conservatives. Nevertheless, practical cooperation across regional lines remains very difficult for a variety of reasons (except for OPEC, such cooperation has been primarily rhetorical) and is not likely to become any easier if the external environment becomes even more threatening. In such circumstances the need for immediate support will probably overwhelm any efforts to construct broader coalitions. The one obvious potential exception might be a coalition of Muslim states, but, apart from religion, the differences have proved and are likely to continue to prove more powerful than the commonalities.

If the creation of substantively significant transregional coalitions is unlikely (although the commitment to collective self-reliance might produce some genuine results at a later date—perhaps the 1990s), and if regional conflicts continue to make large regional coalitions problematic, what is the most probable outcome? What may emerge, and what may provide the focus for external support, are subregional coalitions of like-minded states at more or less the same level of development (Association of Southeast Asian Nations [ASEAN], the Caribbean Group, the Andean Pact, the Organization of Arab Petroleum Exporting Countries [OAPEC]) and/or a few coalitions between a regional great power and its less developed neighbors. The latter coalitions are likely to be less stable than the former, because the great power may not have the resources to buy support and because of resentment against its role or against "backwash" effects. Moreover, the like-minded coalition may be more effective at attracting support from the developed countries.

The potential fault lines that have just been noted are obviously of primarily economic origin. That might well lead to the charge of "economism," as it is clear that political and ideological interests have from time to time dominated or appeared to dominate economic interests and conflicts. It is not my intention to discuss in any direct or detailed fashion the many political issues that affect bargaining within the Third World; doing so would require a very extensive increase in the scope of this study. This is especially true because the conflicts are so variegated and disparate, which implies that an even minimally satisfactory treatment would require an analysis of a large number of different cases. Nevertheless, it is worth asking very briefly what effect the political issues might have on economic fault lines.

One must begin by noting the obvious: The separation between political and economic concerns is largely artificial. Economic outcomes will surely have a massive effect on political outcomes, and political conflicts and friendships have had and will have a massive effect on what can or cannot be done in economic terms (for example, conflicts impeding regional cooperation and friendship occasionally generating acts of economic charity or sacrifice). Still, a rough separation of the two categories is at least analytically feasible. Precise forecasts about the results of political and economic interactions in individual cases are probably impossible, as there is no effective way of specifying beforehand all the factors that might have an important effect. Moreover, not only does influence move in both directions (from political to economic and vice versa), it can also be beneficial, detrimental, or neutral. The key question, consequently, is whether we can indicate a plausible trend line (around which there will be many variations) for the impact of political issues on economic issues or whether we have no choice but to accept a very large degree of indeterminateness.

Political conflicts within and between Third World countries have had a variety of negative effects on development prospects in the past. Regional and subregional cooperation has been impeded, national integration ("nation-building") has been slowed, scarce funds have been diverted to arms spending, domestic inequities between different groups have widened, and so forth. If economic conditions deteriorate (or merely stagnate), an outcome that has been widely forecast for the 1980s, it is surely likely that these political conflicts will be exacerbated, at one and the same time making economic cooperation more difficult (thus worsening economic conflicts) and sharply limiting the economic sacrifices that might be made by relatively well-off developing countries for the benefit of their friends and allies in the Third World.

This is not to argue, of course, that political factors will be unimportant; rather, it is to suggest that existing political conflicts may exert an even more negative effect on development prospects as the international environment becomes more hostile and that political ties that have induced acts of friendship in the past may not be able to produce much more than rhetorical support when even the richer developing countries must expend more of their own resources in managing their own development programs. There will certainly be much variation around this trend, because community feelings within the Third World are high, resentments against the developed countries are widely shared, and in some cases economic desperation might generate some willingness to forget or bypass political conflicts. But it is probably more likely that economic conditions will generate much less cooperation and much more of an effort to steal a march on friends and neighbors. In this sense, one might forecast that political conflicts will only reinforce the major economic fault lines.

Put another way, unless economic conditions improve considerably in the next few years (that is, unless the pessimistic forecasters are wrong), political conflicts may come increasingly to reflect underlying economic difficulties and to be irresolvable without a solution to the major economic conflicts. However, in some cases political conflicts may be so severe or feelings of friendship or community so strong that potential economic fault lines may be obscured or lessened in force. This suggests a mixed and confusing pattern of outcomes, with economic fault lines coexisting with very different political or ideological fault lines. But even if this is the most likely outcome, it probably will not diminish the long-term significance of economic fault lines that reflect real divergences of interest.

Despite divisions and pressures to break away and seek special arrangements with the developed countries, the Group of 77 has managed thus far to maintain its unity. Calculations of self-interest provide part of the explanation for this; the poorest countries have nowhere else to go, and the richer countries see real or potential advantages in supporting a common position. In any case, the bedrock of unity must be self-interest, as poor countries obviously cannot sacrifice real gains for long, no matter how appealing the other forces that sustain unity may be. In addition, of course, even if unity has produced few real gains, the developed countries have not offered enough to make going it alone seem very attractive. As I have indicated, the increasing institutionalization of the Third World coalition has helped to maintain unity. There are also some very general shared interests that unite virtually all of the developing countries, irrespective of other conflicts: All want to alter the international distribution of power (if not always in the same way), all want more external support of various kinds, and all want the income gap narrowed as rapidly as possible.

But these goals are too broad to provide much more than rhetorical guidance. The real glue that has kept the group from disintegrating and that at least delays or dilutes immediate preoccupations with self-interest may well be an emotional commitment to the idea of a Third World—not so much shared interests, but shared problems, a common interpretation of past and present exploitations, a sense of a shared fate in the future, and consequently a strong desire to stand together. In the future, however, if internal and external pressures on weak governments continue to increase, as appears likely, feelings of solidarity may not be strong enough to preserve unity when or if the developing countries are in sharp competition for scarce resources (food and energy imports, access to markets, aid)—when conflicts of interest are real and immediate, not abstract and long-range. At any rate, for the moment the conflict between the powerful forces that encourage disintegration and those that encourage unity has been resolved in favor of unity. More narrowly, the benefits of unity, both tangible and intangible, still seem to outweigh the costs. This is a calculation, however, that will come under constant and increasing pressure.

Should the United States Take the Dialogue Seriously?

The North-South Dialogue responds to one pattern of concerns and one set of influences; bilateral North-South relations respond to a different pattern of concerns and a different set of influences. Of course, there is inevitably some overlap; the two systems are only partially discontinuous. But when they do intersect, usually at grand conferences when ministers from home supplant diplomatic representatives, the concerns of the Dialogue tend to prevail—primarily, as I have noted, because many home ministers do not always take the Dialogue seriously (not expecting many gains from it), because they tend to see it as essentially symbolic (thus making unity important), and because of the strong desire to remain in good standing within the Third World coalition.[13]

These considerations might seem to justify a major shift in emphasis by the United States away from the Dialogue and toward bilateral or regional relationships.[14] The United States could treat the Dialogue, as many on both sides do, as an exercise in ritual, a form of shadowboxing, while concentrating substantive programs on more practical and more promising arenas (bilateral, functional, perhaps regional). This may become necessary if current patterns persist, or if reforms are impossible, but this shift could be very costly and might very well be ineffective. The two levels of North-South interaction are indeed badly integrated. It would be a mistake, however, to take this as a given, thus justifying a shift in emphasis, for neither level can function effectively unless a better degree of integration is achieved.

For poor, weak, and vulnerable governments success at one level will always be threatened by failure at the other; the Dialogue will remain a ritual if it is not more closely connected to domestic concerns in the developing countries, and domestic (or bilateral) policies are more likely to succeed if supported and supplemented by parallel international policies.[15] For example, if commodity prices fluctuate rapidly or if processed commodity exports face heavy tariff or nontariff barriers, domestic decisions on commodity investments or industrialization policies can be significantly affected. Conversely, if external opportunities are created, complementary actions must be taken domestically to increase the capacity to take advantage of such opportunities. External actions are especially important signals for countries that are heavily dependent on trade and, of course, external trends (like inflation) may undermine even effective domestic policies in countries with so few buffers against adversity.

In short, rather than merely seeking to adapt to present circumstances, the developed countries need to seek means to more effectively link the bilateral and the multilateral settings. Another way of making the point is to emphasize that if the Dialogue is to be reformed, the key changes will come not from tinkering with its mechanism in Geneva and New York, but rather from altering perceptions and policies in Caracas, Nairobi, and New Delhi (not to say Washington, Oslo, and Paris). The two levels are inter-related. Changes by home governments will make reform of the Dialogue easier, changes in the Dialogue may have some useful effects on home government perceptions, but the changes at home are clearly the more crucial.

One should also note that UNCTAD, which has been very worried about the failure of "senior government officials" in some developing countries to understand UNCTAD policies and programs, has decided to make a major effort to garner the support of these officials. Thus a new Research and Training Program has been established, financed by the United Nations Development Programme (UNDP) and the OPEC Special Fund. It will hold "high-level workshops on a regional basis on specific key issues of concern to UNCTAD."[16] As the workshops will be staffed primarily by UNCTAD experts, UNCTAD will provide the documentation, and the workshops will last only about five days (because of time pressures on senior officials), it is clear that the intention is only to increase support for programs already devised at UNCTAD and to prevent potential dissidents from defecting or revealing their doubts to Western governments.

From UNCTAD's perspective, this is an intelligent response to the discovery that commitments by diplomats in Geneva and ministers at home are not necessarily identical or equivalent in significance. From the perspective of the United States and the other developed countries, however, this particular effort to more effectively link the Dialogue and domestic patterns of concern might provide the worst kind of linkage: more fervent support for "global bargains" that reflect only one set of interests. To counter this (insofar as it is determined that such proposals are either politically or economically impracticable), the developed countries will have to make a greater effort to devise more coherent policies of their own and to organize a more effective educational effort on their behalf, points to which I shall return in Chapter 7. In the present context, the central point is that the significance of the gap between the two levels of the North-South arena has already been noted and acted upon by the South, but not by the North.

There are other consequences of the disconnections between the two levels. For example, the failure of domestic elites in the developing countries to pay sufficient attention to the Dialogue diminishes the pressure in the Dialogue to devise policies that can be or will be implemented; it gives relatively free rein in the Dialogue to leaders and institutions with their own interests and biases; and it permits grand confrontations to preempt more moderate and pragmatic bargaining. This gives more currency to a gibe occasionally heard in the corridors in Geneva: The only ones who really benefit from the Dialogue are the elites who carry it on. In addition, to argue that the Dialogue can be bypassed or deemphasized because most of the Third World leaders are not very concerned about it obscures the fact that this permits some leaders, either foolishly or cynically, to blame their problems entirely on the international system and that it creates conflict and confusion between apparently divergent sets of policies (as with the familiar example of the NIEO and basic human needs). Moreover, the demonstration effect of ideas is very strong, and the failure of the developed countries to take account of this relinquishes an important means of influence on LDC domestic and international policies—a not irrelevant consideration in a period when ideas that emanate directly from the developed countries are inherently suspect. There are also some issues, and they may be growing in number, for which a wider arena of settlement may be necessary or appropriate.[17] Such arenas need to be built on cooperation and a record of achievement, not improvised in response to crisis. Finally, in such a fluid and changing environment, foreclosing a potential arena of cooperation may be dangerous, particularly when one asks what actions the developing countries that are ignored may undertake in order to attract attention and support.

This argument may be unpersuasive, for it requires understanding of some complex linkages, its effects are long-range and not completely foreseeable, and it requires a commitment by the developed countries to a reform strategy that may not work. One should also remember that effectively connecting domestic development policies and policies in the North-South Dialogue will require not only the cooperation of the developing countries but also a major shift in their approach to North-South negotiations. Doubts that the developing countries will oblige might appear to make an attempt at more effective integration illusory. In addition, this argument does not intersect very saliently with the configuration of forces that affect immediate decisions, especially decisions by governments that perceive the long run as the next press conference. In these circumstances, it is reasonable to ask whether there are other arguments for taking the Dialogue seriously that are likely to be more persuasive.

The Dialogue: Criteria of Importance

Moral arguments about our obligations to help those in need may be very convincing, but they are not very helpful in policy terms. There is no system-wide principle of justice that commands sufficient support to provide guidance for particular decisions. Other ambiguities confuse the issue: for example, the need to give aid or support through governments that may be corrupt or incompetent, the complexities involved in advocating policies that may increase initial inequities (with the promise of diminishing inequities in the long run), the fact that some of the policies of the NIEO may injure some developing countries and some of the poorest citizens within them, the conflict between moral and political interests in various cases, and the extent to which public support in the developed countries is tied to the state of the domestic economy. The moral arguments are critical, and to many of us as individuals they may be compelling, but governments, for better or worse, are likely to see them as only one factor among several.

We must also consider arguments about the nature of the international system. One might argue, for example, that as the developing countries will contain nearly 90 percent of the world's people by 2000, the developed countries cannot assume that they will be able to continue to use more than a fair (proportionate) share of the world's resources, thus suggesting the need for an immediate start to redistribution. Or one could argue that the developed countries need the cooperation of the developing countries to reach agreements in global areas of concern such as the environment, the oceans, and nuclear proliferation, or that failure to cooperate will create a system dominated by terrorism or other deliberately destabilizing acts. To some extent these arguments are undoubtedly overstated. "Global" is a misnomer in most cases, for successful agreements on these issues are possible — and probably more likely — well below the global level. Still, these arguments are hardly irrelevant or utopian. But the problem, once again, is that they do not intersect very well with the configuration of forces that affects immediate decisions. Moreover, in some cases there are real conflicts between different systemic goals or substantial uncertainties about the specific policies entailed by agreement on a particular long-term systemic goal.

The contention that North-South issues will become a major factor in domestic politics in the 1980s, much like the issue of Israel, is hardly new, but the turmoil surrounding Andrew Young's resignation as ambassador to the UN has obviously given it new force. It may very well be that what is called "North-South" is in fact a narrower issue. *Some* North-South issues will surely become domestic political and economic issues, but the more salient intersections are likely to be in the form of blockages by essentially single-issue constituencies, as with Turkey, Greece, Zimbabwe, perhaps Mexico, and indeed Israel. It is difficult to see what effect these issues will have on the substance or even the atmosphere of the North-South Dialogue itself. Still while the congressional Black Caucus has had little influence in the past on, or apparently much interest in, the major economic issues of the Dialogue, this may be changing, as is indicated by recent demands to increase aid to Africa. Hispanics may also become a more influential pressure group on Latin American issues. But it seems highly unlikely that this pressure will be transformed into strong support for the NIEO (not least because of potential effects on domestic welfare expenditures).

An argument that might be more convincing to policymakers concerns the presumed link between OPEC decisions and developed-country responses to North-South issues. In general, recent U.S. administrations have worked on the assumption that the linkage is essentially rhetorical: OPEC's pricing decisions will be made independently of the state of the Dialogue. But as I have already noted, there are significant indications that the developing countries are beginning to be more vocal about the damages inflicted by OPEC pricing decisions. For example, overt conflict between OPEC and a large number of developing countries almost brought UNCTAD-V to a halt (and was compromised only with great difficulty), and it surfaced once again at the Havana summit of the Nonaligned Movement. OPEC might try to diminish pressure upon itself by more fervent support for NIEO demands, by increases in aid, and perhaps by increased investment in other developing countries. There is also a possibility that OPEC might agree to barter oil for goods or to institute a two-tiered pricing system. (There are reports, for example, that the Saudis and others have cut allotments to the oil companies and set aside oil for the developing countries, presumably at a discount.)

Most observers have continued to dismiss possibilities of increased linkage between the NIEO and oil pricing decisions on various grounds: that only the most conservative OPEC countries have resources to spread around, that many OPEC countries (especially the Arab countries) are major losers from some NIEO programs, that a two-tiered pricing system is unworkable, and that the non-OPEC countries lack the power or the will to do much more than complain. Yet again, one should note that, although OPEC is hardly likely to act against perceptions of its own interests, those interests can be defined in different ways, and the emotional and psychological ties that bind the Third World together are very powerful. In short, confronted by rising pressure from its peers, OPEC might be far more amenable to adjusting its strategies than if pressure emanated from the OECD. However, if OPEC's actions cut developed-country supplies appreciably, or if OPEC raised prices even further to compensate for subsidized sales to the Third World, the damage would not be limited to the developed countries — OPEC's "charity" to its friends might turn out to be more apparent than real. Subsidized oil to the other developing countries might also have a perverse effect over the long run if it encouraged continued reliance on imported oil and discouraged necessary shifts in energy consumption and growth strategies.

What all of this implies about the Dialogue is far from clear, especially as the link between the Dialogue and OPEC policies is always bound to be uncertain and problematic. Some optimists have suggested that a more effective Dialogue might facilitate the creation of a North-South coalition against OPEC, but this seems doubtful. OPEC has too many cards, both material and psychic, and could probably destroy any such effort before it got under way. After all, special arrangements for the Third World would be costly, but hardly on a scale to threaten OPEC's prosperity. Still, if a two-tiered system broke down, or if conditions became increasingly desperate for many developing countries, perhaps OPEC would be more amenable to seeking cooperative solutions if the Dialogue was functioning more effectively. This is surely nebulous and, from a policymaking perspective, is unlikely to be more than a peripheral factor in any effort to deal with OPEC. I shall return to the issue of OPEC and the Third World in Chapter 4 as it is obviously crucial in attempting to understand whether present bargaining patterns can persist. In this context the key point is that the presumed connections between OPEC and the Dialogue are too uncertain and unclear to generate much support for a new approach to the Dialogue.

Finally, there is the argument that the developing countries are becoming increasingly important markets for U.S. exports and increasingly important sources of U.S. imports.[18] This is, of course, both true and important, but it is not absolutely clear that the argument leads quite where its most enthusiastic proponents think it does. Trade has gone up sharply, but the great majority of it has been with OPEC and with a relatively small number of advanced developing countries.[19] Much of the increase (apart from oil) has been in labor-intensive manufactured imports. In the short and medium term, it seems likely that these exports will continue to come from the advanced developing countries (and not the other LDCs) and that they will create most or many of the adjustment problems implicit in a situation of rapidly shifting comparative advantage. As a result, it might well be argued that the advanced developing countries — and not the rest of the Third World (except for oil and other raw material exporters) — should become the focus of U.S. Third World policies. This issue is obviously too complex to resolve by a clear choice between global or bilateral emphasis, but again in the present context I mean only to make the point that increased trade with parts of the Third World does not necessarily lead to any simple short-run conclusions about the policies the United States should adopt toward the Dialogue. I shall discuss the trade issue again in Chapters 5 and 7.

The short-run arguments for taking the Dialogue more seriously thus seem inconclusive. These arguments are not wrong, but rather insufficient, especially in light of the difficulties of successfully diminishing the obstacles that currently impede the negotiating process. This is particularly true because most of the developed countries have found it difficult to make a strong case domestically for the political or technical wisdom of programs such as generalized debt reform, legally binding codes of conduct, or large numbers of buffer stocks for commodities of interest to the developing countries. More is at issue than the simple fact that the developed countries may lose in the short run from some of these proposals; it is also important that some experts are uncertain whether many developing countries will actually benefit from the proposal, or that they can or will be implemented.

The picture changes, however, if we try to peer ahead. The key is a judgment about what the international system might look like in the 1980s if the United States and other developed countries allow the Dialogue to remain stuck and if they choose to continue present policies. As already noted in Chapter 1, most experts foresee a system that is less open, less stable, more nationalistic, and more fragmented. This could be a very fragile system, increasingly unable to deal with a number of systemic problems in food, energy, and trade because institutions have eroded, rules have become ineffective, and controls have become impossible to negotiate. Even if the system manages to function on the basis of more or less closed blocs, the loss in welfare could be sharp and the loss of certain amenities of an open system could prove severe. But few of the developed countries are strong enough or imaginative enough to change their discount rates so that judgments about future consequences of present actions are given sufficient weight, and few of the developing countries can afford to do so. The decline of U.S. power reinforces this conclusion, for there are no longer any countries able or willing to pay the collective goods costs of leadership.[20]

A common theme runs through this discussion of the various reasons to take the Dialogue seriously. The theme is worth reemphasizing because it will appear again in the discussion of specific issues. The individual arguments to adopt a new orientation toward the Dialogue do not seem very powerful or persuasive, especially in the sense that they do not carry much weight in the political or economic calculations that tend to determine current policy decisions. This may be either because they reflect trends that are just becoming salient (for example, in trade or in growing resource dependence) or because they reflect a concern with nebulous potential long-term dangers to a stable and orderly international system (for example, nuclear proliferation, the threat to the environment, a viable system of international communications). There is no point in simply asserting the obvious — the need to lower the discount rate on the future — for this well-meant injunction will easily be ignored in the rush to deal with today's crisis ("the urgent driving out the important"). The practical question is how to alter the policy process so that the category of the urgent is expanded to include, perhaps gradually but nonetheless ineluctably, a growing concern for the important issues that must be resolved if the North-South arena—and thus the international arena itself—is to become less bitter and contentious.

This argument implies that the United States *should* take the North-South Dialogue seriously, but before deciding whether it *can* do so we shall need to consider several other issues.[21] What the United States chooses to do is important, but not by itself decisive. We need also to consider the pressures that might come to bear on the developing countries in this decade and the policy responses they might choose (or be compelled) to make. I shall examine several of these pressures in the next three chapters. This should permit a better judgment about what to expect from the developing countries and the Third World in the 1980s and thus about the policy alternatives open to the United States during the greater part of this decade. These latter issues will be analyzed in Chapters 6 and 7.

Notes

1. Some would argue that keeping the game going *is* the Dialogue's triumph. There is a minor point here, but no more. Failure to achieve real progress is not merely costly in its own terms; disguising the failure delays necessary adjustments in behavior.

2. "Both sides" is obviously an oversimplification, for there are groups within each side quite content with the persistence of stalemate: for example, some conservatives in the developed countries are convinced that developing-country demands are irrational and unjustified, and some radicals in the developing countries feel that progress in the Dialogue will only delay revolution and self-reliance.

3. The discussion of the bargaining process in multilateral settings draws upon Robert L. Rothstein, *Global Bargaining: UNCTAD and the Quest for a New International Economic Order* (Princeton, N.J.: Princeton University Press, 1979).

4. Nyerere's speech was reprinted as an appendix to the Arusha Program of the Group of 77 (the major caucusing group of the developing countries within the UN, established at the first UNCTAD conference in 1964), dated February 1, 1979. The Arusha meeting was the Group's major preparatory meeting for UNCTAD-V. Subsequent quotations of the Nyerere speech are from the same source. See *Arusha Programme for Collective Self-Reliance and Framework for Negotiations* (Geneva: UNCTAD, TD/236, May 1979). Similar conclusions are also reached in a recent report by Arjun Sengupta, "A Review of the North-South Negotiating Process," *IFDA Dossier 18* (July-August 1980), which argues that "group solidarity" is the South's principal source of power and that any proposal must compensate Third World losers and "yield a net benefit to all" developing countries. There is obviously an ele-

ment of hyperbole in some of the Third World's "one for all, and all for one" descriptions of unity. In any case, the concept of unity needs to be taken in a "more or less" not an "either/or" sense. The defection of one state or a handful of relatively uninfluential states would not mean that "unity" would no longer be important in the bargaining process. For example, when Burma left the Nonaligned Movement after the Havana summit, the effect was minimal; if Egypt had been expelled or if all the disaffected had quit, the effect would have been profound. In short, all are equal, but some are more equal than others; thus interpretation and judgment are always necessary to determine how much unity there is and whether it will be strong enough to withstand pressure.

5. Thus William R. Cline notes that if virtually all the changes the LDCs demand were enacted, "the result still would be only a moderate increase in the per capita income of the poor countries. For example, the full list of measures might amount to increased benefits to the less developed countries of $35 billion or more. . . . for comparison, the aggregate GNP of the poorest countries . . . is approximately $500 billion; and if the middle-income developing countries . . . are included, the total rises to about $800 billion (1974 figures)." See "A Quantitative Assessment of the Policy Alternatives in the NIEO Negotiations," in William R. Cline, ed., *Policy Alternatives for a New International Economic Order: An Economic Analysis* (New York: Praeger Publishers, 1979), p. 52.

6. For the extraordinary range of demands presented at the most recent UNIDO conference, see *Industrialisation for the Year 2000: New Dimensions* (Vienna: UNIDO/IOD 268, May 1979).

7. This indicates why the least developed countries (mostly African) have become an increasingly powerful "single-issue" constituency in the bargaining process, especially within the Group of 77, usually demanding support for direct resource transfers as compensation for supporting the rest of the Group's demands.

8. This is one reason why I find the assertion that "the North-South Dialogue has contributed to a spirit of realism which is leading to a strategy of mutual accommodation" either misleading or premature. The quote is from *Development Co-operation: 1977 Review* (Paris: Organisation for Economic Co-operation and Development, 1978), p. 7. As I indicated in the last chapter, pressing needs always compel the developing countries to make the best immediate deal that they can. But this is only part of the story, for the "spirit of realism" does not reflect a change in goals or strategy or any shared view of what needs to be done. Nor does it reflect resolution of any of the major issues dividing North and South.

9. The material in this section is based on interviews and my own interpretation of a State Department questionnaire sent to a large number of U.S. embassies in the Third World. The questionnaire asked embassy officials a number of questions about how the North-South Dialogue looked to the developing-country governments at home. I was permitted to read the responses, which varied greatly in length and coverage, but of course I cannot quote directly from them. Thus my comments in the text that relate to this survey must be very general and unattributed. But I think the results are worth specifying, even within these constraints, because material on how the Dialogue looks from home is very sparse. I should add that an official of an international institution, to whom I described my conclusions, indi-

cated that his institution had conducted a similar exercise, with identical results.

10. A number of "NICs" (newly industrializing countries) are illustrative in this regard, for they have taken a gamble on an open-economy, export-oriented strategy and greatly fear increased protectionism by the OECD countries. I have in mind here not only large LDCs like Brazil and Mexico, but also smaller LDCs like South Korea, Thailand, and Taiwan.

11. Brazil is a good example; it fears exclusion from some Latin American markets and/or competition from neighbors like Argentina and Chile. Brazil also now trades more with other developing countries than it does with the United States. Support for collective self-reliance by the advanced developing countries reflects the fact that they are as dominant in South-South trade as they are in North-South trade: The same small group of NICs earns most of the benefits in both cases. In addition, NIC exports to the South are more advanced and less labor-intensive, thus permitting movement out of the familiar North-South trading patterns. For further comment, see Chapter 5.

12. One observer goes even further and argues that the Arab elites won't support Southern demands because they "need the cooperation of the North in order to maintain their own positions" and that these elites "have perfunctorily gone along with prevailing moods, reflecting at once the low importance of these issues for domestic constituencies and the assumption that the resolutions of these meetings will have no binding effects." John Waterbury, "The Middle East and the New World Economic Order," in John Waterbury and Ragaei El Mallakh, *The Middle East in the Coming Decade: From Wellhead to Well-Being* (New York: McGraw-Hill, 1978), pp. 105 and 133. Although probably true for the recent past, these comments also have to be taken with some caution; in some other countries support of the NIEO has been useful domestically, and even in the Arab countries there are elites (and some poor and/or foreign residents) who take the NIEO issues and ties with the rest of the Third World seriously.

13. This also tends to explain one subterranean aspect of the Dialogue. Some of the conservative or moderate countries frequently indicate their disagreement with particular proposals in private communications with U.S. officials but refuse to break publicly with the Group of 77. This reflects, as already noted, real calculations of interest, e.g., access to Third World markets, a desire to keep lines open to the radical countries, the domestic utility of strong support for changes in the international system, and the absence of attractive offers from the developed countries. But the differing public and private positions also reflect the fact that the public and private positions are often stated by different officials: Ministers within the home governments (and their ambassadors in Washington) are more interested in getting something specific and tangible from the United States and less interested in the Dialogue, while diplomats in Geneva and New York are playing a different game and see their success as linked to progress in the Dialogue. But U.S. officials in Washington tend to be more aware of, or to put more credence in, the "silent defectors" in the home governments, which strengthens the feeling that the Dialogue is primarily a charade—especially when even ostensibly radical countries (like Algeria and Jamaica) also indicate privately that the state of Dialogue will have little effect on their bilateral relationships.

14. Only a shift in emphasis is contemplated, not breaking off the Dialogue completely. Nonetheless, the shift could be crucial, for it implies certain judgments not only about how future relationships with the developing countries will be conducted, but also about how to deal with both crises and conflicts in the emerging international system.

15. The general theme about the need to integrate more closely domestic and international policies — to pursue reforms at both levels — is virtually a cliché, but the key intellectual question is not the need for integration per se, but rather why it has been so difficult to achieve and how it might be done. For an analysis of these questions, see Robert L. Rothstein, *The Weak in the World of the Strong: The Developing Countries in the International System* (New York: Columbia University Press, 1977).

16. For the quoted phrases and the other material about the new program, see UNCTAD, *Monthly Bulletin No. 160* (Geneva, April 1980).

17. A wider arena of settlement does not necessarily imply a global arena: What one seeks is an arena that includes all affected by an issue (not merely the most powerful), so that agreements are both effective and legitimate. For discussion on this issue, see Rothstein, *Global Bargaining,* especially pp. 260–262.

18. For an argument in this regard, with recent trade figures, see John W. Sewell, "Can the Rich Prosper Without Progress by the Poor?" in *The United States and World Development: Agenda 1979* (Washington, D.C.: Overseas Development Council, 1979), pp. 45–76. The argument has also become a staple of many recent Third World pronouncements.

19. Note also that the argument that this trade helped to diminish recessionary pressures in the rich countries in 1974–1975 needs to be qualified by the fact that much of it was financed by very heavy commercial borrowing, so the effect may have been only to diminish one problem by exacerbating another. One hopes this is wrong, but the recent oil price rises do not generate much hope that it is.

20. Arguments about the need for leadership and the difficulty of getting it from the weak governments in the developed world are very familiar. But perhaps it should be noted that the absence of effective leadership is also a severe problem for the developing countries as a group. Even the largest developing countries (except perhaps for Saudi Arabia) are too poor to make any sacrifices for the common good, and the international leadership of the Group of 77 is too frequently left in the hands of elites who have little influence in their own countries (or elsewhere) and are sometimes more interested in their own political fortunes than in providing real leadership. As a result, the difficulties of convincing the developing countries that a new bargaining strategy is imperative are considerably enhanced.

21. I should perhaps note that there have been some indications lately that recognition of the need to reform the Dialogue, especially to diminish group confrontations, has begun to spread. Thus the Brandt Commission recently advocated a committee system for actual negotiations, with broad guidelines set by a summit meeting of world leaders. This is surely an improvement over simplistic arguments that the stalemate can be broken by a few compromises on specific issues (which ignore a large number of underlying difficulties) or by replacement of a few recalcitrant bureaucrats in the U.S. government (the failure of the "new" officials in the Carter administration to transform will into effective policy should be warning

enough in this regard). But the weakness of the Brandt Commission approach is that it fails to recognize that delegates on the various committees may be forced to maintain initial group positions (and assiduously to avoid charges of "selling out") and that the quest for global bargains may itself be part of the problem. Insofar as there is a solution to these difficulties, one might venture the guess that it will come from a sharper separation of the actual negotiating process from the guideline-setting process: negotiations among states with a substantive interest in an issue, with negotiators not bound by explicit briefs prepared by the Group of 77 or the OECD, and, at the same time, acceptance by the negotiating parties of the broad guidelines set within the Dialogue and of the need to have any agreement exposed and discussed at the Dialogue level.

3

Food Policy, Foreign Policy,
and the International Politics of Food

An Agenda of Questions

A retrospective view of the success or failure of forecasting is not encouraging. The failures seem especially striking; perhaps they seem obvious in retrospect (as with oil), or perhaps they are simply more salient than the successes. Moreover, the successes may not elicit much enthusiasm, because responses may have been inadequate or because the grounds on which they rest are unclear.[1] In the circumstances, the justification for continuing the enterprise, beyond the pressures generated by the growth of the forecasting "industry" itself, can only be a rough comparison with the alternatives. "Muddling through" or relying on experience have proved increasingly inadequate, and forecasting has some potential — limited, incomplete, unguaranteed — to increase awareness about emerging problems, to diminish surprise, to indicate why some factors that might be ignored should not be, and perhaps to increase confidence in the wisdom of present choices. These are aspirations, not necessarily expectations; the forecast may provide some of the pieces in an unfinished mosaic, but it cannot provide a road map to desired destinations.[2]

As we move into the 1980s, it may be worth recalling what forecasters on the eve of the 1970s failed to foresee. Paul Streeten has recently noted that energy was not even mentioned in most studies, and that no one (at least no one who was noticed) was talking about, for example, resource exhaustion, pollution, the transfer of technology, the control of transnational corporations, or food scarcities.[3] The belief that the distribution issue and the direct relief of poverty were as important as rapid growth and that a new development strategy was thus imperative was confined to a relatively small group of development intellectuals. Inflation was not generally perceived as a systemic problem, and faith in Keynesian demand-management techniques remained high. The systemic implications of the decline in U.S. power and influence were not anticipated, and indeed the problems of the international system were perceived as manageable and not structural. Optimism about future progress, especially if the Vietnam war was brought to an end, was still in fashion, and reform of the old order (and certainly not "new international economic order") would presumably proceed at a leisurely pace within the closed circle of the rich countries and the institutions they dominated. In retrospect, however, the 1970s was a decade of shocks — practical, intellectual, metaphysical — and, as the *Economist* magazine called it, a "decade of unsolved problems."[4]

There is no self-evident means to avoid such failures to foresee the future. The number of methods employed by forecasters has been growing rapidly, but none of the methods appears inherently superior to any of the others.[5] In what follows I shall be concerned throughout with the question of whether and how the basic framework of the North-South relationship is changing, but the method employed is inevitably eclectic: Trends will be extrapolated, hypotheses will be examined, and scenarios will be analyzed and developed, but ultimately the combination of these elements into a coherent argument is limited by the talent and imagination (and luck) of the analyst. My intention is not to provide precise predictions (the Shah will be overthrown in 1979, or the Group of 77 will disintegrate in 1982) or to provide the practitioner with explicit advice about specific choices.[6] Rather, what I hope to do is to suggest an "agenda of questions" that will confront the policy community in the years ahead — perhaps a crucial function in a period when the conventional wisdom no longer inspires confidence — and to discuss some of the "constraints . . . within which policy decisions can be effective."[7]

This and the ensuing chapters on energy and trade follow a generally similar pattern of exposition. In each case I shall begin by examining what the experts perceive as the central problems and what prescriptions they have developed to deal with these problems. I shall then analyze (or, given the difficulties, attempt to examine) whether the developing countries are implementing the prescriptions and, if they are not, whether failure can or should be attributed to the prescriptions themselves, to the developing country governments, to the international environment, or to some combination of the three. I shall then discuss the policy implications for the U.S. government on two levels: first, what might be done to improve the prospects of effective implementation by developing-country governments and second, as many governments will not be able or willing to implement the prescriptions effectively, what might be done to deal with the international environment created by very asymmetric patterns of success and failure.[8] The two levels are only analytically separable; it should be clear that failure at the first level will create difficult foreign policy and international politics problems at the second and that attitudes and policies at the second level will have a significant effect on what developing-country ruling elites are able and willing to do.[9]

The structures of each of the issues that I shall discuss differ in significant ways. They are also connected, however, in the very crucial sense that what happens in one area will be heavily affected by developments in the other areas. And, of course, developments in the international system will probably have a decisive impact on what happens in all of the specific areas of concern (food, energy, trade, and debt). These connections will become clear as I go along, but there are also some themes that appear in each of the chapters that are worth noting at this point, if only to increase prior awareness that the implications of a particular discussion may extend beyond the issue at hand.

All analysts agree that if present trends continue the gap between developed and developing countries is likely to increase in the next two decades. The desire to reduce this gap is directly responsible for a number of normative forecasts that begin by positing a particular goal—say, the reduction of the income gap by 20 percent by 2000—and then attempt to specify the path by which the goal can be achieved.[10] Whether the growth rates of the developing countries will be sufficiently higher than the growth rates of the developed countries, so that relative reductions in various gaps become possible, is not at issue here. The more interesting question, which is somewhat obscured by the focus on North-South aggregates, concerns the growing gap within the South itself. Wherever we look, these gaps are growing: for example, as a result of differential resource distributions between (and within) geographical regions or differential capacities to export manufactures.[11] This seems to be a very familiar point, in the sense that the distinction between the Third World and the "Fourth World" has been a matter of concern for some time. Heretofore the potential conflicts implicit in this trend have been relatively muted and restrained. In effect, except for the rise of single-issue constituencies like the least developed countries, the political implications of the split have not been very salient, either within the South or between North and South. But if external developments in the 1980s become increasingly problematic, if not desperate, for many developing countries, the North-South focus may disintegrate. How probable this is and what it might mean should be one of the central policy concerns of the United States in the near future.

Growing divergences within the Third World have made Third World cooperation increasingly difficult. This is another way of saying that the non-OPEC developing countries are becoming more dependent on the industrial countries, despite vastly increased rhetoric about collective self-reliance. Food importers are dependent on a few developed countries; the newly industrializing countries, which have gambled on favorable terms for integration into the international economic system, are dependent on access to developed-country markets; most of the remainder of the developing countries have nowhere to go (except perhaps to OPEC, a point to which I shall return) for aid and technical assistance other than the developed countries; and even OPEC needs advanced technology from and secure financial markets in the developed countries. Even if efforts to increase intra-Third World trade gradually become important for some developing countries, they would not solve the problem of acquiring the necessary hard currency to pay for food, energy, and capital goods.

A large number of developing countries, some of which will be increasingly desperate, all competing for scarce resources and limited access to Western markets, suggests a very unstable and conflictual system. But it may also imply a movement away from an international class system, in which states may move up or down in class in response to various developments, to an international caste system (or a combination of caste and class), in which divisions between groups of countries are more or less permanent. Perhaps there will be a revival of spheres of interest, especially if the developed countries limit aid and support to countries that they need for economic and strategic reasons. At any rate, this may compel reconsideration of liberal notions of an open and progressive system based on common rules and principles. I shall return to this important and complex issue in Chapter 6.

Another theme concerns trade and the trading system. It appears increasingly likely that all of the issues I shall discuss will be heavily affected by the operation of the trading system.[12] In many areas, the countries with the resources are obviously not the centers of consumption—as in petroleum and raw materials—or, if they are large consumers, they remain the key residual suppliers for the rest of the world—as in the grain trade. Clearly, this means that access to resources and other trading conditions will be very crucial issues. And perceptions of likely trends in the trading arena can have very significant effects on domestic development decisions: For example, fears about continued access to grain may force many countries to invest in the production of more costly domestic substitutes, thus reducing investment in more productive sectors, and fears about rising protectionism may inhibit large numbers of countries from gambling on an export-oriented strategy.

But beyond these familiar examples, the ability to continue to import oil and grain or capital goods, or to pay back existing debts and to receive new loans, are all dependent in large part on increased trading opportunities for the developing countries. This may not be possible, however, not only because of political and economic problems in the developed countries, but also because the kind of decisions necessary to avert trade wars (for instance, harmonization agreements so that overproduction does not become an endemic phenomenon in many sectors) may be beyond the capacity of the existing institutional structure (and perhaps beyond what we know how to do practically and intellectually). Does this suggest that we have been too quick to dismiss a number of second-best options that, with all their recognized imperfections and costs, may do more to prevent an increasingly closed system than the pursuit of the "best" option? In addition, in relation to the previous theme, is it possible that trade among the developing countries can relieve some of these pressures, or is such trade likely to remain peripheral (and dominated by a handful of advanced developing countries)?[13]

A final theme concerns some crucial differences between technical and political forecasts or, stated differently, it concerns the issue of governmental response. In many areas, as we shall see, the technicians tend to agree on what should be done to avert or diminish the force of a number of potential problems or crises. The technicians can be relatively optimistic because they assume (and must assume, if forecasting is to have any utility) that policymakers will act rationally, that states or the system will have the capacity to respond effectively, or that new technologies will emerge as they have in the past to diminish the constraints imposed by finite resources. And in some cases they may be optimistic because they assume that problems in other areas will be resolved or that such problems will not intersect with problems in their own area; the difficulty of resolving interconnected problems simultaneously is obscured by a relatively narrow analytical focus. However, we shall confront a persistent problem: Political forecasts about imminent developments are usually much more pessimistic than their technical counterparts. Indeed, such forecasts rarely foresee more than incremental responses to perceived problems, largely because of the recognized difficulties of changing either institutions or attitudes rapidly. This pessimism is reinforced in the present context by the interrelationship of different problems, which strains both national and international capacities, by the weaknesses of the international political process, which was not constructed to deal with the problems it now confronts, and by growing doubts in the developed countries about the commitment to development of many Third World elites.

Assumptions about institutional responsiveness, especially about the responsiveness of developing-country governments, are absolutely crucial in any attempt to understand the policy implications of the issues I shall discuss. Failure to implement programs effectively at the domestic level increases pressures on the international system to provide external salvation or to deal with the consequences of regional instabilities. At the same time, developing-country governments may lack the resources to deal with a range of massive problems simultaneously. Moreover, the unusual degree of uncertainty that attends decision making in present circumstances, which I have already noted, is even more difficult for poor and weak governments to manage; even if they want to act, it is far from clear exactly what choice makes sense *now*. And they lack the resources to hedge or the flexibility to alter course quickly. In this sense, pessimism about the future of many developing countries is only partly about food or energy or other problems; equally significant are fears that neither governments nor international institutions will respond quickly and effectively and that what begins as a short-term crisis will end by becoming a prolonged long-term crisis. What can be done about this, or in a policy context, what actions can foreign governments or institutions take to increase domestic incentives (and resources) to implement policies and programs effectively? I shall deal with this problem in some detail in each of the next three chapters.

Two points need to be understood about the material in this and the next two chapters. First, my intention is not to provide an original analysis of the technical problems and prescriptions in food, energy, and trade, but rather to discuss the political implications of these issues for North-South relations. Thus I have included only material relevant to these concerns; there is obviously much about these issues that I have not included. Second, the discussion of policy issues in each of these chapters takes as a given the persistence of current policy limitations (in effect, the boundaries set by an essentially incremental, reformist approach) and does not attempt to search for breakthroughs or presumably optimum solutions. This seems the most likely short-term policy response, whatever its obvious inadequacies (which I shall deal with at length in Chapter 7). Perhaps more crucially, to move significantly beyond incrementalism would require a fundamental reorientation of U.S. policy toward the Third World. This is especially true because all the issues are connected and must be dealt with together and because the costs and consequences of attempting to do so could be very large. But whether such a shift is either possible or wise cannot be inferred merely from an analysis of specific issues, but rather must emerge from a wider analysis of ends and means in the North-South arena. In short, in Chapters 3, 4, and 5 I shall look at existing policies and suggest how they might usefully be improved (and what might happen if they are not), but I shall reserve for Chapter 7 a discussion of the more general shifts in orientation that might permit doing more in the more specific areas of concern.

The Political Economy of Food

Food experts tend to share a number of judgments about the world food system. There is wide agreement, for example, that the existing system is badly flawed; that the persistence of current trends will dangerously increase food deficits in many developing countries; that enough food can be produced with available technologies and resources to meet probable needs; and that a viable international food system requires policies designed to increase food production in the developing countries, to establish a reserve system of buffer stocks, and to increase food aid. There is also a reasonably wide consensus about the specific policies that the developing countries must adopt to increase production and about the policies that the developed countries must adopt to avoid destabilizing the world market. To some extent, however, the range of agreement is deceptive. Some of the disagreements that remain are fundamental, and the critical interim question may not be what should be done, but what will be done.

The salience of the food issue obviously has much to do with its moral and humanitarian significance. But the practical implications are equally important. A number of governments in the Third World—Niger, Chad, Ethiopia—have fallen as a direct result of food shortages, and many others have had to alter or curtail development plans because of rising food import bills. Moreover, domestic decisions about the agricultural sector have serious political implications; I need hardly emphasize the familiar conflicts between urban and rural interests or between industry and agriculture. Conversely, all the developed countries share an interest in stable food prices, and the United States, Canada, and Australia have a common interest in preserving valuable export markets (which might be threatened either by increased efforts at self-reliance or by decreased ability to pay for imports). Transforming this mixture of partially conflicting and partially compatible national interests into mutually acceptable international policy agreements—something more than declarations of good intentions—has been predictably difficult. National priorities, which are themselves frequently in conflict, take precedence over systemic priorities, and most agreements are inherently unstable because they cannot satisfy all the interests at stake or provide benefits to all the participants. As we shall see, this inevitably raises questions about second-best strategies.

A number of specific problems must be resolved in any attempt to create a more effective world food system. The most familiar of these is the problem of periodic shortages, but the most difficult is the problem of poverty and lower agricultural productivity in the developing countries. There are also separate but related problems of sharply fluctuating agricultural prices and earnings and high levels of malnutrition.[14] In effect, the food problem is not a single problem but a series of interconnected problems, and indeed one key policy issue is whether to seek solutions that strengthen and improve the connections or solutions that provide some degree of food security by "delinking" from the international system.

This raises implicitly a more general question about the goals and the norms of any world food system: Can a system dominated by the national concerns of so many states at so many different levels of development and with so many different needs and values reach agreement on general systemic norms and specific systemic goals? Obviously experience suggests that the answer is no and that the likely outcome is a system of mixed and shifting goals and norms—"semi-organized anarchy," as someone has described the current international monetary system. But if an integrated global food system with new norms and new practices seems desirable but not possible, and if a retreat into parochialism seems possible but not desirable, what are the policy implications? To answer, we need first to analyze why a global system has seemed desirable, what policies this has implied, and whether or to what degree such policies are likely to succeed. This sets the context for a discussion of two policy issues. The first, more narrowly concerned with food, has two parts: Is the present policy package adequate and, if so, by what means should the United States and other developed countries seek to implement its directives? The second issue is broader in perspective: What are the implications for the international system of success or failure with food initiatives. The two questions are obviously connected, which is merely another way of saying that food policy, the foreign policy of food, and the international politics of food are separable only as an analytical convenience.

Projections and Prescriptions: An Emerging Consensus

During the 1950s and 1960s the developing countries increased agricultural output at a rate of about 3 percent per annum. The developed countries maintained a growth rate of about 2.7 percent per annum (yielding a global rate of about 2.8 percent per annum). But, primarily because of population growth rates, food demand increased at divergent rates: 2.5 percent per annum for the developed countries and 3.5 percent per annum for the developing countries.[15] As a result per capita production was barely rising in many LDCs, and it even began to decline in Africa in the early 1970s (see Table 3.1). One inevitable result was (and is) increasing import dependence (see Table 3.2). Imports supplied about 5 to 6 percent of LDC food consumption in 1960, but the average has steadily increased and might well triple or even quadruple by the end of the decade—if the importers can raise the necessary foreign exchange. Food import costs have increased 200 to 300 percent since 1960.

The potentially disastrous consequences of these trends were somewhat masked (at least for nonspecialists) during the 1960s by the generally upward trends in production, by the large reserve stocks in the United States, by favorable weather, and by the relative moderation of Soviet intrusions into the world market.[16] But a perceptual factor may have been even more

TABLE 3.1 Average Annual Growth Rates of Population and Food
Production in Developing Market Economies, by IFPRI Category and
Region, 1960-1975 and 1975-1990 (in percentages)

IFPRI Category	Population		Food Production		
	1960-1975	1975-1990	Cereals 1960-1975	Other Staples 1961-1974[a]	All Major Staples 1975-1990
Food deficit	2.6	2.6	2.8	2.3	2.7
Low income	2.5	2.6	2.6	1.8	2.4
Middle income	2.8	2.9	3.6	3.1	3.5
High income	2.7	2.7	2.4	...	2.4
Grain exporters	2.6	2.9	4.0	...	4.0
Total developing market economies	2.6	2.7	3.0	2.3	2.9
Region					
Asia	2.5	2.5	3.1	-1.0	2.8
North Africa/ Middle East	2.7	2.9	2.5	2.9	2.5
Sub-Sahara Africa	2.6	2.9	1.8	3.5	2.2
Latin America	2.8	2.8	3.7	3.1	3.6
Total developing market economies	2.6	2.7	3.0	2.3	2.9

[a]Other staples include root crops, pulses and ground-nuts where
these are important components in the diet of the population. The cereal
equivalent of their output, computed on the basis of calorie content, was
used in calculating the combined growth rates.

Source: Food Needs of Developing Countries: Projections of Production
and Consumption to 1990 (Washington, D.C.: IFPRI Research Report 3,
December 1977), p. 33.

Sources of basic data: Population: United Nations Economic and
Social Affairs Department. "Selected World Demographic Indicators by
Countries, 1950-2000" (GSA/P/WP.55), May 1975.

Cereals: USDA, Foreign Agricultural Service, Computer Printout
on Production, 1975.

Other Staples: FAO, Production Tapes, 1975.

critical: The developing countries were so concerned with rapid industrialization and so convinced that it was the only road to development that a
bias against, if not outright indifference toward, the agricultural sector was
inevitable.[17] All of this changed radically with the crisis of 1972 and its
aftermath. A number of immediate factors—bad harvests, a deliberate

TABLE 3.2   Import Dependence

Country	Wheat % Imported (or trade status)	Wheat % of Calories	Rice % Imported (or trade status)	Rice % of Calories	Corn % Imported (or trade status)	Corn % of Calories
Afghanistan	3	54	ss	7	ss	18
Algeria	44	60	70		80	
Angola	85	5	uex	2	e	21
Argentina	e	33	3		e	
Bangladesh	94	14	4	32		4
Bolivia	72	18	ss	4	mss	25
Brazil	66	8	e	18		18
Burma	37	1	ss	72	e	
Burundi	100	1			ss	14
Cameroon	100	2			ss	15
Cen. African Rep.	100	2		1		8
Chad			ss	3		2
Chile	45	47	48	3	39	
Colombia	87	6	uex	22	uex	20
Costa Rica	100	14	uex	14	46	14
Cuba	100	27	60	16		
Dahomey				1	mss	32
Dominican Rep.	100	6	mss	15	41	3
Ecuador	69	8	uex	16	uex	12
Egypt	63	10	e	13	8	
El Salvador	100	6	uex	3		37
Ethiopia	70	10			mss	13
Gabon	100	6		2		2
Gambia	100	2	32	36		
Ghana	100	3	48	4		22
Guatemala	66	1	uex		5	56
Guinea	100	2	10	32		22
Guyana		21	mss	35		
Haiti	100	5		3	uex	24
Honduras	98	5	36		mss	49
India	10	14	uex	32	3	4
Indonesia	100		8	46	uex	14
Iran	17	49	19	12	65	
Iraq	30	39	uex	9		
Ivory Coast	100	5	41	20	mss	16
Jamaica	100	25	94	8	94	6
Jordan	50	49	100	5		
Kenya	uex	3			uex	46
Khmer Rep.			uex	73		
Korea (S.)	89	9	12	47	89	
Laos			11	85		3
Lebanon	86	45	100	4	95	
Liberia	100	1	28	53		

effort to cut the size of reserve stocks, the Soviet decision to enter the market in force—joined with more pessimistic interpretations of long-run trends in yields, emerging supply constraints in land, water, energy, and fertilizer, and environmental dangers to create fears of a double crisis: immediate starvation or severe malnutrition for millions of poor citizens in the Third World and a long-run inability of food production to keep up with food demand. World food problems suddenly became a major political issue, testimony for which was provided by the World Food Conference of 1974, and study of the world food system became a major growth industry.

TABLE 3.2 (Cont.)

Country	Wheat % Imported (or trade status)	Wheat % of Calories	Rice % Imported (or trade status)	Rice % of Calories	Corn % Imported (or trade status)	Corn % of Calories
Libya	85	44				
Madagascar				64		
Malawi	100	1			mss	84
Malaysia (west)	100	10	16	46	99	
Mali		1	16	9	mss	8
Mauritania		4		5		2
Mexico	24	9	uex	2	uex	43
Morocco	29	40	ss		6	6
Mozambique	91	3	uex	4	uex	20
Nicaragua	100	5	e	9	12	34
Niger				1		
Nigeria			1	2	1	7
Pakistan	14	20	e	47	99	2
Peru	85	16	uex	9	23	9
Philippines	100	6	8	44	5	12
Rwanda						7
Saudi Arabia	67	27	99	13		
Senegal	100	4	72	30	41	5
Sierra Leone	100	3	4	52		2
Singapore	100	11	100	35	100	
Somalia	100	3		7		22
Sri Lanka	100	10	29	48		
Sudan	53	5				
Syria	uex	49	99	3		
Tanzania	44	2	uex	4	uex	23
Thailand			e	72		
Tunisia		54			100	
Turkey	uex	50	mss	2	mss	1
Uganda		2			mss	7
Uruguay	uex	29		3		
Venezuela						
Vietnam (S.)	100	3	9	76	60	
Zambia	100	3			uex	60
Zaire	98	7	15	2	25	2

Key: ss = self-sufficient (production with neither imports nor exports)
uex = uncertain exporter (exports alternating with imports or no net trade)
e = exporter (steady exporter)
mss = marginally self-sufficient (imports alternating with years of self-sufficiency)

Source: Cheryl Christenson, "Food and National Security," in Klaus Knorr and Frank Trager, eds., Economic Issues and National Security (Lawrence, Kansas: Regents Press of Kansas, 1977), pp. 300-301. Trade figures computed from unpublished printout USDA, ERS. Calorie figures computed from the Food and Agriculture Organization, *Food Balance Sheets* (Rome: FAO, 1965).

The studies that began to appear in this period agreed on a number of major conclusions. All the experts agreed that a continuation of past trends was impossible. Developing-country demand in the 1980s and after would increase much faster than developing-country supply (the former increasing at roughly 3.6 percent per annum, the latter at 2.6 percent per annum).[18] Although there was some disagreement about amounts, there was no disagreement that the gap between supply and demand meant sharply rising import dependence for many developing countries — depending on a number of circumstances, the aggregate developing-country food deficit in 1985 was likely to fall somewhere between 40 and 100 million metric tons of cereals (see Table 3.3).[19] These projections rested on the assumption that LDC production rates would more or less match the rates achieved during the previous twenty years. They took no account of the additional amounts of cereals needed to diminish malnutrition nor did they include any judgments about policy changes, relative prices (although increasing demand surely meant sharply higher prices), or any other new development. They were simply extrapolations of likely growth rates for population, income, and production.[20] Still, with all the qualifications, these were very ominous projections, for it was improbable that many developing countries could export enough to pay the likely import bill or that food aid (which supplied between 30 and 45 percent of total LDC food imports in the 1960s) would do much to diminish the deficit. And the alternative of cutting consumption was neither morally nor politically acceptable.

The great majority of studies also agreed that the food problem was not a physical one: Enough food was being produced to feed everyone and food production could be increased enough to feed everyone in the future.[21] Consequently, the problem, both domestically and internationally, seemed essentially one of distribution, of providing the people who need the food with the purchasing power to buy it or the physical power to grow it. As we shall see in the next section, this raised a number of very crucial issues for developing-country governments. In any case, even if the developing countries sharply increased their production growth rates, they could not entirely eliminate the projected deficits by their own efforts.[22] Almost all the studies agreed, however, that the developed-country exporters would be able to meet whatever level of demand—*effective* demand—materialized.[23] But this judgment obviously also raised several important policy issues: about food aid, about the possibility of increased demand from developed-country importers driving the LDCs out of the market, about increased market instability from the increased number of market participants, and about the dangers of rising levels of external dependence (symbolized by the "food as a weapon" debate).

A widely shared diagnosis of the nature of the world food problem also led to widely shared prescriptions for dealing with it. There was (and is) nearly universal agreement that the first need was a set of policies that permitted and encouraged increased agricultural output in the developing countries. This was especially true for the deficit countries that seemed unlikely to be able to pay for necessary imports, as distinct from deficit countries that were earning enough foreign exchange and that might lose more than they gained if forced to divert investment funds from export industries to agriculture. As deficits would persist for some time, even if all

TABLE 3.3 Net Cereal Deficits in Less Developed Regions
(million metric tons)[a]

Region	Actual aver. 1969-71	Actual 1974-75	Projected[b] 1990
Asia	8.3	15.1[d]	41.2[d]
North Africa/Middle East	7.9	12.0	29.7
Sub-Sahara Africa	1.5	2.1	23.9
Latin America	(1.0)[c]	4.2	(8.4)
Total	16.7	33.4	86.4

[a]Figures represent net deficits--i.e., larger gross deficits minus the predicted surpluses of potential exporting countries in the region.

[b]Projected on the basis of 1960-1974 production trend in cereals which averaged 2.5 percent per year; consumption projected on the basis of assumed population growth, income growth and income elasticities of demand for food grain and feed grain. Income assumptions that produced the projections in this table reflect "low growth" variants (between 1.5 and 2 percent per year); if higher economic growth occurred, the projected demand and the consequent size of the deficits would be even larger (unless *growth* in production increased, growth already higher than in developed countries).

[c]Parentheses indicate net surpluses for region. Argentina is projected to remain a net exporter and Brazil will become a net exporter by 1990.

[d]Developing market economies only. Excludes Japan and Asian Communist Countries.

Source: Hopkins and Puchala, "Perspectives on the International Relations of Food," International Organization, Vol. 32, no. 3 (Summer 1978), p. 587. Based on data presented in Meeting Food Needs in the Developing World (Washington, D.C.: International Food Policy Research Institute, Research Report 1, February 1976), p. 27; and Nathan Koffsky, "Food Needs of Developing Countries," IFPRI mimeo, April 1977.

LDCs made a major effort to encourage increased agricultural output, and as some LDCs lacked sufficient resources to make the effort, continued food aid was imperative, and conventional aid programs would have to shift a higher proportion of their grants and loans to the agricultural sector. In addition, market instability, which creates problems for both exporters and importers, was likely to persist and perhaps to increase; thus, a reserve system consisting of either international or coordinated national buffer

stocks of cereals seemed necessary.[24] Finally, because the domestic
agricultural policies of the developed countries had a decisive impact on the
size of the necessary stocking system and indeed on the likely degree of
market instability itself, the final element of the emerging consensus was
agreement that those domestic policies also had to be changed.[25]

A world food system that incorporated the policies reflected in this consensus would certainly constitute something of a normative triumph. Even
apart from the obvious fact that achievement is surely likely to fall well
short of aspiration, the implicit norms of this new system are a substantial
improvement on the essentially nationalistic and uncoordinated norms of
the old (and, in practice, still existing) system. For the developed countries,
there is clear movement toward recognition of the need to take account of
international consequences in domestic policy decisions and toward acceptance of some *continuing* responsibility to provide support for agricultural
development in the Third World. Moreover, even the effort to increase
agricultural productivity within the developing countries (perhaps even at
some long-run danger to developed-country exports) may well implicitly
reflect a better understanding of the practical implications of interdependence: Only the ability to provide sufficient food for their own people
will permit the great majority of developing countries to avoid becoming
permanent charges (financial and moral) on the international system and to
be effectively integrated into the international economy. Finally, there is
also a new operational norm, for central guidance or central management—of stocks, of markets, of investment—must presumably supersede national control and the (ostensibly) free market.

Raymond Hopkins and Donald Puchala thus seem quite right when they
argue that the normative content of the world food system is in flux and that
the new norms that are emerging imply international scrutiny of domestic
actions, the need to take development implications into account in all policy
decisions within the system, and perhaps an increasing degree of global
responsibility for achieving sufficient levels of investment in agriculture.[26]
It need hardly be added that these are norms that are not everywhere
accepted, especially in the current environment, and that a certain asymmetry in responsibilities between developed and developing countries (for
example, do the developing countries really accept international scrutiny of
their policies?) is bound to create friction. From a policy perspective,
however, there is another question that may be more important. Even if we
agree that a world food system that reflected the new norms would be in the
interest of both developed and developing countries, we need to ask
whether the policies that presumably reflect the norms can or will be implemented. Or, put another way, what is the distance between the emerging
normative and policy consensus at the international level and the definition

of interests and needs by the different national governments? What answer we give to this question will permit some judgment about whether the emerging norms will provide the basis for an effective world food system or whether they are likely to become rhetorical camouflage for the continued pursuit of short-term national interests.

The Political Economy of Implementation

A number of food experts are optimistic about the long-run prospects for most developing countries.[27] Their optimism essentially reflects two judgments: that there are no inherent physical constraints on producing enough food to meet expected needs, even with existing technology, and that the developing countries will very quickly and very effectively adopt the necessary policies to increase their own agricultural output (or, alternatively for some, to earn enough foreign exchange to pay for imports). From this perspective, the problem is primarily transitional, and food aid and other aid for the agricultural sector are meant to ease the path to a viable food system, both nationally and internationally. If these judgments are correct, the support of the developed countries for the elements of the new world food system seems both wise and necessary; if they are not correct, however, the policy implications may be very different.

The only way for the developing countries to avoid massive and unmanageable food deficits in the 1980s is to sharply increase their own food production. As already noted, if demand increases at roughly 3.6 percent per annum and supply increases at roughly the historic rate, disaster impends. Merely maintaining past production growth rates is insufficient. Meeting expected needs will require more than a doubling of current output and unprecedented growth rates of something like 4–5 percent per annum. Several major studies contend that such rates are possible, but others doubt that they are possible and even question whether historic production rates can be maintained.[28]

The pessimists argue that production and productivity growth rates have been declining, that the amount and quality of land on which food could be grown is diminishing, that irrigation projects have slowed, that there may be water and fertilizer shortages, that energy costs are increasing, and that unfavorable changes in weather and climate (either a cooling or warming trend or merely increased variability) may be imminent.[29] Continuing high rates of population growth, as well as the effects of previous population growth, also threaten to erode (or continue to erode) whatever gains in production are possible. In addition, increasing demand from developed-country importers (Japan, Eastern Europe, and the Soviet Union) will make buying food even more costly and may cut into surpluses that could be used for aid.[30]

These are persuasive arguments, but they are not necessarily decisive.

Thus the optimists argue that sufficient land is available, that yields in the developing countries are much below the point at which they will begin to level off, and that fertilizer use is low and that relatively small increases will have much more effect than equivalent usage in the developed countries. In addition, they believe genetic research has much promise, energy costs are relatively less significant in the small-scale, labor-intensive agriculture that *should* dominate in the developing countries, and the food "shock" of 1972 increased awareness of the importance of the agricultural sector in development policies.[31] Recent evidence that fertility rates are declining and that family planning programs (and not merely socioeconomic development) have had an independent effect on the decline is also very encouraging.[32] This suggests two important points: Projected demand growth rates may be too high, particularly over the long run, and governments need not wait until development has progressed before they can do anything useful about population pressures. At any rate, taken together, these factors suggest that "the food problem of the developing countries is not a problem of limited resources, but rather a problem of mobilizing existing ones."[33] This also clearly implies that any judgment about the debate between optimists and pessimists must rest on a prior judgment about how governments and political leaders have responded and will respond to food problems—their own and those of the world food system.[34]

The evidence we have on recent performance must be treated with great caution, because the food problem (and food production) has a tendency to shift rapidly between scarcity and surplus, even in "normal" periods, and because the (presumably) unique features of the past five years may have undermined or inhibited even strong governmental commitments to agricultural restructuring. In any event, not enough time has passed since the World Food Conference to determine whether new trends have or have not been established. Nevertheless, the record is worth a brief comment, both because awareness of the need to reduce import dependence and increase production has been widespread and because we have no better evidence on which to base judgments.

The record of the past five years does not provide much ground for optimism about the food situation in the next decade. Favorable developments have certainly occurred, but what needs emphasis is that these developments have had little to do with policy actions by the developing countries themselves. Thus food production has increased in parts of the Third World and food stocks have been replenished in the United States and elsewhere, but this has been due primarily to good weather. And the annual production growth rate in the lower-income developing countries has declined sharply (from 2.6 percent in 1969 to 1.7 percent in the mid-1970s). In any case, the goal of achieving a 4 percent per annum production growth rate, which was emphasized in the UN World Food Conference's *Assessment of the World Food Situation,* was not achieved; the best that could be done, even with favorable weather, was about 3 percent per annum (1974–1978). Moreover, per capita output is no greater than it was in the early 1970s, and in some regions (Africa and the Middle East) it has actually fallen. In view of the conference's emphasis on reducing hunger, malnutrition, and import dependence, several other statistics may be even more alarming: The number of hungry and malnourished has increased significantly since 1974, the degree of self-sufficiency in cereal production has declined for the developing countries in the aggregate, and foodgrain imports have reached about 70 million tons (against 48 million tons in 1974).[35]

Investment in agriculture has increased sharply since the World Food Conference (by about 70 percent from 1974 to 1978), but most of the funds have come from external institutions like the World Bank and the UNDP, not from a shift of domestic resources out of other activities. One recent study concludes that "agriculture did not have very high priority in investment in a number of countries in the period under review" and that "it is significant that agriculture's share of total investment was lower than its share of GDP [gross domestic product]" in the great majority of countries examined.[36] In addition, national food reserves remain well below target levels; only eleven countries have established minimally adequate reserve stocks. Thus the pessimistic conclusion that "actual progress in implementing comprehensive agrarian reform programmes has been limited" seems amply warranted; so too does the judgment that the "World Food Conference target [for abolishing hunger and malnutrition] . . . in practice has been ignored."[37]

The international response to the goals and prescriptions of the World Food Conference has not been much better. Foreign aid for agricultural development has increased, but it is not much more than half the target. The proportion of total aid spending devoted to agriculture has also increased, but it is still only about 20 percent of the total — and most of the increase has come from shifts in World Bank spending patterns and not shifts in bilateral aid programs. Direct food aid is also still below the annual target of 10 million tons. It has proved difficult, as predicted, to reach agreement on a system of reserve stocks for stabilization purposes, and discussions have currently been suspended (although they are likely to resume). The smaller emergency stock has also fallen short of its goal of 500,000 tons. Finally, the domestic policies of the developed countries are still designed primarily to protect domestic farmers and/or consumers. In short, there may be increased awareness of the importance of the food issue and of the common interests at stake, but conflicting interests, divergent

perceptions, and economic fears and uncertainties have made it very difficult to transform awareness into new national and international policies.

The record of performance, taken by itself, is important, because it
clearly suggests the likelihood of some kind of food crisis in the decade
ahead and it means that more time has been lost and more resources will
have to be expended to compensate. From a policy perspective, however,
we need to ask why such failures have occurred. Clearly, some part of the
responsibility must be attributed to external forces beyond the control of
developing-country governments. But this is far from the whole story.
Some governments have not done what *is* within their power and resources,
and even where resources are very scarce and external developments very
adverse, some rough judgments can still be made about degrees of commitment and performance by different governments. Moreover, I must
strongly emphasize that the domestic performance of developing-country
governments is central to any attempt to understand why failures have occurred in the past and whether they are likely to occur in the future. Even a
benign and generous international response will not produce consistently
beneficial results if LDC governments fail to adopt sensible domestic food
policies, and even a malign and selfish international response will be
relatively less disastrous for governments that have invested their own
resources wisely.

Radical versus Reformist Approaches

As I have already indicated, there is something of a consensus about the
policies that developing-country governments should adopt if they want to
increase agricultural production. Why so many have not done so will be a
central theme in what follows. There is another theme, however, that will
be of nearly equal importance. Radical analysts argue that such policies will
fail unless they are preceded by political and social revolution; by contrast,
moderate analysts contend that the policies will work (in *most* cases) even
without massive revolution if the governments receive sufficient support
(and pressure) and if the external environment becomes less hostile. This is
an important conflict, for if the radicals are generally correct, the policy
implications for developed country governments are severe, but if the
moderates are generally correct, problems will persist but there will also be
policies available that are both politically feasible and economically sensible
for all concerned. At the conclusion of this discussion I should also be able
to say a bit more about the debate between optimists and pessimists.

Assessment of the World Food Situation argued that agricultural output and
productivity could be increased in the developing countries if governments
mobilized financial and other resources, if they accelerated a variety of
institutional reforms (for example, access to credit and to the market, in-

creased training and research, support for irrigation), if they maintained political stability, and if sufficient international aid was provided. Because the agricultural sector must bear much of the burden of reducing unemployment and absorbing population increases, support should be given to small-scale, labor-intensive farming. Indeed, support for the family farm on both employment and efficiency grounds is a nearly universal recommendation.[38] Moderate land reform, or at least the elimination of absentee landowners, has also received a great deal of support.

These are sensible measures that might succeed in reforming the agricultural sector and increasing output. But they have not worked well in the past, and a growing number of critics maintain that they are not likely to work in the future, even if external conditions become more favorable. The burden of their argument is that the food problem in all its dimensions—as distinct from merely raising output—cannot be resolved without a much more fundamental and radical restructuring of each country's socioeconomic and political institutions. This argument cannot be dismissed out of hand; not all of its proponents are radical ideologues, and there is a good deal of persuasive empirical evidence to support it. This is not to say, however, that the evidence is either complete or totally convincing—in fact, much of the argument is extrapolated from a few cases—or that the policy implications are quite as simple and straightforward as many of the argument's proponents suggest.

The argument for more radical change rests on a number of propositions. The interconnected problems of rural poverty and low agricultural productivity are attributed to unequal ownership of land and other assets, to governmental allocative mechanisms that discriminate in favor of the wealthy, and to investment and technological patterns that are biased against labor.[39] Government policies, it is alleged, are deliberately designed to sustain these inequalities and biases, because the governments are committed to rapid industrialization, the power of most governments is urban-based, and the governments receive support from the wealthy landowners and farmers. As Keith Griffin argues:

> The initial distribution of wealth and income has a decisive influence over the pattern of growth and hence over the rate of amelioration or deterioration in the standard of living of the lowest-income groups. Furthermore, given the initial conditions, it is difficult to change the distribution of income by manipulating standard policy instruments—tax, subsidy and expenditure levels, exchange rates and trade controls, monetary variables, etc. It follows from this that a "grow now, redistribute later" strategy is not a valid option in most countries; it is necessary first to "get the structure right."[40]

The argument could be restated in a different fashion: The social and political relationships implicit in underdeveloped societies tend to virtually guarantee that the normal instruments used to reduce or eliminate inequities will not function effectively. As Lance Taylor asks, how can you channel resources to the poor when markets are badly flawed, the price system is distorted, the tax system is regressive and corrupt, and the transmission of information and knowledge is difficult?[41] In effect, the conventional incentives to alter behavior do not work, and only those capable of taking risks and grasping new opportunities — that is, the wealthy — really benefit. Concrete evidence is well provided by the record of the green revolution: While production went up, rural inequities actually increased because the process was capital-intensive and biased toward the interests and capacities of the rich farmers.[42]

This argument clearly implies that conventional reform strategies must fail and that only a revolution that creates a new political order and a major redistribution of wealth — particularly (where economically justified) via radical land reform — will establish the conditions for a genuinely effective food system. Changes in the world food system and the policies of the developed countries are also imperative but, if such changes are not possible, the new domestic agricultural base will at least provide increased security against reliance on the vagaries of the world market by cutting import needs and by shifting agricultural production for export into domestic food crops. Insofar as this argument is correct (or is widely believed to be so), it confronts the governments of the developed countries with an extraordinary dilemma: Either they can continue to support reform proposals that will not work and that ultimately will create massive problems for the world food (and political) system or they can support revolutionary upheavals in many developing countries that will guarantee conflict and confrontation, that will generate much domestic conflict in the developed countries, and that might not in any case produce the anticipated outcomes. In sum, the developed countries confront a choice between the inept and the impossible.

The radical argument is important not only because there is some evidence to support it, but also because belief in its validity may generate increased pessimism (and perhaps apathy) on the part of the developed countries about the effectiveness of their support and increased revolutionary rhetoric by Third World intellectuals and leaders. There are a number of reasons, however, to doubt that the real choice is always between reaction and revolution. In the first place, there are a reasonably large number of developing countries that have increased agricultural production substantially without undergoing a revolution or that have increased their ability to pay for necessary imports.[43] In the second place, no one — self-styled revolutionaries or not — knows exactly how to create or control a revolution or to insure that it achieves its intended aims.[44] The assumption that revolution will succeed because reform has failed is dangerously naive, for it ignores too much of the historical record—some reformist successes, some revolutionary disasters—and mistakes a statement of faith for a statement of fact. Moreover, as it is unlikely that a massive firestorm of revolutions is imminent, and as some of the revolutions that do occur will make matters worse for the poor (as in Ethiopia, Benin, Uganda), it seems morally and politically irresponsible not to do what one can for the poor by whatever means are possible *now,* even if it delays the "revolution." Still, as we shall see, there are "more or less" distinctions along a very complex spectrum that are worth making in this context. These distinctions will be made more effectively if we admit that our knowledge and foresight are sharply limited; as Taylor notes, the poor are short of food and other resources, but "there is *not* an obviously effective way to attack this problem."[45] In a situation with so many complexities and uncertainties, the best strategy may not be an all-or-nothing gamble on revolution.

There is one last point about the conflict between radicals and reformers that seems particularly important. A revolution may change a regime and decimate the old ruling class, but it does not by itself remove the conditions responsible for underdevelopment. Poverty, malnutrition, unemployment, and all the other familiar afflictions of underdevelopment still persist, although a genuine revolutionary movement may be able to begin the process of removing them without the need to overcome the resistance of a corrupt and reactionary ruling class (if such indeed dominated). But it is of some importance that (with a few exceptions like Cambodia) the new revolutionary elite has had to adopt the moderate and evolutionary policies it previously denounced; such policies make sense, once a new set of initial conditions has been established, because there is no magical key by which underdevelopment can be made suddenly to disappear. This means that one is not arguing about policies per se but rather about which government is able or willing to create the conditions in which such policies can be effectively and *gradually* implemented. This suggests a way out of the apparently insoluble dilemma of choosing between unacceptable extremes.

Conclusions

What conclusions emerge from this discussion? Government performance has obviously been extremely uneven and generally disappointing. Neither the food crisis of 1972 nor the enhanced awareness of the importance of the agricultural sector has seemed to generate much genuine commitment to rural reform and modernization. Perhaps the good harvests of the past few years, which provided an opportunity for movement, deflected attention to other matters — hardly surprising, given the other demands on scarce resources. How much of the failure should be attributed to the external shocks of the last five years — oil, inflation, monetary turbulence — and how much to governmental ineptitude and biases is impossible to determine; the two are not really separable and have affected individual countries in widely differing ways. Nevertheless, whatever the difficulties, for policy purposes a number of crucial judgments must be made about the likely performance of developing country governments in the next decade.

The food issue, taken by itself, does not provide grounds for great optimism; neither does it provide grounds for apocalyptic pessimism. If fertility rates continue to decline, if aid increases, and if awareness of the centrality of the food problem continues to grow, the worst outcomes seem unlikely and a number of LDCs may do very well. And in the longer run, if those who are optimistic about physical potentials are correct, prospects for diminishing hunger and malnutrition may be reasonably bright. But there are obvious difficulties with this argument: The food issue cannot be sensibly treated in isolation, and some factors suggest that surviving the transition may become increasingly problematic for large numbers of developing countries.

The case for optimism ultimately rests on the judgment that developing-country governments will adopt, at the very least, the package of reform measures necessary to increase agricultural production and the purchasing power of the poor. The case for pessimism rests on the fact that few have done so and — most critically — the judgment that not enough will do so in the future even if increased external resources are provided. Governments in the Third World generally are too weak and unstable politically and too unskilled and inflexible economically to change course quickly and effectively; given the existing commitment to rapid industrialization, the power of vested interests, and the bias against agriculture and rural modernization, the prospects for conversion to a new strategy are limited by insufficient resources and power and/or insufficient willingness to change the distribution of benefits. Fear of generating instability is likely to be exacerbated by a more general propensity to avoid risks on the part of both government elites and rural interests. The key policy point concerns government incentives: What actions can foreign governments or international institutions take to alter the risk calculus so that rural reform seems less dangerous than repression and the maintenance of the status quo? I shall return to this issue in the next section.

Most of the nonoil LDCs also lack the financial resources to make a major new commitment to agriculture in the face of massive and mounting balance of payments deficits. In the short run, this suggests that the food problem is in large part financial. Deficit countries with financial resources will obviously be able to buy what they need, even if prices begin to rise. For other countries, both financial and food aid will be imperative. Even if such aid doubles in real terms, however, this would probably be at the expense of other kinds of aid (for energy, industrial development, etc.). In addition, although the focus on a new agricultural strategy based on the small farmer is very widespread, in the near term progress in increasing output is likely to require the adoption of the energy- and capital-intensive, science-based techniques so prominent in developed-country agriculture. Whatever else they may be, these techniques are very expensive.[46] In short, when the financial resources needed to increase food production and to pay for food imports are added to the resources needed for other purposes, the situation looks grim. This is true in an immediate and graphic sense for the poor countries that cannot feed their own people, but the effects may be much more widespread and long-term if they lead to repudiation of debts, sharp cutbacks in imports from developed countries, forced adoption of increasingly inward and inefficient development strategies, and perhaps deliberately destabilizing actions as a form of blackmail. I shall discuss the resource question again in the next section.

The argument that the food problem cannot be dealt with in isolation because it is part of a larger systemic financial problem does not mean that specific policy actions within the food sector are irrelevant. It does mean that such actions are likely to be insufficient; perhaps for most states, especially the poorest, little more than holding actions at best. Still, there are degrees of both success and failure in these circumstances and better or worse choices can be made. Effective use of available resources may diminish the need for very scarce external resources and provide some building blocks for more extensive action later. But a short-run crisis seems likely in the next four or five years because these minimal policy actions may be the *most* that can be anticipated unless the larger financial issue is resolved.

Successful efforts to deal with the food problem will also require coordinated policy responses at both the national and international levels. But pessimism about achieving the necessary degree of coordination seems amply warranted, especially if we look at the structure of the prevailing arguments. The developed countries blame the food problem primarily on ineffective policies in the developing countries. The developing countries blame the domestic policies of the developed countries and the international system that reflects those policies. Both agree that international institutions are not doing enough, but the developed countries refuse to give the institutions more resources and the developing countries refuse to give them more authority within their own countries. The international institutions blame their members, but refuse to question their own competence or their proper role in the development process. In sum, each believes that it is doing enough and that the real problem lies elsewhere. This does not provide much ground for cooperative and coordinated policy responses, either now or in the future.

These comments suggest that a food crisis is quite likely in the mid-1980s, unless luck with the weather persists or a massive international aid effort suddenly becomes feasible. As the effects of the crisis are likely to be very asymmetrical, one clear need will be for prior policy judgments about which countries to help in what manner. The major danger is not a massive, system-wide shortage of food, but rather a series of smaller crises that might or might not be cumulative. Food crises in India and Bangladesh are obviously not of the same order as food crises in the Sahel, but even a smaller crisis could have disproportionate external effects in some circumstances unless containment actions had been prepared in advance.[47] Two other probable developments should be noted: a continued widening of the gap within the Third World and continued and escalating pressures by the Third World on the international system for increased resource transfers and radical changes in operating rules. The first of these developments will obviously make cooperation in the second more difficult, and both together raise important questions about the wisdom of seeking global North-South solutions to what may not be global North-South problems.

The Foreign Policy of Food

Many experts attribute the major problems of the world food system to the fact that national concerns override the wider concerns of the system.[48] In particular, pricing policies in the large developed countries are primarily aimed at achieving domestic price stability, usually by manipulating exports and imports, even at the cost of increased pressures on world market prices. Consequently the first imperative for an improved world food system is a decision by the developed countries to allow domestic prices to reflect world market prices; the second imperative is agreement on a system of international stocks to stabilize the market and to insure the availability of sufficient imports for the developing countries. This is surely sensible; after a period of adjustment, it would probably permit both groups of countries to achieve their aims, if the developing countries simultaneously managed to increase domestic food output.[49]

Unfortunately, there is little persuasive evidence that such proposals are about to be implemented. They require of the developed countries a willingness to accept some short-run risks and costs and to weigh long-run and systemic concerns more heavily. There are clearly some signs that the developed countries are moving (or being pushed) in this direction as a result of new perceptions of, and new pressures from, the growth of economic interdependence. Thus there is increased recognition that all are likely to benefit from price stabilization; that an unreliable food system that forces the developing countries toward uneconomical forms of self-sufficiency may ultimately harm developed-country food exporters (and diminish international trade in general as a result of misallocated resources); and that the stability of the international system itself may be threatened if some developing countries become increasingly desperate. Nevertheless, the translation of these emerging perceptions into new policies has been inordinately difficult and is likely to remain so until such policies can also be justified in terms of short-run benefits to the developed countries and acceptable policy responses from the developing countries. Current economic conditions obviously make the transformation even more difficult, and the current policy failures of the developing countries may make the systemic focus itself increasingly questionable. At any rate, for the 1980s we must assume that we are seeking food policies for a very second-best world, one in which the market distortions created by the primacy of domestic stabilization decisions will persist, any reserve system that may be created is unlikely to be large enough to deal with all needs, and the agricultural policies of the developing countries will fall well short of what seems necessary.

Policy in these circumstances must have several different dimensions. There is, for example, a distinction — and a connection — between the short run and the long run that must be kept in mind. Short-run crises can be dealt with by such measures as emergency food stocks, an improved disaster relief system, and a fund to finance necessary imports. At the same time, such crises will tend to become permanent and perhaps unmanageable unless long-run policies are successful in increasing agricultural output and stabilizing the market. If the latter are unsuccessful, or if international agreement on relevant policies is impossible, short-run responses may also have to be reconsidered — which, at a minimum, will raise several very difficult political and humanitarian questions.

Another rough distinction must be made between food policy, the foreign policy of food, and the international politics of food. Food policy, which must rest upon the conventional package of measures that has received wide support from experts, governmental agencies, and international institutions, can be divided into two categories: measures that can or should be implemented by international institutions or foreign governments to help the developing countries to deal with their food problems and measures that must be implemented by the developing countries themselves. Again, these are separate but connected; failure at one level is likely to lead to failure at the other (or at least to make success much more difficult). This implies that one of the central issues for foreign governments and institutions will be whether incentives can be incorporated into external policies that will encourage governing elites in the developing countries to implement dangerous and perhaps unpopular reforms. Even in the best of circumstances, there will be a gap between what needs to be done and what developing-country governments seem able or willing to do, and this also raises questions about the implications of varying degrees of success or failure within and between regions. I shall return to this issue momentarily.

All of these food policy measures have an indirect effect upon foreign policy insofar as they structure responses and attitudes within the Third World toward the developed countries and the international system. Food policy and foreign policy are directly connected, however, on the issue of which governments to support by what means.[50] Scarce resources and varying degrees of success with implementation will require complex judgments about priorities and about trade-offs between bilateral, regional, and global initiatives. The multiple and occasionally conflicting goals that the United States seeks to achieve through its Third World policies will obviously complicate the process of choice. For example, the United States cannot actively support political and social revolution against existing governments — short of taking chaos as a norm — and must work with and through existing governments. Obviously this does not imply that all governments should be supported or that governments that come to power by revolution could not be supported if they were genuinely committed to development or even if other national interests made it imperative (for instance, a revolutionary government in Saudi Arabia — or Iran — that continued to produce and sell oil). In any case, the essential point here is that the United States will have to make choices about food policy and those choices should reflect prior judgments about broader foreign policy interests.[51]

The international politics of food concerns those aspects of the food problem that are likely to affect the stability or the operation of the international system itself. Localized food crises seem more probable than a single, global crisis, although the latter is not wholly improbable. These crises will probably force the developing countries to demand sharply increased resource transfers and a centrally managed international food system. The ensuing debate will raise some profound questions about the kind of international system that is desirable and possible. As we shall see, the issue may come to focus on whether a permanent and automatic international social welfare system — roughly parallel to domestic welfare systems — is either necessary or feasible. (The debate may also greatly increase animosities if it generates or exacerbates suspicions that aid will be used primarily for the maintenance of stability and control, rather than for rural reform and that international management is sought as a means of avoiding domestic change.) Systemic questions may also arise in another way. Crises in some countries or some regions might have a major effect on the stability of the international food system (and perhaps derivatively on the whole system) as well as on perceptions of how the international system must be regulated. As food policy, foreign policy, and international politics are all likely to be affected by this issue, it may be useful to preface the policy discussion with a brief analysis of the most likely, or the most crucial, regions of potential crisis. The analysis does not lead to any surprising conclusions, but it may be helpful in suggesting patterns and questions of some policy interest.

Food experts have tended to divide the developing countries into a number of distinct groups.[52] One group includes countries that do not produce enough food to meet domestic demand, but nevertheless earn sufficient foreign exchange to pay for necessary imports. The OPEC countries and some of the successful exporters of manufactures are obviously examples, but a few mineral exporters may also qualify (for example, Bolivia, Morocco, and Tunisia). Potential crisis points within this group include large OPEC countries like Nigeria and Indonesia and a number of smaller countries whose export earnings might be impaired through economic developments or domestic political upheavals (for example, South Korea, Bolivia, and Morocco).

A second group includes countries that are self-sufficient or even manage to export food. The self-sufficient include two important large countries—Pakistan and Brazil—and a group of smaller countries with a somewhat shifting membership. For example, Cameroon, Kenya, and Uruguay have remained on the list for some time, but Ethiopia, Tanzania, Turkey, Zimbabwe, and Burma are questionable inclusions. Still, the capacity for sufficient production is there, provided untoward events do not occur, as they have with Ethiopia and Tanzania, and that their governments are not overwhelmed by the financial crisis. The exporters include Argentina, Thailand, Burundi, and Mexico.

The remainder of the developing countries can be divided in various ways, but the essential point is that they are all very vulnerable: They do not produce enough food and they cannot afford to pay increasing food import bills. Some have serious production problems because food production has not kept up with population growth; others have simply not made much effort (or have made unsuccessful efforts) to exploit existing potential for increased production. These countries might also be divided according to the degree of import dependence. Alberto Valdes and Barbara Huddleston, for example, distinguish a group of dependent importers, including OPEC countries like Venezuela, Algeria, and Libya and important non-OPEC countries like Malaysia and Sri Lanka, from marginal importers (that is, countries whose imports as a percentage of total consumption are small) like India, Indonesia, the Philippines, Ghana, Bangladesh, Nigeria, Egypt, Chile, Taiwan, and South Korea.[53] For policy purposes, however, this list is somewhat less useful. Some of the dependent importers can well afford to pay their import bills, and some of the marginal importers are so large that even relatively small shortfalls could have disproportionately large effects on the world market and on the system of reserve stocks (and, in any case, several will have difficulty in paying for even marginal imports). In the circumstances, the World Food Council's list of forty-three "Food Priority Countries" (see Table 3.4) seems to me the best indicator of potential areas of crisis. It does not include countries likely to be able to buy what they need, and it does include countries that might confront a crisis in the next decade, even if they are currently marginal importers (India), self-sufficient (Pakistan), or exporters (Burundi) on another list.

The food priority countries need to be further disaggregated. India is projected to have about one-third of the total Third World food deficit in the mid-1980s. Nigeria alone is projected to have about two-thirds of the African deficit. Other countries with a large share of the projected deficit include Bangladesh, the Philippines, Indonesia, and Egypt.[54] These six countries could have more than 75 percent of the total deficit over the next decade. The magnitude of their needs, either in a short-run crisis or as a result of long-run failures to increase production, could easily overwhelm whatever security measures are built into the world food system. A disaster in these countries could also generate a great deal of regional instability, not least in the sense that smaller neighbors in need of imports might be driven out of the market or treated as residual recipients of whatever aid is available. What happens to these countries will have a significant effect not only on the viability of the world food system but also on the entire North-South relationship. There is no doubt, then, that these countries must be the focus for food policy initiatives. But what this means in practical terms must be carefully considered.

Several points are worth noting. None of the large deficit countries are in Latin America, which suggests that food crises there can probably be contained relatively easily. The pattern in Africa is different, with one large deficit country — Nigeria — and a great many small deficit countries. A Nigerian food crisis would almost certainly affect its immediate neighbors, but short of a continent-wide crisis, probably would not have a major impact on North or East Africa. In any case, virtually all of Africa will face persistent deficits — which is to say, persistent local crises — for several decades. The Middle East has one major deficit country — Egypt — but otherwise a different pattern obtains: a few relatively rich countries where

TABLE 3.4   World Food Council Food Priority Countries

ASIA	AFRICA (cont'd)
Bangladesh	Mauritania
Burma	Mozambique
Democratic Kampuchea	Niger
India	Nigeria
Indonesia	Rwanda
Laos	Senegal
Nepal	Sierra Leone
Pakistan	Somalia
Philippines	Tanzania
Sri Lanka	Uganda
	Upper Volta
AFRICA	
	NORTH AFRICA/MIDDLE EAST
Benin	
Cameroon	Afghanistan
Cape Verde	Egypt
Central African Empire	Sudan
Chad	Yemen Arab Republic
Ethiopia	Yemen People's Democratic Republic
Gambia	
Guinea	LATIN AMERICA
Guinea Bissau	
Kenya	El Salvador
Lesotho	Guyana
Malagasy Republic	Haiti
Malawi	Honduras
Mali	

demand is outpacing production (Saudi Arabia, Iran) and several poorer countries in which both demand and population are growing faster than production (Jordan, Syria, Iraq, Yemen, as well as North African states like Algeria and Tunisia). South and Southeast Asia, conversely, have many potential major deficit countries: India, Bangladesh, Pakistan, Indonesia, the Philippines. Smaller countries in the area, such as Sri Lanka, Nepal, Burma, and Cambodia, have significant problems of their own, but will also be heavily affected by what happens in the large countries. Divergent patterns within regions are almost as salient as the divergences between regions.[55]

Most studies implicitly assume that all of these problems can be dealt with in the context of a reconstituted world food system. In the abstract, this seems to make a good deal of sense; for example, consistent principles and practices could be applied in all cases, and some savings might result from the creation of a single reserve system. Nevertheless, as the range and depth of the food problem differ so widely between regions, it may make more sense to try to build integrated regional or subregional food systems with partial links to a global system than a dominant global food system, at least at this time. Supply shortages usually occur in single regions, not simultaneously throughout the world.[56] This provides the obvious linkage with the rest of the food system: Regions in surplus sell to regions facing a shortfall. But it seems both financially and politically more practical to create a small, regionally sited emergency stock (i.e., not a stabilization stock), a regional fund to finance necessary imports, and a much smaller international stock to serve as a supplier of last resort, rather than a single massive buffer stock system to stabilize prices and supply.[57]

The argument is *not* that regional cooperation is always easier to achieve; old animosities and the lack of functional ties may make it as difficult as any other attempt at cooperation. But if the problems are regional, if regional needs (and food tastes) are similar, and if there is already some movement toward cooperation — as there is in all regions — it may be easier to negotiate a regional food system. Such a system may operate more effectively and may increase awareness of common interests and problems. It may also provide a degree of protection for the smaller states within the region. At any rate, given the enormous difficulties and costs of creating a centrally managed global system, we ought at least to make sure that a regional system cannot be created or that it would be too inefficient before we gamble everything on a global system.[58] From another perspective, if policy changes in the North-South arena are to remain largely incremental, which seems likely but which also seems to guarantee a series of small-scale crises (small for the system as a whole), the narrower focus may make both crisis-aversion and crisis-management more feasible.

The international response to the food problems of the developing countries is important — whether the focus is regional, subregional, or global — but the response of developing-country governments is even more important. As already noted, there is general agreement among the experts about the specific measures that governments should be implementing, although radicals and reformers disagree about whether it will be possible to get governmental and other elites to reverse the prevailing bias against agricultural development and whether reform measures will suffice. There is no way to resolve this issue in the abstract; the factors encouraging either optimism or pessimism are too balanced. One point worth noting is that this indicates how vast the uncertainties are — not only in food, but also in energy and trade. This suggests that the pattern of success or failure will be highly differentiated and that one crucial variable will be governmental performance (although as we shall see, even good performance may be overwhelmed by external forces). In this situation developed-country governments will thus be able to exert some influence on outcomes. And in making decisions about whom to help — about who is genuinely committed to increasing production and reducing poverty — two issues are likely to be crucial: how to give governments that are short of resources and concerned with their own survival incentives to implement a major reform program and how to make rough but reasonable judgments about whether implementation is genuine. If incentives cannot be given and if implementation can be faked, the radical argument about the need for revolution may very well turn out to be justified.

Increasing the incentives for poor and insecure governments to give food production the highest priority is far from simple. Merely providing more external resources is insufficient. They may be misused (or used as a substitute for, rather than a complement to, domestic resources) unless the government itself is committed to a new approach — that is, unless the new approach reflects government priorities and not just the priorities of foreign donors. And many developing-country governments, perhaps inevitably, are concerned with immediate problems and are so short of resources that long-term questions of food security are rarely salient. Foreign governments, pursuing their own political ends, have not made much effort to encourage policy changes by developing-country governments. The power of foreign governments is clearly limited in such circumstances. This is not to argue that the case is hopeless, but to gain leverage and to increase power to persuade, external donors will need to think more contextually about the problems confronting the elites who must accept and then implement the policies that the donors advocate. Too frequently, when developed-country analysts discuss the politics of policymaking, they have in mind the problems of winning domestic support in the developed countries for particular policies and not the problems confronting developing-country governments. Or external analysts concentrate on narrow studies, such as the means of convincing peasants to adopt new techniques, without worrying enough about how to convince the government to support such programs with its own resources — and I must emphasize that most of the resources in any program must come from domestic sources.

Thinking contextually requires understanding that developing-country governments must deal with multiple challenges simultaneously and that they confront a "capabilities paradox": The poorest and weakest states, with new and untried institutions, carry the heaviest burdens.[59] This means that feasible policies must be much more than technically correct. They must also reflect some consideration of whether they are justified in light of competing demands — in, say, energy — for limited resources. Beyond this, the policy process must also take account of who must accept and support particular policies and what their needs and attitudes happen to be. In short, political feasibility is as crucial as technical feasibility.

Within this context, perhaps some additional support for giving food production a very high priority might be generated by emphasizing certain matters that are likely to be of great concern to ruling elites. Thus the connection between stability and the capacity to provide citizens with sufficient food is worth noting, as well as the fact that some of the most successful Third World producers (for example, South Korea and Taiwan, which produce as much grain per acre as the United States) have also been successful in other aspects of development and have been relatively stable. Given the strong commitment to industrialization, great stress should also be placed on the fact that industrialization is probably impossible without a strong agricultural sector to provide food and savings and to buy industrial goods. This point is especially important because many elit s want to reduce external dependence, obviously an impossible goal if food imports continue to grow. In addition, the provision of external resources is crucial, but only if the commitment is relatively long-term. In this sense, the shift in aid strategy from projects to programs (and perhaps even some financing of local and recurrent costs), whatever its economic rationale, may also give the donor more leverage over a longer period: Governments may be reluctant to see support withdrawn from programs that have been initiated and that involve a great many citizens (as distinct from most projects). Government intentions to perform may also be reinforced if it is clear that performance will be regularly evaluated by the donor. But that brings us to the complex question of how performance can or should be evaluated.

The possibility of generating primarily rhetorical or counterfeit commitments to agricultural development cannot be dismissed, not only because of the dangers of agrarian reform but also because competing demands are so strong. Indeed, the desire to get more resources and to please donors may be great enough to induce apparent conversion to any new doctrine. One need only recall how frequently "development plans" have been created, not to be used but to be displayed for visiting aid missions. Subjective judgments about intentions are unavoidable in these circumstances, but perhaps they could be supplemented by a rough index of commitment. The index could be based on such things as shifts in investment patterns toward agriculture, increases in production, changes in import dependence, and governmental ability to extract domestic resources. Foreign donors might also insist that each aid recipient prepare a national food strategy as a precondition for aid (or at least strongly encourage them to do so)—even if the developing countries object. As I have noted, allowance has to be made for the "capabilities paradox" and for the impact of uncontrollable external factors like worldwide inflation. Moreover, care has to be taken in how success is measured: If most of the developing countries that do well seem to be those that did well in the past and that have a relatively high level of per capita income, different measures and different definitions of success may be necessary for the poor countries that are doing badly.[60] None of this is completely satisfactory, but it may be a useful starting point and, above all, it may provide some indication that the developed countries are serious about making (and acting upon) judgments of performance. As resources become increasingly scarce, need alone will not suffice as a criterion for aid. Almost all the developing countries will be in need, and available resources will probably go first to those that seem most likely to make effective use of them.

What has been discussed thus far is essentially a food policy response to several near-term dangers. The need for a quick response and for more effective allocation of very scarce resources seems to dictate a shift in emphasis within the available package of measures to deal with food problems: The focus, from this perspective, should be more regional or subregional, in hopes of developing practical programs of cooperation, and more selective, in suggesting more concern with performance and with the needs of the large countries that could affect the operation of the whole food system. Over the medium and longer term, the emphasis must be on increasing government incentives to implement reform proposals. In a narrow sense, this is a food policy measure, but in a broader sense, it is the most promising means of containing the short-term crisis — and thus containing the foreign policy and international politics implications of world food problems. For the U.S. government, the most difficult aspect of this approach is not with the policy means themselves (increased aid, technical assistance, support for various reserve stocks), but rather with the effort to distinguish genuinely reform-minded governments from the others and to determine priorities not only among countries, but also among competing needs in an environment of multiple and conflicting political, strategic, and economic goals.

The desirability of an improved world food system is not at issue here, but the means of achieving it surely is. Implicitly, the argument is that a new system will not emerge merely because it seems desirable, but rather that immediate needs must be met first (and cannot await the complex negotiations for a new order) and that immediate responses must be designed, as far as possible, so that they become practical building blocks for continued reform. This is a modest goal, and an unsatisfactory one in terms of perceived needs, but it must be noted that, although many experts have designed models of an improved world food system, none has indicated how to achieve it.[61] For that matter, it is not self-evident that a world food system that requires massive buffer stocks and centrally controlled markets and that does not have the power to intervene within developing countries to impose necessary reforms will perform better than a more modestly reformed system.

One major problem with the kind of pragmatic reform strategy that I have outlined is that it does not promise to help all who need help or perhaps even all who deserve help. The strategy is most useful to those countries that have some capacity to help themselves; even in the worst of circumstances, the measures proposed will at least permit these countries to diminish the force of either an internal or external crisis. The notion of choosing among developing countries on the basis of merit (and U.S. needs) is morally unattractive and can be justified only by the even more unattractive consequences of alternative strategies. But to do more will require a vastly greater commitment of resources than most of the developed countries seem willing to contemplate. Moreover, even a sensible reform strategy might become increasingly futile or irrelevant in the next decade, not because the radical argument is necessarily correct, but rather because neither radical nor moderate arguments will make much difference in the context of the massive financial crisis that may loom ahead for most of the nonoil developing countries.

In what follows, I shall look only at the financial problem in the food arena (and not in relation to energy and other needs) and then return very briefly to the question of whether a vast commitment of resources to help these countries (as in various proposals for a new "Marshall Plan") must be considered more seriously. The discussion thus far has been largely in terms of existing policy responses and of the various constraints that inhibit implementation of those policies and that make the acceptance of more fundamental policy responses seem improbable. By implication, the ensuing discussion prepares the ground for the broader policy issues that will be considered in Chapters 6 and 7. The crucial point is that, whether the United States merely continues present policies or makes an effort to alter current policies in a number of important ways, the stance that it adopts toward the food issue cannot be treated apart from its stance toward the whole North-South arena.

Although it is difficult to attach dollar figures to projected import deficits, even the most moderate projections of future price trends and future deficits are potentially catastrophic. For many countries, especially the least developed, even maintaining current nutritional levels may become increasingly difficult.[62] The amount of financing projected as necessary to increase investment in agriculture so that growth rates can approach the target of 4 percent per annum — which will be necessary to reduce import costs — is also substantial. For example, a recent study by the World Food Council estimates that domestic investment for the whole agricultural sec-

tor would have to reach roughly $16–20 billion per annum over the
1975–1985 period—about double current levels of investment.[63] Foreign
aid, which would have to provide perhaps one-third of the investment
spending, would also have to double, increasing 8.5 percent per annum in
real terms in the 1980s.[64]

Both aid and investment are currently well below targeted levels, but the
amounts by themselves are not inconceivable. Taken in context with other
needs and with prevailing attitudes toward foreign aid, however, they make
for a grim prognosis.[65] This means that attempts to influence LDC governments or to make judgments on the basis of performance will probably be
ineffectual and misleading. Most countries will simply not have the
resources to undertake any new programs, and available resources are
likely to be spent disproportionately on maintaining stability (current consumption, buying arms, pacifying the colonels, etc.).[66] What developing-
country governments have not been able or willing to do in the relatively
benign international environment of the 1960s and early 1970s, they are
not likely to be able or willing to do in the probably menacing environment
of the 1980s.

Put another way, the argument simply means that food policy can no
longer be discussed in isolation from the other elements of the current
systemic crisis: energy, trade, and debt. In this sense, the genuine reasons
for a *moderate* degree of optimism about the long-range food problem—particularly increased awareness and concern and the most recent population
figures—may be counteracted by an inability to take absolutely necessary
actions during the transition period.[67] The more general implications of
this for North-South policies will be discussed in Chapters 6 and 7. But in
the context of food policy itself, it tends strongly to support the arguments
of the pessimists, if for a somewhat different reason. The uncertainties at
the root of the debate between the optimists and pessimists have not really
been resolved—the outcome in relatively "normal" circumstances is still
unclear—but the pressure of events seems increasingly likely to simply
overwhelm even genuine efforts to reform the agricultural sector.

The unity of the developing countries may be increasingly strained by
these developments. Some countries, particularly the "success stories" in exporting manufactures, will probably be compelled to seek even closer integration with (or dependence on) the developed countries, and they may
be less willing or less able to make concessions in trade to the poorer LDCs
(and may also outbid the latter for available food supplies). Many of the
poorest countries may be forced into self-reliance by lack of an effective
alternative. Even countries that have reasonably good export prospects for
some agricultural commodities may feel compelled to use the land for the
production of food for domestic consumption. Fears about the risks of ex-

ternal dependence may outweigh the potential gains from increased trade. Certainly the movement toward collective self-reliance will become even more prominent, but it is doubtful that many countries will make the sacrifices or provide the leadership to convert rhetoric into meaningful practical cooperation. Finally, between a small group of countries that might not remain viable, there is a third group that is likely to vacillate between the extremes, doing nothing well. In short, this could be an increasingly stratified and increasingly unstable international system. It could also be a system in which most of the developing countries become more dependent on the developed countries, to assure continued access to markets, to receive various kinds of aid, or to receive protection against internal and external enemies. The common interests and perspectives of the Group of 77 may not be strong enough to maintain unity.

This is a grim forecast. It might also be wrong. However, prudence suggests that it be taken seriously, for many of the actions that might be elicited if it is correct could be very harmful to the United States and the other developed countries: debt default, a rise in terrorism, domestic conflict over which countries should be helped, a sharp decline in welfare in both developed and developing countries, and a major setback to the effort to establish a more stable world order. The policies that I outlined earlier would provide only very limited relief in these circumstances, perhaps helping some countries to cope and perhaps permitting some progress in developing patterns of regional and subregional cooperation. The model of the international system implicit in this forecast is obviously unappealing: It would be a closed system, perhaps dominated by something akin to spheres of interest, and run according to fragmented and discontinuous principles and rules.

As I have already noted, the alternative to this seems to be a massive transfer of resources to the developing countries. There have been many suggestions for a new Marshall Plan for the Third World or for a "Global New Deal," and more recently the Brandt Commission has proposed even more far-reaching measures.[68] The political feasibility of such proposals is virtually nil, but they raise additional problems that should be noted.[69] Some advocates of global restructuring, for example, have proposed not only major increases in conventional aid, but also the creation of an international fund, based on various kinds of taxes, that would automatically and continuously provide resources to all countries in need (or perhaps according to some prorated formula). But should all countries receive aid automatically, irrespective of behavior (e.g., Idi Amin and Emperor Bokassa) and performance? After all, except for short-term or humanitarian purposes, the mere provision of external resources is not very helpful: Some control has to be established over who gets the resources and how they are employed. But the developing countries might not accept this (note, for example, their demand at the most recent UNIDO conference for a $300 billion fund *entirely* under their control), which is why they have so persistently demanded automatic aid — and why it should be resisted. Controls are imperative, if only because wasted resources could have been usefully expended elsewhere (including on the poor in the developed countries) and because continued waste will inevitably create a climate even more hostile to further resource transfers.

Negotiation of such an agreement would also take many years. This is true not merely because the idea of an international social welfare system has not yet been widely accepted, but also because there is no longer a dominant state (the United States as an "ordinary state") capable of imposing its will and pacifying dissidents with side payments. At any rate, this implies that the crisis that looms ahead may well strike before the foundations of a new order can be laid.

For the moment, then, the only viable alternative seems to be a reform strategy designed to cope with the emerging crisis and to diminish or contain its scope. Within this context, if the United States wanted to add to the policy measures already discussed — primarily to facilitate the transition to a more stable system — initiatives in three areas could be very useful. First, it should seek "standstill" agreements that try to prevent abandonment of existing principles or to enforce some degree of international accountability before abandonment or violation. The stabilization of gains and the prevention of further deterioration must be the first order of business. Second, it should be thinking more seriously about emergency and stopgap measures to deal with immediate crises as they arise — for example, by creating a larger emergency reserve stock or a larger fund for financing of necessary imports. An improved disaster relief system is also imperative.[70] In addition, perhaps the United States could offer direct support to a number of the largest countries to finance a national stock program. Third, it should aim at negotiating as many practical, small-scale agreements as possible, as in the recent ASEAN commitment to create a regional rice buffer stock. At the very least, such agreements could cushion the shock of adverse external developments; they could also make wider efforts at cooperation easier — if they become possible.

The United States and the other developed countries must also begin to think more clearly about development strategies and their relationship to the stratified, dependent, and hostile international system that may dominate the next decade. Incoherence and uncertainty about what the United States is advocating wastes resources, encourages confusion, and facilitates the evasion of commitment. For some countries, the conventional strategy of rapid industrialization and an export orientation may still make sense. For others, a partially closed strategy and an emphasis on agricultural reform may suffice. Still others may require a more radical strategy, implying a substantial degree of isolation from the international system. The United States also needs to ask what strategy, if any, makes sense for countries that do not appear able to adopt any coherent strategy — that simply lack sufficient resources or rational leadership to cope with their problems — and that may become permanent charity cases of an international system without an institutionalized welfare component. These are not academic issues in a universe of increasingly and perhaps desperately scarce resources.

Notes

1. If one holds to the following definition of success, the problem resolves itself, as we are unlikely to have any successes: "A successful forecast must account for at least the following: the direction of the activity modeled, the direction of sharp breaks or reversals, the extent of change, the period over which change is likely to persist, the points in the system most amenable to manipulation, and the costs of manipulation." Nazli Choucri, "Key Issues in International Relations Forecasting," in Nazli Choucri and Thomas W. Robinson, eds., *Forecasting in International Relations: Theory, Methods, Problems, Prospects* (San Francisco: W. H. Freeman, 1978), p. 4. One could satisfy all of these conditions only (or perhaps) in a model so oversimplified as to be irrelevant — thus hardly a "success."

2. There are many discussions of the limits of forecasting. I have found the following useful, if in different ways: Oskar Morgenstern, Klaus Knorr, and Klaus P. Heiss, *Long Term Projections of Power: Political, Economic and Military Forecasting* (Cambridge, Mass.: Ballinger, 1973); and Daniel Bell, *The Coming of Post-Industrial Society — A Venture in Social Forecasting* (New York: Basic Books, 1973).

3. See Paul B. Streeten, "Summary of S.I.D. Conference," draft report on the 1979 Conference of the Society for International Development, to be published in the conference proceedings.

4. *Economist,* December 29, 1979, p. 40.

5. Choucri and Robinson, *Forecasting in International Relations,* includes many examples of the current state of the art.

6. The demand for precision and explicit policy guidance can never be satisfied by social scientists, at least until they develop grounded theories. Misunderstanding of what each can and cannot do for the other is at the root of much of the unhappiness that attends the relationship between theorist and practitioner. For extended comment, see Robert L. Rothstein, *Planning, Prediction, and Policymaking in Foreign Affairs* (Boston: Little, Brown, 1972).

7. Bell, *Coming of Post-Industrial Society,* p. 4.

8. It is conventional to say that the central issue in forecasting is not whether a particular forecast is right or wrong — as it may be self-fulfilling or self-

negating—but whether it helps in making a better decision about an area of concern. There is a good discussion of this in Choucri, "Key Issues in International Relations Forecasting." I have no major disagreement with this view, but I am somewhat uneasy with the notion of "better" decisions. Better in whose judgment and in what time period? How do we know what is better in many complex issues? Perhaps it would be wiser to be more modest and to accept a more nominal interpretation of what makes a forecast useful—perhaps that it merely encourages discussion or self-consciousness about long-range consequences of present actions or merely that the decision maker takes it into account when making a decision.

9. On the general problem of the interconnections between domestic and international changes and of the need for parallel reforms at both levels, see Robert L. Rothstein, *The Weak in the World of the Strong: The Developing Countries in the International System* (New York: Columbia University Press, 1977).

10. Wassily Leontief et al., *The Future of the World Economy* (New York: Oxford University Press, 1977) is illustrative. So too is the work of the Bariloche Foundation in Argentina on basic needs—one of the few forecasting exercises that is not growth-oriented. Some work by UNIDO on industrial restructuring (which will be cited later in this chapter) and by the Food and Agriculture Organization (FAO) on food prospects (see Chapter 5) is also illustrative. These are all useful and technically sophisticated works, but they are also politically naive, not only in leaving out any concern with the policy process (how to achieve desired ends), but also in ignoring the extent to which normative forecasts can be transformed—especially within the UN system—from statements of what ought to be into statements of what will be. They may thus divert attention from some very pressing and difficult immediate needs.

11. See, for example, *World Development Report, 1979* (Washington, D.C.: World Bank, 1979), p. 18.

12. Almost all scenarios of the future, whatever the ideological underpinnings, see rapid growth rates in trade as critical, although they obviously differ on such matters as the role of multinational corporations or the market versus planning. Different assumptions about developed-country growth rates decisively affect trade projections, but, as the previous theme emphasizes, the differential effects on different parts of the Third World should be noted: slower growth of the OECD countries hurts the advanced developing countries most, the poorest least.

13. I shall treat the issue of South-South trade and its political and economic implications in Chapter 5.

14. There is a good introduction to all these issues in Raymond F. Hopkins and Donald J. Puchala, "Perspectives on the International Relations of Food," *International Organization,* Vol. 32, no. 3 (Summer 1978):581-616.

15. From 1953 to 1971, food production did not keep up with population growth rates in 24 of 71 LDCs and in 17 others it did not keep up with the growth of domestic demand. See Sterling Wortman and Ralph W. Cummings, Jr., *To Feed This World* (Baltimore, Md.: Johns Hopkins University Press, 1978), p. 20.

16. See Fred H. Sanderson, *Japan's Food Prospects and Policies* (Washington, D.C.: Brookings Institution, 1978), pp. 68-69.

17. I have discussed this in Robert L. Rothstein, *The Weak in the World of the Strong: The Developing Countries in the International System* (New York: Columbia University Press, 1977), Chapter 3.

18. See the *Assessment of the World Food Situation — Present and Future* (Rome: United Nations World Food Conference, E/Conf. 65/3), November 1974, p. 114.

19. Ibid., pp. 191ff. See also *Food Needs of Developing Countries: Projections of Production and Consumption to 1990* (Washington, D.C.: International Food Policy Research Institute, Research Report 3, December 1977); and Shahid Javed Burki and T. J. Goering, "Food Problems of the Low-Income Countries," *Finance and Development*, Vol. 14, no. 2 (June 1977):15ff. A more recent study projects a deficit of 145 million tons by 1990. See *Toward a World Without Hunger: Progress and Prospects for Completing the Unfinished Agenda of the World Food Conference* (United Nations, World Food Council, WFC/1979/3, March 1979).

20. A technical analysis of various projections calls them "simple-minded, technically deficient, and rather expensive" and is not sure "if the projections have any particular meanings." Romesh Diwan, "Projections of World Demand for and Supply of Foodgrains: An Attempt at Methodological Evaluation," *World Development*, Vol. 5, no. 5-7 (1977):501, 503. Nevertheless, these were the best large-scale studies available, and they had a major role in structuring perceptions of, and responses to, the food crisis.

21. There is a good review in Pauline K. Marstrand and Howard Rush, "Food and Agriculture: When Enough is Not Enough—the World Food Paradox," in Christopher Freeman and Marie Jahoda, eds., *World Futures—The Great Debate* (London: Martin Robertson, 1978), pp. 79-112. Also very useful is Harry Walters, "Difficult Issues Underlying Food Problems," *Science*, Vol. 188, no. 4188 (May 9, 1975):524-530.

22. This was in part because of lead time, as it would take nearly a generation for all the necessary reforms to be implemented effectively, and in part because some countries simply lacked the resource base and would thus always be substantial importers.

23. See especially the *Assessment of the World Food Situation* and Sartaj Aziz, "The World Food Situation and Collective Self-Reliance," *World Development*, Vol. 5, no. 5-7 (1977):657. The reference to effective demand in the text simply highlights the obvious fact that what exporters *will* produce depends on what importers can afford to buy; in effect, the distribution question is as important internationally as nationally.

24. This was in addition to a smaller stock for emergency use.

25. There was also a consensus that population growth rates would have to come down in many countries, but there was some debate about how significant this was, as aggregate production had not been outpaced by population growth rates in the past. In any event, lower population growth rates would make it easier to achieve a food-population balance, even if lower growth rates by themselves did not "solve" the food problem.

26. Raymond F. Hopkins and Donald J. Puchala, "Toward Innovation in the Global Food Regime," *International Organization*, Vol. 32, no. 3 (Summer 1978): 862-863. They also noted (p. 866) that "internationally regulated market-sharing

might be necessary" and that rural modernization "requires planning global strategy and mobilizing global resources." Although I share most of the norms, I have doubts about their political feasibility and about whether we know enough to run such a system more effectively than a reformed version of the present system. Thus I have a different perspective on how to create the conditions to make such norms ultimately both effective and implementable.

27. See especially Sanderson, *Japan's Food Prospects and Policies,* and Wortman and Cummings, *To Feed This World.* Of course, if one gets sufficiently above the battle, anything is possible: "If we can deal successfully with the next 25 years, we can deal with the next 200." This is irrefutable, but somewhat less than helpful, unless as a piece of unintentional irony. See Marylin Chou et al., *World Food Prospects and Agricultural Potential* (New York: Praeger Publishers, 1977), p. 11.

28. *Assessment of the World Food Situation* sees a 4 percent per annum growth rate in production as possible. Wassily Leontieff et al., *The Future of the World Economy* (New York: Oxford University Press, 1977) believe that a 5 percent per annum growth rate is physically possible and that it is necessary to achieve their projected GNP growth rate of 7 percent per annum in the decade ahead. I have found no expert who agrees.

29. See, for example, *World Food and Nutrition Study: The Potential Contributions of Research* (Washington, D.C.: National Academy of Sciences, 1977) and the various critical essays, all of which attack the excessive optimism of the *Assessment of the World Food Situation,* in Sartaj Aziz, ed., *Hunger, Politics and Markets* (New York: New York University Press, 1975). Also useful is Selwyn Enzer, Richard Drobnick, and Steven Alter, *Neither Feast Nor Famine—Food Conditions to the Year 2000* (Lexington, Mass.: Lexington Books, 1978).

30. See Sanderson, *Japan's Food Prospects and Policies;* and Alec Nove, "Can Eastern Europe Feed Itself?" *World Development,* Vol. 5, no. 5-7 (1977):417–424. Other factors that generate pessimism include the declining size of the world fish catch and the potential dangers to crops from a loss of genetic diversity.

31. Wortman and Cummings, *To Feed This World,* pp. 226–230, have a good brief discussion of most of these factors.

32. See Amy Ong Tsui and Donald J. Bogue, "Declining World Fertility: Trends, Causes, Implications," *Population Bulletin,* Vol. 33, no. 4 (1978).

33. Sanderson, *Japan's Food Prospects and Policies,* p. 74.

34. To a certain extent this is even true for several imponderables that seem beyond the control of governments—like climatic changes or the outcome of genetic research efforts—as governments can at least take actions in these cases to increase information and to decrease the potential effects of adverse developments. Still, it is obviously much easier for rich governments with sufficient resources to take out some insurance against long-range threats.

35. For the various figures cited, see *Toward a World Without Hunger* and Burki and Goering, "Food Problems of the Low-income Countries," pp. 15–18. The Caribbean area may be indicative of the general problem: Per capita food production has declined in the last decade and agricultural production for export (which might balance or diminish the import deficit) fell by 40 percent between the mid-1960s and mid-1970s. Thus the net deficit in food trade has sharply increased.

Efforts at regional integration have barely touched agriculture, as exports go out of the area and the countries in the area are competitive rather than complementary. The Regional Food Plan, created in 1975 to reduce the food import bill, has foundered. See Sidney E. Chernick, *The Commonwealth Caribbean: The Integration Experience* (Baltimore, Md.: Johns Hopkins University Press for the World Bank, 1978), pp. 118–131.

36. *Current World Food Situation,* Note by the Executive Director, World Food Council (United Nations, World Food Council, April 15, 1979), pp. 20–21.

37. The first quote is from *Toward a World Without Hunger,* p. 3; the second is from *Agriculture: Toward 2000,* an unpublished Food and Agriculture Organization (Rome) paper, July 1979, p. xv. The latter attempts to update the various targets set by the World Food Conference and to indicate normatively what will be necessary to achieve the targets. Its assumptions, even as norms, are *very* optimistic — perhaps dangerously so.

38. See *Assessment of the World Food Situation,* pp. 210–221. On the family farm, see Wortman and Cummings, *To Feed This World,* p. 8; Gunnar Myrdal, *The Challenge of World Poverty* (New York: Vintage Books, 1970); and Kenneth R. M. Anthony, Bruce F. Johnston, William O. Jones, and Victor C. Uchendu, *Agricultural Change in Tropical Africa* (Ithaca, N.Y.: Cornell University Press, 1979).

39. See Keith Griffin, *International Inequality and National Poverty* (London: Macmillan, 1978), pp. 131ff.; and Michael Lipton, *Why Poor People Stay Poor — Urban Bias in World Development* (Cambridge, Mass.: Harvard University Press, 1977).

40. Griffin, *International Inequality,* p. 132.

41. Lance Taylor, "The Misconstrued Crisis: Lester Brown and World Food," *World Development,* Vol. 3, no. 11-12 (1975):837.

42. See Keith Griffin, *The Political Economy of Agrarian Change — An Essay on the Green Revolution* (Cambridge, Mass.: Harvard University Press, 1974); Thomas T. Poleman, "World Food: Myth and Reality," *World Development,* Vol. 5, no. 5-7 (1977):383-394; and Thomas T. Poleman and Donald K. Freebairn, eds., *Food, Population, and Employment — The Impact of the Green Revolution* (New York: Praeger Publishers, 1973).

43. Some of these countries will be noted in the next section.

44. Lipton notes in *Why Poor People Stay Poor* (p. 329), "How to make revolutions, how to ensure that they benefit the rural poor — social scientists neither know these things, nor have the right to sacrifice human life to their ignorance." I concur strongly, for some of the armchair revolutionaries, happily leading the assault on poverty and hunger from one or another watering-spot on the international poverty circuit (Geneva, Nyon, Cuernavaca, Arusha, Bellagio, etc.), seem more interested in making speeches to each other than in actually accomplishing something.

45. Taylor, "The Misconstrued Crisis," p. 836. Italics in the original.

46. All the developing countries that have achieved high growth rates of production have done so by increasing yields rapidly, while the countries with slower growth rates have depended much more on expanding arable areas. Increasing yields have come from increased use of energy and capital inputs, as in the developed countries. Moreover, there is not much room for increasing arable areas in the future, and what room there is will come at increasing cost. See *Agriculture:*

Toward 2000, p. 7. There are also some doubts in the World Bank and elsewhere about the practicality of concentrating on increasing production on small farms, despite the advantages in employment-creation — which again implies a continuing emphasis on large-scale and capital- and energy-intensive agriculture. See Richard E. Stryker, "The World Bank and Agricultural Development: Food Production and Rural Poverty," *World Development,* Vol. 7, no. 3 (March 1979):331.

47. Given India's importance in the general scheme of things, one should perhaps note one reason for some optimism: India did quite well in 1977–1978, with a GDP growth rate of 5 percent and a growth rate of slightly over 3 percent in food production. The latter was twice the rate achieved in 1970–1975 — a result attributed both to good weather and to other factors such as increased irrigation. See *World Development Report, 1979* (Washington, D.C.: World Bank, 1979), pp. 12–13. Of course, increasing doubts about India's political stability may mean that optimism is premature.

48. For example, Tim Josling, "Grain Reserves and Government Agricultural Policies," *World Development,* Vol. 5., no. 5-7 (1977):603–611.

49. Domestic and international policies are directly connected on the issue of reserve stocks, because the degree of world-market instability and the size of the stock are both larger if the rich countries concentrate only on domestic price stability. Similarly, if the developed countries rely increasingly on long-term contracts to guarantee supply availability, the rest of the countries must compete for remaining supplies, thus increasing instability.

50. Using food as a weapon is an obvious means of linkage, but I want to put that question aside in this study. Food can provide leverage and influence, but the popular notion that it can be used as a weapon against OPEC (an increasingly important importer) seems delusive: Dollar values of food and oil imports are hardly equivalent, OPEC could easily buy what it needs elsewhere (and raise oil prices to compensate), and the real losers — as usual — would be the poor. Moreover, using food in this way would encourage new producers and perhaps result in the loss of valuable export markets. And there is a moral question involved, especially if the weapon misses its ostensible target. In any case, for one advocate of the food-as-weapon approach, see Dan Morgan, "Using Wheat Against OPEC: Not as Farfetched as You Think," *Washington Post,* July 8, 1979, p. C1.

51. Thus the argument "that the United States Government make the elimination of hunger *the primary focus of its relationship with the developing countries"* seems to me misleading, if not naive, and perhaps more likely to increase misunderstandings than to decrease hunger. Unfortunately, North-South relationships are not now, nor are they ever likely to be, quite that simple. (The quotation is the major recommendation in *Preliminary Report of the Presidential Commission on World Hunger* [Washington, D.C.: Presidential Commission on World Hunger, December 1979], p. 1. The italics are in the original.)

52. See *The World Food Situation and Prospects to 1985* (Washington, D.C.: U.S. Department of Agriculture, Economic Research Service, Foreign Agriculture Economic Report No. 98, 1975); and Alberto Valdes and Barbara Huddleston, "Agricultural Exports in Selected Developing Countries: Their Potential for Financing Increased Food Imports," in Jimmye S. Hillman and Andrew Schmitz, eds.,

International Trade and Agriculture: Theory and Policy (Boulder, Colo.: Westview Press, 1979), pp. 183–208.

53. See Valdes and Huddleston, "Agricultural Exports in Selected Developing Countries." There is obviously some overlap between different categories and lists, which indicates not only the different purposes in view but also how rapidly perceptions in the agricultural area can change.

54. See *Food Needs of Developing Countries,* pp. 17–20.

55. A regional or subregional focus may be imposed by the fact that the agricultural systems of each region tend to differ, thus making a global system feasible only at a level of great generality. In addition, the magnitude of the projected deficits in each region is very different: For example, most studies indicate that Asia may have over 40 percent of the deficit, North Africa and the Middle East about 25 percent, Africa close to 20 percent, and Latin America only 10 percent. Finally, China's refusal to join an international reserve system or the World Food Council (instead relying on national stocks and long-term supply contracts)—not to mention doubts about Soviet participation—also makes a global system problematic. On China, see A. Doak Barnett, *China and the World Food System* (Washington, D.C.: Overseas Development Council, 1979), pp. 4–5.

56. See Shlomo Reutlinger, "Food Insecurity: Magnitude and Remedies," *World Development,* Vol. 6 (1978):798.

57. A number of proposals favor a funding facility to finance import purchases when they fall below agreed levels, combined with a smaller buffer stock than the one favored by the World Food Conference. Reutlinger, "Food Insecurity," is a prominent exponent of this idea. See also R. S. Weckstein, "Food Security or Exchange," *World Development,* Vol. 5, no. 5-7 (1977):613–621. Given the record of previous experiences with buffer stocks, the difficulty of reaching agreement between producers and consumers, and the costs, this approach seems very sensible to me. My suggestion differs primarily in advocating regional stocks and a regional financial facility, rather than global institutions. What the regional institutions lose to the global in potential savings, they may regain in increased practicality.

58. Perhaps the developing countries themselves are beginning to move in this direction—and even greater movement may result from the increasing strains within the Group of 77. Thus the ASEAN countries have recently agreed among themselves to establish a rice buffer stock and some Latin American countries have begun to talk (privately) about the fact that Argentina alone could fill projected Latin American deficits if its surplus increases as projected. By contrast, Aziz has recently suggested a system of reserves controlled and financed entirely by the Third World (i.e., OPEC), as this would cut the size of stocks from 60 million tons (if each state established a stock) to 12–16 million tons. But it might be easier to negotiate and operate this stock (or a funding facility) on a regional basis—and time is becoming an increasingly critical factor. For the original proposals, see Aziz, "The World Food Situation and Collective Self-Reliance," p. 659.

59. There is some discussion of this in Donald Rothchild and Robert L. Curry, Jr., *Scarcity, Choice, and Public Policy in Middle Africa* (Berkeley: University of California Press, 1978), pp. 38ff.

60. For a discussion of success in implementation that emphasizes the two factors

noted, see Frances Stewart, "Country Experience in Providing for Basic Needs," *Finance and Development,* Vol. 16, no. 4 (December 1979):23–26.

61. The most prevalent tactic is simply to assert that only the absence of a mystical something called "political will" prevents creation of a new order; but this is simply a way of avoiding serious discussion of the substantive problems that impede agreement. For a recent example, see *Preliminary Report of the Presidential Commission on World Hunger,* pp. II-2.10.

62. *Assessment of the World Food Situation* calculated that the projected deficit for 1985 of 85 million metric tons would cost $17–18 billion (1972 dollars) for cereals alone. According to some private estimates, that figure should be doubled now. But all such calculations of dollar costs are very uncertain.

63. *Overcoming the Constraints on Increasing Food Production in Developing Countries — Investment Requirements for Food Production,* Report by the Executive Director, World Food Council (United Nations, World Food Council, WFC/1979/4, April, 1979), p. 8.

64. Ibid, p. 22. See also *Agriculture: Toward 2000,* p. xxxvii.

65. For a recent analysis of public support for aid, see Burns W. Roper, "The Limits of Public Support," *Annals,* Vol. 442 (March 1979):40–45. Roper's polls show that seventeen times as many people feel the United States is spending too much on aid as feel that it is spending too little. In fact, only the lack of salience of aid as an issue allows even present aid levels to persist — less apathy, less aid.

66. The possibility that increased trade or increased lending will provide the help not provided through aid is also very unlikely, except for a limited number of countries. I shall return to this issue in Chapter 5.

67. Slower income growth rates might also cut demand in the future (although most increased demand in poor countries has come from increased population), but slower growth may also slow agricultural reform as it will cut into government revenues. It is thus difficult to forecast what effects slower growth will have on food availability.

68. The Brandt Commission report will be discussed in Chapter 7. For an analysis of some of the other proposals, see H. G. Braun, "A Marshall Plan for the Third World or a 'Global New Deal'?" *IFO-Digest,* Vol. 1, no. 4 (December 1978):16–20.

69. I pass by here several technical problems related to sudden and short-term transfers of vastly increased resources, such as the issue of absorptive capacity or the inflationary consequences for small economies.

70. There are some practical proposals for such a system in Stephen Green, *International Disaster Relief — Toward a Responsive System* (New York: McGraw-Hill, 1977). But my notion of proper system extends beyond improving immediate response capacities: Emergency funding facilities would also be necessary, and much more effort needs to be devoted to early warning mechanisms and containment mechanisms, as well, of course, as to preventive mechanisms.

4

The Developing Countries
and the Energy Crisis

Massive and continuing increases in oil prices have had a devastating impact on the economic — and perhaps political — prospects of the nonoil developing countries (NOLDCs). Each time that prices have increased $1 a barrel the NOLDCs together have had to expend about $2 billion more to pay for oil imports. Oil import bills have sharply escalated to more than $50 billion annually and consume (on the average) about 26 percent of NOLDC export earnings, with much higher figures for many countries, such as Turkey, Brazil, India, and Jamaica. The most immediate effect has been slower gross national product (GNP) growth rates, but other longer-term effects may be even more damaging. Development plans have obviously had to be scrapped and revised, and indeed development planning itself has become more problematic — but also more imperative.[1] Slower growth rates in the developed countries have sharply diminished the prospect of compensating for increased oil costs by increased exports or by an increased transfer of resources. Moreover, vast and potentially crucial uncertainties have been generated by the need to adopt new development strategies that reflect difficult judgments about trading prospects in a decade of (potentially) slower growth and increased concern with political and economic security. Finally it bears emphasizing that the full weight of escalating oil prices may not yet really have struck many developing countries: Borrowing at high rates and short maturities has put the adjustment crisis off for a few years, but this may not have been very wise and it may not be repeatable.

The food problems and the energy problems of the developing countries are obviously connected, but there are also similarities and dissimilarities between them that are worth noting. Energy, at least in the forms now dominant commercially, is not renewable and, unlike food, it cannot be easily stored against a crisis.[2] Supply shortages in food and energy increase prices, needless to say, but there is also a *relative* difference in the response of suppliers: Energy, especially oil, is already close to capacity supply rates, and new energy has a long lead time before it can be brought on line; the supply response in food is still well below physical capacities and can be generated more quickly.[3] There may also be an increasing difference in scale between the two issues, as oil imports are beginning to cost much more than food imports, and oil and energy investments may be much more costly than investments in the agricultural sector. Nevertheless, there is one very crucial similarity between the two problems: In both cases the developing countries are being asked to undertake a massive restructuring of production, distribution, and consumption relationships, all of which will require new institutions, new investments, new technologies, and massive infusions of financial and technical aid.

These comments set the context for the discussion that follows. As with food, I shall need to be concerned with the implications of what developing-country governments are being asked to do—what the risks and costs appear to be—and how well they seem to be performing. I shall again discuss the most likely regions of crisis and the policy implications for the United States in the narrower context of energy itself and the broader context of the foreign policy or international relations of energy. The latter will also require some discussion of the relationship between OPEC and the other developing countries, which may serve to emphasize not only potential conflicts within the Third World but also the importance to the developed countries of the politics of energy within the Third World. Before turning to these matters, however, I shall briefly summarize some energy projections for the developing countries and the policy prescriptions that have been drawn from them.

Projections and Prescriptions for Energy in the Developing Countries

The future energy needs of the NOLDCs will depend on their economic growth rates, the energy alternatives they choose to emphasize, and the structural changes they make in their economies. Merely continuing 1960–1974 trends in energy production and consumption, which implies continuing to develop according to an energy-intensive, oil-intensive model, is likely to lead to disastrous outcomes. Demand will rise sharply as development procedes (because of its close relationship to income growth rates, urbanization, industrialization, etc.), commercial energy use will increase, the share of energy investment in the gross domestic product (GDP) will escalate, and external dependence will be even greater than it has been in the past. For example, one study, which extrapolates 1960–1974 trends, concludes that by 2000 the share of energy investments in the GDP would increase five to seven times (to 8.2 percent of GDP), that domestic resources would cover only 62 percent of consumption (against 79 percent in 1974), that the trade deficit in fuels alone would be $90 billion (1975 dollars), and that the external deficit of the energy sector would be about 17 percent of total exports (against 9.6 percent in 1970).[4] It is necessary to emphasize that these are relatively optimistic forecasts, especially in terms of oil prices: Fuel imports for the NOLDCs accounted for 7.3 percent of total imports (and cost about $6 billion) in 1970, but 15 percent of total imports (and $37 billion) by 1975, a rate of increase that cannot be sustained for very long without severe consequences for growth and development.

The share of oil in the total consumption of primary energy in the developing countries is also much higher than it is in the developed countries.[5] This is important because it provides a crucial perspective on the fact that the energy sector is likely to increase its share of the GDP: that development becomes problematic primarily if a large part of that share is imported and if import costs are rising. And two-thirds of the oil importers in the Third World depend on oil for at least 90 percent of commercial energy use; in only four countries (India, South Korea, Pakistan, and Zambia) is the figure less than 50 percent.[6] In general, the developing countries are also likely to find conservation more difficult than the developed countries because consumption is already low, early aspects of development are very energy-intensive, and higher shares of domestic energy use are expended on the transportation and industrial sectors than on the residential and commercial sectors (which are relatively easier to cut back).[7] Consequently, if development is to continue, growth rates in energy consumption in the developing countries must continue to rise, and at faster rates than in the developed countries, but this is likely to be possible only if there is an alternative to increased and increasingly costly oil import dependence.[8]

Projections of the supply and demand balance in oil for the NOLDCs over the next decade are even more uncertain than projections for the developed countries. Most of the uncertainties seem to be on the demand side, if only because all the forecasters seem to rely on the same sources for supply projections.[9] But models of future demand in the developing countries are especially weak because the data base is insufficient, economic structures change rapidly in the process of development, and there is great diversity among the developing countries. In these circumstances the basic assumptions on which any forecast of supply and demand must rest — income growth rates, elasticities, price trends, government policies, resource availabilities — are inherently unreliable: Relatively small variations in any of the assumptions can have relatively large effects on outcomes.[10] It should come as no surprise, then, that one major survey of energy projections found great variation and no clear pattern in estimates of NOLDC oil imports in 1985.[11]

Too much emphasis on the great diversity of forecasts might, however, be misleading. There is widespread agreement that increasing growth rates and high elasticities of demand mean that the developing countries will provide an increasing share of world energy demand in the next twenty years, perhaps rising to 25 percent of world demand by 2000 (as against about 10 percent in 1973).[12] The key question consequently is not whether there will be a net import deficit in primary energy, but rather how large that deficit will be. Tables 4.1 and 4.2 provide two recent World Bank estimates of the deficit for all primary energy in 1985 and 1990. The most recent projections of the World Bank suggest a growth in commercial energy consumption by the oil-importing LDCs from 12.4 million barrels of oil per day equivalent in 1980 to 22.8 million in 1990; domestic production is expected to grow from 7.8 mbd to 15.2 mbd—a widening gap that would double import costs in constant dollars. It is again necessary to emphasize how dependent these projections are on very uncertain assumptions about growth rates and other variables.[13] Nevertheless, these are among the best and most recent analyses available, and they do not differ greatly from other analyses by authoritative institutions. There is very little reason to assume that they are unduly pessimistic, and there are some reasons (in terms of basic assumptions and institutional biases) to think that they may be too optimistic. But how should the governments of the NOLDCs respond—or how can they respond?

Just as with the developed countries, there is no great mystery about the policies that the NOLDCs should adopt; the mystery in both cases is how to get governments to act. But the analogy cannot be carried too far, since developed-country governments have the resources (both financial and technological) to act if they so choose, the inevitable political and social conflicts that will emerge on particular issues are relatively easier to contain, and the risks and uncertainties are more bearable (and probably can be hedged in most cases). None of this is true for any developing country, least of all the NOLDCs.

Increased conservation is an obvious imperative for the NOLDCs. As already noted, this is difficult because consumption levels are already low, a much smaller share of commercial energy is consumed by sectors that can readily be cut back, and life-styles cannot be quickly altered. Still, there is some evidence that the developing countries use energy inefficiently—more so than the developed countries in similar activities—so that there is much room for improvement.[14] There is little or no evidence, however, that more than a handful of developing countries have begun to take conservation seriously.

Equally imperative is a policy to shift away from more energy-intensive activities in the industrial and agricultural sectors. In industry this clearly implies foregoing the production of energy-intensive basic materials (such

TABLE 4.1 Commercial Primary Energy Balances, 1976 and 1990 (in millions of barrels a day of oil equivalent)[a]

	1976		1990	
	Production	Consumption	Production (Projections)	Consumption
Industrialized countries	46.5	69.8	70.7	109.7
Centrally planned economies	37.9	34.4	66.7	64.3
OPEC countries	33.0	3.1	49.0	7.7
Developing countries	26.5	16.8	51.3	38.4
Developing OPEC countries[b]	16.9	2.3	23.5	5.4
Non-OPEC oil exporters	3.1	1.9	9.3	4.5
Oil-importing developing countries	6.5	12.6	18.5	28.5
Bunkers and other		5.3		7.0
World total	127.0	127.1	214.2	221.7

[a]Primary energy here refers to coal, lignite, crude petroleum, natural gas, natural gas liquids, hydro and nuclear electricity, expressed in barrels a day of oil equivalent.

[b]Included also in OPEC countries above.

Source: A. Lambertini, "World Energy Prospects and the Developing World," Finance and Development, December 1979, p. 2. Based on data from World Bank projections; United Nations, World Energy Supply, Series J, actual.

as steel, metals, fertilizer, and paper) and importing them instead. Given rapidly increasing energy prices, very few developing countries are likely to have much choice in the matter.[15] This surely will reduce energy demand, but there may not be much saving if all basic materials need to be imported. Moreover, this also implies a pattern of industrial development that is historically unique — which is not to say impossible or unnecessary — but that may create problems of its own (for example, in terms of which industries to develop or in the possibility of serious overproduction in some low-energy industries). And in agriculture, although there is an obvious need for a new labor-intensive, small-scale approach to raising production and reducing poverty, most of the improvements in yields have come from energy- and capital-intensive, science-based techniques. In addition, the small-scale approach, although very attractive in conception and intent, has run into a great many practical difficulties.[16] Still, in present circumstances the move to a new and less energy-intensive form of agriculture may be imposed by force majeure.

A third policy for the NOLDCs would aim at increasing exports to compensate for the foreign exchange costs of oil imports. This is a very conventional suggestion, sanctioned by both textbooks and institutions, and it confronts a very conventional obstacle: Slower growth rates in the developed

TABLE 4.2 Preliminary Projections of Non-OPEC Developing Countries' (NODCs) Energy Balance, 1975-1985 (million barrels per day of oil equivalent)[a]

	1975	1980	1985	Growth Rates (% per annum)		
				1976-80	1981-85	1976-85
Oil-importing developing countries (OIDCs)						
Consumption: Oil	4.33	5.35	7.20	4.3	6.2	5.2
Non-oil[b]	3.73	4.95	7.30	5.8	8.1	6.9
Total	8.06	10.30	14.50	5.0	7.1	6.0
Production: Oil	1.21	1.66	2.85	6.5	11.4	8.9
Non-oil	3.62	4.88	7.35	6.2	8.5	7.3
Total	4.83	6.54	10.20	6.2	9.3	7.8
Net energy imports[c]	3.23	3.76	4.30	3.3	2.7	3.0
Oil imports	3.12	3.69	4.35	3.4	3.4	3.4
Oil imports as % of total imports	14.4	12.6	7.2			
Value of oil imports (current $ billion/year)	14.3	24.3	38.3			
Non-OPEC oil-exporting developing countries[d]						
Consumption: Oil	1.14	1.36	1.88	3.6	6.7	5.2
Non-oil	0.49	0.85	1.37	11.6	10.0	10.8
Total	1.63	2.21	3.25	6.3	8.0	7.1
Production: Oil	2.36	4.09	5.55	11.6	6.3	8.9
Non-oil	0.61	1.14	1.91	13.3	10.9	12.1
Total	2.97	5.23	7.46	12.0	7.4	9.6
Net energy exports	1.30	3.02	4.21	18.4	6.9	12.5
Oil exports	1.22	2.73	3.67	17.5	6.1	11.6
Oil exports as % of total exports	22.0	29.6	32.1			
Value of oil exports (current $ billion/year)	4.3	13.8	25.0			

TABLE 4.2 (cont'd)

Total non-OPEC developing countries

Consumption:	Oil	5.47	6.71	9.08	4.2	6.3	5.2
	Non-oil	4.22	5.80	8.67	6.6	8.4	7.5
	Total	9.69	12.51	17.75	5.2	7.2	6.2
Production:	Oil	3.57	5.75	8.40	10.0	7.9	8.9
	Non-oil	4.23	6.02	9.27	7.3	9.0	8.2
	Total	7.80	11.77	17.67	8.6	8.5	8.5
Net energy imports		1.90	0.75	0.08	-17.0	-36.1	-27.2
MEMO ITEM[e]							
Bunkers (all oil)		0.46	0.57	0.67	4.4	3.3	3.8

[a]Refers to commercial energy sources only and assumes that OPEC crude oil prices remain constant in real terms through 1985 ($11.50 per barrel in 1975). OIDCs are projected to grow at 5.3 percent per annum in 1976–80; 6.4 percent in 1981–85; and 5.8 percent per annum for the whole of the decade. Corresponding growth rates for non-OPEC oil exporters are 5.5 percent, 6.6 percent, and 6.1 percent; and for all NODCs the growth rates assumed are 5.4 percent and 5.9 percent. Totals may not add due to rounding.

[b]Non-oil includes coal, gas, and hydropower, nuclear and geothermal. The breakdown for energy from these sources (in million barrels per day of oil equivalent) for all NODCs is:

	1975		1985	
	Production	Consumption	Production	Consumption
Coal	2.17	2.30	3.74	3.75
Gas	0.85	0.71	2.53	1.92
Hydro, nuclear, and geothermal	1.20	1.21	3.00	3.00
Total Non-oil	4.23	4.22	9.27	8.67

[c]As indicated, the bulk of energy imports is in the form of oil; coal and gas account for almost all of the remainder.

[d]Non-OPEC oil exporters include: Angola, Bahrain, Bolivia, Congo, Egypt, Malaysia, Mexico, Syria, Oman, Trinidad and Tobago, Tunisia, and Zaire.

[e]Deliveries to bunkers (for fueling vessels) are excluded from net imports and net exports.

Source: A Program to Accelerate Petroleum Production in the Developing Countries (Washington, D.C.: World Bank, 1979), p. 4.

countries, and the attendant rise of protectionism, make its prospects rather limited in the near term (and perhaps much longer). In any case, the gains to be expected from increased exports, although surely substantial and important, are hardly on a scale to compensate for massively increased oil prices and are not likely to be made by those countries most in need. Widespread adoption of such an export orientation at this time, whatever its justification, would probably only generate a hostile reaction by most of the developed countries. In addition, if many of the developing countries attempted to export the same range of labor-intensive goods, the most likely outcome would be rapid saturation of the market, followed by intense price competition, which would benefit only consumers in the developed countries. Finally, the development strategy implicit in an open-economy, export orientation may be in sharp conflict with the need to create a new development strategy that is not only much less energy-intensive, but also breaks sharply with some traditional notions of development. I shall return to this issue momentarily.

More intensive exploitation of existing energy resources and a more intensive quest for nontraditional energy sources are also imperative. As many studies have emphasized, although the NOLDCs have only about 7 percent of present oil reserves, they have more than 50 percent of the world's potential reserves and a very low rate of exploratory drilling.[17] Unfortunately, such exploration is both risky and expensive and probably requires some kind of agreements with foreign oil companies with the necessary capital and technical skills. In some cases, these agreements have already been negotiated, but in other cases either the prospects have not been sufficiently attractive to the companies or the risk has seemed too great. The World Bank's increased involvement in oil development (and possibly oil exploration) may facilitate the negotiation of more mutually satisfactory agreements; at the moment, however, progress has been very limited.

Two other crucial points need to be emphasized here: First, even if these agreements are negotiated, it will be at least seven to ten years before they begin to have much effect on the energy balance; and second, if the NOLDCs attempt to produce more domestic energy on their own, the investments will be very capital- and import-intensive. And the creation of new forms of renewable energy also seems likely to be very costly and very import- and capital-intensive, at least in the initial stages.[18] This is not to argue that the attempt to finance indigenous energy development is mistaken, for imported energy is likely to be much more costly and may not even be available for many more years.[19] But it does indicate that there are no "quick fixes." The alternatives are almost as costly, they are frequently very risky, and they do not provide instant relief.

None of these policy measures promises quick returns. Even if the growth rate of energy production increases sharply in the next decade — as it must — consumption growth rates will not be far behind (or may even be ahead of production increases if remedial measures are not taken) because of income growth and high elasticities of demand. Furthermore, the growth in production is likely to be concentrated in a relatively small number of countries. Thus by 2000, even if most of the policy measures are implemented, oil, a diminishing and increasingly costly resource, will still provide about 55 percent of total Third World energy consumption (against 61 percent in 1975). In any case, even if the NOLDCs exploit indigenous resources *very* aggressively and increase conservation greatly, the real oil import bill by the end of this decade could still be larger than the current import bill — not least because of consumption growth rates.[20] Consequently the NOLDCs will face slower growth as more resources have to be diverted to pay for imported oil, severe balance of payments difficulties, and, probably, a need to cut food and capital imports. Many observers, therefore, see a much more radical policy change as necessary: a fundamental shift in development models away from rapid industrialization and rapid growth, both of which tend to be energy- and capital-intensive, and toward what has been called "another development" (slower growth, an emphasis on agriculture, the reduction of poverty, "appropriate" technology, etc.).[21] Whatever else this strategy would accomplish, it would presumably lower energy demand.

Choosing by Not Choosing: Policy Dilemmas

Virtually all oil experts believe that there are important but undiscovered deposits of fossil fuels in the developing countries. But there are widely different estimates about how much recoverable fuel will be found and about how to go about finding it. Less than 5 percent of total drilling has taken place in the developing countries, but the central issue is why drilling has been so heavily concentrated in a few locations. Optimists about future levels of production, who believe that the developing countries could have as much as 15 percent of the world's ultimately recoverable reserves (against 2 percent presently), argue that most of the developing countries were not explored for oil because the oil was not needed, governments were unwilling to allow access, or the oil companies feared driving prices down or risking investment in unstable areas or jeopardizing their role as marketers for OPEC. Pessimists, who foresee declining productivity as more wells are drilled, contend that previous exploration and drilling was efficient (i.e., went to the best sites first) and that the areas that were unexplored are in very harsh, unpromising, and costly environments.[22]

The explosion in oil prices in the past few years presumably provided strong incentives to settle the argument between optimists and pessimists by encouraging sharply increased exploration and drilling in the non-OPEC developing countries. After all, what may seem small and inconsequential from a global perspective may be very important for many small and medium-sized developing countries. And indeed, as the oil companies increasingly lose control over OPEC supplies, they too may be forced to reconsider the virtues of even small or expensive sources of oil. Nevertheless, the record of the past five years is not very encouraging. As D. G. Fallen-Bailey and T. A. Byer note, "Most developing countries have some kind of indigenous energy resource which could be developed to help ease the strain of petroleum imports but, with a few notable exceptions, little is being done to develop the resources."[23]

Exploratory drilling in the NOLDCs has actually declined by 20 percent since the early 1970s. The World Bank has also noted that in the seventy-one non-OPEC LDCs in which there was some drilling between 1967 and 1976, only ten had been adequately explored (and only seven of the twenty-three countries considered most promising).[24] This is one major reason why there has not been much new production since 1972 and why what production there has been tends to be concentrated in a few countries (as Table 4.3 indicates, Mexico, Peru, Egypt, and Congo are the exceptions). The situation might improve somewhat in the future, as the incentives to develop indigenous resources are hardly diminishing, but very few developing countries are likely to be able to afford much exploratory drilling, which is risky, expensive, and import-intensive, unless the World Bank provides some of the financing and some guarantees to both the companies and the host government.[25] But the companies (and initially the U.S. government) oppose World Bank financing of exploration, as distinct from development of known reserves. This will only guarantee that there will be little to develop and that what there is will be in a few conservative, stable countries. I shall return to this issue in a subsequent section.

Conservation and increased efficiency in use, as well as efforts to increase fuel substitution possibilities, seem dependent on the prior creation of an energy development plan. For example, substitutes for imported oil—coal, natural gas, hydropower—can replace only heavy oil; there is no substitute for gasoline or diesel fuel. Thus a plan to allocate gasoline and diesel imports to priority uses is imperative. But as two World Bank experts sadly note, "Few countries have a conscious energy policy."[26] This is, however, a manifestation of a larger issue: There is probably no way for the NOLDCs to have a viable plan for the energy sector in the present (and probably future) resource environment as long as conventional development models continue to dominate.

TABLE 4.3 Oil Production in Non-OPEC Developing Countries, 1972 and 1978 (in thousands of barrels per day)

Countries by Region	1972 Production	1978 Production	Percentage Change
Latin America:			
Argentina	435.0	450.0	3
Barbados		0.7	
Bolivia	32.0	30.0	-6
Brazil	167.0	160.0	-4
Chile	32.5	20.0	-38
Colombia	192.0	130.0	-32
Guatemala		0.7	
Mexico	440.0	1,270.0	189
Peru	60.2	150.0	149
Trinidad and Tobago	143.0	240.0	68
Africa:			
Angola	135.0	130.0	-4
Cameroon		10.0	
Congo	7.5	28.0	273
Egypt	227.0	490.0	116
Morocco	0.3	0.1	-67
Tunisia	80.0	100.0	25
Zaire		20.0	
Middle East:			
Bahrain	72.0	56.0	-22
Israel	120.0	10.0	
Oman	280.0	320.0	14
Syria	120.0	170.0	42
Turkey	65.0	50.0	-23
Far East:			
Burma	20.0	25.0	25
Brunei-Malaysia	278.0	420.0	51
India	151.0	230.0	52
New Zealand	2.7	13.0	381
Pakistan	9.5	9.3	-2
Thailand	0.2	0.2	
Total	3,070	4,533	48

Source: A Strategy for Oil Proliferation: Expediting Petroleum Exploration and Production in Non-OPEC Developing Countries (Washington, D.C.: Congressional Budget Office, February 1979), p. 10.

Can developing-country governments devise and implement a new, less energy-intensive development plan? Governmental decisions are determinative in this regard not merely because only the government can set national goals but also because energy sector investment is usually a direct government responsibility. Unfortunately, "there is no evidence that these countries have altered their investment plans on account of higher energy prices, nor any evidence that the industrialization patterns of the recent past are being revised to allow for additional energy production."[27]

The developed countries can hardly criticize the NOLDCs too severely for the failure to devise and adopt new energy plans and development strategies. They have done no better (and with much less excuse), thus exacerbating the policy dilemmas of the NOLDCs. But a difference in scale and impact remains, whatever the degrees of responsibility for the current crisis. Policy failures by the developed countries may lead to prolonged recession, regime instability, and a loss of confidence in existing institutions, but they are unlikely to lead to mass starvation and revolutionary upheavals; policy failures in some developing countries seem quite likely to generate such outcomes.

That the NOLDCs have not made much effort to create new energy and development models or to sharply increase the exploitation of indigenous energy resources is important information, for it provides a crucial insight into the probable range and depth of a mid-1980s energy crisis, a point to which I shall return. It is equally important, however, to ask why they have not done so, for this may provide some understanding of the nature of the policies that may or may not succeed.

There is virtually no disagreement with the argument that "the degree to which the developing nations of the world can or are willing to take a developmental path that is different from the Western industrialized nations will be a fundamental issue."[28] Nevertheless, even if the need for a new development model seems self-evident, changing direction in mid-course puts extraordinary demands on poor and weak governments. Governing elites have been taught for nearly a generation that rapid industrialization is the path to modernization and reduced dependence, they have created and profited from political and economic structures that would resist change, and they have invested available resources in an infrastructure that cannot be easily or quickly converted to a new pattern of response. The grudging and suspicious reaction of so many Third World elites to U.S. support for a basic human needs strategy is perhaps symptomatic. What the United States saw as a sensible response to rising levels of poverty was viewed by many elites as an attempt to thwart the creation of a New International Economic Order and to keep the Third World as an economic backwater.[29]

Risk aversion is bound to be very high in these circumstances, and sensibly so. Moreover, it is necessary to strongly emphasize that the new strategies are untested and in some cases inconsistent or incomplete. The results of such strategies are not (and cannot be completely) known and there is no certainty that they will be better than the results of following conventional paths.[30] Additional uncertainties must be recognized. For example, many developing countries are just building their energy sectors and consequently could adopt the best technology available in order to take advantage of new factor prices. But what is the "best," not merely in the sense that efficiency may not be the only goal sought, but also in the sense that no one yet knows — no one can predict the effects of future technologies — what the best choice really is. Put another way, the developing countries cannot gamble on technological breakthroughs, even though their prospects may be decisively affected by such breakthroughs (if they come), and they lack the resources to hedge against risk by building redundant or alternative systems. In effect, they must choose now in the midst of great uncertainty and with very little chance of reversing a mistaken judgment; they lack the flexibility to make quick changes and they lack (and will continue to lack) the resources to invest in new equipment, new infrastructure, and new conversion processes.

From this perspective, the attempt to avoid or delay a decision — to muddle along, plead for massive resource transfers, or simply gamble that something will turn up — is pernicious, but understandable. In addition, as in the food arena, it is difficult to attribute responsibility for present failures; even governments that desire to change course may not be able to do so because they lack financial resources. Still, again as with food, there are actions that even governments with limited resources can take to improve their situation, and distinctions can be made between governments that need and deserve external support and governments that may only dissipate resources or use them for repression. At any rate, I shall leave the financial question until the next section.

This discussion sets the context for an analysis of policy options and foreign policy implications in the energy arena in the next decade. The failure of most NOLDCs to devise new energy and development plans means that they will need oil increasingly desperately in a period when prices are unlikely to soften (except in certain short-term periods), when a conservationist ethic in parts of OPEC may become more prominent, and when no *major* new supplies of oil are likely to become available. This is all the more true because there has been little increase in capacity in OPEC itself in recent years (except for a very recent and somewhat ambiguous announcement by the Saudis of an intent to increase capacity by 2 million barrels per day [mbd] by 1981).[31] In any case, even if major new oil fields are discovered, in OPEC or elsewhere, it would be some years before they could begin to affect the market. Perhaps the most likely source of "new" supplies is successful conservation within the developed countries (as reflected in the sharp and surprising drop in the energy/GDP ratios of several OECD countries in recent years), but even this may not help the NOLDCs very much, especially if OPEC reduces production to maintain prices.

One policy problem that must be considered concerns the identification of the countries and regions that are most likely to be directly threatened by developments in the oil market. Obviously, the effects are likely to be very asymmetrical; some countries are making a major effort to develop indigenous resources (or have other means of compensation), while others are doing very little and/or lack the means to do very much. This may simply be another way of saying that the oil problem is making a major, and perhaps decisive, contribution to the growing gap within the Third World.

The second policy problem that must be considered concerns the financial issue. Even if oil is available in the 1980s, it is far from clear that many NOLDCs will be able to pay for it. The price of oil doubled in real terms in 1980, which is relatively much smaller than the 400–500 percent increase in 1974. In absolute terms, however, the increase is staggering because it comes on a much larger base. As a result, financial recycling mechanisms may be strained, perhaps beyond capacity, and it may also become increasingly difficult for the surplus countries in OPEC to respend what they earn. In addition, the NOLDCs must borrow to pay their import bills, but this is much more problematic now than in 1974–1978: Debt service ratios have increased sharply for some countries and banks are more cautious (and somewhat more regulated) than in the past. Still, there is no alternative to lending the money (or, more precisely, the alternatives seem even more unappealing) and the money will probably be available—unless OPEC production is radically cut, for whatever reasons. Another aspect of the financial issue must be considered: aid for investments in the energy sector, including exploration and development of indigenous resources. Finally, the financial problem concerns not only paying for imports and financing necessary investments, but also the allocation of resources between competing needs.

The third policy problem concerns OPEC's response to the problems that it has created or exacerbated for the NOLDCs and the implications of this response for the international politics of energy.

From a foreign policy perspective, the issues that I shall discuss need to be understood on two levels. The first level, with which I shall be primarily concerned in the next section, pertains to energy problems in a fairly narrow sense. Here I shall be concerned with how to respond to the immediate problems raised by the oil crisis and how to begin taking actions to deal with long-run issues. But these responses may not work well because they are badly implemented, reflect mistaken judgments, or are overwhelmed by unforeseen events. Thus the United States also needs to think about a second level of foreign policy in the energy arena, a level that is concerned with the problems of dealing with a world in which much of what should have been done was not done.

The two levels are not completely separate, either in time or in substance: Thus actions at both levels can and should go on simultaneously, and success or failure at one level can have a significant effect on the other. Nevertheless, the immediate emphasis must be on the first level, as the worst disasters may still be avoidable; the second level, however, may become increasingly prominent by the middle of the decade — unless we are lucky. At any rate, second-level issues will be implicit in some of the material in the next section, especially in the discussion of likely areas of crisis, but will become increasingly prominent in later sections. Still, I should emphasize that, while responses at the first level tend to be very similar irrespective of more general policy orientations, second-level responses will not be very effective unless they are integrated into a wider policy framework, which will be the focus of Chapter 7. In this chapter, however, the discussion will concentrate primarily on issues that arise only in the energy area.

Energy Policy: Rising Needs and Insufficient Resources

The World Bank has projected an annual growth rate of 8.5 percent in energy production to 1985 for the non-OPEC developing countries and a growth rate of consumption of 6.2 percent.[32] Net imports for these countries would thus decline appreciably (from 1.9 mbd in 1975 to 0.08 mbd in 1985). But this is a very misleading figure, as it masks a significant distinction between non-OPEC oil exporters and the rest of the developing countries. The former would increase their oil exports sharply (12.5 percent per annum, even with a 7.1 percent per annum increase in domestic consumption) and would perhaps get 30 percent of their total export earnings by 1985 from oil and other energy exports. Included in this group are Angola, Bahrain, Bolivia, Congo, Egypt, Malaysia, Mexico, Syria, Oman, Trinidad and Tobago, Tunisia, and Zaire. Nothing much ties these countries together except geological good fortune (as with OPEC). The remainder of the developing countries, however, even if conservation and increased efficiency permit some reduction in imports, would have not only a large import deficit (nearly 5 mbd) but also nearly a tripling in their oil import bill (and this estimate was based on 1975 prices).[33]

Trade dependence (net imports as a percentage of total commercial energy consumption) is a useful indicator of potential crisis areas in the next decade. Table 4.4 provides a breakdown of varying degrees of trade dependence for 104 developing countries, but it also adds two other critical characteristics: per capita energy consumption (which provides an indication of what dependence may mean internally) and domestic energy resources (which may determine energy strategies). This very informative table is worth some comment.

Groups VII, VIII, and IX are obviously the most vulnerable to adverse external developments. They include 61 countries, 28 from Africa, 17 from Latin America, 9 from Asia, and 7 from North Africa and the Middle East. In Group VII only Burundi was not on the World Food Council's list of Food Priority Countries and both African countries in Group IV were also on the list. Only Zaire (which is not a food priority country — yet) and perhaps Niger and the Central African Empire (which have uranium deposits) may be able to compensate for oil import costs, although a few other countries have some unexploited potential in oil. Nigeria, Gabon, Congo, and Angola are the only African oil exporters thus far, and they, along with Zaire, may face increasing pressures from neighbors to share their wealth or at least use it for some common purposes. But none of these relatively resource-rich countries has yet gone much beyond rhetorical support and none is likely to have surplus resources to give away. If these countries maintain political stability — a very big if, especially for Nigeria and Zaire — the gap between them and their neighbors is likely to increase significantly, particularly if they receive large amounts of external capital and their neighbors receive very little (both of which seem likely, the stability issue aside). Intraregional tensions are likely to rise (note the geographical proximity of the resource-rich to each other), but the more important point is that the food-energy nexus is rapidly creating a class (or, more accurately, a caste) of permanent charity cases.

Bangladesh, the Philippines, Sri Lanka, Laos, and Nepal are the major Asian countries with serious problems in both food and energy. But Pakistan, India, and Indonesia, which are food priority countries, have somewhat better prospects in energy (as do Thailand and Malaysia because of domestic resources). It would be incorrect, however, to interpret this too optimistically. These countries face other problems, in terms of both political stability and socioeconomic constraints, and the necessary investment funds to convert potential resources into immediately available resources may not be available and/or will reduce necessary spending on other needs. Many of the Asian countries, because they have relatively large industrial sectors, are also among the top fifteen Third World energy users (for example, India, Indonesia, South Korea, Pakistan, Taiwan,

Thailand, and the Philippines).[34] In any case, because of the relative size of most of these countries, they will need extremely large amounts of foreign assistance — more than they are likely to get, especially if the bias in aid-giving toward small countries persists — and their tribulations, which seem inevitable, are likely to become major systemic concerns (in terms of both North-South and East-West relations). At the same time, the countries of the region are so divergent in size, level of development, resource endowments, and ideology that policies that focus on subregional or bilateral relationships may be more practical (that is, may help to maintain sufficient political and economic stability for development to continue) than policies with either a global or regional focus.

Only four small Latin American countries — Haiti, Guyana, Honduras, and El Salvador — were on the list of food priority countries, and they all confront major problems in energy as well. Many of the large Latin American countries are oil exporters or are in a relatively good position in terms of unexploited domestic resources. Conversely, the great majority of the small countries, especially in Central America and the Caribbean, are both heavily dependent on imports and in a weak resource position. This necessarily suggests a further widening of the gap between rich and poor (both countries and citizens) in Latin America.

However, it should be noted that many of the large countries that do not export oil, even if they have good resource potential, have been hit very hard by the massive oil price increases because they have relatively high per capita energy consumption levels; Argentina, Brazil, Chile, and Colombia are among the Third World's top fifteen energy users. This has created balance of payments difficulties, debt problems, and difficulties in raising investment funds to finance resource development. Consequently, they face severe transition problems that may be exacerbated by decreasing export prospects (as the OECD economies grow more slowly) and by the increasing tendency to limit aid to the least developed countries. Increased tension with oil-exporting neighbors (Venezuela, Mexico, Trinidad and Tobago, Bolivia, and Ecuador) may be likely, but there is also an important potential for regional energy cooperation, particularly if the international economy becomes more closed and unstable.

There may also be increasing conflict over export markets for manufactured goods among the advanced Latin American countries themselves and between them and other developing-country manufacturing exporters. The historical record would justify a great deal of pessimism about the possibility that the arguments for regional cooperation will prevail over centrifugal forces, although an increasingly threatening international environment may begin to compel reconsiderations about how to achieve national interests. Still, in policy terms it might be prudent again to concentrate ini-

TABLE 4.4 Energy Position of Developing Countries and Territories by Levels of Energy Consumption, Import Dependence, and Reserves (Figures in parenthesis denote the net energy imports expressed as percentage of total commercial energy consumption)

Per capita commercial energy consumption for 1975
(in kilograms of coal equivalent)

Net imports of energy as percentage of total commercial energy consumption for 1975 — Less than 25%

Less than 200 kg

Country/territory	\	\	Reserves[a]	\	\	\
	SF	O	OS	H	NG	U
Group I						
Afghanistan*	X	X		X	X	
Angola*		X	X	X	X	X
Burma (23)		X		X	X	
Indonesia*	X	X		X	X	
Nigeria	X	X		X	X	

200 - 1,000 kg

Country/territory	\	\	Reserves[a]	\	\	\
	SF	O	OS	H	NG	U
Group II						
Algeria*	X	X		X	X	X
Bolivia*	X	X		X	X	
China*	X	X		X	X	
Colombia*	X	X	X	X	X	X
Congo*	X	X		X	X	
Ecuador*		X		X	X	
Egypt (20)	X	X		X	X	
India (19)	X	X		X	X	X
Iraq*	X	X		X	X	
Malaysia (12)		X		X		
Oman*		X				
Syrian Arab Rep.*	X			X	X	
Tunisia*	X			X	X	

More than 1,000 kg

Country/territory	\	\	Reserves[a]	\	\	\
	SF	O	OS	H	NG	U
Group III						
Argentina (16)		X	X	X	X	X
Bahrain*		X	X		X	
Brunei*		X	X		X	
Gabon*		X	X	X	X	X
Iran*	X	X			X	
Israel (21)		X	X	X		
Kuwait*		X			X	
Libyan Arab Jamahiriya*		X	X		X	
Mexico*	X	X	X	X	X	
Democratic People's Rep. of Korea (5)	X	X		X		
Qatar*		X	X		X	
Saudi Arabia*		X		X		
Trinidad and Tobago*		X	X	X	X	
United Arab Emirates*		X	X		X	
Venezuela*	X	X	X	X	X	

Net imports of energy as percentage of total commercial energy consumption for 1975 — 25 to 75%

Less than 200 kg

Country/territory	\	\	Reserves[a]	\	\	\
	SF	O	OS	H	NG	U
Group IV						
Mozambique (75)	X	X		X	X	
Pakistan (40)	X	X		X	X	
Rwanda (68)		X				
Viet Nam (49)	X			X		

200 - 1,000 kg

Country/territory	\	\	Reserves[a]	\	\	\
	SF	O	OS	H	NG	U
Group V						
Brazil (70)	X	X	X	X	X	X
Chile (64)	X	X		X	X	
Peru (37)	X	X		X		
Zambia (62)	X			X		

More than 1,000 kg

Country/territory	\	\	Reserves[a]	\	\	\
	SF	O	OS	H	NG	U
Group VI						
Mongolia (36)	X			X		
Rep. of Korea (57)		X				

Table 4.4 (continued)

Net imports of energy as percentage of total commercial energy consumption for 1975

Group VII

	Country/territory	SF	O	OS	H	NG	U
More than 75%	Bangladesh (76)	X					
	Benin (100)				X	X	
	Burundi (100)				X		
	Central African Empire (89)						X
	United Republic of Cameroon (79)		X				
	Chad (100)				X		
	Ethiopia (96)				X		
	Gambia (100)				X		
	Ghana (78)				X		
	Guinea (99)				X		
	Guinea-Bissau (100)				X		
	Haiti (86)				X		
	Kenya (97)				X		
	Laos (85)						
	Madagascar (98)				X		
	Malawi (89)				X		
	Mali (97)				X		
	Mauritania (99)				X		
	Nepal (91)				X		
	Niger (100)				X		X
	Paraguay (87)				X		
	Senegal (96)				X		
	Sierra Leone (100)				X		
	Somalia (100)		X				
	Sri Lanka (120)				X		
	Sudan (100)				X		
	United Republic of Tanzania (100)				X		
	Togo (100)	X					
	Uganda (84)				X		
	Upper Volta (100)				X		
	Yemen (100)				X		
	Zaire (76)	X	X	X	X	X	X

Group VIII

Country/territory	SF	O	OS	H	NG	U
Belize (100)						
Costa Rica (87)				X		
Dem. Yemen (99)						
Dominican Republic (101)						
El Salvador (103)				X		
Fiji (102)						
Guadeloupe (100)						
Guatemala (94)				X		
Honduras (99)	X			X		
Ivory Coast (98)						
Jordan (114)			X			
Lebanon (100)						
Liberia (105)				X		
Mauritius (98)				X		
Morocco (86)	X		X			
Nicaragua (105)	X			X		X
Panama (125)	X			X		
Papua New Guinea (97)	X				X	
Philippines (93)	X					
Thailand (97)	X		X	X		
Uruguay (100)	X		X	X		X

Group IX

Country/territory	SF	O	OS	H	NG	U
Barbados (101)	X					
Cuba (103)					X	
Cyprus (106)						
Guyana (100)				X		
Jamaica (95)						
Malta (100)						
Singapore (120)						
Surinam (86)						

a SF = Solid fuels   OS = Oil shale   NG = Natural gas
  O = Oil   H = Hydro resources   U = Uranium

Marking an "X" for a given resource in a given country symbolizes "at least some endowment" of proved reserves or of resources. "Some endowment" means 100 million barrels of proved reserves for oil, 1,000 billion cubic feet of proved resources for natural gas, and similar estimates for the other resources.

*Net exporters of energy

Source: Energy Supplies for Developing Countries: Issues in Transfer and Development of Technology (Geneva: UNCTAD, TD/B/C.6/31, 1978), p. 18.

tially on subregional cooperation, especially in the Caribbean and Central America, where Mexico, Venezuela, and Trinidad and Tobago have non-energy interests that might induce cooperation on energy.

Sudan and Yemen are the only countries in the Middle East and North Africa that are both deficient in energy and on the list of food priority countries. Most of the other countries — Jordan, Lebanon, and Israel are exceptions — either are oil exporters or possess substantial domestic energy resources (for example, Morocco). As the countries that are deficient in food and/or energy also tend to be recipients of relatively large amounts of foreign aid from various sources, a crisis in this area would probably look considerably different from crises in other areas. Except possibly for food problems in Egypt, the lines of major tension remain political and ideological (and perhaps religious). But the countries in this region also face another complication, for their attitudes and responses will probably determine whether OPEC makes and sustains a major initiative to relieve the oil-importing developing countries of some of the oil burden — and thus perhaps whether the Third World can maintain unity in the coming decade.

A number of relatively familiar points emerge from this discussion. First, the growing gap between rich and poor countries in the Third World will be considerably widened by emerging energy developments. Indeed, the major fault line may well come to divide those with energy resources from those without them. In addition to the obvious questions this raises about Third World unity and about the need for new development strategies (and incentives to implement such risky ventures), there is another question for the international system itself: how to deal with a large group of states for whom the rhetoric and the assumption of growth and progress may be becoming increasingly irrelevant. A second point concerns the very wide divergences and asymmetries between countries and regions in terms of their energy situation. Oil and energy are certainly global issues, in the sense that all are competing for the same supply of diminishing resources, but situations are so different and the need for a quick response so imperative that it seems prudent to concentrate initially on subregional cooperation. The need for a quick response also suggests a third point. Even if a new development strategy can be implemented, it will take a great deal of time to alter existing practices and institutions. In the interim there is an enormous transitional problem involved in providing the NOLDCs with the financial resources to keep afloat — more than that will probably require good fortune with the weather and technological breakthroughs in energy — during a very dangerous period. This brings us to our second policy problem.

The financial problem is not a single phenomenon (except in the broad sense that resources are scarce in every sector), but rather a series of interlocking problems. The enormous deficit created by escalating oil import costs is the most immediate problem. The NOLDCs cannot earn enough foreign exchange to pay the bill, which must be financed. This was successfully accomplished through recycling of OPEC earnings in 1974 and 1975. But "success" is a very relative term in the circumstances, as massive short-term commercial bank lending obviously creates serious problems, not only in terms of the ability to repay the loans in a period of generally slow growth but also in the sense that subsequent lending becomes progressively more difficult. Still, failure to lend in the past would only have exacerbated the oil crisis, and failure to lend in the present and future would probably lead to political and economic instability, widespread defaulting, and reduced production by OPEC. In effect, recycling is a dubious policy justified only because the alternatives seem worse. One should also note the crucial connection between the recycling problem and domestic energy policies: Failure to provide immediate financial help means that none of the medium- or longer-term problems will be resolved, but failure to begin dealing with the latter problems means that the immediate financing problem will ultimately become overwhelming and insoluble.

The NOLDCs also must make a major effort to develop their domestic energy sectors. Estimates of how much this will cost vary enormously, largely because of very different assumptions about growth rates in consumption, energy coefficients, price developments, definitions of the energy sector, and other matters.[35] Because of the uncertainties, the specific projections are not very useful. Nonetheless, they all agree that energy investments must increase sharply and that the amounts needed are massive. For example, in Table 4.5 spending of over $160 billion (1975 dollars) per annum by 2000 is projected. This contrasts with investments in oil and power of $22 billion in 1975. And a recent World Bank estimate has projected capital costs for power facilities alone from 1977 to 1990 as $446 billion (the foreign exchange component of which is $267 billion) and per annum costs of around $52 billion in 1990. At any rate, whatever the amounts, the share of energy investments in the GDP must increase sharply by 2000 (perhaps to more than 8 percent of the GDP, which is more than seven times the 1970 level).[36] It is important to note that these estimates are only for commercial energy, that they will deflect spending from other purposes, and that there is a very large foreign exchange component in all Third World energy investment. Thus either major increases in foreign aid and/or very significant increases in export earnings will be necessary.

Domestic energy production in the NOLDCs is important in itself if the development process is to continue. It also has some importance as a means

TABLE 4.5 Investment in the Energy Sector by the Developing Countries Not Members of OPEC (reference variant)

	For the Period 1975–2000 as a Whole		Per Annum, Around the Year 2000	
	Total (in billions of 1975 dollars)	Per-cent	Total (in billions of 1975 dollars)	Per-cent
Exploration and extraction of mineral resources	170.5	10.6	13.1	8.2
of which: oil	(135.6)	(8.4)	(10.4)	
Oil Pipelines, gas pipelines, refineries	88.9	5.5	8.6	5.4
Generation of electricity	886.4	55.2	93.5	58.4
of which: nuclear power	(442.2)	(27.5)	(61.1)	
Transmission and distribution of electricity	461.4	28.7	44.9	28.0
Total	1,607.2	100.0	160.1	100.0

Source: Investment by Developing Countries in the Energy Sector: A Preliminary Analysis of Long-term Financing Requirements (Geneva: UNCTAD, TD/B/C.3/146, September 1978), p. 9.

of reducing pressure on world energy supplies. But finding the necessary funding will be extraordinarily difficult for most of the NOLDCs, whose potential resources may not be large enough to attract private financing. The World Bank's energy program, which is expected to account for about 10 percent of total World Bank lending (or $1.2 billion) by 1983, will be very important, but it will still provide only 10-20 percent of estimated needs. Other foreign aid commitments are uncertain, especially because such aid is increasingly aimed at agricultural development and basic human needs, but—as a very rough guess—it might amount to another 10-20 percent of estimated needs. The rest will have to come from domestic resources and foreign private investment, both of which present problems.[37]

Private investment by major foreign oil companies is likely only where the prospects of discovering large fields are good and where governments seem stable and reliable. Smaller oil companies, either national or independent, may lack the capital to invest in very risky exploration projects. As a result, many of the developing countries may have a potential large enough to justify exploration and development in terms of domestic needs, but not large enough to attract the oil companies. A fund to finance exploration in these countries, recently suggested by the World Bank, would seem to make a great deal of sense, but opposition by the oil companies and (initially) the U.S. government prevented action. The position of the companies, who obviously fear the competition that such a fund might generate, is understandable, but the U.S. position, although also understandable, is much more debatable.

The United States apparently objected because of fears that investments in the exploration fund would be too risky and that the availability of funds might encourage drilling in very unpromising sites. In addition, Edward Fried, the U.S. director on the bank's board, contended that "if a field is promising, the oil companies will bid" and that "our major objective should be to reduce some of the political problems that plague exploration and development."[38]

In response, one might argue that the risks are well worth taking, that funds need not be lent for drilling in the most unpromising areas, and that what is promising to the companies is not necessarily what is promising to the NOLDCs, as the figures on drilling densities amply testify. More critically, the political problems that worry Mr. Fried are not going to be solved by a policy that effectively leaves all power of decision in the hands of the oil companies. The discovery and exploitation of even relatively small domestic energy resources may provide some desperately needed foreign exchange savings and a domestic emergency stock in case of an external crisis and may help to ease the transformation to a new energy strategy.

And the World Bank's imprimatur on the fund should increase the probability that the agreements between countries and oil companies will be kept.[39] Mr. Fried's position, conversely, may help to solve some of the political (and economic, if it discourages competition) problems of the companies, but it will not help enough of the NOLDCs, and those that it does help may not be the (only) countries that need and deserve help.

A third aspect of the financial problem concerns the allocation of investment resources between and within different sectors. If a new, less energy-intensive strategy is imperative, presumably investment should be directed toward renewable forms of energy, rural development, and small-scale industry. However, in present circumstances immediate needs and the needs for a transitional period — perhaps the next decade — must dominate long-run transformation strategies. The central concern must be to find the means to pay for necessary imports of fuel (and food) and to expedite the exploitation of domestic resources; failure at these tasks probably means that many of the NOLDCs will barely survive as viable economic entities. Moreover, many aspects of "the" new development strategy are unclear and some may require energy-intensive techniques (for example, increasing agricultural yields). Consequently there is no contradiction between an immediate emphasis on paying for and developing traditional, nonrenewable energy resources and the evident need for a shift in development strategies: Only the first will permit the second.

This argument also implies that the implementation issue is not and will not be as crucial in the next decade in the energy area as it is in food production. The emphasis on immediate and transitional needs does not conflict with the interests of the governing elites, as it implies support for the existing structure of activities. Nevertheless, the implementation issue (structuring programs so that they are in the interest of development, but also so that the elites have an incentive to make them work) will become increasingly important over time, as the adoption of a new development strategy is bound to threaten existing interests.

For the most part, the immediate policy implications of this discussion are clear. Increases in aid to the NOLDCs will not solve the energy problems of these countries, but they may help in devising a sensible coping strategy for the next decade. Also, opposition to the World Bank's exploration fund should be reconsidered, despite the opposition of major oil companies, because most of the NOLDCs will not be able to compete for diminishing supplies in the world oil market. And, of course, the recycling mechanism will need to be bolstered, perhaps by some form of cofinancing with the International Monetary Fund (IMF) or a change in the lending conditions of the IMF itself.

I believe we should also be putting much more emphasis on conservation strategies in the NOLDCs, even though there is apparently less scope for such strategies in these countries. Even limited gains in conservation are important—and clearly possible—for many of the oil importers (for example, by substituting labor for energy where possible). And, in fact, a number of experts believe that gains are especially likely in the industrial sector (where much of the end-use is concentrated), either through the adoption of the latest energy-saving technology or through increased efficiency in the use of existing technologies.[40] Conservation is especially important because it may be less costly than increasing production, its benefits are more certain, and it may have a much quicker effect. Consequently a program of technical assistance in conservation strategies would seem very sensible.

Finally, over the longer term, support for research on Third World energy strategies should be increased and, perhaps above all, a major effort should be made to determine the feasibility, the requirements, and the consequences of alternative development strategies. Without the latter effort, repeated calls for "another development" will remain essentially rhetorical, and the NOLDCs may muddle into a disaster. At any rate, such policies provide the central elements of the first level of response to the energy crisis.

These are sensible policies, but they are clearly insufficient. There is more to this than the obvious fact that some of the policies will not be effectively implemented, for this would at least imply that the policies, if implemented, would be sufficient and that a great many of the NOLDCs would be helped by them. But incremental policies seem out of scale with the set of interlocking problems confronting most of the NOLDCs. They are committed to development strategies that clearly imply rising import deficits for food, energy, and capital goods; new development strategies are risky and uncertain and may require very high rates of investment; and priorities are very difficult to set when all needs are legitimate and all resources scarce. In this sense, the energy problem, like the food, debt, and trade problems, cannot be treated in isolation, but attempting to treat all problems together may lead only to futility and frustration.

One can hardly fail to recognize that this is a dangerously unstable state of affairs. From the perspective of the governing elites of the NOLDCs, the most critical aspect of this situation is also the most immediate: paying for energy and food imports. Given the magnitude of these import costs, there is very little likelihood that more than a handful of the developing countries can increase their own exports enough to balance the import deficit. Sharply cutting either food or energy imports—or having them cut by suppliers—is, of course, disastrous for development prospects, dangerous for political stability, and morally unpalatable. Another alternative is to borrow recycled OPEC surpluses, but this has problems of its own, not least the exacerbation of long-run difficulties. Finally, there is another alternative, perhaps the most attractive of all, as it delays (but does not eliminate) the need to devise a new approach to development: pressure on OPEC for special treatment. What are the prospects that such an approach can succeed?

OPEC, the Nonoil Developing Countries, and the Quest for a Global Oil Agreement

OPEC strongly supported the Third World's demands for a New International Economic Order (NIEO) in the immediate aftermath of the first oil price explosion in 1973–1974. This was most clearly manifested in OPEC's support for broadening the agenda of the Conference on International Economic Cooperation to include many NIEO proposals. OPEC also sharply increased its own foreign aid commitments. These actions deflected a good deal of Third World pressure away from OPEC, but they became progressively less effective. It became apparent that most of the developed countries did not believe that concessions on the NIEO would have much effect on oil prices, that OPEC aid was initially directed primarily to a few Muslim states, that such aid was bound to decline as OPEC surpluses declined, and that aid levels were much below the level of damage inflicted by rising oil prices. Nevertheless, open rebellion against OPEC remained relatively muted; indeed, one analyst has recently argued that the non-OPEC LDCs "as a group have already ruled out the possibility of breaking up their common front with OPEC and siding instead with the industrial countries on the issue of oil prices."[41] It is unclear who—if anyone, other than the analyst—made this decision; but the degree of unity between OPEC and the rest of the Third World has always seemed surprising, if not perverse, to many Western (and some Third World) observers.

There is no single explanation of the continuation of strong ties between OPEC and the non-OPEC LDCs. One factor may well have been the decline in the real price of oil (by about 20 percent) from 1975 to 1978, which lulled all the oil importers, both developed and developing, into a dangerous degree of inertia. And of course many others found that they could delay necessary but painful domestic adjustments by heavy borrowing, a course of action facilitated by the optimistic assumption that the oil deficits were temporary. Hopes of emulating OPEC and satisfaction at the damage it was inflicting on the developed countries were also consequential. Perhaps more critically, it was very difficult to establish a common position against OPEC because some of the developing countries (the non-

OPEC oil exporters) were benefiting from OPEC's actions and others thought they could cope reasonably well by increasing other exports (especially of manufactured goods to OPEC and OECD countries). OPEC aid and the promises of increased trade with OPEC were also important, as was the assumption that only OPEC could induce or compel substantial movement on other North-South issues. Above all, however, one must understand that the nonoil LDCs had very little choice in the matter. OPEC was inflicting harm, but it was also providing some compensation and promising (or talking about) more; the developed countries were in disarray, providing little and promising not much more. In short, gambling on OPEC's generosity and seeking special arrangements with OPEC (bilaterally and multilaterally) seemed more prudent than gambling on the developed countries.

Signs that the common front was cracking began to appear, both privately and publicly, in 1979. At an Economic Commission for Latin America (ECLA) meeting in April, the Central Americans protested that "we are being strangled" by OPEC, and a little later, at the inauguration of the new Venezuelan president, the Dominican Republic, Costa Rica, Bolivia, and Colombia protested that they had become "prisoners of oil prices." All demanded some form of price relief for developing-country importers.[42] Public protest also began to appear in Africa. As one illustration, an editorial in August in a Nairobi newspaper noted,

> Among the members of the neck-strangling club called OPEC are our "brothers" from Arab countries and other African nations such as Nigeria. Whenever we meet these brothers in other forums . . . they do everything possible to make us support their cause of backing the Palestinians. But apparently when they meet in their other club — OPEC — they tend to forget our brotherhood.[43]

And both UNCTAD-V in Manila and the Nonaligned summit meeting in Havana were almost brought to a halt by open conflicts, which were barely resolved, between oil haves and have-nots. Finally, there have been a number of private or semi-official inquiries from some NOLDCs about the potential for joint initiatives to induce moderate pricing policies from OPEC — none of which, as yet, has produced any results.

OPEC has been very conscious of these developments, and there have apparently been many internal discussions of how to respond. This surely reflects more than brotherhood with the rest of the Third World, for OPEC also fears isolation and is aware that the consequences of increasing desperation among the NOLDCs could be dangerous for OPEC itself. Thus the Caracas meeting of OPEC in December 1979 was presented with a number of proposals, including several joint Algerian-Venezuelan initiatives, to provide new and larger measures of relief for the NOLDCs. To understand why these proposals did not gain complete support from the membership of OPEC, we need to examine very briefly certain aspects of OPEC's current and prospective patterns of behavior.

As has been noted many times, the members of OPEC are very heterogeneous. They have different interests, different levels of development, and different resource endowments. They have managed to remain unified in spite of these differences because they have been able to agree on a few common goals—maintaining a floor price under oil, increasing national control over oil production—and, perhaps above all, because they share an awareness of the dangers to themselves of disunity.[44] These goals might not have sufficed to maintain unity, however, because the achievement of agreement in practice has always been threatened by different short-term and long-term interests. Consequently, with so many real and potential conflicts, I should perhaps note that one of the strongest supports for unity has been entirely exogenous. Consumers have never effectively challenged unity by cutting demand sufficiently, by devising coherent energy strategies, or by establishing an important degree of unity among themselves. In effect, OPEC unity has not required much sacrifice by any of its members.

Many analysts in recent years (before the doubling of prices in 1979) believed that OPEC would remain unified and that future price increases would be moderate.[45] A number of factors seemed to indicate that the crisis would recede (at least until the surplus of production over demand began disappearing in the late 1980s or thereafter): lower growth rates in the developed countries, increased conservation, less use of energy, and new sources of oil.[46] There was also an implicit or explicit judgment that political conflicts, either within particular countries or between different countries, would not threaten OPEC's unity or alter its strategy—OPEC's "economic logic" would prevail, whatever the political differences.[47] Two other judgments were even more crucial: the first, that there would be no major supply shortage (that a buyer's market was in the offing), and the second, that Saudi Arabia would remain a dominant and moderating force within OPEC.

Saudi moderation has frequently been treated in the United States (and Saudi Arabia) as a "gift," as something the Saudis do, against their own interests, to accommodate profligate Western consumers. This is misleading. The Saudis, with the largest reserve position in OPEC, need to worry about the future consequences of present pricing policies. Moreover, they cannot invest all of their earnings domestically, and the surplus must be deposited in Western financial institutions or invested in Western assets. Thus actions that undermine the Western economic system, such as drastic or erratic price increases, also undermine Saudi economic interests. In short, the optimal long-run price and production strategy for the Saudis would seem to require relatively low and predictable price increases and sufficient production to clear the market. This kind of strategy would maintain a dominant market position over the medium and long term by discouraging investment in substitutes, and it would help to stabilize the international financial system. Saudi support for such a position is not a gift or a bribe to induce new policies in the Arab-Israeli conflict, but simply a reflection of its own long-term national interests.

The Saudis and the other surplus countries (Kuwait, Qatar, United Arab Emirates, and, with a different position, Libya) have dominated OPEC, merely by having the means to destroy pricing strategies that they opposed, but that domination has never been complete.[48] Presumably the Saudis also valued OPEC unity, perhaps because of the gains that OPEC had helped to provide and fears about the consequences of an OPEC split. Such a split might either raise prices too high as consumers began a bidding war to ensure supply or drive them too low (even below the Saudi's own rising revenue needs) as producers competed with each other for markets. The latter is perhaps more likely, especially after initial reactions, because most of the rest of OPEC seems to be indifferent about long-run oil prices (having limited reserves) and under great domestic pressure to increase and spend available resources. This would depress prices, as long as the overall supply and demand situation is more or less balanced. At any rate, an OPEC split would signal a period of great instability in the world oil market. A unified price was clearly preferable, and only OPEC provided the Saudis with a good forum to exercise some influence over the price radicals. But this also meant that the Saudis had to compromise and accept a price somewhat higher than its own economic interests dictated. How much higher, however, depended on a number of other factors.

The relative price stability of the period from 1975 to 1978 rested on a precarious *im*balance within OPEC in which price moderates managed to restrain price radicals (perhaps also because the latter, and some of the former, took a few years to digest and sometimes waste early gains). Analysts in this period tended to speculate about what OPEC would do if (or really when) production exceeded demand; presumably OPEC would then require a difficult internal agreement on production shares and profit-sharing (determined previously by the oil companies). OPEC itself, which had in the past limited itself to discussion and coordination of policies, would thus be compelled to accept an entirely new role as a forum for formal decisions on who benefits and how much. Agreement would be particularly difficult if, as some analysts argued would happen, Saudi Arabia gradually lost its ability to absorb all or most of the necessary cutbacks in production because of its own rising need for revenue.[49] But the events of 1979 and the Iran-Iraq war that began in the autumn of 1980 seem to make discussions of OPEC's problems during a period of excess supply very academic. There may well be transitory periods of excess supply in the next few years, if only from a prolonged and synchronized recession in the OECD countries, but the probability of supply shortages (from "another Iran," more severe conservationist strategies within OPEC, a leveling-off in recent improvements in the energy/GDP ratios, etc.) seems to have risen sharply — or at least seems to be the most prudent assumption about likely developments.

The revolution in Iran and the subsequent cutback in production (whether this was deliberate or due to inefficiency) has compelled most experts to reassess near- and medium-term projections of supply and demand. The Iranian events are important in and of themselves, but they are perhaps more important in shaping perceptions of future developments elsewhere, as illustrated by the Carter administration's sudden enthusiasm for the Rapid Deployment Force and by increasing public fears about continued dependence on obviously unstable, if not hostile, regimes. What can or should be done about this is less clear. Military power is not likely to be of much use, and what might be of most use — an effective energy policy by the developed countries — seems beyond the power of existing governments. Still, the point to emphasize here is that instability in various members of OPEC, which seems inevitable, need not be harmful to the oil consumers *if* new regimes continue to produce oil after they consolidate power.[50] This suggests that the (or a) crucial question may concern the development strategies of new regimes and not their ideologies.

The decline in Iranian production has indicated the limits of Saudi power. That power has always tended to reflect the level of excess capacity controlled by the Saudis. But the Saudis have not significantly increased capacity in the past decade, and only very recently have they indicated any intention to increase capacity in the near term (from about 10 mbd to 12 mbd).[51] As a result, the Saudis could not fully compensate for the withdrawal of some Iranian supplies and thus could not restrain the recent price increases generated by a tight market and fears of future shortages. The increased prices have also had another crucial effect, as several other countries (Iran, Iraq, Libya, Venezuela) can now afford to cut their own production back if the Saudis attempt to produce at maximum levels. Whether the Saudis have chosen not to increase capacity for political or technical reasons is unclear, but the outcome has been a significant loss of short- and medium-term leverage — in effect, a major defeat for price moderation and a long-run perspective.

Other economic and socioeconomic factors suggest continued dominance during the 1980s of a strategy of higher prices and limited production. All the OPEC countries are sharply increasing their own use of energy and are fearful of exhausting domestic supplies that they themselves will require.[52] In any case, countries with limited reserves are likely to slow extraction rates as reserves deplete, if only to retain some leverage within OPEC. In addition, fears of social unrest as development, with its attendant consequences of waste, corruption, and domestic inflation, proceeds are likely to continue to escalate — although it should be noted that the failure to develop rapidly may now be as dangerous as rapid development itself.[53] The probable result is somewhat slower growth rates, plus heavier spending on arms.

Growth expenditures may also slow in many OPEC countries for more narrowly economic reasons. The small populations and limited opportunities for investment in nonoil sectors may slow spending in the surplus countries such as Saudi Arabia and the United Arab Emirates, especially if the best investment opportunities have already been exhausted. There may also be considerable slowing of investment in petrochemicals and other oil-sector activities as the market becomes saturated. The Iranian decision, if such it is, to follow a different development strategy (or no strategy at all if chaos continues) will also be important: Iran is the largest economic actor in OPEC, with 25 percent of its total imports and GDP. There are also several forecasts that even some of the countries with very large absorptive capacities, like Indonesia and Nigeria, may have somewhat lower growth rates (and thus lower import growth rates) in the 1980s.[54] At any rate, even if current growth rates are sustained, the necessary imports can be purchased with a smaller volume of oil exports, unless there is something more than a transitory drop in the real price of oil.

The developed countries have done their part to facilitate the victory of OPEC's price hawks. The failure to develop effective energy policies means that the only economic weapon the OECD countries have is to cut demand by a prolonged recession (or by much more profound efforts at conservation), and it means that the world oil market remains at the mercy of wayward events in a number of very unstable countries. Worse yet, persistent inflation, which depreciates the value of OPEC investments in the OECD countries, further encourages a conservationist ethic. Oil in the ground looks like a better investment, and the fear of encouraging the development of substitutes (which would devalue oil reserves) is considerably allayed by immediate price gains, by the ability to lower prices if substitutes begin to appear, and by the ever-increasing projected costs of alternatives to OPEC oil.

The Saudis seem caught between at least partially incompatible aims. Some of the leadership seems inclined to adopt a conservationist trend, thus reducing Saudi ability to flood the market to lower prices and preserve long-term goals, but others clearly desire to reestablish Saudi preeminence within OPEC by increasing the capacity to manipulate supply in order to control short-term prices. But a genuine reassertion of Saudi dominance is likely only if there is a prolonged supply surplus, which seems unlikely or perhaps merely an imprudent assumption on which to base policy. For the moment, however, OPEC can decrease production, conserve supplies, and still earn what revenue its members need (or want). The OPEC meeting in September 1980, which *apparently* reestablished a unified pricing system for OPEC and which might also seem to have reestablished Saudi leadership, does not invalidate these judgments. That agreement was probably transitory as the decline in world oil demand is unlikely to persist and as supply might be endangered (or appear endangered) by the immediately ensuing Iran-Iraq conflict. Indeed, if the Saudis had previously maintained a high level of production (in the relatively "soft" market of from 1979 to the autumn of 1980) in an effort to reestablish some control over world oil prices, the Iran-Iraq war seems certain to embolden the price "hawks" (note the December 1980 increase of roughly $4 a barrel, despite a soft world market), with incalculable consequences for international economic stability and the economic prospects of the NOLDCs.

The period of relative price stability from 1975–1978 led several analysts to the conclusion that OPEC's influence on the world market was essentially beneficial to the oil-importing countries. Thus Edith Penrose argued that "to attempt the destruction, or even weakening, of OPEC as an organisation would be folly. If OPEC did not exist, it would be in the interest of the industrial world to promote its creation in some form."[55] This argument rested on the assumption that OPEC provided the moderates with a large degree of influence over the radicals. Some analysts also assumed that supply shortages and increased prices were more likely without OPEC, if only because the oil companies' loss of influence, which was already significant, was likely to be accelerated (presumably national oil companies would be less efficient and more hawkish on prices). The current situation, however, makes all of these assumptions debatable. The Saudis have lost (or foregone) considerable influence, supply shortages and surpluses have not resulted from OPEC actions (as distinct from national decisions or external events), and many analysts believe prices will fall if OPEC splits.[56] What do these divergent judgments suggest about OPEC's prospects in this decade?

Precise predictions about OPEC's future are obviously impossible. The difficulty is that OPEC's own actions are not necessarily decisive: What consumers do with their energy policies is equally crucial. And, of course, the discovery of new oil, increased use of substitutes, technological breakthroughs, and political or military "shocks" might also alter or invalidate prior calculations of likely outcomes. Nevertheless, within these very substantial constraints, it seems clear that the factors that have seemed most likely to weaken or undermine OPEC cohesion — excess supply and increasing revenue needs and the consequent need for an agreement on production sharing — seem less probable (except in periods of general recession), and the factors that have facilitated unity — increased demand, the cost of substitutes, supply shortages — seem more probable. There will certainly continue to be price conflicts within OPEC during the next decade, as discount rates and reserve positions still differ, but the key point is that supply does not appear likely to increase enough or demand to decrease enough to make the price issue threatening to OPEC's unity. The debate is only likely to be about how much to increase real prices.[57] In these circumstances, OPEC can avoid difficult decisions about shares and quotas and can remain largely consultative, perhaps setting a floor price, exchanging information, and coordinating policies toward world energy problems and foreign aid.

The burden of this argument is that OPEC is likely to persist and remain important, but not as a forum in which the moderates exercise influence over the radicals. Price moderation may dominate again as a result of (probably) transitory external developments or, later in the decade, as a result of the reemergence of Saudi dominance because of its control of so much reserve potential. But secular price trends are likely to be steadily upward, and the central questions are likely to concern how — not whether — prices are increased and whether supply capacities are increased. And from this perspective OPEC could be very crucial in providing a forum for agreement on predictable, consistent, and system-wide patterns of price changing and supply control. Consumers might then have the confidence to rely on the world oil market (and producer fears of military intervention if the market is chaotic might be diminished). In short, Penrose and others may well be right in arguing that the developed countries need OPEC, but the primary rationale is predictability; moderation is a secondary consideration.

Unfortunately, even if OPEC wanted to play this role (and it is not clear that it does) it may not have the power to do so: The crucial factors will be consumer actions, the occurrence or nonoccurrence of supply interruptions, and nationally determined decisions on production strategies. OPEC is not likely to have much difficulty in maintaining a floor under prices, but its power to maintain a ceiling will depend on external factors that it cannot control or if external factors are relatively favorable (no more Irans), on joint agreement (both within OPEC and with the OECD) to follow new and different price and production strategies. In effect, OPEC is unlikely to split but it is also unlikely to be unified enough to agree on the terms of an oil bargain or to be able to effectively implement such a bargain if it became possible.

OPEC has thus lost some of its power because its members need it less. The decline in Saudi dominance, the diminished power of the major oil companies, and prices that are already high enough to make production cutbacks relatively painless hardly imply much need for price hawks to compromise merely to maintain OPEC unity. The inability of the Western countries to move much beyond limited and essentially hortatory cooperation reinforces this judgment, as does the tendency of buyers in the oil market to panic at the first rumor of trouble. Increasing doubts about the ability to continue to recycle funds to the nonoil LDCs add another element of gloom to increasingly credible forecasts of "the decline of the West" or simply of prolonged instability and depressed prospects throughout the global political and economic system in this decade.[58]

In these circumstances, the need for some kind of global oil settlement seems ever more imperative and ever less likely. The United States and other developed countries need to think about how this calculus might be altered—or, if it cannot be altered, how to deal more effectively with an international system that will remain in permanent crisis. This quest may not be successful, but one needs also to add that neither the current approach (essentially piecemeal, a holding action that focuses on minimal cooperation and ad hoc stopgaps) nor the military approach (reportedly enthusiastically supported by some of Ronald Reagan's defense experts) offers any higher certainty of success. And growing fears that we are on the verge of chaos may be a more effective catalyst for agreement than rational statements about mutual long-term benefits.

The Prospects for a Global Oil Agreement

If we set aside the case of a major loss of production capacity, against which consumers would probably have to rely on sharing arrangements and sharp cuts in consumption, we need to ask what might induce OPEC to follow price and production strategies (moderate price increases, assured supply, increases in spare capacity) that are more compatible with the interests of the developed countries and the NOLDCs? Put another way, why should OPEC give up the advantages of a tight market in which it can conserve supply and maintain (or increase) earnings without much difficulty? As I have already argued, the developed countries lack the economic leverage to persuade OPEC to change direction, and military leverage (preventive war or, as Bismarck described it, suicide for fear of death) is neither credible nor likely to guarantee an assured flow of oil—its ostensible purpose. Nevertheless, although the OPEC leadership is well aware that most of the leverage is in its hands, in recent months there have been many indications, both public and private that OPEC (or some key countries within it) might be willing to come to some kind of arrangement with the developed countries and the NOLDCs.

Why this is so can only be a matter of speculation, but there are some reasonable inferences worth noting. In the first place, the near-chaos in the oil market during 1979 was obviously not in the long-term interest of OPEC — especially, of course, of the member countries that hoped to preserve the value of their oil reserves. But uncontrolled price increases could also harm OPEC's short-run interests, because the consequences of a worldwide economic slump (or desperate actions like military intervention) would also be disastrous for countries intent on industrialization and the protection of their earned assets. Some degree of market stability is thus in everyone's interest, but it is difficult to see how this can be achieved without the cooperation of consumers.

In the second place, OPEC's greatest fear, partly because of feelings of solidarity and partly because of the dangers of radicalization, has centered on the possibility that the rest of the Third World would turn against it. Although the OPEC countries are divided in many ways and on many issues, they share a strong desire to help the NOLDCs. Major efforts have been made to retain Third World support, but they have been increasingly inadequate. The NOLDCs could not afford the initial price explosion, and the more recent increases not only play havoc with NOLDC development plans but also make it very difficult for OPEC to pacify desperate countries with incommensurate amounts of aid. OPEC clearly wants to respond to these developments and it clearly wants help in doing so, but achievement of these goals will probably require the support of the developed countries. Consequently, the question of whether such joint support for the NOLDCs can be negotiated or whether OPEC support by itself will suffice will be a major issue in the early 1980s. A brief analysis may permit some tentative conclusions about the likely state of the relationship between OPEC and the NOLDCs in the 1980s.

I should begin by noting that OPEC will surely defend its economic interests, but what that means in practice is uncertain. Economic interests can be interpreted very differently by states with different goals, different discount rates on the future, and different perspectives on issues like domestic stability and obligations to the international system. If the market is dominated by a condition of tight supply and rising prices, individual producers will have a wider margin (but not carte blanche) within which to follow political inclinations without sacrificing economic goals. This point obviously holds more for countries that cannot invest all their earnings domestically. Many of the other countries will confront increasingly difficult balance of payments constraints either because spending exceeds revenues (Algeria, Indonesia) or because oil revenues and oil reserves begin to decline (Iran, Nigeria, Venezuela); but even the latter countries will have relatively more room to follow political inclinations (especially for short periods of time).[59]

The decision to help the NOLDCs must be primarily political, as these countries can do little to harm OPEC in economic terms. The crisis confronting the NOLDCs is likely to increase in intensity throughout the 1980s, and rising oil prices will play a very substantial role in exacerbating that crisis. None of the options open to the NOLDCs looks very appealing; most are very risky, and all are difficult to implement successfully. One analyst lists the following options: allying with OPEC against the industrial countries; seeking special deals from OPEC; allying with the industrial countries against OPEC; defaulting on all international obligations; constructing cartels in other raw materials; and undertaking a crash program to exploit domestic energy resources.[60] Exploiting domestic energy resources is certainly imperative, but it is very costly, not all the NOLDCs have enough resources to exploit, and it would be some years before beneficial results could be expected. Defaulting does not make much sense (although it may be imposed by events if further external support is not provided), and no other cartels could possibly match or compensate for OPEC's success. OPEC is not interested in an alliance, and an alliance with the developed countries is not much more probable. Nor would it be very effective unless both groups of countries adopted effective domestic energy policies.[61] That leaves the effort, already well under way, to extract preferential concessions from OPEC as — apparently — the only real option open to NOLDCs. But this also is likely to prove problematic, and we need to ask whether yet another option exists.

The OPEC countries are definitely intent on providing some price relief for the rest of the Third World, but they confront several difficulties in attempting to do so. A two-tiered pricing system, for example, is difficult to operate without complete control of the oil distribution system and may generate widespread cheating. Some fear has also been expressed that subsidized prices will encourage NOLDCs to increase demand and discourage necessary adjustments to an oil-short world — although in present circumstances this is like telling a drowning man to reject a lifesaver because he won't learn to swim as quickly. At any rate, these problems have led OPEC in its recent discussions to consider other means of helping the NOLDCs.

The most prominent of these has been an Algerian-Venezuelan proposal to create a $20 billion bank that would finance oil imports (and perhaps other needs) of the NOLDCs. Details have been very sparse, but apparently the bank was (or is) to be funded by a levy on each barrel of oil sold (Libya had already proposed a $0.50 tax on each barrel of OPEC oil to subsidize LDC oil purchases).[62] The Caracas meeting of OPEC in December 1979 could not agree, however, and the bank proposal was put aside for "further study." According to Bijan Mossavar-Rahmani and other sources, the OPEC package for the NOLDCs also included support for oil and gas exploration and development and guarantees of secure, relatively low-cost supplies of liquid fuel.[63]

OPEC did not indicate why the bank proposal (or any other form of preferential treatment) was rejected, but some of the reasons are perhaps apparent. For one thing, setting up another institution, staffing it competently, and determining its operating rules takes time and resources, both of which are obviously scarce, especially in a period when the NOLDCs need help *very* quickly (particularly because so much of their debt is due to be repaid in the next few years). In the second place, some OPEC countries are fearful of losing a certain amount of leverage over aid recipients if aid is collected via an automatic tax and dispensed according to presumably neutral criteria. Bilateral programs may (or may not) be more inefficient, but they are more useful to the donor.[64] There are, however, two other and more important reasons for OPEC's reluctance to act.

OPEC wants to help the other developing countries, but not at its own expense. Thus the Libyan delegate to OPEC, while noting the need for "a policy that would permanently lift the burden from the developing countries" also added that "the industrialized countries should pay more for the oil" (to compensate for subsidized prices to the NOLDCs).[65] And at a news conference at OPEC's Caracas meeting, the Algerian oil minister noted that the OPEC countries "have proposed to examine the problem of security and supply and maybe more than the security — we will talk about a priority" for the rest of the Third World.[66] The difficulty with proposals that cut prices and guarantee supplies for the NOLDCs, while raising prices and endangering supplies for the developed countries, is that they take away with one hand what they give with the other. As long as the prosperity of the developing countries (both OPEC and non-OPEC) is linked to the prosperity of the developed countries, the developing countries may lose more in aid and trade from recession and inflation in the developed world than they gain from lower-priced oil. And OPEC does not appear willing, and many of its members cannot afford, to subsidize Third World oil purchases without compensatory increases for the developed countries.

Put another way, analysts such as Mossavar-Rahmani concentrate solely on the OPEC-NOLDCs connection and are very optimistic that OPEC can thwart resistance by means of a relatively small aid package (roughly $4 billion in 1981). But they fail to understand that the position of the

NOLDCs will become progressively more desperate—even if OPEC doubles its aid—if growth rates in the developed countries decline, if protectionism increases, and if aid levels continue to sink. In these circumstances, OPEC aid to the NOLDCs may help to keep them afloat for a few years, while OPEC policy toward the developed countries assures that keeping the NOLDCs afloat is the most that can be achieved. The point of this argument, and it is a very crucial point, is that OPEC may be able to help its Third World friends only by a tripartite agreement with *all* oil importers; otherwise it risks an increasingly desperate confrontation with the NOLDCs.

The other reason that OPEC may find it difficult to develop a major program to help the NOLDCs is that the conservationist trend that has become increasingly attractive—because of inflation, fears of the consequences of unchecked growth, and higher revenues from oil exports—is directly contrary to the interests of the NOLDCs. The latter need cheaper prices and increased oil supplies, but in a tight market not only can they not afford to buy oil, they may not get much chance to do so if they must bid against the industrial countries. As the NOLDCs buy a relatively small share of total OPEC exports, OPEC might try to alter its conservationist policies for Third World importers. But once again, this generates fears that the NOLDCs will become locked into an increasingly precarious oil economy and that necessary changes will be postponed until they are even more costly and difficult. And oil subsidies will not be very useful if general conditions in the world oil market further depress economic activity in the developed countries and thus diminish the prospects for Third World exports.

This analysis apparently implies that the other option that the NOLDCs should be pursuing—indeed that all should be pursuing—is a tripartite agreement that seeks to protect each group's central interests. A number of experts have emphasized that the long-run interests of all converge on a stable oil system in which the oil producers have their gains preserved and are helped to prepare for development without oil revenues, the developed countries are assured sufficient supply at predictable prices, and the NOLDCs are guaranteed enough oil at subsidized prices to survive a transitional period to a nonoil future. It should perhaps be noted that the NOLDCs are an important component of an agreement not only because of OPEC's concern for their fate but also because they are likely (short of economic catastrophe) to become an increasingly important element of world oil demand and because their behavior might have a significant impact on the stability of the international financial system. Nevertheless, the difficulties of negotiating a tripartite "global bargain" are evident, in terms of its elements as well as its timing.

The elements of the bargain are not mysterious, but they are problematic. Consumers and producers would have to agree to establish and maintain a balance between supply and demand, but this would require very complex internal negotiations for each group. The difficulties might be even greater for OPEC than for the OECD countries, as the members of OPEC, split every which way, would have to agree on production shares (and perhaps even the sharing of cutbacks, although this hardly seems likely at the moment). Apart from this, there would also have to be an agreement on pricing policy. Maintaining the real value of oil by the indexation of prices (against a "basket" of import prices) might be possible, but indexation does create some difficult technical problems. And, of course, it raises issues of equity, not only in terms of why only oil should be protected against inflation, but also in terms of differential effects on individual producers and consumers. Finally, some provision would also have to be made for a fair rate of price increases—perhaps, as some in OPEC have suggested, by relating such increases to OECD growth rates, rates of inflation, and currency changes.

There are three major difficulties with these measures: The proposed pricing formula would increase inflationary and recessionary pressures on the developed countries (and, more specifically, on the dollar); it is not clear that OPEC is sufficiently united to develop (and implement) a common position; and, in any case, OPEC does not really need any external help at this time to set effective production and pricing policies or to protect the real value of its export earnings. In effect, such measures would provide consumers with an assured supply of oil (barring another supply "shock") and predictable price increases, but they provide too little to OPEC that it cannot get by itself. Thus other elements would have to be added to the package.

These are also familiar and do not require extensive comment—which is not to say that they would be easy to negotiate and put into effect. Two measures have been widely discussed: support for OPEC's industrialization, including guaranteed access to OECD markets for its industrial exports (mostly petrochemicals), and some form of guarantee for OPEC's financial investments in the developed countries (perhaps by indexed bonds). This would presumably allay the growing fear within OPEC that oil in the ground is a much safer investment than financial assets that are being eroded by inflation; only a guarantee of equivalent purchasing power might induce continued production levels above OPEC's own current needs. These measures raise a number of difficult problems, especially in terms of industrial policy and political response, but the problems might be resolved or diminished by careful planning and (presumably) by a shift in attitudes attendant upon the realization that all sides were genuinely in quest of a mutually acceptable agreement.

Apart from these measures, however, what might be most attractive to OPEC is a joint agreement to help the NOLDCs. This would have to entail immediate balance of payments help so that the NOLDCs could pay for necessary imports, perhaps by an agreement to relax IMF conditionality or by some form of cofinancing of private bank loans. It must also include longer-term support for indigenous energy development, perhaps by increased support for World Bank programs to finance exploration and development or by creation of a new fund financed by an oil tax (or the more general tax on exports suggested by the Brandt Commission). An agreement such as this, apart from the details, seems in everyone's interest, as it reduces pressure on OPEC from the NOLDCs and it reduces supply pressures (and perhaps the danger of a debt crisis) for the OECD countries.

The idea of a global bargain of this kind is attractive, but one is compelled to be pessimistic about its prospects. There are a common long-run interest in a stable system and some mutual short-run interests in averting irrational actions — and a worldwide recession or depression; but there are also conflicting short-run interests, vast uncertainties about the best course of action, and potentially crucial long-term conflicts about values and purposes. In addition, global agreements will require sharp increases in international coordination of national policies and in national willingness to sacrifice some autonomy and to accept international surveillance. There are few persuasive signs yet of movement in this direction. Furthermore, although OPEC seems increasingly nervous about the consequences of its own actions, internal OPEC disarray may make agreement impossible. At any rate, if OPEC cannot impose restraint on its members — and it appears too weak to do so in present circumstances — the agreement would be unstable; poor producers would always be tempted by the gains to be earned in the spot market and rich consumers would continue to panic at the first hint of trouble. Finally, one should add that the Arab members of OPEC (as well as several others) might ask for political concessions in the Middle East or in the North-South Dialogue that were unwise or impossible — or perhaps simply more costly than the probable benefits from an agreement that, if negotiable, might prove very unstable (or irrelevant, if there is another Iran).

Some advocates of a global oil agreement will admit the force of these arguments — especially in light of the Iran-Iraq war — but nevertheless maintain that a "near equivalent" of a global agreement still remains possible with Saudi Arabia and its conservative allies in the Persian Gulf. If this is true, such an agreement would certainly be worth pursuing, not only because of its potential effects on the oil market but also because only the

Saudis and the Gulf states (and Libya) have the surplus funds to invest in projects designed to reduce some of the burden on the NOLDCs. Still, even this truncated version of a global agreement may be impossible to negotiate or, if negotiated, may not be very stable. Proponents of such an agreement tend to overestimate *current* Saudi leverage in the oil market as well as Saudi willingness to break openly with the rest of OPEC. Moreover, Saudi willingness to take large investment risks in and for the rest of the Third World has yet to be convincingly demonstrated. It should also be noted that the Saudis seem no more disposed than any other member of OPEC to cede some degree of control over oil production and pricing — control that they have only recently achieved.

Doubts about the wisdom or feasibility of negotiating a global bargain may be justified, but something more needs to be said about the matter. In the first place, if only at a tactical level, it would be a mistake to appear too negative, as this might provide some of OPEC's radicals with a convenient rationalization for hostile actions. Moreover, continued discussion may prevent OPEC from buying off or frightening the NOLDCs into silence or into acceptance of an OPEC-NOLDCs coalition against the industrial countries, which is in neither side's interests.

In the second place, the sense of imminent worldwide crisis may grow in the next few years and perhaps alter conditions enough to permit meaningful negotiations. There is, after all, increasing recognition that the failure to control the factors responsible for pessimism — rising demand, tight supplies, panic buying, undisciplined producers — can only generate a disaster of the first magnitude for the global system. We need to keep patching the system together until a strong government takes the lead (perhaps by sacrificing some of its own short-term interests) or until a disaster actually occurs and belatedly permits a settlement. It could be important in these circumstances to have planned ahead; to have discussed the issues with allies, with OPEC, and with the NOLDCs, and to have worked out some of the technical details of the various proposals. In the third place, one can only expect the unexpected in this system. Saudi Arabia and the moderates may reassert their dominance in a few years, some of the radicals (Iraq?) may have a change of heart or leadership, or something else may intervene — any of which might make a package deal not only desirable but also possible.

For the moment, however, the prospects for the relationship between OPEC and the NOLDCs must be considered very uncertain. OPEC will certainly make a major effort in the next few years to compensate the NOLDCs for the effects of rising oil prices and to prevent an OECD-NOLDCs alignment against itself (one of the few agreements at Caracas was to create an information office to make OPEC's case better). But this effort is not likely to succeed, primarily because responses may take too long to devise and implement and because OPEC will probably be unable or unwilling to compensate the NOLDCs for the full effects of rising prices and tight supplies (not the least of which are the effects on growth rates and political attitudes in the OECD countries). The prognosis is grim: OPEC in disarray, mixing elements of greed, self-interest, charity, and fear into inconsistent policies; the developed countries turning inward and accepting a lower standard of living or gambling that guns can extract oil; the NOLDCs retreating into *sauve qui peut* policies or trying one or another form of blackmail to attract support; and no one concerned enough about stability to sacrifice a few short-run interests — or perhaps no one capable of making the sacrifice.[67] Can the United States diminish the likelihood or at least the effects of such an outcome?

The International Politics of Energy

None of the options to deal with the problems of the NOLDCs looks very promising. Even if those that seem to make the most sense were to be adopted — rapid exploitation of indigenous energy resources, a new approach to energy development, a quest for a tripartite energy agreement — there is no guarantee that they would produce consistently beneficial outcomes or that even good policies would make much difference if the external environment gets much worse. Some NOLDCs obviously will be able to deal with external effects better than others, but none is likely to do very well; success may consist of staying afloat. In any case, gaps within the Third World will grow, conflicts between different Third World countries are likely to increase, domestic stability may become even more precarious and even more dependent on repression, and the possibility of intra-Third World cooperation to diminish the impact of some adverse external developments may become even more problematic. The OPEC countries may not enjoy their prosperity for very long, because they will become increasingly nervous and insecure as the international environment deteriorates, and because it is unlikely they will have created the conditions for post-oil development.

Two additional points about the emerging crisis are worth noting. First, in a very real sense the conditions of the crisis have already been set. Things not done now, sins of omission like failing to increase investment or decrease oil consumption, will be more costly and more difficult to implement at a later date, perhaps compelling sins of commission that are dangerous for both national and systemic stability. In short, the crisis is already here, if as yet primarily in a latent form. Second, the crisis may appear less severe than it actually is because some of the projected import deficits in oil (or food) apparently do not materialize. But the deficits *should* appear if real needs are to be met. Consequently, if the actual deficit is (say) only half as large as the projected deficit, and if major efforts to increase domestic supplies have not been made, this means that demand has been artificially suppressed. In effect, to discover what the real deficit is, one needs to add unmet domestic needs to the actual deficit. In these circumstances, it would be an illusion to assume that great progress had been made in containing the crisis confronting the NOLDCs.

Perhaps this forecast is sufficiently grim and sufficiently credible to induce cooperative responses that may avert the most disastrous outcomes. As I have already argued, the first level of policy response by the United States must reflect the need to cope with the immediate crisis—to limit damage to the developing countries by devising or improving mechanisms that provide quick relief and by encouraging Third World elites to adopt new energy policies (and perhaps new development policies). The elements of this coping strategy have already been discussed at various points—more aid, new forms of recycling, increased research, etc. They are familiar, but they need more determined and more extensive support. So too does the effort to establish a consensus on the need for, and the content of, a new development strategy; failure in this regard assures a continuing and escalating crisis for the NOLDCs.

But it is worth reemphasizing that these initiatives, although necessary, are unlikely to be sufficient. The energy crisis cannot be effectively dealt with in isolation; solutions must form part of an integrated approach to food, trade, and debt problems (not to say other problems) as well. But even on its own terms, solutions to the energy problem of the NOLDCs will require a range of cooperation and support from (and between) OPEC and the developed countries that seems improbable. Moreover, what the developed countries do with their own energy policies is likely to be more decisive for both groups of countries than anything the NOLDCs do or do not do. Still, although no one can pretend that this first level of response is adequate, and although it must be recognized that responses within the Third World will vary enormously, it makes sense to help those countries that can be helped. It should diminish the severity of the emerging crisis, and it would provide some important evidence that the United States wants to maintain and increase its commitment to Third World development despite its own economic difficulties.

Much more effort also needs to be made to bring the NOLDCs into the OPEC-OECD energy discussions—not in order to construct an alliance against OPEC (which the latter, in any case, could easily foil), but rather to increase pressures against OPEC from friendly sources and to emphasize more clearly the effects of OPEC pricing decisions on NOLDC development prospects. After all, the fear of creating a worldwide depression is not the only limitation on OPEC: Well before a depression occurred, OPEC could inflict irremediable damage on its allies and peers. In this sense more support might be gotten for the effort to induce OPEC to invest directly in the developing countries (diminishing some recycling pressures) and to support the World Bank's energy program more generously (which support has been limited by OPEC doubts about the wisdom of creating new suppliers).

In addition, apart from the OPEC connection, the NOLDCs ought to be included in efforts to establish some sort of emergency allocation system for oil supplies in the event of a supply crisis. Research and discussion about new development strategies also need much greater emphasis and could be usefully emphasized in this context. Finally, greater understanding might be encouraged among the NOLDCs for the proposition that an oil settlement must take precedence over the demands for simultaneous negotiation of a settlement of many other North-South issues. I do not mean to suggest that the latter issues are unimportant, but rather that they cannot be dealt with (at least in a political sense) without a prior settlement of the oil issue and that dealing with all issues in the same conference is too complex and too time-consuming.

It is necessary to reemphasize that the point of these efforts is not to split the NOLDCs away from OPEC. Rather, in a negative sense, the point is to prevent the solidifying of an OPEC-NOLDCs alliance that cannot by itself resolve the problems created by the oil situation. More positively, the effort should be perceived as an attempt to create new perceptions of possibilities and to alter OPEC's interpretation of how it can help the NOLDCs. One obvious reason why the NOLDCs have continued to support OPEC is that they do not see a viable alternative, especially one that guarantees them a supply of oil at a bearable price. Thus efforts to establish a worldwide allocation system (in contrast to an allocation system limited to the countries in the International Energy Agency), to increase foreign aid, IMF resources (as well as the conditions of access to such resources), funding of the World Bank energy program, and spending on research on alternative energy sources might help create a feeling that pressure on OPEC is not bound to be futile. At the same time, the United States might be more forthright in indicating that there is no possibility of serious movement on North-South issues until there is an acceptable oil agreement. The implicit OPEC argument that only its support guarantees concern for NIEO issues needs to be directly resisted: The point needs to be made that OPEC, by its policies, stands in the way of movement, not toward the NIEO, but toward sensible compromises on a number of important issues (especially the possibility of increasing aid levels).

The limitations of the first level of response obviously imply the need for a second level—policies to protect U.S. interests in an international environment that is unstable and fragmented, in which a global oil agreement is desirable but probably not possible in the near term, and in which the United States lacks the power and the resources to impose order (or policies) on others. This might become a second-best world heading into a third-best world, but the United States can at least establish priorities of concern and attention. With resources scarce, and with virtually all non-OPEC developing countries needing and wanting help, North-South policy may become less salient than bilateral or subregional ties with "like-minded" states or with economically and strategically important states. This will be especially true if conflicts within the South continue to grow. In any case, a more selective and discriminating policy ("delinking," after all, is a policy open to both sides) may be necessary because the United States will be able to promise less to (and expect less from) the developing countries than the rhetoric of past and current policies imply. I cannot discuss the implications of this here, but I would like to conclude with a brief word about the most significant external aspect of U.S. energy policy in the context of this second level of response.[68]

There is no point in belaboring the obvious fact that a successful energy policy must begin at home: conservation, the development of new energy resources, and a serious effort to create an adequate emergency petroleum reserve (and perhaps also a reserve of natural gas). Continued efforts to improve planning and coordination with our allies in the International Energy Agency is also imperative. But the United States will remain dependent on imports for a crucial amount of supply, no matter how successful it is with domestic energy policies. This means that the greatest danger is likely to come from a supply shortfall or interruption from or by one or more major producers. If this comes because of another embargo—perhaps because of an Arab-Israeli war—there is very little the United States can do about it (except to bear the burden or, *faute de mieux*, risk military intervention). But if the supply interruption is a result of domestic instability and not a result of a deliberate OPEC decision, the decisive factor in getting through the crisis without a disaster will be the existence of spare producing capacity (and of course a reserve system) in a number of oil-producing countries (not only OPEC; Mexico, Great Britain, and Norway might also be candidates). Spare capacity could be used in an emergency to supplement petroleum reserves (or as a *short-term* substitute if no reserve has been established—as is true for almost all the LDCs) and perhaps as a means of diminishing panic in a crisis. A broad agreement on allocation could also be very important. The immediate U.S. policy aim, consequently, should be to urge the creation of enough shut-in capacity to ride out a crisis—perhaps

2 to 4 mbd for a period of six months. The United States should offer to share in the cost of construction of this capacity and should seek prior agreements on trigger points for its release and its allocation as well as firm agreement that it will not be used simply because supplies are tight. The United States need not approach all of OPEC on this matter: The Saudis and the smaller Gulf states are the key, and they might well agree because of fears about the consequences of a crisis or because of the offer of other inducements. If not, or as an additional safety valve, an approach to U.S. allies is imperative.

As I noted earlier, a number of reports appeared in the spring of 1980 that Saudi Arabia is rapidly increasing its production capacity to 12 mbd.[69] The apparent aim is to have the extra 2 mbd available before the end of 1981 (the earlier target date was 1986). The decision to increase capacity, despite the growth in conservationist sentiments, presumably reflects a number of calculations. The Saudis want to restore their leverage within OPEC by reacquiring the ability to flood the market, thus providing a means of defending a price ceiling as well as a price floor. They also need to meet their own rising revenue needs and increased domestic demand for oil. Lastly, they want to provide their national oil company (Petromin) with larger supplies — to be used for economic or political purposes — without diminishing the amount available for foreign oil companies (thus increasing the incentive of the companies to invest in joint ventures).

But I should note that, if these reports are true, the Saudis apparently intend to *use* this capacity (unless demand continues to drop because of a prolonged worldwide recession), which suggests that it might not be available as spare capacity in case of a supply crisis. I need hardly add that unpredictable events within Saudi Arabia itself might also make the increased capacity unusable or unreliable. This suggests a strong need to seek a private agreement with non-OPEC producers (especially Great Britain and Norway) to develop spare capacity and an even stronger need to increase the U.S. emergency reserve system (despite Saudi and OPEC reluctance to sell oil that is, effectively, put back into the ground). The latter can surely be done quietly but steadily, as the oil market is hardly completely transparent. The unwillingness of the Carter administration to support the emergency reserve is virtually irresponsible. But Congress finally decided to force the Carter administration's hand and presumably will maintain the pressure if the Reagan administration seems indifferent to the need for a large reserve. It needs emphasis that not only is a reserve very useful if a crisis occurs but it may also have a deterrent effect in warding off deliberate actions like an embargo. And although a reserve will be expensive (especially, of course, if a supply interruption never occurs), it has the virtue of providing a rapid response, it is an easily reversible policy, and it is probably less costly than the available alternatives (quotas, tariffs, subsidies). In any case, the costs must be borne as long as we judge the likelihood of a supply shortfall as reasonably high.

More effective policies at both of these levels — coping with the immediate crisis, preparing for continued deterioration — are important on their own terms. They are also interrelated, in that progress at one level facilitates progress at the other. Nevertheless, without OPEC's active cooperation in seeking a global oil settlement, such measures must ultimately fail: They are stopgaps for the NOLDCs and are damage-limitation measures for the developed countries. Still, the most critical point about these policies may well be that they will increase the possibility of an international agreement that benefits OPEC, the NOLDCs, and the developed countries. Successful domestic energy policies, enhanced cooperation within the OECD on emergency reserves, spare capacity, an allocation agreement (including an effort to take the needs of the NOLDCs into account), and a stronger effort to emphasize to the NOLDCs that international progress is impossible without new policies from OPEC may generate enough pressure on OPEC to elicit a positive response. And prior efforts to work out the details of such an agreement and to establish working groups (within and among the three camps) could be a useful supplementary step. The intent of these measures would be to establish a more effective two-track strategy: on the one hand, measures to protect U.S. interests in an unstable environment, and on the other hand, simultaneous efforts to begin preparing the ground for movements that might encourage OPEC to accept the need for a genuine tripartite agreement.

In this sense, advocates of a global agreement with OPEC are not so much wrong as premature: The ground for such an agreement must be carefully prepared, which is to say, it must rest on a deliberate political strategy that seeks to protect both short-term and long-term interests. No one needs to be reminded that the prospects for success are poor and that it will take time — and strong leadership from the United States — to put the elements in place. But it would also be irresponsible to act as if the prospects for success were nil or as if more extreme actions could succeed (at what, one might ask).

Notes

1. For example, Kenya had to scrap at least 30 percent of the programs in its newest development plan because of increases in the price of imported oil — and this

was before the latest price surge. And Turkey, which imports 85 percent of its oil, now expends *all* of its export earnings on oil—and "another" 45 percent on debt payments.

2. In any case, few developing countries have built, or can afford to build, much storage capacity for imported oil; too much has to be spent on current needs to build a hedge against shortages.

3. There is also a difference between food and energy in terms of developed-country responses, as the energy issue more directly affects developed-country interests, especially in the context of potential links between OPEC's behavior and Third World needs and demands. Another difference is that the LDCs produce a much larger proportion of their food than of their energy needs domestically (although there are some exceptions).

4. See *Investment by the Developing Countries in the Energy Sector: A Preliminary Analysis of Long-term Financing Requirements* (Geneva: UNCTAD, TD/B/C.3/146, September 1978), pp. 4–9.

5. Ibid., p. 2.

6. *A Program to Accelerate Petroleum Production in the Developing Countries* (Washington, D.C.: World Bank, 1979), p. 23. These four countries rely fairly heavily on other resources like coal and hydropower.

7. See Robert S. Pindyck, *The Structure of World Energy Demand* (Cambridge, Mass.: M.I.T. Press, 1979), pp. 252–258. It is also harder to reserve energy patterns in developing countries because they lack the economies of scale necessary to make some investments profitable, and they frequently lack the transport system necessary for other fuels (like coal).

8. I should note that I will concentrate only on the oil problem and ignore many other aspects of the energy problem (for example, the noncommercial sector, the development of renewable energy forms, etc.), all of which are important, but not in the immediate context of the need for oil to run economies that have copied the oil-intensive techniques of the developed countries.

9. For sophisticated analyses of the various projections, see Juan Eibenschutz and J. Wallace Hopkins, Jr., "Summary Report of the Workshop Discussions," in *Workshop on Energy Data of Developing Countries* (Paris: International Energy Agency, 1979); and Edward L. Allen et al., *A Comparative Analysis of Global Energy Models* (Oak Ridge, Tenn.: Institute for Energy Analysis, 1979).

10. See Pindyck, *Structure of World Energy Demand*, pp. 249ff., for an analysis of this issue.

11. John R. Brodman and Richard E. Hamilton, *A Comparison of Energy Projections to 1985* (Paris: International Energy Agency, 1979), p. 9. See also the table in *Investment by Developing Countries in the Energy Sector*, p. 6.

12. See the estimates in Carroll L. Wilson, *Energy: Global Prospects 1985–2000* (New York: McGraw-Hill, 1977), p. 97. These figures do not imply, however, much increase in per capita usage, primarily because of population growth rates.

13. One should be careful to note the distinction between non-OPEC oil exporters and the rest of the non-OPEC developing countries; as we shall see later, lumping the two groups together as a single non-OPEC category can be very deceiving. In the text, the category of NOLDCs excludes the non-OPEC oil exporters.

When I discuss both groups together, I use the more generic term "developing countries."

14. See Arjun Makhijani with Alan Poole, *Energy and Agriculture in the Third World* (Cambridge, Mass.: Ballinger, 1975), pp. 16ff. There is similar evidence in regard to industry, although, as with agriculture, there are some important exceptions. The World Bank, as well as many other institutions and analysts, was initially very doubtful about the potential for conservation in the developing countries. But a recent World Bank report estimates that conservation (through realistic pricing and other measures) might reduce estimated energy consumption in 1990 (30 mbd) by about 15 percent—a substantial reduction indeed. See *Energy in the Developing Countries* (Washington, D.C.: World Bank, 1980).

15. See Pindyck, *Structure of World Energy Demand*, p. 253.

16. See *Agriculture: Toward 2000* (Rome: Food and Agriculture Organization, July 1979, preliminary draft) and Richard E. Stryker, "The World Bank and Agricultural Development: Food Production and Rural Poverty," *World Development*, Vol. 7, no. 3 (March 1979):331.

17. See *Program to Accelerate Petroleum Production,* pp. 14-22.

18. See Pindyck, *Structure of World Energy Demand,* pp. 257-258.

19. For one estimate that the financing burden of additional oil imports will be greater than the financing required to develop indigenous energy resources, see *Energy Supply and Demand Balances in Non-OPEC Developing Nations* (Washington D.C.: U.S. Department of Energy, February 1979), p. 12. And a recent World Bank study estimates that domestically produced oil is unlikely to cost more than $25 a barrel (against over $30 for imports) and that domestically produced coal would be much cheaper than either imported oil or imported coal supplies. See *Energy in the Developing Countries,* pp.6-8.

20. *Programmatic Areas for U.S. Assistance for Energy in the Developing Countries* (Upton, N.Y.: Brookhaven National Laboratory for the Agency for International Development, 1978), p. 11. For estimates of the import bill at the end of the decade, see *Energy in the Developing Countries,* pp. 21-23. It should be noted that even if the real import bill in 1980 is larger than the current bill, taking the actions noted (exploiting indigenous resources, conservation) would keep the claim of oil imports on export earnings close to present levels of roughly 25 percent—a not inconsiderable achievement, given rising energy demand.

21. One of the best discussions of this is in Philip F. Palmedo et al., *Energy Needs, Uses and Resources in Developing Countries* (Upton, N.Y.: Brookhaven National Laboratory, 1978), pp. 107ff. Also useful is *Investment by Developing Countries,* pp. 23ff.

22. For a discussion of this argument, see *A Strategy for Oil Proliferation: Expediting Petroleum Exploration and Production in Non-Opec Developing Countries* (Washington, D.C.: Congressional Budget Office, February, 1979), pp. 3-7.

23. D. G. Fallen-Bailey and T. A. Byer, *Energy Options and Policy Issues in Developing Countries* (Washington, D.C.: World Bank Staff Working Paper No. 350, August 1979), p. 4.

24. See the various tables on exploration in *Program to Accelerate Petroleum Production,* pp. 18-19. There has also been no major increase in exploration for coal.

25. Exploratory activity may already be on the upswing, particularly in highly promising areas. Thus there have been a number of recent small discoveries of off-shore oil in West Africa, that is, in the same general area as much of the oil from Nigeria, Gabon, and Angola. *Economist*, November 24, 1979, p. 94.

26. Fallen-Bailey and Byer, *Energy Options and Policy Issues*, p. 4.

27. Adrian Lambertini, "World Energy Prospects and the Developing World," *Finance and Development*, Vol. 16, no. 4 (December 1979):22. Current investment plans indicate that the NOLDCs will be able to supply only 25 percent of their projected energy needs in 1990 from indigenous resources.

28. Palmedo, *Energy Needs, Uses and Resources*, p. 86.

29. There is another parallel worth noting, if only as a warning. The Carter administration, which initially seemed very committed (rhetorically) to a basic human needs approach, was extraordinarily naive in its understanding—or misunderstanding—of the economic and political complexities of basic needs and was thus apparently surprised by the negative reactions of many LDC elites. The point is that there is need for care in suggesting energy alternatives to the NOLDCs, both in the sense of making sure that all the consequence⌐ have been thought through and in understanding the issues raised for governing elites by the new approach.

30. For a brief discussion of the uncertainties, see *Programmatic Areas for U.S. Assistance*, p. 3. The uncertainties, as well as the political and economic factors cited in the preceding paragraph, indicate why the optimism of some analysts about the availability of "soft" energy options for the LDCs may be misplaced or excessive. At any rate, analysts who advocate this option ought at least to indicate how the political and intellectual obstacles can be overcome. But most seem content to indicate that other alternatives exist or may exist, which is only part of the problem. See, for example, Amory B. Lovins, L. Hunter Lovins, and Leonard Ross, "Nuclear Power and Nuclear Bombs," *Foreign Affairs*, Vol. 58, no. 5 (Summer 1980):1171–1172. One might also note that the "soft" energy options tend to rest on decentralized and disaggregated initiatives, which is advantageous in some senses, but is unpopular with governing elites who prefer centralized and aggregative schemes that enhance government power and control.

31. On OPEC capacity, see Lambertini, "World Energy Prospects," pp. 20–21. Lambertini notes that most expansion in capacity took place in the 1960s and that future increases are likely in only a few of the capital-surplus countries. Various doubts about Saudi capacity are also discussed in *The Future of Saudi Arabian Oil Production* (Washington, D.C.: Subcommittee on International Economic Policy of the Committee on Foreign Relations, April 1979).

32. See *A Program to Accelerate Petroleum Production*, pp. 3–4.

33. Ibid., pp. 4ff.

34. As with food, there is a very heavy concentration of Third World demand in a relatively small number of countries: Sixteen countries provide 75 percent of total Third World energy demand (six countries provide 75 percent of food demand). Most of the countries are very large and/or have a relatively large industrial sector; several are in OPEC (Iran, Venezuela, Indonesia) or are oil exporters (Egypt, Mexico); none are in Africa. South and Southeast Asia are major areas of potential crisis, not only because of the size of the countries involved, but also because of the

intersection with the food problem.

35. For various estimates, see *A Program to Accelerate Petroleum Production* and Palmedo, *Energy Needs, Uses and Resources.* These studies and the Department of Energy study, *Energy Supply and Demand Balance in Non-OPEC Developing Nations,* provide estimates well below UNCTAD estimates of financing needs; beyond the obvious differences in underlying assumptions, this may also reflect institutional biases and perspectives.

36. For the World Bank estimate, see Fallen-Bailey and Byer, *Energy Options and Policy Issues,* p. 77; for the share of GDP estimate see *Investments by Developing Countries in the Energy Sector,* p. 10.

37. The Brandt Commission has proposed a "World Development Fund," based on various kinds of universal taxes, to increase lending to the developing countries. The Commission has also proposed sharp increases in aid (to reach the target of 0.7 percent of GNP by 1985), a doubling of World Bank lending, increased IMF lending to middle-income LDCs, and an SDR(special drawing right)-aid link, all of which would raise the net flow of resources to the developing countries by at least $50 billion (1980 prices) by 1985. This would represent roughly a doubling in real terms of current resource transfers (and might go much higher, depending on the acceptance and the details of the proposed World Development Fund). All of these ideas have been in circulation for some years and all can be justified by real needs and by the argument that they will also benefit the developed countries. They are not likely to be implemented quickly (and some, like the proposed fund, perhaps not at all), which makes it necessary to assume that resource transfers will only increase moderately at best. Still, acceptance of some of these ideas would make the long-run investment picture in both energy and agriculture look considerably less bleak.

38. Quoted in *New York Times,* August 22, 1979, p. D5.

39. Funding could also be limited to the poorest LDCs, which could not attract private financing or raise the funds domestically. I should add that, since writing this paragraph, there has been some indication that the United States will shortly end its opposition to the bank's financing of exploration. Moreover, the United States seems willing to support a bank initiative to create a special fund or institution to double the bank's energy lending (from about $13 billion to about $25 billion). But even this commitment, which would be helpful although hardly decisive, will depend on OPEC agreement (which has been delayed by a dispute over Palestine Liberation Organization representation, among other things).

40. See Lovins, Lovins, and Ross, "Nuclear Power and Nuclear Bombs," p. 1165 (and the technical material cited there).

41. See Bijan Mossavar-Rahmani, "OPEC and NOPEC: Oil in South-South Relations," *Journal of International Affairs,* Summer 1980, p. 40.

42. See *New York Times,* April 24, 1979, p. D2, and *Washington Star,* May 28, 1979, p. 2.

43. Quoted in Carey Winfrey, "Oil Price Rises Put Kenya's Economy in Jeopardy," *New York Times,* August 20, 1979, p. 8.

44. Rustow and Mugno described OPEC's primary economic task as securing maximum monetary returns in the medium term for oil exports, but this formulation seems to mask a key internal conflict. Obviously the members want maximum

monetary returns, but the central question is when — the different discount rates on present and future returns must be taken into account. This is why I believe the goal is better stated as maintaining a floor price, as this is in the interest of all members. See Dankwart A. Rustow and John F. Mugno, *OPEC—Success and Prospects* (New York: New York University Press, 1976), p. vii.

45. See Pindyck, *Structure of World Energy Demand*, p. 279; and Charles Blitzer et al., "A Dynamic Model of OPEC Trade and Production," *Journal of Development Economics*, Vol. 2 (1975):363-386. The latter analysis noted (p. 375) that all the studies examined implied that "the current price of oil is higher than consideration of OPEC's long-run interests would dictate, and that prices ought to fall in the not too distant future." So much for models.

46. For the argument that the crisis was receding, see Edith Penrose, "OPEC's Importance in the World Oil Industry," *International Affairs*, Vol. 55, no. 1 (January 1979):18-32.

47. For the "economic logic" argument, which is obviously simplistic, see Rustow and Mugno, *OPEC—Success and Prospects*, pp. 97ff.; for an interesting discussion of the political conflicts, see Paul Jabber, "Conflict and Cooperation in OPEC: Prospects for the Next Decade," *International Organization*, Vol. 32, no. 2 (Spring 1978):378-399.

48. There have been many analyses of the different groups within OPEC, most of which center on the distinction between "surplus capital" and "high absorber" countries. One of the most useful discussions is in Paul Leo Eckbo, *The Future of World Oil* (Cambridge, Mass.: Ballinger, 1976). See also Ali Ezzati, *World Energy Markets and OPEC Stability* (Lexington, Mass.: Lexington Books, 1978).

49. See Theodore Moran, *Oil Prices and the Future of OPEC* (Washington, D.C.: Resources for the Future, 1978).

50. I do not mean to imply that instability is beneficial; rather, my point is that how harmful it is will depend on the price and production strategies of the new regime (or the reactions to instability by the old regime).

51. See Lambertini, "World Energy Prospects," for Saudi actions in respect to capacities in the past decade. For recent reports of intentions to increase capacity to 12 mbd, which will be discussed in this chapter, see *Economist*, April 19, 1980, pp. 63-64.

52. For one of the many comments on OPEC needs, see Abdelkader Sid Ahmed, *Development and the Members of the Organization of the Petroleum Exporting Countries* (Geneva: UNCTAD, TD/B/C.3/145, October 4, 1978).

53. There was clearly a policy failure on the part of the developed countries in not warning OPEC countries about the dangers of too rapid growth, but short-run pressures to relieve balance of payments difficulties were obviously so strong that worries about long-run consequences were even less salient than usual. See *New York Times*, January 28, 1980, pp. D1 and D5, for a recent assessment of the problems created for the Gulf states by poorly planned and massive spending on industrialization, including social unrest, unrealistic projects, and neglect of traditional economic activities (especially agriculture).

54. See Farid Abolfathi et al., *The OPEC Market to 1985* (Lexington, Mass.: Lexington Books, 1977).

55. Penrose, "OPEC's Importance in the World Oil Industry," p. 18. See also Peter R. Odell and Luis Vallenilla, *The Pressures of Oil—A Strategy for Economic Revival* (London: Harper & Row, 1978).

56. See Pindyck, *Structure of World Energy Demand,* p. 279.

57. This implies that if OPEC does split, prices might not drop very much (if at all) and would probably recover in fairly short order.

58. The quoted phrase is from Walter J. Levy, "Oil and the Decline of the West," *Foreign Affairs,* Vol. 58, no. 5 (Summer 1980):999–1015.

59. On the balance of payments projections, see Abolfathi, *OPEC Market to 1985,* pp. 10–17.

60. Oystein Noreng, *Oil Politics in the 1980s—Patterns of International Cooperation* (New York: McGraw-Hill, 1978), p. 75. This list does not include the most important option—adoption of a new development strategy—perhaps because it can begin to affect matters significantly only later in the decade. Moreover, it places too little emphasis, even in the short term, on cutting domestic demand (which may become *the* major alternative for the poorest countries, despite its pernicious effects on growth and development). This is one reason why I emphasized conservation in the earlier policy discussion.

61. There is a tendency on the part of both developed- and developing-country importers to use the quest for an alliance as an excuse to avoid adopting painful domestic energy policies. But no external policy will work (including the increasingly popular military option) if major domestic changes are not instituted quickly.

62. See *New York Times,* December 5, 1979, p. D5. The difference between a two-tiered price system and increased lending through a bank is somewhat like the distinction between price stabilization and compensatory financing of export shortfalls (as in the commodity debate). The latter is easier, does not affect market operations, and provides some donor control over who gets support. Some OPEC countries are making individual efforts to help the NOLDCs. For example, Iraq has reportedly made agreements with fifteen very poor countries to provide long-term, interest-free loans equivalent to the price increases of 1979. The recipients include Tanzania, Somalia, Sri Lanka, India, Pakistan, and Bangladesh. But this is at best a limited stopgap measure and does nothing to deal with the long-term problem of developing indigenous resources. Venezuela has also announced a program to subsidize oil purchases by some of its Caribbean neighbors.

63. Mossavar-Rahmani, "OPEC and NOPEC," pp. 32–33.

64. Based on interviews with several officials of OPEC aid programs.

65. *New York Times,* December 5, 1979, p. D5.

66. Quoted in *New York Times,* December 17, 1979, p. D4.

67. Some recent events—for example, the sharp drop in the energy/GDP ratio, the decline in oil imports, and the apparent glut in oil supplies—seem to suggest that a more optimistic picture might be appropriate. But the danger in interpreting such developments too optimistically is not merely that they might be transitory phenomena but that they provide another excuse for delaying or avoiding hard choices, as in 1975–1978, when the decline in the real price of oil encouraged a return to "normal" behavior.

68. I shall discuss more general aspects of U.S. policy in Chapters 6 and 7. After

completing this analysis, I read Joseph S. Nye, Jr., "Energy Nightmares," *Foreign Policy*, no. 40 (Fall 1980):132–154, which discusses these issues from a broader perspective and employs somewhat similar arguments about the unlikelihood of a global oil agreement and the elements of a successful U.S. energy policy. Professor Nye also discusses other energy matters, and his article deserves to be widely read.

69. The comments in this paragraph are drawn from *Economist*, April 19, 1980, pp. 63–64, and from private discussions with various officials.

5

The Developing Countries
and the Trading System

Perspectives on Trade

Trade was once perceived as the "engine of growth" and then, more modestly, as the "handmaiden of growth."[1] In the past decade, however, some analysts have argued that trade was and is an enemy of growth — and equity — for most developing countries. Nevertheless, as autarky is an extremely costly, if not hopeless, alternative for small and poor countries, especially those that cannot avoid some degree of contact with a very complex and sophisticated international system, trade policies and trade issues are not likely to diminish in importance for the developing countries. Indeed, without expanded opportunities for trade, development prospects throughout the Third World will be increasingly grim, food and energy problems will be insoluble, and a major debt crisis will be inevitable. Consequently, it is not surprising that virtually all of the scenarios for the next two decades, whether conservative, reformist, or radical, project increasing growth rates for Third World trade and an accelerated transfer of many activities and skills to the Third World.[2] From this perspective, the question is not whether to trade, but with whom, in what products, and under what terms.

The factors primarily responsible for developing-country dissatisfaction with the trading order will still be present in force in the 1980s. In fact, it seems increasingly likely that they will be more rather than less powerful. The notion of a liberal trading order with special exemptions from the rules for the developing countries has come under attack not only from the "new protectionism" (voluntary export restraints, "organized free trade," etc.), but also from the creation of principles, such as graduation and selectivity, designed to limit the gains of particular developing countries.[3] Increased concern by the developed countries for questions of economic and strategic security may also make an open system less likely, as there will be less willingness to give up certain mature industries that have a historical relationship with security.[4] Moreover, the long-term gains for growth from restructuring may be outweighed, especially for rich countries, by the short-term costs of adjustment and political conflict.[5] And additional uncertainties will be generated by the need to make changes in a context of slower growth, the conversion to a new energy strategy, the development of challenges to new and more capital-intensive industries, and perhaps challenges by several very large developing countries (such as India and China).

The trading system has also been attacked by many developing countries on other, more specific grounds. Most of the indictment is a variation on the theme of the unfair and exploitative relations of the "center" with the "periphery": The center establishes export enclaves that have little connection to the rest of the economy; the exports left to the periphery lack technological dynamism or confront declining terms of trade (although the argument has shifted recently from primary products to the terms of trade for labor-intensive manufactured goods); and the multinational corporations that are crucial to exporting, especially of relatively advanced products, earn excessive profits, control the transfer of technology in order to maintain dominance, and impose inappropriate technologies on poor and labor-surplus economies. In sum, trade becomes a form of "unequal exchange" in which only a few benefit and resources are transferred from poor to rich. Increased trade might also have a negative effect on equity, as in some cases it might benefit a few industrialists and a small number of highly paid developing-country workers at the expense of the poor in the developing countries and the lowest-paid workers in the developed countries (who tend to be in low-skilled, labor-intensive activities).

There have been, and there are, cases in which all of these charges have been justified, but as a general case the indictment is not persuasive. Some developing countries have done very well within the trading system, in terms of growth as well as equity; multinational corporations are not omnipotent and uncontrollable; technology transfer has not always been "inappropriate," whatever that term may imply; and the terms of trade have not always deteriorated for the developing countries. Whether trade will or will not be beneficial consequently cannot be answered in either theoretical or ideological terms: One must examine the external environment in which trade will take place and the internal conditions and policies of individual countries. In short, trade *may* increase inequality or have very little effect on either growth or development, but it need not do so; moreover, a severance of external ties is hardly a guarantee of progress.[6] In any case, developing countries have a high and growing import propensity; there is thus no alternative to trade to get necessary items that are not produced domestically. And of course the traditional arguments about the welfare benefits implicit in specialization, economies of scale, and competition—if they can be earned—are incontestable. The desire of the developing countries to minimize or eliminate the factors that limit, or seem to limit, benefits from trade will obviously be difficult to achieve in an environment of slower growth and increased uncertainties. This is especially so because the developing countries want more than a reform of the old trading order. They want a new and restructured trading system that takes "developmental responsiveness" as its guiding principle, that seeks an increasing share of the benefits of trade for an increasing number of developing countries, and that proposes to achieve its ends by central direction and by rules that explicitly legitimize a partially closed and preferential trading system. These are not irrational demands, as merely reconstituting the old system will not provide enough gains to a group of countries that desperately need to increase foreign exchange earnings, not only to pay for crucial imports of food, oil, and capital goods, but also to overcome the inherent limitations of size and poverty. Moreover, substantial changes are imperative if the benefits of trade are to be spread beyond a small number of advanced developing countries and if movement into more promising exports is to become possible. Nevertheless, it is far from clear that such massive restructuring is possible or that the means by which the developing countries hope to proceed are either feasible or wise.

The 1975 UNIDO Conference at Lima set the target for the developing countries: 25 percent of world industrial production by 2000. The January 1980 UNIDO Conference in New Delhi provided detail and direction for the achievement of this goal. I shall discuss this effort after first examining some of the general problems of North-South trade. In addition to restructuring North-South trade, the developing countries have indicated a strong desire to increase trade among themselves. I shall also discuss some aspects of this movement. These discussions of the problems and prospects of North-South and South-South trade should provide some perspective on whether trade will be a major factor in reducing the impact of the food, energy, and debt crises for the developing countries and on the tensions likely to appear in one part of the North-South arena. I shall then comment briefly on some of the policy implications of the analysis for the U.S. government.

North-South Trade: Problems and Prospects

World trade increased by about 8.5 percent per annum between 1963 and 1973, and trade in manufactures increased by about 11 percent per annum.[7] From 1973 to 1978, however, both figures were halved. Still, despite the growth of the "new protectionism," developed-country imports of manufactures from the developing countries grew by about 15 percent per annum, about twice as fast as imports of nonfuel raw materials. At the same time, the developing countries have become increasingly important markets for developed-country exports: By 1978 exports to the LDCs were larger for the United States, Western European countries, and Japan than exports to each other. Moreover, reversing the pattern of the 1960s, North-South trade during the 1970s grew faster than North-North trade. The trade surplus in manufactured goods of the industrial countries increased from $12.3 billion in 1973 to $54.6 billion in 1977 with the OPEC countries and from $23.9 billion to $42.2 billion in 1977 with the oil-importing developing countries (although with much variation among the OECD countries as to shares of the surplus). It is useful to keep the aggregate surplus in mind as we examine some of the problems created by Third World manufacturing exports.

The rapid growth rate of manufactured exports from the developing countries did not create many problems for the developed countries before 1973. After all, the developing countries were following the "outward" strategy sanctioned by Western theories — as had Japan — and they had only a small share of the world total of manufactured exports (less than 10 percent). And the vast majority of their exports were in the same mature, labor-intensive industries that the developed countries would abandon "naturally" as they shifted, in the course of growth itself, to more capital-intensive and highly skilled activities. In this sense, developing-country exporters merely contributed to, but did not cause, an inevitable adjustment problem for dynamic, growing economies. This also provided the ground for a theory of "stages of comparative advantage" in which countries rapidly shifted out of activities in which they were losing comparative advantage (usually because of different labor costs) and moved on to more sophisticated activities.[8] But this very optimistic interpretation of present and future developments in the international trading system rested on a number of crucial assumptions: that growth rates in the developed countries would remain high; that *both* developed and developing countries would readily abandon activities in which they had lost comparative advantage; and that such a process of change would provide enough benefits to enough developing countries to defuse demands for a radical restructuring of the trading system. All of these assumptions are eminently challengeable.

That growth rates in the developed countries are likely to be lower in the next decade is by now a widely shared assumption.[9] Obviously this assumption might be overturned by events, but for planning purposes it needs to be taken seriously, even at the risk of generating a self-fulfilling prophecy. At any rate, the implication is clearly lower demand for exports and perhaps the growth of protectionism (or diminished support for continued liberalization).[10] In addition, in a context of slower growth, the likelihood that the initial developing-country entrants into a market may swallow all the opportunities, especially for low-level activities in which market saturation is always a danger, seems bound to increase.

This also creates problems in terms of the need for countries to abandon activities in which they have lost comparative advantage: The normal uncertainty about which products to develop as an alternative will be exacerbated by perceptions of generally narrowing opportunities. In any case, risk-averse developing countries are even more likely than developed countries to be reluctant to give up activities in which they have developed some capacity, not only because of uncertainties about what the replacements should be, but also because of political pressures from vested interests or nationalist pressures to maintain certain industries as a symbol of modernization (such as iron and steel or automobiles).[11]

The third assumption, that enough developing countries will receive enough benefits to accept the existing trading system, is neither more nor less doubtful than the first two, but it may be more important because it relates to the structure of the trading relationship itself and not to more uncertain and changeable factors such as growth rates or individual state behavior. But to understand this issue we need to understand which developing countries have benefited from the trading system and which products they have exported.

Ten developing countries had 90 percent of the increase in the share of the Third World in total world manufacturing value added from 1966 to 1978.[12] Eleven developing countries had more than half of total LDC industrial production and more than 75 percent of LDC manufacturing exports.[13] The newly industrializing countries (NICs), also had very high GDP growth rates (7–10 percent per annum before 1973), export growth rates of 16–20 percent per annum, very high domestic investment rates, and an increasing share of the OECD import market for manufactures (the share increased more than 3 times from 1963 to 1976, but still amounted to only 8.1 percent of OECD imports). The following are conventionally described as NICs: Greece, Portugal, Spain, Turkey, Yugoslavia, Hong Kong, South Korea, Singapore, Taiwan, Brazil, and Mexico.[14] There is obviously some doubt about the accuracy or utility of including the first four countries, but the addition of potential NICs tends to diminish the sense of strangeness. There is some debate about who the new NICs might be, but India, the Philippines, Argentina, Thailand, and Malaysia are most often mentioned; Chile, Pakistan, and Egypt are sometimes mentioned; and several of the OPEC countries are treated as a special case (because of the emphasis on capital-intensive petrochemical exports).[15] The original list of NICs, even apart from the inclusion of the southern European countries, is hardly representative of the Third World: Most are small (except for Mexico and Brazil), politically conservative, stable, closely tied to the United States, and committed to an outward strategy. These are not characteristics likely to generate much support in the rest of the Third World, although broadening the number of NICs may diminish some of the potential conflicts.

The problems implicit in the rise of the NICs have usually been attributed to the export strategy that they have adopted. Concentration on a limited number of primarily labor-intensive exports has created specific and deep — rather than general and superficial — problems for a number of mature industries in the developed countries. The familiar examples include clothing, textiles, footwear, leather goods, and wood products. One study, for example, notes that fifty items accounted for 80 percent of NIC exports to the OECD area and over 17 percent of OECD imports of these items (against a share of total OECD imports of 8.6 percent).[16] But, although these imports surely cause severe adjustment problems, it should be noted that they are mostly in products (consumer goods, some engineering products with standardized technologies) that the developed countries should be abandoning (in economic terms) and that the overall balance in manufactured trade is still — and is likely to remain — very favorable to the OECD countries. In effect, were it not for the slowing of growth and the turmoil in the international economy since 1973, the transitional problems created by concentration on a few export products, and perhaps even the problems created by the inevitable movement into new products, could be dealt with relatively easily and in terms of mutual long-term interests.[17] This necessarily implies that the export strategy itself is not the root of the problem; rather, external growth rates are the central issue. Presumably, then, the exporters should follow a holding strategy, fighting within the system to maintain existing gains and to open future opportunities, until growth rates return to their historic (1960–1973) path. But this oversimplifies, for there are other problems associated with the rise of the NICs.

It may be useful to begin with the problems of the NICs themselves, not least because, once again, they highlight the close connections between domestic and international problems. There is general agreement that the external successes of the NICs have masked some important domestic failures. Leaving aside special cases like Hong Kong and Singapore, several of the NICs have neglected their agricultural sectors and been confronted with rising food import bills.[18] In addition, while exports to the developed countries have been primarily labor-intensive (in contrast to exports to other developing countries) and have thus made some contribution to employment, in overall terms the export orientation has had only a slight effect on the problem of unemployment in NICs and is not likely to have much more effect in the future.[19]

The neglect of agriculture and the failure to diminish significantly the employment problem have been major contributing factors to a more general failure: The domestic markets of all the NICs have expanded (GNP growth has been export-led, but domestic demand has also increased), but not enough to diminish the need for continuing high rates of export growth.[20] But to increase the domestic market for industrial products would require not only substantial investments to increase agricultural output and employment and to provide the necessary infrastructure but also a shift in industrial strategy away from exportable products to products for domestic use. Such a strategy is obviously impossible for small countries that must export to grow, but even for the larger NICs the investment funds are not available, foreign exchange needs would still be high (to pay back debts, for necessary imports, etc.), and the willingness to shift to a more inward-oriented strategy may not be present. In any case, if the import bill for oil and food (among other things) continues to escalate, the need for massive amounts of foreign exchange merely to keep afloat during the present turbulence may not permit a shift away from an export orientation.

The failure to increase domestic markets and the need to increase exports to pay for very costly imports sharply exacerbate the problems that the NICs cause for the rest of the trading system. The difficulties created by heavy concentration on a small number of labor-intensive exports have been difficult enough, especially in a period of slow growth, and the addition of several larger NICs (like India, Pakistan, and perhaps China) may increase the likelihood of protectionist reactions — even if the exports of the larger NICs are much smaller, proportionally, than the exports of the smaller NICs. Apart from this, as the initial NICs are losing comparative advantage in many labor-intensive goods to other developing countries and as they are moving into more advanced goods, the pattern of competition — and thus the nature of the NIC challenge — is shifting for both the developed countries and the non-NIC developing countries. I shall briefly examine some of the problems this creates or may create for both groups of countries.

The NICs have responded extremely well to the deteriorating economic environment of the past six years and in fact have managed to increase export growth rates — at a slower rate than previously, but still much above the rates of the developed countries and the nonoil LDCs. They have diversified both products and markets. There have been increasing shifts toward capital- and skill-intensive products with mature technologies (like ships, iron and steel, engineering products, machinery, and transport equipment) and toward the markets of OPEC and the NOLDCs. One should emphasize that although the share of labor-intensive manufactured exports in total NIC manufactured exports declined (from roughly 78 percent to 68 percent between 1968 and 1976), labor-intensive manufactured exports were still dominant, and that although new markets were opened, the OECD market still took about two-thirds of NIC manufactured exports.[21] Nevertheless, new patterns are clearly emerging and with them, new problems (or potential problems). In narrowly economic terms, increased diversification implies increased competition and, consequently, increased efficiency, more rapid growth, and reduced inflationary pressures. But there are other problems, both political and technical, that suggest that all the benefits of diversification may not be achieved and that diversification itself may not get very far.

In one sense, diversification into more advanced products reduces the impact of NIC exports on the OECD countries, as import pressures are spread across a wider number of industries. In another sense, however, it merely intensifies the range of difficulties for the developed countries. In effect, developed-country exporters struggle with each other for high technology markets, they compete with the NICs for markets for advanced manufacturing goods, and they still confront challenges from a combination of NICs and the new developing-country exporters in traditional labor-intensive goods.[22] Advocates of theories of "stages of cooperative advantage" perceive this as normal and beneficial—as it would be if "economic logic" always prevailed. But the movement by the NICs into more advanced goods confronts both political and economic obstacles, and movement by other developing countries into labor-intensive exports may not be as wise or beneficial as theory suggests.

One problem that the NICs may confront as they move into more advanced exports is that such exports may create even more severe adjustment problems for the developed countries. There is widespread agreement that the developed countries should be abandoning declining, labor-intensive industries such as clothing and footwear. But in an environment of great insecurity (with perhaps a reassertion of nationalism), phasing out traditional industries that have a historic connection with security—iron and steel, ships, some machinery, etc.—is an entirely different matter.[23] This is especially so because the benefits of adjustment tend to be long-term and the security focus is near-term. One thing that this means, as we shall shortly see, is that the NICs may be compelled increasingly to find their markets for such advanced goods in the rest of the Third World.

Another factor of some importance in this context is that the benefits of trade with the NICs are very asymmetrical. In the aggregate, the OECD countries have maintained a considerable surplus in manufacturing trade with the NICS. Disaggregated, the picture looks much different: The surplus is increasingly concentrated in Japan, West Germany, and Italy; the United States, the United Kingdom, and Canada have moved into a deficit position.[24] Japan is the key problem; the Japanese doubled their share of exports to the NICs from 1963–1977 (from 13 percent to 27 percent) and had about 55 percent of the total OECD surplus with the NICs. Japan has also placed a much higher share of its foreign investment in the developing countries (60 percent from 1966 to 1976, against 14 percent for the United States and 30 percent for France and West Germany) and thus directly or indirectly controls a relatively higher proportion of NIC exports.[25] This is not meant as criticism of the Japanese, who have had no choice but to invest abroad, but rather to indicate why the frequent references to the OECD surplus with the NICs are somewhat misleading: The aggregate surplus is not likely to deter the various countries in deficit from protectionist reactions, particularly if they already have a bilateral deficit with the Japanese.

Some trade specialists have suggested that the NICs may confront serious technical problems if they attempt to increase advanced exports to developed-country markets. Trade among the developed countries themselves has tended to follow different patterns from trade between developed and developing countries. For a variety of reasons, the former has emphasized intraindustry specialization, while the latter—more closely resembling the traditional factor proportions theory—has emphasized interindustry specialization. However, if the NICs move on to more advanced exports to the developed countries, they must increasingly shift to the complex patterns of intraindustry specialization.[26] This trade pattern demands sophisticated skills in marketing, product differentiation, technological innovation, quality control, and the like—all of which are in very short supply in developing economies.[27] This implies, again, that the market for such exports must be other developing countries. But it also seems to imply that trade between developed and developing countries, which will still be crucial because of developing-country foreign exchange needs, should concentrate on the traditional exchange of primary products and labor-intensive goods for capital- and skill-intensive goods.

The argument that trade with the developed countries should continue (or revert to) traditional patterns of exchange is not necessarily reactionary, at least if the terms of trade for primary product exports improve and if the returns from labor-intensive exports seem likely to be favorable. Primary products are not my concern here, but I should note that the prospects for the labor-intensive, standardized exports of the NICs and other developing countries are not especially promising. For example, Keesing notes that such products suffer from narrow profit margins, unstable markets, low income elasticities of demand, excessive competition, and threats from technological progress. As some markets are already glutted and as such exports will be major casualties of slower growth rates, it seems quite likely that their terms of trade will fall against other *manufactured* exports.[28] Movement to more advanced exports thus seems imperative, despite the problems discussed in the previous paragraph. But this is obviously possible—if at all—only for the NICs and a few other advanced developing countries. The rest of the developing countries may be left to compete among themselves for declining shares of an increasingly saturated market for low-level goods. This is hardly fair, but even if one chooses to leave questions of fairness aside, the poorer countries are not likely to be able to afford or to be willing to accept more advanced exports from the NICs and the developed countries if they cannot sell their own goods. The problem is exacerbated by the tendency of both NICs and non-NICs to emulate each other's successes—which is not surprising for risk-averse countries, but which does quickly circumscribe initial gains.[29] A solution would presumably require some kind of broad agreement on harmonization, but determining which countries should get what industries (and on what grounds) may be beyond the current state of the art in either politics or economics.

Finally, a few comments are necessary at this point (although I shall discuss South-South trade in greater detail in the next section), if only in reference to some of the problems created by diversification. In 1976, seven NICs had 7.2 percent (against 2.5 percent in 1963) of total world manufactured exports; the rest of the developing countries had 1.6 percent, down from a share of 2.7 percent in 1963.[30] In effect, the NICs had increased their share primarily at the expense of the other developing countries. The great majority of these exports went to the developed countries, as other LDCs produced their own labor-intensive goods for domestic consumption. But as the NICs shifted to relatively more capital-intensive exports (almost a quarter of manufactured exports by 1975), the need to diversify markets was apparent. Home markets were usually not large enough to absorb production, but many of the new exports were either not competitive in OECD markets or confronted various restraints on trade. As a result, many of the newer exports had to be sold in Third World markets; for example, in 1976 over 40 percent of NIC exports of machinery and transport equipment went to other developing countries.[31] South-South trade, however, has been as concentrated as North-South trade; the same group of NICs has earned the great majority of benefits (thus five NICs have almost 70 percent of intra–Third World trade in capital goods). Moreover, the NICs are increasing their share of trade with OPEC and the socialist countries (as well as the other LDCs) even faster than they are increasing their share of OECD trade. As the OECD countries have maintained their share of OPEC, socialist, and nonoil LDC markets, this means that NIC gains have come, once again, at the expense of the other developing countries.[32]

These factors, taken together, indicate why there must be substantial doubts that a "stages" theory of comparative advantage will lead, gradually but steadily, to an international trading system that maximizes global efficiency and welfare. The problem is not merely the likelihood of increased protectionism by the developed countries. Indeed, it may well be that vacillations around the status quo are more likely than a general retreat into a "new" or "old" protectionism, if only because awareness of the costs (and memories of the 1930s) is so salient and institutional surveillance of national policies so commonplace (which is not to say, of course, that surveillance is sufficient by itself). Still, one must be cautious; growing fears and perceptions of the likelihood of increasing deterioration within the international economy may generate some dangerous self-fulfilling prophecies.

Beyond this, the preceding discussion suggests two major factors that may well impede movement toward a relatively more open and rationalized system—or perhaps even maintenance of present patterns. The first of these is the sharp asymmetry of benefits both within and between the different groups of countries. In the past this could be finessed by side-payments (e.g., preferences, bending of General Agreement on Tariffs and Trade [GATT] rules) or simply overwhelmed by the general pattern of widespread and rapid growth. This may no longer be possible, which means complex and perhaps insoluble questions of fairness and harmonization must be dealt with *from the start*. The second factor relates to the nature of the choices confronting both NICs and non-NIC developing countries. For the former, giving up many labor-intensive industries will be politically and economically difficult, and moving into more advanced efforts will require a new range of skills in penetrating developed-country markets (or competing in other markets with developed-country firms) and an enhanced willingness to accept and attract foreign investment. For the latter, there are the danger of moving into exports that may confront declining terms of trade (ironically, such exports have some of the negative characteristics of traditional commodity exports) and the need to reach difficult agreements with other developing countries on who shall produce what. There are also serious questions about the availability of finance and about the allocation of whatever funds are available among equally important needs.

Each group of countries thus faces severe pressures and major risks in choosing an outward orientation. The NICs, faced with rising domestic demands and a sharply increased import bill for oil and other natural resources, must continue to improve their export performance, but they are losing comparative advantage for some exports and confront sharp competition in gaining or maintaining access to markets for more advanced exports. They will probably continue to resist "graduation" into developed-country status, both to maintain preferential access to developed-country markets and to remain eligible for special status in intra-LDC trade. This implies a mixed system in reference to the developed countries (preferences for traditional exports, but trade liberalization for newer exports) and an increasingly closed system in reference to the Third World. It will require a very difficult balancing act, but it also suggests that developed-country efforts to split the NICs away from the other developing countries are not likely to succeed, unless the offer to the NICs is much more generous than currently seems likely.

The developed countries, facing increased competition on all sides, are likely to continue to seek to control the NICs by graduation, selective application of safeguards, and various other forms of "voluntary" and involuntary restraints. But there is also likely to be more intra-OECD conflict over NIC markets and more bilateral conflict with the NICs for other markets. Some foresee the outcome as increased regionalization of trade, but perhaps equally likely are cross-regional and selective ties with particular groups of countries.[33]

It seems unlikely that many other developing countries will actually move into the NIC category, especially if the international environment remains as menacing as now seems probable. One reason is that few are likely to be able to match the conditions generally considered to be responsible for the success of the NICs: political stability, a disciplined labor force, a supply of entrepreneurs, and a government able and willing to impose the "right" policies (restraint on wages, incentives for foreign investment, etc.).[34] What developing countries will probably want is a closed, centrally directed system (with an increased generalized system of preferences [GSP], directed redeployment of industries, more South-South trade, and a sharing of benefits with NICs) that removes some of the risks they confront by guaranteeing market access and outcomes.

At best, this could be a very unstable and unpredictable system; at worst, divergent interests and rising uncertainties could force a retreat into protectionism, spheres of interest, and open conflict. Given the difficulties, there is no point in simply emphasizing the obvious fact that genuine cooperation would make everyone better off—someday. The response of the U.S. government has been to discount or minimize the threat and to emphasize dealing with issues as they arise. This is an understandable response to a universe of such uncertainty, but it may also guarantee a disastrous outcome. But before commenting on this, I should examine the two major developing-country proposals to overcome some or all of the difficulties that we have discussed: restructuring of the world industrial order to achieve the Lima goal and increased collective self-reliance.

The Lima Goal and Industrial Redeployment

Increasing the developing countries' share of world industrial production to 25 percent (and their share of world manufactured exports to 30 percent) by the year 2000 would require massive changes not only in the world's industrial geography, but also in the socioeconomic structures of both developed and developing countries. As one UNCTAD study put it, reaching the Lima target "will involve vast, sustained and concerted action by peoples and governments throughout the world."[35] But if the goal could be achieved, or even reasonably approximated, many of the problems of the developing countries would be considerably diminished, as, presumably, necessary domestic changes would have to be implemented, foreign exchange earnings would increase substantially, and questions of domestic and international equity would be less salient.

Some degree of restructuring is inevitable merely through the internal dynamics of the growth process and the rate of technological change. But much more is necessary to bring the Lima goal within sight. Extrapolation of historical growth rates from 1960 to 1973 suggests that allowing the process of change to follow its "natural," unaided course would not greatly alter the developing countries' share of world industrial production: The current share of roughly 9 percent would increase only to 11–14 percent.[36] Moreover, if economic decisions on industrial location are left entirely to individual firms, not enough industries would relocate and a very high percentage of those that did would choose the same small group of stable, conservative, relatively advanced developing countries — the NICs. Consequently, achievement of the goal would require direct government intervention into the decision-making process and extensive supervision and surveillance by various international institutions (especially UNIDO and UNCTAD).

A number of studies have attempted to analyze whether and how the Lima goal might be attained.[37] As they are normative studies that simply take the goal as a given and work backwards to estimate the changes that must occur to achieve it, they are of primarily academic interest — or perhaps one should say that they are merely indicative. At any rate, the necessary assumptions about future growth rates and other variables are eminently challengeable, and none of the studies are much concerned with policy questions (how the changes will be made), so that there is not much point in extended examination or comparison of the different studies. It suffices to point out some areas of agreement.

It is generally conceded that the goal can be achieved only if world conditions are extraordinarily favorable (much more favorable to the developing

countries than in the 1960–1973 period). Most of the studies see an improvement over historical patterns as possible (perhaps a share of 17–20
percent as distinct from 11–14 percent) but doubt the likelihood of reaching
25 percent; and all agree that the developing countries in the aggregate will
still have a substantial deficit in manufactured trade in 2000 (imports increase faster than exports so that, for example, the nonoil LDCs might
have a $150 billion deficit in 2000). All other sectors of developing-country
economies will also have to increase output significantly. In a rough sense,
most projections assume that the developing countries must achieve double
the growth rates of the developed countries in GDP, industrial production,
and manufactured exports to 2000, which implies, inter alia, that manufacturing output in the developing countries would have to be about twenty
times larger in 2000 than in 1972 and that growth rates would be about
twice the rate achieved between 1960 and 1973. In addition, there would
probably be a small loss in per capita income for the developed countries, a
change in the composition of the GDP for both groups of countries, and a
steady shift to intraindustry trade between developed and developing countries.

All of this will require a massive increase in domestic investment rates in
the developing countries. All agree that the amounts will be large and unprecedented, but there is wide disagreement on what the exact figures must
be, largely because of different assumptions. But a very recent study provides some indication of magnitudes: "Under plausible assumptions, it is
estimated that net annual industrial investment in the South would have to
reach a level of about $450 to $500 billion by the year 2000 if the Lima
target is to be attained, about one-third of which may have to be covered by
external flows."[38] According to this study, foreign direct investment would
have to be ten times present levels and total annual capital inflows (both
public and private) would have to amount to about $750 billion (in 1975
dollars). In 1977, total capital inflows reached about $60 billion.[39]

I need hardly emphasize the extraordinary implications of these studies.
They assume a degree of directed and controlled change not only in industrial structures and world trade but also in domestic societies and the
relations between groups of states that is quite unique. Nevertheless, it
would be too simple to dismiss the Lima goal as utopian or as another indication of the rhetorical excesses of the quest for a New International
Economic Order. In the first place, major changes in the industrial order
are necessary, inevitable, and potentially beneficial to all the countries
involved. In the second place, the Lima goal may be extremely ambitious,
but it is also a within-system goal; that is, because of the need for cooperation and aid from the industrial states, the achievement of the goal is also a
means of more effectively integrating the developing countries into the in-

ternational system. In this sense, the implications for the international system of not achieving the goal or at least not making a significant effort to move toward it must also be considered.

Finally, while the numbers associated with the achievement of the goal (growth rates, foreign investment, shares of production, etc.) appear vast, two further points should be noted. The actual gap between "normal" changes and the goal are not as overwhelming as might first appear (especially when one becomes accustomed to the magnitude of the aggregates for even normal industrial adjustment over two decades), and the 25 percent goal is only a target that needs to be increasingly approximated. Thus, reaching 18–20 percent instead of the expected 11–14 percent would still be useful and beneficial—even if denounced as a "failure." Unfortunately, however, there are other problems with the Lima goal.

One problem concerns energy. The various studies of how to achieve the Lima goal largely ignore the energy issue. But it seems quite clear that the energy transformation now under way will require new patterns of industrial development. For example, energy-intensive basic materials industries, which have been the foundation of the industrialization process in most of the developed countries, may not be economically or financially feasible for energy-poor developing countries in the next two decades.[40] What the new pattern of industrial development should be is uncertain, but if it requires dependence on imports of basic materials and exports of complex intraindustry goods, many developing countries will find it extremely difficult to cope with the demands of the trading system. At any rate, merely projecting future patterns on the basis of historical patterns, as most of these studies do, is unsatisfactory. This issue may or may not be correctable, either analytically or practically, but it would be imprudent to ignore it.

Another issue that needs more explicit consideration than it has received heretofore concerns the relationship between a strategy of rapid industrial development and other development strategies (or needs). This is obviously an issue of such complexity that it can be only noted here, but it is clear that the failure to consider whether an emphasis on industrialization is wise for many developing countries or what the priorities should be between (say) industrialization and basic needs could be very costly. Many questions could be raised in this context. For example, what benefit is it for the poorer developing countries to enter a trading system in which their main advantage is cheap labor, which is hardly in short supply? Will the export-oriented, trade-dependent, aid-dependent strategy implicit in the Lima goal, which will require both great charity and great farsightedness from the developed countries, make it more difficult to increase cooperation among the developing countries themselves? Some have argued that there is no necessary contradiction between the Lima goal and basic needs, either because basic needs is only a phase (or part) of development or because basic needs also requires industrialization.[41] But this ignores some crucial issues of timing and priority as well as the fact that basic needs implies a different kind of industrialization (especially an industrialization which is not export-oriented).

I do not mean to suggest that there are simple answers to these questions or that the Lima strategy is necessarily mistaken. We must recognize, however, that there are crucial choices involved, that they need to be weighed very carefully, and that the answers are likely to differ considerably for different countries. These judgments tend to be obscured by the tendency of advocates of one or another strategy to act as if they had discovered *the* key to development—everywhere and always. Suspicion about such claims seems particularly justified when or if they reflect self-serving interpretations of the universe by international institutions. For example, a major UNIDO study has recently argued, "It is important that industry should be recognized as the most dynamic sector of most developing economies, and that it is industrial development which is most likely to accelerate economic growth. Present aid policies [basic needs aid] merely serve to perpetuate the status quo, the old international economic order."[42] But industrialization may not be such a panacea (especially when a large number of poor countries seek to develop the same industries and to export the same products in an environment of slow growth), economic growth is not the only aim, and aid for basic needs may ultimately create better growth and development prospects than aid for industry.

The final problem, or perhaps set of problems, concerns implementation: how the Lima goal is to be achieved. According to UNIDO, industries should be redeployed from developed to developing countries, the process should be buttressed by the creation of a large number of new institutions and funds to finance, guarantee, and supervise specific decisions on relocation, and disputes should be settled according to principles that include "developmental responsiveness."[43] Redeployment has been defined as "a form of international industrial cooperation for resource transfers" and would involve "the transfer of capital, technology, know-how, plants and other resources by an operating industrial enterprise in a developed country to a developing country in order to establish a manufacturing capacity in that country."[44] But the hidden presumptions in this design of a "new world industrial order"—about what we know, or what we can do, and perhaps what we should do—are quite extraordinary.

The developing countries, unhappy with a redeployment process controlled by the decisions of individual firms, want developed-country governments to intervene to compel firms within their jurisdictions to move to "assigned" locations; they want guaranteed access to developed-country markets for the exports of these firms; and they want *anticipatory* adjustment policies by the developed countries to defuse protectionist reactions by firms and workers threatened by these exports.[45] The political difficulties of such a program are obvious, but an effort to overcome them might be justified *if* the practical and technical obstacles were less severe. Successful redeployment requires prior knowledge of future shifts in comparative advantage. Most experts believe this is impossible (except at a very high level of generality) because of the complexities of forecasting technological developments, monetary changes, shifts in trading patterns, changes in social and economic goals, and so on. Moreover, because of a variety of factors — including the increased rapidity of communications and transport, the spread of learning, and the growth of multinational corporations — the pace of shifts in comparative advantage may be accelerating. This will obviously strain the adaptive capacities of states (and entrepreneurs), but it also raises questions about who would pay for incorrect decisions on redeployment. In any case, given the time lag between a decision to redeploy and actual production by the redeployed firm, the likelihood that the original decision will have been "overtaken by events" is not small.

Indeed, centrally planned redeployment could work only if, as a recent UNIDO study suggests, North and South closely coordinated macroeconomic policies, if guaranteed access for Southern products was increased, if South-South trade increased sharply, and if international financing and control was effectively institutionalized (including introducing "a new international dimension to the risk assumption process").[46] It is taken for granted that the developing countries will make the necessary domestic changes (in agriculture, enlarging internal markets, etc.) to take advantage of the new external opportunities. In short, in an effort to eliminate future uncertainties and to guarantee better outcomes for the developing countries, the Lima goal is to be attained by the creation of a centralized global planning structure that would determine, finance, insure, and supervise industrial decision making.

It would have to be decided not only which industries to relocate, but also where they should be relocated. Most of the obvious candidates for movement are labor-intensive industries with mature and standardized technologies. This is clearly oversimplified in many cases — labor-intensiveness is not the only factor determining location — but it can be used here as a first, rough approximation of potential redeployments. Such industries could go to many developing countries, but careful and complex choices would be necessary to avoid the dangers of overproduction. How, then, would the choice be made? There is no answer in any of the studies of redeployment. Presumably the industries would be parceled out according to some formula that guaranteed each country at least one industry before another country could get a second (as with some "harmonization" agreements in regional arrangements). The notion that such a process which will be very politicized, will create an industrial order that is more efficient and more equitable than — as distinct from merely being different from — the old order is surely problematic, if not naive. As one small illustration of the difficulties that are likely to be encountered in reaching agreement, when the regional economic commissions attempted to determine how the 25 percent target should be divided, the outcome was a division of shares that added up to 27.3 percent of world manufacturing output.[47]

Western officials and economists have reacted predictably to these demands. An official of the European Economic Community noted that the "practical problems of identifying firms or industries for elimination are insoluble, and the political difficulties would be insuperable." He also warned of the dangers of "freezing patterns of production" (leaving the LDCs with low-productivity industries) and described anticipatory (as distinct from ex post facto) adjustment as a "delusion."[48] The OECD has argued that the effort "to spot the winners" is doomed to failure and that "governments should mainly concentrate on trying to create the general conditions conducive to industrial adjustment, leaving it to market forces to determine its direction of change."[49] And a recent World Bank study has argued that identifying vulnerable industries before market changes have actually occurred is not possible, but that it is also unnecessary as long as one anticipates that "import surges will occur, and, therefore, policies must exist that tell the government and the industry affected what is to happen."[50]

The outcome of this exchange of manifestos is familiar to an observer of the North-South Dialogue. The South demands massive changes to create a new order with a new pattern of benefits; the North responds that the demands are technically flawed, politically impracticable, and probably inequitable even within the South; the ensuing negotiations, with one side demanding increased resource transfers and immediate acceptance of new principles and the other offering incremental adjustment and case-by-case reform, yield little beyond verbal formulas to keep the game going. But insofar as reform can be justifiably perceived as in the interest of both sides, and insofar as the negotiating system inhibits the concluding of meaningful agreements, we must ask whether some means can be found to move toward common ground — a negotiating space between case-by-case adjustments of the status quo and demands for the kind of change that are beyond the current state of the art in politics and economics.[51]

In the present context, substantial changes in what the United States and the other developed countries are able and willing to do in the trading system do not appear probable. The economic environment is simply too dismal and perceptions of the future too pessimistic. Still, perhaps some useful small steps could be taken that at least keep open the possibility of movement. What I have in mind here is something more than continued support for the conventional package of trade measures (adjustment assistance, reduction of tariff and nontariff barriers, etc.). The key issue is how to adjust or prepare to adjust to rapid shifts in comparative advantage at least cost, both political and economic. UNIDO's implicit assumption that such changes can be forecast with enough assurance to justify imposed redeployment may be incorrect. Nonetheless, certain general patterns of change remain probable (despite the vast uncertainties, there are still structural inheritances and technological rigidities that impose some order on developments) and continued research may permit something more than educated guesses about industries that may be losing comparative advantage.[52] The Dutch and the Norwegians have created national commissions to examine this issue, and the United States (as well as other countries) might consider doing the same. This might be conceived as an early warning measure to encourage actions to improve competitiveness or to move to different activities. The OECD has advocated "positive" adjustment in response to developing-country demands for anticipatory adjustment, and this may be a useful first step insofar as it implies active efforts to facilitate and initiate adjustment, rather than merely responding to it in an ad hoc or defensive fashion. An example is the Japanese effort to support "structurally depressed" industries by creating a fund to finance scrapping of excess capacity or efforts to finance movement into more advanced activities.

But national actions by themselves, although useful and important, are insufficient. International action is also imperative, not only to avoid some unpleasant conflicts but also to provide the developing countries some assurance that their interests and needs are not being ignored. Given existing political and economic difficulties and given the technical difficulties of redeployment, perhaps the most that can be expected in the near future is increased consultation, strong support for research and for expert groups to increase knowledge and awareness, and diminished rhetoric about the market as the only "solution" to these problems (as it is not a solution for most of the developing countries). Increases in the exchange of information, which have been advocated by a number of officials, might also be useful, especially if they alerted policymakers in the developing countries to new opportunities—or pointed out opportunities that had already been seized by others and were no longer available. These are limited and unsatisfactory responses, but if some effort is not made to move beyond stalemate, we may drift into the trade wars that seem a likely outcome of present patterns of development.

The other side of this is the response of the developing countries. Why have they made a set of demands that are obviously impracticable and unrealistic? One answer is that their needs are massive and only massive changes will suffice. But this vastly overestimates what can be achieved by changes in the international order. Another answer is that such demands are built into the negotiating system. Programs have to be devised that promise large transfers of resources to all the developing countries and that give control over the process to the institutions that they dominate. In addition, the influence of the advanced developing countries in devising international programs from which they at least will benefit should not be underestimated.

There is little sign that this process is changing — or that any process that must satisfy so many countries with so many needs can function effectively. I should add that although there is much discussion at the international level of the need for new development strategies, at the national level most developing countries are still pursuing strategies of rapid growth and rapid industrialization. Such strategies may no longer be appropriate (because of rising concerns for equity or because of energy implications or balance of payments implications), but the failure to consider alternatives more seriously means that the negotiating process may reinforce the quest for the impossible or the premature. Perhaps these comments suggest that we should take a less jaundiced look at some efforts to provide the basis for a more stable system by nonmarket means, a point to which I shall return.

The pessimistic conclusion, for the moment, must be that the North-South trading system is not about to be fundamentally transformed to benefit primarily the developing countries and that the benefits earned in it are likely to continue to go to the same small group of developing countries. We need to ask whether South-South trade might be a viable alternative for some or all of the developing countries.

South-South Trade:
Hopes, Realities, and Possibilities

Efforts to increase trade — as well as other forms of cooperation — among the developing countries have been much discussed in recent years. In part, this reflects the judgment that

> it is not realistic to expect that cooperation between developed and developing countries, i.e., co-operation between parties unequal in economic opportunities and power, can result in equitable and just relationships. International co-operation for development . . . must therefore be premised on the collective self-reliance of the developing countries.[53]

This "horizontal cooperation" presumably will be facilitated by the existence of different levels of development within the Third World. "Mutual complementarities" thus exist and can provide the basis for increased and more equitable trading relationships.[54] This is surely true, but there are strong practical impediments to cooperation, and there are no guarantees that the different levels of development within the Third World will not reproduce the injustices and inequities (real and imagined) of North-South trade.

The desire to reduce dependence on trade with the developed countries also reflects other considerations. Even if North-South trade is not inherently unjust, the fact remains that growth prospects in the South have always been closely connected to (and sometimes virtually a residual of) growth rates in the North. Thus South-South cooperation is especially attractive because it has the potential to "accelerate the growth prospects of developing countries, independent of developments in the developed countries."[55] As we shall shortly see, there is some evidence that this is not an entirely illusory goal, although it must be treated with *great* caution. The ability of some developing countries to increase growth rates in spite of dismal economic performance in the North since 1973 has had much to do with their ability to borrow in Eurocurrency markets, which meant that they could delay adjustment to, but not avoid, oil price increases. It should also be noted that enthusiasm for South-South cooperation reflects the fear that "delinking" will simply be imposed, whether the South wants to reduce dependence or not, by slower growth and increased protectionism in the North.

The share of South-South trade in total world trade actually decreased from 1955 to 1970, from 6.2 percent to 3.5 percent. But this trend was sharply reversed in the 1970s, and South-South trade increased at 36 percent per annum (24 percent excluding oil) from 1970 to 1978. Growth was much higher than for trade flows among the developed countries and between North and South, thus increasing the South-South share of world trade to about 6 percent. Manufactured exports were the most dynamic element in this revived South-South trade.[56]

Trade with the OECD countries is, of course, still dominant, but in recent years about 20 percent of LDC nonoil primary products exports and about 30 percent of manufactured exports have gone to other LDCs. Historically, the only major exception to the dominance of North-South trading patterns has been in fuel: 90 percent of fuel imports in the South have come from other developing countries and fuel alone accounts for close to 60 percent of South-South trade.[57] Aggregate summaries of South-South trade are useful, for they give some sense of emerging trends, but they also conceal great diversity within and between regions. I shall examine a few of these differences, if briefly, because they provide some indication of existing trends as well as of potential areas of conflict.

Most South-South trade is intraregional, but there has been some increase in interregional ties during the 1970s.[58] This is somewhat deceptive, however, because trade in fuels tends to skew the figures. Thus the intraregional share of South-South trade declined from 76 percent in 1955 to 50 percent in 1976, but if fuel is excluded, the intraregional share declined only to 68 percent. In any case, interregional trade has been dominated by OPEC, and every region increased its exports to West Asia from 1970 to 1976 (all were net exporters to West Asia, but were still in deficit because of the disproportionate rise in oil prices). The remainder of interregional trade was dominated by the same group of NICs that successfully penetrated OECD markets, but the product mix was different in the two cases, as will be shown later in this chapter.

Intraregional trade as a proportion of total South-South trade was highest in Latin America (79 percent) and Asia (70 percent) but quite low in Africa (33 percent) in 1978. Obviously the figures are reversed for interregional trade, and Africa's 67 percent was the highest (in value terms, however, Asia led the way). Africa's large share of interregional trade reflects the composition of its exports: Most of its commodity exports went to more advanced developing countries and not to African neighbors. Nonetheless, Africa was still in deficit in its interregional trade (even excluding fuel), because it had and has heavy food import bills from Latin America and a large deficit in manufactured trade with Southeast Asia. Conversely, South and Southeast Asia have a relatively large surplus from manufactured exports to Africa and West Asia, and Latin America has a smaller surplus from food exports to Africa and West Asia.[59]

The composition of South-South trade may be as important as the fact that it is increasing. Manufactures are likely to be the key in terms of future increases in South-South trade.[60] They have increased from 27 percent of South-South trade in 1970 to 46 percent in 1976, but much of this trade remains intraregional and dominated by a few suppliers. Southeast Asia has led the way, both in total amounts of South-South manufactured trade and in interregional trade. Latin America has also increased its share (but still largely within the region), and Africa has lagged behind. But a much higher percentage of South-South manufactured trade has occurred in relatively advanced capital goods (nonelectric machinery, transport equipment, chemicals, automobiles, etc.) that are not competitive in developed-country markets. Conversely, there has been very little South-South trade in the kind of consumer goods sent to the developed countries; for example, less than 10 percent of clothing and footwear exports went to other LDCs.

This pattern of trade suggests that there is a large and growing market for South-South trade in manufactures. Moreover, as this trade is in relatively sophisticated goods, it might facilitate the creation of more advanced capital goods production and the development of some indigenous technological capacity. But there are also some negative factors to be taken into account. In the first place, much of the trade in advanced goods is controlled by multinational corporations (MNCs): While developing-country exports of manufactures have increased, the proportion controlled by MNCs has increased even faster.[61] This does not decrease dependence, it means equitable sharing of potential gains between countries is unlikely, and it suggests continuing conflict over MNC behavior. In the second place, South-South trade in this pattern may not make much contribution to employment. Because intra-LDC exports are relatively more capital intensive and less labor intensive, they actually make less contribution to reducing the mass of unemployed and unskilled labor than do the more labor-intensive exports to the developed countries.[62] In the third place, even if South-South trade continues to increase, it cannot be much more than an addendum to North-South trade for at least the next decade. Foreign exchange needs are too large, and many necessary goods and services can only be gotten from the developed countries.

Finally, there is the fact that dominance by a small group of southern countries, most of whom are unlikely to be able or willing to compensate their trading partners with aid or other concessions, will probably become as unappealing—perhaps more so—than dominance by a few developed-country partners. If the latter begin to compete seriously with the NICs for trade in these relatively advanced goods, continued NIC success is not assured (nor is NIC failure).[63] The effort to "graduate" the NICs into a new status, after all, reflects concern with NIC exports (and tactics—subsidies, etc.) to both developed- and developing-country markets. In any event, NIC-LDC trade currently repeats the pattern of dependence in North-South trade—except that the LDCs cannot sell their labor-intensive goods to the NICs for foreign exchange. Much of South-South trade, consequently, is rich-poor trade: Only 20 percent takes place among countries at similar levels of development (and most of that is with OPEC).[64]

These arguments clearly imply that South-South trade may be potentially significant in the long run, but prospects are much more limited for the next decade. Moreover, only a small number of countries are likely to benefit more than marginally and, unless they are able to come to an agreement on the distribution of benefits with their customers, the likelihood of a backlash is reasonably high. It should come as no surprise that the strongest advocates of South-South cooperation are the NICs and near-NICs (like Brazil, India, and the Philippines) that need Southern markets for their advanced goods (many from uncompetitive import-substitution industries); there is little sign that they perceive the need to share their own markets with the other developing countries. The next decade in South-South trading relations must concentrate on laying the foundation for future gains, but it is not clear that the necessary long-run perspective will or can be adopted or the sacrifices made. And, as usual, the rhetoric attendant on discussions of South-South cooperation in the UN system promises so much more than can be delivered that the resulting disappointments may make the construction of a foundation (in infrastructure, currency arrangements, credit schemes, etc.) even more difficult. Still, there are experienced voices suggesting the need to move slowly and carefully and to build up from local cooperation rather than down from global visions, so complete pessimism is unwarranted.[65]

The United States has not been a strong supporter of these efforts because of doubts about the wisdom of constructing another preferential system and because of a refusal to support Third World meetings within the UN system from which developed countries have been excluded. In any case, the Third World has found it difficult to articulate exactly what the developed countries should do in support of collective self-reliance, beyond what they are already doing in other contexts (aid, technical assistance, interest-rate concessions, etc.). There has been some discussion of changing U.S. policy because, in the long run, increased South-South trade will enlarge LDC markets sufficiently so that all will benefit and because such trade will decrease pressures on OECD markets. Both of these judgments may be correct, at least over time, but it is also true that enlarged markets will not help the developed countries if they are excluded from them and that the exports the developing countries currently send to the developed countries (labor-intensive consumer goods) are not sold in great volume to other developing countries.

There are, however, other factors that might make a change in policy sensible. In the last analysis, South-South cooperation cannot be built solely on feelings of solidarity. The discussion must concentrate on practicalities—on specific actions that governments must take in order to cooperate with other governments. This is likely to be an improvement over the North-South Dialogue's tendency to degenerate into ideological posturing. In addition, such discussions are bound to give more influence (gradually) not only to more moderate governments but also to ministers of home governments concerned more with practical results than rhetorical confrontation. Certainly, U.S. support for collective self-reliance may encourage the creation of a preferential bloc, but it is unlikely that it can be more than partially closed and, in any case, the United States may be forced to reconsider its stance toward such arrangements. Finally, if conditions in the international system deteriorate radically, the small movement toward cooperation might provide the developing countries, especially the poorest ones, a degree of support and protection against a very hostile environment.

In short, the argument to support South-South cooperation because of specific gains to the United States seems uncertain and ambiguous to me; the argument to support it because of what Arnold Wolfers called "milieu goals"—goals aimed at affecting the systemic environment—seems more convincing. Anything that the developing countries can do for and among themselves is likely to contribute to the construction of an international system that is relatively less dominated by conflict and confrontation, and it is difficult to make a strong case that this cooperation will be greatly harmful to specific developed-country interests. But, as I have indicated, none of this is likely to make much difference in this decade, except perhaps if it slowly affects the systemic climate.

East-South Trade

A word about whether trade with the socialist countries or China could alter these conclusions might be useful. In brief, the answer is no. Indeed, East-South relations may become increasingly competitive, rather than increasingly cooperative.

Less than 5 percent of total LDC trade has been with the socialist countries. East-South trade has never been very important to either group, despite much rhetoric in institutions like UNCTAD (where the socialists have sought to increase East-West, not East-South trade). In a real sense East-South trade is essentially a residual of East-West and North-South trade: When there are no markets in the West, East and South become (minor) markets for each other.[66] There are two exceptions to this: First, socialist developing countries have benefited very substantially from trading and other ties with the more advanced socialist countries. Second, the East in a number of cases has been a major arms supplier to some developing countries (not all within the bloc).[67]

East and West have generally similar patterns of trade with the South. Both exchange manufactured goods for raw materials, although the West is taking an increasing amount of manufactures also. East-West trade is largely similar, which means that with the West, the East is like the South, but with the South, the East is like the North.[68] The East has increased its manufactured exports to the West, but more slowly than the developing countries and in essentially the same products.[69] This competition is the key reason why the East has consistently complained about trading concessions by the West to the developing countries.[70] Prospects for increased East-West trade may be diminishing, not only because of recent events in

Afghanistan, but also because of the heavy debt burden of most of the Eastern countries (which will cut future access to credit). The combination of difficult domestic economic problems and the need to expend hard currency on imports of food and advanced technology goods (and perhaps oil) suggests an inward turn within the Eastern bloc (to sharply limit imports to necessary items) and very limited opportunities to increase East-South trade. In effect, East and South will compete for food, credits, and market access, and neither will have surplus foreign exchange to expend on what the other has to offer. Finally, without discussing details, it should be noted that China's trade with the developing countries is much like the East's — manufactures for raw materials — and tends only to reinforce the South's dependence on traditional exports.[71]

Conclusions: Are Trade Wars Inevitable?

Potentially severe and disruptive conflicts could appear throughout the trading system within the next decade. The complexities and uncertainties are enormous, but it is difficult to be optimistic that the international environment will be sufficiently benign or national leadership sufficiently farsighted to avoid increased trading tensions between North and South, between East and South, and within both North and South (and perhaps East). But competition is an intrinsic and a beneficial part of any trading system, and one might well argue that the notion that competition will degenerate into trade wars is far too pessimistic.

The general pattern of the trading system implicit in current trends is not difficult to discern. Left to work itself out in response to "natural" shifts in comparative advantage, the international division of labor around 2000 *ought* to look something like this: Labor-intensive and raw materials–intensive industries will be located in the non-NIC developing countries; capital-intensive products in the late stage of the product cycle will be dominated by the NICs; capital-intensive products in the early stages of the product cycle will be in various developed countries; and human capital–intensive industries (sophisticated services, R&D facilities, highly skilled labor) will be in the most advanced developed countries. The outcome would be increasing intraindustry specialization on a world scale and increasing regional specialization.[72]

Perhaps we shall be able to advance, stage by stage, to this very elegant division of labor. But those who believe that we can arrive at this destination simply by letting economic logic determine individual decisions may be relying on a number of untenable judgments or assumptions. The most significant underlying assumption is that growth rates will at least approximate those achieved during the 1960s. But if world trade slows, conflict will be exacerbated. This is likely to be especially true if some of the countries that are planning particularly large increases in exports (almost all projections forecast a much higher growth rate for Japanese-LDC and NIC-LDC trade than for world trade) attempt to carry out their programs. The backlash by countries losing traditional shares of world trade (or, for the LDCs, not increasing their share) might be severe. In addition, of course, security and employment concerns in the developed countries might slow adjustment in a number of mature industries, and potential capital shortages (because of energy needs and the need to restructure some domestic industries) may cut sharply into resource transfers to the developing countries.[73]

The assumption that states and industries will be able to make necessary adjustments in response to a rapidly shifting comparative advantage may also reflect a simplistic or inappropriate analogy with the adjustment process in earlier trading systems. The current and emerging system is far more complex, not only in the need to deal with many industries that many countries are capable of developing (because of converging factor costs), but also simply because there are so many more countries at so many different levels of development. And it should not be assumed that the non-NIC LDCs are indifferent to developments in the trading system: For example, by 1975 more than forty non-NIC LDCs each had at least $100 million worth of manufactured exports.[74] The key point is that all LDCs (and some of the NICs) will find it difficult to react quickly and effectively to external changes—or perhaps even to know what their reaction should be. This is especially true because shifts in comparative advantage appear to be occurring with increasing rapidity. The tendency to copy each other will also create problems, soluble only by prior agreements on who should do what. But discussion of the basis of such agreements has barely begun, and the record of earlier attempts at "harmonization" in regional schemes does not provide much ground for optimism. In short, these states may constitute a very rigid component within a system requiring great flexibility.

It hardly seems realistic to assume that such states—desperately short of resources, confronting rising domestic demand pressures, without sufficient technical skills, and compelled to deal with a difficult external environment—will choose the correct industries to develop or be willing to give up those that no longer seem viable. Or, put differently, there may not be many more countries with the skills (and the opportunities, if markets contract) of South Korea and Taiwan. Perhaps one should also note that slower growth rates in the developed countries will make developing-country markets increasingly attractive (as in 1974-1975)—if, of course, the developing countries have the financial means to purchase more than bare necessities (if that, for some). But the struggle for these markets will exacerbate already existing conflicts and asymmetries between the developed countries over North-South trade and perhaps engender a tendency toward closed "preserves" and special "deals." The resulting configuration of these forces would hardly be very "rational."

Another factor makes the achievement of a "rational" international division of labor improbable. The likelihood of slower growth means fewer opportunities, especially for new entrants into the system. This suggests that questions of fairness may become increasingly prominent, but as there is no agreement on what fairness means, only the international political process will be able to provide acceptable answers: What is fair is what emerges from a mutually agreed bargaining process. The emphasis on the political process will be reinforced by the lack of economic answers to many of the questions about which developing countries should specialize in what activities, but an answer must be given if economic benefits are to be achieved. In effect, decisions about the elements of the division of labor will not be either completely economic or completely political, but rather a complex mix of the two, in which the political, in a great many cases, will have the final say. But it would certainly be easier if these decisions could follow a primarily economic rationale, as the absence of an agreement on values and on the rules of the game means that the international political process does not always (or even generally) produce outcomes that are equitable, wise, or timely.

This means that we are likely to be in a very second-best world during the 1980s. The developing countries are unlikely to be able to increase North-South trade sufficiently to greatly diminish their problems; worse yet, without difficult agreements within the Third World, South-South conflicts might reduce the scope of whatever gains are possible. Acting as if we can escape from this world by a leap of faith into a "planetary bargain" may only make matters worse; we know too little about future consequences of present choices, and the quest for a utopia distracts from the pressing business of the day. Moreover, no state has the power to impose either imperial or global solutions. At the same time, simply drifting along, responding to events, is not ambitious enough and carries dangers of its own.

I cannot here lay out the details of what this implies, but it may be useful to ask whether the primacy of a second-best system (perhaps for decades) suggests the need to reconsider "organized free trade" and its many variations. We can recognize without dissent the textbook virtues of the liberal order (and the textbook vices of its opposite: challenges from new producers, freezing the market, instability, etc.), but in a second-best world we have only a choice between more or less closed systems. Furthermore, as long as the system contains states at many different levels of development, and as long as special concessions are made to those at the lower levels—whether out of fairness, a desire to encourage stable behavior, or whatever—the system will always be at least partially closed. The United States needs, however, to do more than simply recognize and take account of this fact; it also needs to respond to it in ways that do the most to keep open future possibilities of moving toward a liberal order.

The rules appropriate for a second-best world must concentrate initially on creating and maintaining stable expectations by emphasizing accountability, dependability, and precise and specific obligations.[75] Rather than seeking primarily to eliminate measures that restrain or limit openness, such rules must seek to control and limit these measures, perhaps by legitimizing external scrutiny of national actions, by constraining their scope and duration, and by encouraging in some cases the quest for agreement on fair shares (as between the developing countries themselves). The latter point is especially important, because unless the developing countries can agree among themselves on the distribution of gains, systemic rules that restrain unregulated behavior will still benefit only a few.

In any case, while the rule-making effort needs to recognize the *provisional* legitimacy of second-best efforts to control and direct some aspects of the trading system, care must be taken to assure that the provisional does not become permanent. Distortions and obstacles to freer trade must be limited and predictable (which is to say, accountable within wider forums and not wholly nationally determined), and special exemptions for the developing countries must be defined and extended. Different sets of rules for differently situated states (including graduation for the NICs) are probably more realistic and perhaps more meaningful than a single set of very general global rules. This at least suggests that narrower agreements with particular groups of countries may be more successful than global bargaining at UNCTAD or UNIDO—provided that the narrower agreements accept the legitimacy of accountability to the wider forums (i.e., negotiations at one level and "collective legitimization" at another). Still, even if such an approach is possible, it would take many years to negotiate. This implies that for the period that concerns us the kind of limited holding actions suggested here probably means that major gains from the trading system are not probable for either North or South, although individual countries may do reasonably well (or less badly than their peers). The real struggle for the majority may be how to avoid major losses, especially in the South.

Postscript: The Debt Problem

Deficits exist only if they are financed. If financing is not available, external needs—the fulfillment of which creates the deficit—are simply not met. The massive deficits run up by the NOLDCs since 1973 have been financed, if largely by something of a shotgun wedding, with commercial banks, thus achieving, against all odds, perhaps the only successful reaction to the OPEC "shock." But it was very much a short-run success. The recent oil price increases, which will again generate massive deficits ($60 billion projected for the NOLDCs in 1980), raise very serious questions about whether and how the new round of recycling can be accomplished. And as I have indicated in the last three chapters, apart from the immediate financing problem, there is a need for a massive infusion of foreign capital to help finance the long-term investments that will diminish dependence on food, energy, and capital goods imports. It is not my purpose here to deal with these issues in detail, but I would like to add a comment about the relationship between the debt and financing issues and the material that has appeared in the preceding chapters.

The recycling of the OPEC surplus from 1974 to 1979 was more successful than initially anticipated. Foreign aid increased (to about $20 billion in 1978), OPEC aid provided a new source of funds (about $6 billion at its zenith in 1977), and special oil funds in various international institutions were helpful, but the bulk of the funds came from the commercial banking system. The banks served as intermediaries, selling low-risk assets to risk-averse OPEC countries and lending at high interest rates to needy NOLDCs. By 1979 the NOLDCs alone owed almost $200 billion to multinational banks (70 percent to be repaid or refinanced by 1982) and another $125 billion to governments and international institutions. As is well-known, the prolonged recession in the OECD area sharply lowered loan demand and left the banks with a great deal of excess liquidity; the NOLDCs, in desperate need of funds and with export growth rates cut by the recession, were thus both needy and necessary recipients of a massive surge in bank lending. But only a relatively small number of multinational banks were heavily involved in the process and only a relatively small number of countries were major recipients of funds (twenty countries had 80 percent of the debt and about half went to just five countries).[76]

The mere size of the deficit has not appeared too worrisome especially as debt-service ratios have remained relatively stable (in most cases export growth rates have kept up with or exceeded increases in debt). Indeed, one analyst has argued that the policy objective should be "to keep expanding the edifice of credit, but to do so steadily and surely. It is not a balloon that is more apt to pop the more it is blown up. On the contrary, the bigger the credit structure, the stronger it is likely to be."[77] This is, however, somewhat misleading; whether the "edifice of credit"—irrespective of its size—is sound depends on its structure and on the uses to which loaned funds have been put.

There are obviously three factors that determine the repayment prospects of a loan. The first of these, which has received the greatest share of attention, concerns the terms of the initial loan. The high interest rates and the short maturities of private bank loans create severe problems: For example, 95 percent of the Eurocurrency debt of the NOLDCs is due by 1983, and by 1985, $2 out of every $3 borrowed will be used simply to repay old debts.[78] In addition, because both interest rates and maturities shift in response to market forces, the NOLDCs may be pushed out of the market if the developed countries recover and, if the developed countries remain in recession, credit will contract because the export prospects of the NOLDCs will look grim. Moreover, some banks are already near their loan limits with a number of developing countries and may find it increasingly difficult to discover good lending risks or to liberalize the terms of lending. Still, there is a kind of implicit assumption that these problems will be resolved, if only because the banks presumably have no choice but to keep on lending (or face default) and the LDCs have no choice but to keep on borrowing (or do without critical imports). The real force behind these assumptions, however, may be somewhat different: If the banks do not lend, they cannot accept massive infusions of OPEC funds; OPEC consequently might receive additional encouragement to leave its oil in the ground.

The precarious nature of a situation in which potentially overextended banks (borrowing short and lending long) lend to potentially unstable countries in a potentially unfavorable environment hardly needs emphasis. One useful set of suggestions concerns various means of involving the IMF or the World Bank in cofinancing or guaranteeing of credits with the private banking system. New international facilities to refinance existing loans or to provide new sources of funding have also been suggested.[79] But even if some of these suggestions are implemented (which seems most likely for the cofinancing proposals), they are not likely to be of much use if the recession continues and if the borrowers do not use the funds productively. This brings us to the other two factors that determine repayment prospects.

If loans are used only to repay old loans, to finance goverment spending on unproductive activities (such as buying foreign arms), or to pay for immediate consumption (as with oil), the long-term prospects for repayment are obviously grim. There is thus a difference between borrowing for development to finance infrastructure (ports, railroads, etc.) or capital goods and borrowing merely to stay afloat. And although the evidence is not conclusive, it does appear that much of the recent borrowing—perhaps of necessity—has been used to survive the present crisis, not to build a hedge against future crises. Bankers reputedly never really desire to be repaid (and thus compelled to find new targets for lending) and would much prefer to keep refinancing old loans, but sooner or later this happy charade must come to an end if imports continue to grow faster than exports and if there is no imminent prospect of reversing the prevailing patterns. Default is clearly bad for both sides, but if the debtor sees a diminishing possibility of new funds or the flow out is greater than the flow in and if the lender sees a decreasing chance of even interest repayment and is straining against any standard of prudence, how long can the game go on? The answer seems to depend on the export prospects of the debtor, and this brings us to our final factor.

Optimism about the debt problem has rested, either explicitly or implicitly, on a number of assumptions about the external environment during the period of repayment. The most important of these is that the recession will end and the export prospects of the NOLDCs (especially of course the heavy debtors) will once again improve markedly. But there is very little near-term indication that growth will begin to accelerate rapidly. Moreover, the kind of labor-intensive exports that the developing countries rely upon are generally the first casualty (and the last recovery) of a recession and the most prone to oversupply. Three other assumptions have been nearly as crucial — and nearly as doubtful. The first is that new mechanisms for resource transfers will be established, particularly to help the poor LDCs that have not received much private lending. The second is that the banks will continue to lend and will not increase the severity of the conditions under which they do so. Nevertheless, terms have already hardened and, at best, the banks will be able to do relatively less to relieve the crisis than they did from 1974 to 1979. Finally, there has been the assumption that the price of oil would remain relatively stable — that OPEC would not take advantage of its pricing power. Recent price increases have already undermined this assumption and may make the debt situation unmanageable. Future increases will certainly do so.

One conclusion must be that the NOLDCs will not be able to "export their way out of debt."[80] The implications are ominous, for more than a debt crisis is at stake. The development prospects of the NOLDCs will deteriorate, industrialization will be sharply impeded if oil imports must be quickly cut, and the consequences if food imports are unavailable or too costly are clear. At the same time, if (or as) the developing countries cut back on their imports, the prospects for developed-country exports obviously decline, thus generating or helping to generate a global recession. Moreover, if OPEC is confronted with circumstances in which it exchanges oil for increasingly dubious financial paper, extreme conservation strategies will surely become more likely, thus exacerbating the very crisis that threatens OPEC gains. Perhaps this is a forecast that is, as Keynes once noted, "too bad to be true," but it is sufficiently credible to compel some consideration—or reconsideration—of the choices before the United States.

An examination of the long-term financial situation leads to a similar conclusion. Even very moderate estimates indicate that the need for external capital will grow by 12 to 16 percent per annum through this decade. Other estimates, aimed at one or another kind of fundamental restructuring of the economies of the developing countries, are much more extreme. There is no point in summing all the demands—in agriculture, energy, industrial redeployment, debt relief, infrastructure, program aid, trade, etc.—because they reflect very different assumptions about priorities, needs, and goals and because each set of demands seems to be made in ignorance of other, competing demands. I should note however, that if all these demands were met, resource transfers would substantially exceed 1 percent of the GNPs of the developed countries—depending on assumptions, perhaps reaching 2–3 percent (against current levels of less than half of one percent). This would mean an entirely different kind of international system, one run according to welfare principles and animated by a fairly wide sense of community. This is obviously not politically feasible, but it also raises serious questions about external intervention and control—unless one assumes that the aid, however collected, will be passed on automatically to all developing countries (via some formula of disbursement), irrespective of performance either before or after receiving aid. Still, there is another side to this argument, for we must also ask what will result if resource transfers are not sharply increased.[81]

One result will be to perpetuate and increase the gap between the few that can cope and the many that probably will not be able to do so. Merely maintaining the existing level of resource transfers will help primarily the countries most able to help themselves and will do little to deal with the underlying structural problems that will make the North-South arena even more hostile in the future. The linkage between issues creates additional difficulties, as none of the problems—in food, energy, trade, and debt—can be effectively isolated from the others. Thus the debt issue is also obviously a trade issue; only increased trading opportunities provide some means of repaying loans (perhaps this is why the banks have been such strong supporters of free trade). But this creates problems for the developed countries, because accepting more imports is difficult in current circumstances. Not permitting greater access, however, forces the developing countries to deflate and to cut imports from the developed countries. The dilemmas are acute, for there are neither clear nor simple choices for either group of countries.

Perhaps the greatest danger in these circumstances is that concentration on solving crucial short-term problems will do nothing to alleviate long-term problems. In policy terms, the United States needs to think constantly about devising short-run responses that contribute directly to diminishing long-run problems or at least do not make long-run solutions more difficult. Thus merely providing the NOLDCs with the means to finance their deficits is necessary but not sufficient. In this context efforts to induce OPEC to lend directly to the NOLDCs seem eminently sensible. This would relieve some of the burden on the private banking system, and OPEC might be somewhat more inclined to follow moderate and predictable pricing strategies when its own money would be endangered if its pricing strategies injured the NOLDCs.[82] The latter point provides some indirect linkage with the quest for more effective long-term measures.

Increasing the role of the IMF in financing oil deficits, although eminently sensible (even imperative), must also be evaluated in terms of the nexus between short-run and long-run responses. The recent 50 percent increase in the fund's quotas means that the NOLDCs would have potential access to about $75 billion, but they do not yet appear enthusiastic about using these funds. As has been noted frequently, the IMF has not been a net lender in recent years and the NOLDCs have used only minimal amounts of their quotas, but this is already beginning to change as lending to some NOLDCs has increased during the first half of 1980. The reluctance to borrow remains despite the IMF's adoption in 1979 of new rules on conditionality, including the proposition that the fund "will pay due regard to the domestic social and political objectives" of borrowers.

If a crisis comes (or deepens), and if commercial banks are unable or unwilling to increase lending, there will be no choice but to go to the IMF. Nevertheless, if current revisions of conditionality are considered insufficient, and if the developing countries insist on further relaxation of the rules, severe difficulties may arise. The key point is that continued loosening of conditions to serve short-term needs may not be in the long-run interests of the developing countries themselves, if it permits excessive expenditure on immediate consumption and facilitates avoidance of long-term adjustment considerations. The issue is difficult and complex, as the developing countries have genuine grievances about previous applications of conditionality. Adjustment via deflation (the standard IMF package in the past) is obviously insufficient, especially when so many countries are in great difficulty simultaneously—they cannot all deflate at once without creating substantial dangers for systemic stability. Thus the IMF may have to adjust conditionality to take account of the need for growth and efficiency. This will be hard to do, as it will necessarily make the IMF's role more difficult and intrusive.[83]

The difficulties of financing oil deficits have generated a great many innovative proposals, although it is unclear whether OPEC will cooperate (by direct lending, increased aid, or price moderation) or whether any of the proposals will go much beyond dealing with the immediate crisis. But it should also be noted that most of the proposals, which involve new roles for the IMF and the World Bank, have much wider implications. If the IMF moves away from being a lender of last resort and becomes more concerned with the long-term development needs of poor countries that confront major structural problems (as distinct from its traditional concern with short-term adjustment problems), its role in the system will shift markedly. It will become more of a development bank, and it will begin to accept a higher degree of risk in its activities. At the same time, if the World Bank begins to finance short-term trade deficits, as it has recently done in a limited fashion, its role will also shift. It will also begin to accept a higher degree of risk in its activities and the distinction between the functions of the bank and the fund may begin to blur.

These changes are occurring primarily because of the need to respond quickly to immediate financial pressures and because other alternatives seem worse or infeasible. They do raise questions, however, about whether the traditional roles of the bank and especially the fund should be altered in this way, whether a new financing institution might be more appropriate, and whether adequate rules can be established to prevent the misuse or abuse of new practices by the fund and the bank. These issues are not my concern here, but I should note that discussion and debate of new roles for the bank and fund are not likely to be concluded for some time. This means that the immediate policy focus is likely to remain on resolving short-term problems and that very little will be done to deal with long-term structural problems. In effect, responses during the period that concerns us are likely to be short-term, improvisational, and fragmented, and conditions during the decade may become increasingly difficult and dangerous. This sets the framework for a discussion of U.S. policy options toward the Third World during the 1980s.

There seem to me to be several policy orientations that are worth considering. One would simply try to improve and clarify the present approach to policy, which has some severe costs but may also reflect the limits of the possible. A second would take seriously the need for major structural reform and actively seek support for such changes. I do not mean by this an acceptance of the NIEO, which is both badly flawed and too narrow in focus (with its sole concern for development) to serve as a guide, but rather a broader effort to seek the operating rules, management principles, and institutional foundations for the kind of international system that seems to be emerging. This effort would require many difficult trade-offs between efficiency and equity or stability and change, and it is far from clear that it is feasible, that we know how to achieve such an end, or that the outcome will be an improvement over the evils it seeks to avert. But the benefits could also be great, perhaps great enough to justify the risks.

A third policy orientation would be much more selective and discriminating and would seek to build up from subregional and cross-regional groups of "like-minded" states working to establish patterns of cooperation and stable expectations among themselves. This moves away, at least initially, from universal principles and global agreements and toward a more differentiated system of world order. But this orientation has costs and dangers of its own and can only be justified as a necessary response to a second-best world. Finally, there is another orientation that might seek to navigate through present difficulties by choosing to combine elements from the other policy orientations into an effective interim strategy. I shall discuss these policy issues, as well as some other factors that might affect the choice of policies, in Chapter 6.

Taken by themselves, problems in food, energy, trade, and debt are complex and formidable, but potentially manageable. Taken together, however, and in the context of a deteriorating international environment, the problems seem much worse and indeed potentially unmanageable. The difficulties confronting developing-country governments will be extraordinary; these governments will be required to undertake fundamental socioeconomic reforms in the face of rising domestic pressures, insufficient resources, and external pressures that may compel domestic austerity. I should also reemphasize an earlier point: The failure of many developing countries to adjust to new economic circumstances, although understandable, means not only persistent crises during the 1980s but also higher costs (both financial and political) for even more difficult adjustments in what may be an even more difficult international environment. At any rate, the attempt to "muddle through" the 1980s with the development strategies of the 1970s seems—to put it mildly—very problematic. Reconciling such conflicting pressures may be impossible for many countries, thus suggesting the likelihood of instability, inconsistent and erratic policymaking, and perhaps an increased propensity for irrationality and adventurism.

The connection between domestic policies in the developing countries and the international policy process is so crucial that it deserves to be reemphasized. International pressures—from worldwide inflation and recession, from the oil crisis, from the pace of change, and from the complexities of growing interdependence—sharply exacerbate the difficulties of devising effective domestic policies. At the same time, domestic failures (usually emanating from a mixture of external pressures and internal weaknesses) redound on the international policy process by generating massive, escalating, and continuous demands for international relief efforts. Such demands strain the response capacity of an international policy process that has been constructed (or is able) to act primarily in an incremental and residual fashion, particularly on matters of development. The pressures on the international system are especially severe both because of existing economic circumstances and because many developing countries are in genuine need of a range of massive and continuing support that can fairly be called revolutionary (in terms of conventional notions of what the international system can do to facilitate domestic development).

Thus the two levels of change, which must be effectively linked, are now largely out of focus. Unless the demands of the developing countries on the international system can be moderated or the international policy process can be very rapidly and fundamentally reformed, the North-South arena will become an even more hostile, suspicious, and futile setting for the negotiation of meaningful agreements. But it should be clear that the kind of massive reforms of the international policy process demanded by the developing countries (and the Brandt Commission) are not now feasible. Even if they were, however, it is not clear that such reforms would suffice unless profound domestic reforms were undertaken simultaneously. Certainly some would be helped by such reforms, but many would not or could not respond effectively, which implies that the "fundamental" reforms would shortly be followed by demands for even more "fundamental" reforms. I note this here because this dialectic between the domestic and the international process will be a major theme for the 1980s and later decades and because the assumption that the necessary (and parallel) reforms at both levels will *not* be made during the period that concerns us must be, unfortunately, a premise of U.S. policy toward the Third World during the 1980s.

Notes

1. The first notion was developed in the writings of the English economist D. H. Robertson and the second in the writings of Irving Kravis.

2. There are obviously degrees of difference between various scenarios. The normative scenarios that rest on assumptions of relatively high GDP growth rates and relatively rapid improvements in international income distributions tend also to assume the highest growth rates for trade, with LDC trade expanding at roughly twice the growth rate of developed-country trade.

3. For a good, brief discussion of what these terms mean and the controversy surrounding them see John A. Mathieson, "The Tokyo Round Trade Agreements: What Effect on the Developing Countries?" Overseas Development Council, *Communique,* 1979/3.

4. Thus some of the background papers prepared for the recent Interfutures program within the OECD discussed openly the question of whether it was wise for the

OECD countries to subsidize exports of plants and capital goods and to guarantee investments in the developing countries when the result was exports back to the OECD in increasingly sensitive sectors. The answer was unclear, but seemed to be, maybe, so long as the exports were not "premature" (a notion that was left undefined). More concern for security may also generate increased reluctance to lower trade barriers on some uncompetitive products (e.g., food and steel) and an increased propensity to search for synthetic substitutes or "safer" sources of supply.

5. See William Diebold, Jr., "Adapting Economies to Structural Change: The International Aspect," *International Affairs,* Vol. 54, no. 4 (October 1978):573–588.

6. For a good, brief discussion of many of these issues, see Kathryn Morton and Peter Tulloch, *Trade and Developing Countries* (London: Croom Helm, 1977), pp. 20–32. Yeats argued that the cases in which trade has had a negative effect usually involve a form of economic dualism in which the foreign trade sector is an enclave with little connection to the rest of the economy. There have been many such enclaves in the past and others have been created more recently (e.g., the export-processing zones in Mexico and elsewhere), but they are only one part of the trading universe and may gradually begin to develop links with the rest of the economy. See Alexander J. Yeats, *Trade Barriers Facing Developing Countries* (London: Macmillan, 1979), pp. 11ff.

7. See *Economist,* November 10, 1979, p. 83. I shall concentrate entirely on trade in manufactures (now 40–50 percent of the Third World's nonoil exports), not only because it has been the most dynamic trading sector, but also because it reflects well so many problems raised by the developing countries' efforts to reorder the international system. North-South trade crossed a symbolic dividing line in 1980: For the first time exports of manufactures by the non-OPEC LDCs were greater than exports of raw materials.

8. For an elaboration, see Bela Balassa, *A "Stages" Approach to Comparative Advantage* (Washington, D.C.: World Bank Staff Working Paper No. 256, May 1977); and Anne O. Krueger, "LDC Manufacturing Production and Implications for OECD Comparative Advantage," paper prepared for the Conference on Prospects and Policy for Industrial Structural Change in the U.S. and other OECD Countries, Department of State, January 1979. But a recent study notes: "In terms of the movement of developing countries along a scale of comparative advantage . . . there are, so far, few examples." *World Industry Since 1960: Progress and Prospects* (New York: United Nations, 1979), p. 165.

9. Except for normative studies that simply posit or assume imaginary growth rates, the most optimistic studies that I have been able to find suggest that it *might* be possible to return to the growth rates achieved in the 1960s. Recent oil price increases may have destroyed this possibility; in any case, "success" on these terms (a return to 1960s trends) would be inadequate, if not disastrous, for a great many developing countries.

10. This implies—at best—the kind of mixed, ambiguous, and uncertain agreements that emerged from the recently concluded Tokyo Round.

11. On the reluctance of some of the successful exporters to give up certain activities as they lose comparative advantage, see Hollis B. Chenery and Donald B. Keesing, *The Changing Composition of Developing Country Exports* (Washington, D.C.:

World Bank Staff Working Paper No. 314, January 1979), p. 47.

12. *Industrial Redeployment in Favor of Developing Countries,* Report by the Executive Director of UNIDO (New York: United Nations, A/34/288, June 1979), p. 12.

13. "Those Other Japans," *Economist,* June 10, 1978, pp. 84–85.

14. The most useful study of the NICs is *The Impact of the Newly Industrialising Countries on Production and Trade in Manufactures* (Paris: Organisation of Economic Co-operation and Development, 1979).

15. Ibid., p. 22. Chenery and Keesing, *The Changing Composition of Developing Country Exports,* pp. 50–53, see only India and the Philippines as potential NICs in the next five years or so, but others are more optimistic. Of course, many of the more optimistic estimates were made before the latest round of oil price increases. Disagreement about which countries to include also reflects definitional difficulties (how much of what has to be exported to whom, etc.) and various other uncertainties about proper categorization. I need hardly stress here that the NICs differ in many crucial ways, that any list that ties together Hong Kong, South Korea, Brazil, Yugoslavia, etc., must rely on very broad and general characteristics, and that in some cases the differences are more important than the similarities. But not here, as I am primarily interested in a common effect the NICs are having on other LDCs and on the developed countries.

16. "Those Other Japans," p. 84.

17. There is presumably some upward limit to this, in the sense that if China or India had exported proportionately as much to the OECD countries (which received two-thirds of NIC exports), as, say, Hong Kong, protectionist reactions would have surfaced earlier.

18. See *Industrialisation for the Year 2000: New Dimensions* (Vienna: UNIDO, IOD 268, May 1979), pp. 15–16. It should be noted that this criticism does not hold for South Korea and Taiwan, which have done very well agriculturally. It does hold for the large NICs and for several of the European NICs.

19. See especially Donald B. Keesing, *Trade Policy for Developing Countries* (Washington, D.C.: World Bank Staff Working Paper No. 353, August 1979), p. 202. Employment for manufactured exports is not expected to go much beyond 15–20 million factory jobs by the 1990s — about the amount that the total work force will grow each year. Also, if future export growth is tied to productivity increases (as is likely if the NICs move to more advanced capital-intensive products), the employment effect will be even smaller.

20. South Korea is planning for an average annual growth rate of exports of manufactures of 14.9 percent from 1977–1991; Taiwan plans 15.8 percent per annum over the next few years; and Brazil is aiming at growth rates of well over 10 percent. This is obviously problematic, not only in terms of slower growth in the OECD area but also in terms of leaving room for other LDC exporters. For the figures, see Bela Balassa, *The Changing International Division of Labor in Manufactured Goods* (Washington, D.C.: World Bank Staff Working Paper No. 329, 197), p. 40.

21. For the figures, see *World Industry Since 1960,* p. 153.

22. For a discussion of this three-cornered challenge, see Stephen B. Watkins and John R. Karlik, "Anticipating Disruptive Exports," *New International Realities,* Vol. 3, no. 2 (Summer 1978):9–20.

23. Note the comment by Edmund Dell, formerly secretary of state for trade in the United Kingdom: "We have our own new international economic order to promote . . . which gives us a greater feeling of security." Quoted in Martin Wolf, *Adjustment Policies and Problems in Developed Countries* (Washington, D.C.: World Bank Staff Working Paper No. 349, August 1979), p. 38. Wolf also indicated (p. 39) that the belief is strong that "an industry in the hand is worth two in the bush."

24. See *Impact of the Newly Industrialising Countries*, pp. 31ff.

25. See K. Billerbeck and Y. Yasugi, *Private Direct Foreign Investment in Developing Countries* (Washington, D.C.: World Bank Staff Working Paper No. 398, July 1979). For a good analysis of the Japanese situation, see Lawrence B. Krause and Sueo Sekiguchi, "Japan and the World Economy," in Hugh Patrick and Henry Rosovsky, eds., *Asia's New Giant — How the Japanese Economy Works* (Washington, D.C.: Brookings Institution, 1976), pp. 382–458.

26. These matters are discussed in Seev Hirsch, "Hypotheses Regarding Trade Between Developing and Industrial Countries," in Herbert Giersch, ed., *The International Division of Labour — Problems and Perspectives* (Tübingen: J.C.B. Mohr, 1974), pp. 65–82. In general, complementary trade, as between developed and developing countries, is based on the superiority of a key factor on each side (e.g., natural resources or unskilled labor in exchange for physical and human capital), while substitutive trade is based on more complex differences (e.g., taste, style, marketing, etc.).

27. This also raises the issue of the role of multinational corporations, as they possess the requisite skills and are in a much stronger position on these LDC exports than they are on traditional labor-intensive exports (which tend to be dominated by local firms). There is thus a trade-off: more advanced exports, more of the gains to foreign corporations. One should also note that tariff barriers against the products exported by the MNCs tend to be lower, at least in part because of the political influence of the MNCs. This *may* increase the gains to both the MNCs and the host country, but complex trade-offs, once again, are involved. On these points, see Keesing, *Trade Policy for Developing Countries*, p. 130; and Gerald K. Helleiner, "The New Industrial Protectionism and the Developing Countries," *Trade and Development*, no. 1 (Spring 1979):15–37.

28. See Donald B. Keesing, "Manufactured Exports from Developing Countries," in Khadija Haq, ed., *Equality of Opportunity Within and Among Nations* (New York: Praeger Publishers, 1977), pp. 98–103. This also assumes that the fall in the terms of trade will not be compensated for by other benefits (for example, increased quality of imports or increased volume of exports).

29. Thus, "whenever a non-traditional exporter achieves a breakthrough on an industrialised country market for a given product by obtaining consumer acceptance, his example will be quickly followed by rivals not able or willing to take the initial risk." *Impact of the Newly Industrialising Countries*, p. 26. For earlier comments on the follow-the-leader syndrome, see Robert L. Rothstein, *The Weak in the World of the Strong: The Developing Countries in the International System* (New York: Columbia University Press, 1977), p. 244.

30. Krueger, "LDC Manufacturing Production," pp. 18ff.

31. *World Development Report, 1979* (Washington, D.C.: World Bank, August 1979), pp. 5–6. The developing countries sent 31 percent of their total manufac-

tured exports to each other in 1977, so the 40 percent for advanced exports is well above the general level of trade in manufactures.

32. *Impact of the Newly Industrialising Countries,* p. 27.

33. Robert T. Green and James M. Lutz, *The United States and World Trade: Changing Patterns and Dimensions* (New York: Praeger Publishers, 1978), pp. 83–95, have some comments about possible patterns of regionalizaton (the United States increasingly a Western Hemisphere power, Japan an Asian power, etc.). But, although regional patterns are still strong, they have declined in recent years, and the United States has increasing trade ties with ASEAN countries. Thus regionalism joined to selective relationships with extra-regional (and "reliable") LDCs seems more likely.

34. For a discussion of the reasons for success, see *Impact of the Newly Industrialising Countries,* p. 48. Keesing, in *Trade Policy for Developing Countries,* pp. 151ff., laid great emphasis on the need for strong government action (usually by nondemocratic governments) to impose sacrifices (and quoted one official's suggestion of the need for "technocrats backed by tanks"), but the issue cannot be resolved in narrowly economic terms. In any case, it is not clear even on such terms; some democratic governments have chosen the "right" policies and some nondemocratic ones have chosen incorrectly.

35. *The Dimensions of the Required Restructuring of World Manufacturing Output and Trade in Order to Reach the Lima Target* (Geneva: UNCTAD, TD/185/Supp. 1, May 1976), p. 1.

36. See *World Industry Since 1960,* p. 55.

37. In addition to the works cited in notes 35 and 36, see *Industrialisation for the Year 2000;* Wassily Leontieff et al., *The Future of the World Economy* (New York: Oxford University Press, 1977); and *International Division of Industrial Labor* (Paris: OECD Interfutures, 1977).

38. *Industrialisation for the Year 2000,* p. 114.

39. Ibid. The $750 billion figure covers the needs of the whole economy, not simply industrial development.

40. For a good discussion, see Robert S. Pindyck, *The Structure of World Energy Demand* (Cambridge, Mass.: M.I.T. Press, 1979), p. 253.

41. See Ajit Singh, "The 'Basic Needs' Approach to Development vs. the New International Economic Order: The Significance of Third World Industrialisation," *World Development,* Vol. 7, no. 6 (June 1979):585–606.

42. *Industrialisation for the Year 2000,* p. 129.

43. Ibid., p. 273.

44. *Industrial Redeployment,* p. 3.

45. Close to 90 percent of the redeployment in the past decade went to the same small groups of NICs that had cornered most of the benefits from the trading system. On the policy demands noted, see ibid., pp. 15–17, and Santosh Mukharjee, *Restructuring of Industrial Economies and Trade with Developing Countries* (Geneva: International Labour Office, 1979), p. 78.

46. See *Industrialisation for the Year 2000,* pp. 212ff. The quoted phrase is on p. 280.

47. See *World Industry Since 1960,* p. 51. William Diebold, Jr., *Industrial Policy as an International Issue* (New York: McGraw-Hill, 1980), which I read only after com-

pleting this study, has many interesting comments on these issues. In addition to noting that "it is difficult to believe that any given pattern of location can be lasting" (p. 105), he argued that it is very difficult to "determin[e] what pattern to move toward, even if one can be quite clear what to move away from" (p. 110).

48. Ferdnand Braun, "The European Economic Community Approach to Adjustment," in Helen Hughes, ed., *Prospects for Partnerships: Industrialization and Trade Policies in the 1970s* (Baltimore, Md.: Johns Hopkins University Press, 1973), p. 208.

49. *Impact of the Newly Industrialising Countries,* p. 15.

50. Wolf, *Adjustment Policies and Problems,* p. 213.

51. This paragraph reflects themes in Robert L. Rothstein, *Global Bargaining: UNCTAD and the Quest for a New International Economic Order* (Princeton, N.J.: Princeton University Press, 1979).

52. Most of the adjustments that take place constantly in response to shifts in comparative advantage appear to go on within sectors and subsectors — which partially explains why future developments are difficult to foresee. But it may be easier to spot broader shifts (between sectors) and to develop timely and coherent responses to them (which is not to say ordering the affected industries to move, even if such an order was economically — and legally — justified). For an interesting effort to work out the details of a new world industrial geography, see Bohuslav Herman, *The Optimal International Division of Labor* (Geneva: International Labour Office, 1975). But he discusses none of the policy issues.

53. *Report of the Conference on Economic Co-operation among Developing Countries* (Geneva: UNCTAD, TD/B/628, October 1976), p. 10. It should be noted that collective self-reliance is a very broad concept that includes efforts to increase Third World cooperation at all levels (local, regional, global) and by many means (including a Third World preference scheme, payments arrangements, joint purchasing operations, the creation of multinational firms, etc.). But as all of these means are still only in the discussion state, I shall concentrate on the general problems of increasing trade between the developing countries.

54. Ibid., pp. 10ff.

55. *Steps to Be Taken to Facilitate the Carrying Out of UNCTAD's Programme of Work on Economic Co-operation among Developing Countries* (Geneva: UNCTAD, TD/B/C.7/14, September, 1978), p. 2.

56. *Trade among Developing Countries by Main SITC Groups and by Regions* (Geneva: UNCTAD, TD/B/C.7/21, September 1978), p. 5.

57. See *Steps to Be Taken to Facilitate the Carrying Out of UNCTAD's Programme,* p. 5. In 1970 fuels were about one-third of total South-South trade.

58. The statistics in this and the following paragraphs are drawn from *Trade among Developing Countries by Main SITC Groups and by Regions* and from an unclassified CIA study, *Preliminary Notes on Trade Among LDCs* (December 1978).

59. There are substantial regional differences in shares of LDC trade in total trade (Southeast Asia 32 percent, Latin America 21 percent, Africa 14 percent) and great differences between individual countries (for example, in 1977 Hong Kong and South Korea sent about 15 percent of their manufactured exports to LDCs; Pakistan sent 54 percent and Argentina 60 percent).

60. Fuel trade will presumably level off, either by necessity or from increased use of indigenous resources. Food exports are almost as important as manufactures in terms of value, but have not been rising rapidly (and much of the increase has been in a few key commodities like sugar).

61. See *Industrialisation for the Year 2000,* p. 224. This study estimates that about half of LDC exports are controlled by transnational corporations.

62. See Anne O. Krueger, "Alternative Trade Strategies and Employment in LDCs," *American Economic Review,* Vol. 68, no. 2 (May 1978):270–274. This should be qualified by noting that, as indicated earlier, the export of manufactures will make only a small contribution to the overall employment problem.

63. Various preference schemes also favor continued North-South trade, as does the very high level of protection in many developing countries. Collective self-reliance seeks to diminish both of these problems (e.g., by South-South preferences).

64. Many other factors also impede South-South trade, including the lack of institutional and financial infrastructure, different currency zones, and the absence of traditional trading ties. Again, collective self-reliance seeks to deal with these problems, if over time.

65. Two UNCTAD studies by consultants stress the need to concentrate on national action first (government commitment to export promotion) and then on subregional cooperation rather than on very complex global preference schemes or payments unions. See Fasih Uddin, *Preferential Trade Measures within the Integration and Co-operation Schemes in the Regions of ESCAP and ECWA* (Geneva: UNCTAD, TD/B/C.7/19, September 1978); and Felix Pena, *Review of Experience to Date with Preferential Measures in the Context of Latin American Integration Schemes* (Geneva: UNCTAD/ TD/B/C.7/22, November 1978).

66. See Richard Portes, "East, West, and South: The Impact of Eastern Europe," paper prepared for the OECD Interfutures project, December 1977.

67. On the benefits to socialist LDCs, see the various essays in Deepak Nayyar, ed., *Economic Relations between Socialist Countries and the Third World* (London: Macmillan, 1977). It should also be noted that India is something of a special case; it benefited substantially from trading relations with the socialist countries but could not be considered a member of the bloc.

68. See Portes, "East, West, and South," p. 25.

69. *World Development Report, 1978* (Washington, D.C.: World Bank, 1978), p. 14.

70. Apart from some relatively muted rhetoric, the East has been closer to the West than to the South on most of the NIEO issues.

71. See Carol Fogarty, "Chinese Relations with the Third World," in *Chinese Economy Post-Mao* (Joint Economic Committee, Congress of the United States, November 1978), pp. 851–859.

72. For a brief discussion of this division of labor, see *Industrial Redeployment,* p. 7. There would need to be some relocation because of energy factors, but there is no mention of this in this or other studies of "rational" redeployment.

73. The employment issue, which I heard mentioned in a recent discussion with a black pressure group in Washington, refers to the fact that black employment pros-

pects in this country might be considerably affected by the movement of many labor-intensive industries to the developing countries and the resulting concentration on advanced-technology industries. How severe this problem would be is unclear, but it does imply an interesting conflict between domestic needs and the desire of black pressure groups to increase U.S. support for the Third World.

74. This is a small sum globally, but not so trivial for the LDCs. For the figure, see Helleiner, "New Industrial Protectionism," p. 18.

75. I have made a similar argument, if in a broader context, in the last chapter of Rothstein, *Global Bargaining.*

76. The foregoing draws on a number of sources, especially Miguel S. Wionczek, "The LDC External Debt and the Euromarkets: The Impressive Record and the Uncertain Future," *World Development,* Vol. 7, no. 3 (1979):175–187; and *Some Aspects of the Impact of Inflation on the Debt Burden of Developing Countries* (Geneva: UNCTAD, TD/AC.2/4, June 30, 1977). The five large borrowers were Brazil, Mexico, Argentina, South Korea, and the Philippines.

77. Susan Strange, "Debt and Default in the International Political Economy," in Jonathan David Aronson, ed., *Debt and Less Developed Countries* (Boulder, Colo.: Westview Press, 1979), p. 24. Other factors that generated optimism included the facts that international lending has not been more risky than domestic lending (in part because of the possibility of choosing only the best risks) and that debt growth rates did not exceed earlier growth rates (in the 1960s).

78. See Wionczek, "LDC External Debt," p. 178.

79. For discussion of various proposals, see Jessica P. Einhorn, "Cooperation between Public and Private Lenders to the Third World," *World Economy,* Vol. 2, no. 2 (May 1979):229–241; and Gordon W. Smith, "The External Debt Prospects of the Non-Oil-Exporting Developing Countries," in William R. Cline, ed., *Policy Alternatives for a New International Economic Order: An Economic Analysis* (New York: Praeger Publishers, 1979), pp. 285–329. Perhaps the most important element in these efforts would be OPEC's willingness to invest directly in the NOLDCs or to supply much greater amounts of its surplus to the World Bank to lend. This would probably require some kind of international guarantee, but this, in turn, is unlikely without a major agreement between oil producers and consumers, which does not appear imminent.

80. David C. Beek, "Commercial Bank Lending to Developing Countries," *Federal Reserve Bank of New York Quarterly Review,* Vol. 55 (Summer 1977):5.

81. I do not mean to imply an either/or choice between current aid levels and the full demands—if they could be established—of the LDCs, but rather a choice between more or less existing levels and an increase of, say, 100–200 percent.

82. Another alternative that has been discussed involves the World Bank in packaging loans to the NOLDCs and then reselling the package to OPEC, as banks now resell mortgage-backed securities. Among the many other suggestions for new means of financing are a proposal for a new supplementary financing scheme and a proposal to sharply increase amounts available in the IMF's compensatory financing facility. Many of these proposals rest on the assumption of direct OPEC cooperation, but it may take a major financial crisis to overcome OPEC's reluctance to make the necessary commitments.

83. The IMF staff has itself been reluctant either to become involved in cofinancing arrangements or to see the terms of conditionality loosened. In terms of the former, the staff has feared being implicated in bad loans by private banks, being denied access to all information if governments fear it will be divulged to private creditors, or being identified by the developing countries as debt collectors for private banks. As for conditionality, they fear that the degree of surveillance necessary to make judgments about growth and efficiency will be unacceptable to the developing countries—not to mention the technical difficulties of such judgments. These points are well taken, but they fail to recognize sufficiently the dangers created by the present crisis and the need for an adjustment of roles by all the international institutions. It is doubtful that the debate over the range and timing of these adjustments will be resolved quickly or successfully—which is to say, in time to be of much help during the early 1980s.

6
The Search for a Policy
Framework for the 1980s

The Context of Decision

The quest for a viable policy toward the Third World will be a recurring theme in U.S. foreign policy throughout this decade. "Recurring" is used deliberately, because the probability of a successful end to the quest is not high, and the salience of North-South issues is unlikely to diminish. Recent events in Iran and Afghanistan, whatever their other consequences, may illustrate some of the difficulties that the United States will confront: Events within the Third World can now have a direct and major impact on important U.S. interests, but U.S. power to protect those interests is limited and there is no clear domestic consensus behind a particular set of policy responses.

Devising a consistent and coherent policy toward a large group of countries that is extremely variegated (and is becoming even more so) is obviously extraordinarily complex. One need not rehearse the additional difficulties created by current economic circumstances and by prevailing trends in food, energy, trade, and debt. The complexities and the uncertainties set the bounds for this discussion: I shall concentrate on general orientations, on the relationships between various issues, and on the factors that must be taken into account in determining policy choices, but the details of specific policies toward particular countries and issues must be left aside. Moreover, the fit between general policy orientations and specific decisions is always imperfect, and surprises are inevitable; thus there will still be much need for operational innovation and improvisation. What follows, then, is at best the beginning of policy analysis, not the end. The limits of this enterprise must be recognized, but it does have the virtue of providing a framework for discussion and some sense of the questions that the United States confronts in the years ahead—if not the answers.

In the next section I shall briefly examine several scenarios of North-South relations in the 1980s. Chapter 7 will discuss the range of policy choices open to the United States. Before turning to these matters, however, I must discuss a number of issues that seem likely to influence the choices it has and the choices it makes.

Discussions of future developments in food, energy, and trade are dominated by uncertainty. This is hardly unusual; projections of future trends are never certain and are always (necessarily) oversimplified. But uncertainty in its current manifestations seems wider and deeper than ever before and more consequential in its practical effects — a difference in kind, not merely in degree. We do not know how to determine which medium- or long-term choice is best or whether expected outcomes will fall within an acceptable range. Furthermore, with so much at stake, the risks of choosing incorrectly are magnified. And the normal policy means of dealing with uncertainty not only seem inadequate (or unavailable to poor countries), but may succeed only in worsening the situation. The management of uncertainty by new means may thus become a crucial issue in the next decades.

The conventional tactics for dealing with uncertainty are familiar. They include hedging, increasing the liquidity of assets, avoiding commitment to a single policy until there is more clarity, and an emphasis on gradualism and the short run.[1] The growing emphasis on economic and military security tends to reinforce the concern for the short run and for protection of narrow national interests. But if present uncertainties are unique in some important senses — if the crisis we face has few reliable precedents — the adoption of conventional tactics may only exacerbate the difficulties. Delaying action may be particularly costly if it encourages or permits continuation of patterns of behavior that are themselves at least partially responsible for the present crisis. This is especially true if we confront a supply crisis — as we do in many areas — because delay wastes existing supplies without facilitating the creation of alternative supplies.

These considerations have a double effect on the developing countries. In the first place, the dominance of short-run perspectives makes it much more difficult to increase aid levels or to establish a more effective relationship between North and South, one that must inevitably rest on some short-run sacrifices by the developed countries. In the second place, the prevailing tactics to deal with uncertainty implicitly reflect two assumptions: that spare resources exist to develop alternative strategies (or capacities) and that the period of delay before a situation clarifies will not be too costly or dangerous. Neither of these conditions holds for poor and weak governments that confront multiple crises and control too few resources to do much more than struggle to survive. Governmental elites may well understand the need to restructure the domestic socioeconomic framework and to adopt major reform strategies to cope with existing problems, but when they are short of resources and power and when the results of alternative strategies are both risky and uncertain, the most likely choice is to procrastinate — to choose by not choosing. Mortgaging the future is hardly an unusual political tactic, and one needs a special degree of compassion for elites confronted by nothing but bad choices, but one must also understand the consequences for the international system. Avoiding today's crisis by measures that assure an even more severe crisis in a few years means that pressures on the international system for a massive rescue effort will intensify at what may be an even more difficult time to elicit a charitable response.

The extraordinary difficulty of dealing with the problems engendered by the oil crisis, inflation, and recession has concentrated attention on short-run coping mechanisms. What must be understood from the preceding discussion, however, is that the combination of insufficient resources and uncertainty about future choices virtually guarantees — barring unforeseen technological innovations — that the short-run crisis will simply persist (in effect, coping with present difficulties is necessary but not sufficient) or, put differently, that many of the NOLDCs will be in permanent crisis throughout the 1980s. That crisis may manifest itself in different ways — from desperate and irrational acts of terrorism to extreme repression and internal sacrifice — but it seems unavoidable. Even if a global oil agreement that took account of the interests of the NOLDCs were to be negotiated, this would only alleviate, not avert, the crisis. The time already lost, as well as the costs of adjusting to a new energy strategy, assures a period of very limited, very painful, and perhaps very destabilizing choices.

The policy implications for the United States and the other developed countries can be broadly stated. If the developed countries merely persist in present policies, the most likely outcome is a continuing series of relatively small-scale (to the developed countries) crises. These might cumulatively escalate into a large-scale systemic crisis, but in any case they would guarantee something like a rigid international caste system. Moderate and steady improvements in present policies (perhaps including increased aid and more innovative insurance schemes to spread the risks of expensive and uncertain policy choices) will improve matters considerably by helping more countries to cope, but will not deal with underlying structural problems. The ability to manage crises may improve, but not the ability to avert (enough) crises. A more radical response, which would involve massive and automatic resource transfers and major changes in the role and powers of international institutions, raises serious questions of political feasibility. It might, however provide the basis for a more stable international order. But there is no guarantee that any of these choices will produce intended effects, because the connection between theory and practice is unclear, because external support is only one factor among many in determining outcomes, and because there is leverage, but not control, over how developing-country governments implement policies. As we shall see, these uncertainties are exacerbated by other difficulties or potential difficulties.

Another issue that is likely to have a significant effect on both perceptions and possibilities in the North-South arena is the diminishing capacity of the United States to play a dominant leadership role. This is a complex issue, because it mixes judgments about the persistence of trends and policies, both of which can be altered, and because the nature and consequences of international leadership are neither perfectly clear nor independent of the socioeconomic context of decision. Still, there is widespread agreement that international systems seem to function better when dominated by a strong leader committed to system maintenance and willing or able to provide guidance and to sacrifice some of its own short-run interests and benefits.[2]

The decline of U.S. power and influence has a double effect on North-South issues. In the first place, the United States, acting as an "ordinary country," is clearly more inclined or more compelled to protect its own immediate interests (for example, by increased protectionism and more concern for security than for development issues). The result is increased difficulty in negotiating broader and more generous North-South agreements.[3] At the same time, of course, the lowered status of the United States, the stagnation of aid levels, the apparent decline of the dollar, and an appearance of inconstancy in defense of friends obviously encourages a tendency among some countries to look elsewhere for support and guidance. The relative decline in U.S. power may also make central control or guidance of the international system, a goal intrinsic to many Third World demands, more difficult: There is no dominant leader willing or able to sacrifice its own short-run interests for the good of the system.

In the second place, and more critically, U.S. policy alone can no longer structure either process or outcome in the North-South arena. While the United States still retains a good deal of blocking (or "negative") power, in that a U.S. failure to agree tends to insure that the initiatives of others cannot succeed, it has also lost much of its "positive" power to impose its own policies or choices on others. The United States must undertake much more detailed and early consultations if its aim is to influence movement and direction in large parts of the Third World, as distinct from bilateral contexts. But this degree of consultation is difficult for three familiar reasons. One is the complexity of reaching agreement within the bureaucracy and with Congress on less-than-salient Third World issues. There are also the difficulties of reaching agreement within the OECD when economic performance varies, when political schedules are uncoordinated, and when the benefits and losses of cooperation with the Third World are distributed asymmetrically. Finally, there is the need to reach prior agreement on what to do and how to do it with Third World groups that have a unique world view and a strong commitment to a very problematic negotiating style. This probably means that, short of a dramatic turnabout in the normal diplomatic process, the quest for quick agreement on massive restructuring of the international system is doomed to failure.

At the same time, however, it should be emphasized that while U.S. power and influence may have declined, the United States is still something more than merely *primus inter pares*. Its choices may be more limited in present circumstances, but it is neither necessary nor wise to assume that the only choice is immobility and the defense of narrow interests. Indeed, the United States may not need to sacrifice the broader goals that it has (sometimes) sought in the past if—and it is a very big if—consultations can produce agreement on *how* to pursue common interests. I shall return to this issue.

A number of related issues concerning potential fault lines in the international system are also worth noting at this point. It may be useful to begin with a general point about strategies of "delinking." In its more moderate forms, delinking is a sensible strategy for a group of countries that are the first victims of adverse external trends and that frequently bear heavy costs for excessive dependency on countries that they do not control and that do not place the highest priority on Third World needs.[4] Efforts to increase ties among the developing countries are a prominent component of this strategy. Of course, given the strength of existing patterns of interaction and the difficulties of constructing new patterns, delinking can be only partial and incomplete for many decades. Nevertheless, even within these very severe limitations, it is difficult to avoid the conclusion that the basic trend is in the opposite direction: The great majority of the developing countries are becoming more, not less, dependent on the developed countries.

Growing dependence is implicit in rising import deficits in food and energy and an ever-increasing need for access to Western markets and increased transfers of resources and technology. This raises three issues that need to be kept in mind as we go along. First, while only a few crises within the Third World—OPEC apart—have the potential to destabilize the international system, all crises within the developed world will have a significant, perhaps decisive, effect on Third World fortunes. Put differently, from the Third World's point of view all crises are systemic: Third World countries cannot effectively isolate or protect themselves. Second, competition within the Third World for shares of whatever the developed countries are willing to offer will surely rise. Finally, increased dependence on a complex, sophisticated, and troubled international system may be exacerbated by some of the prevailing development strategies, especially those that seek to integrate the developing countries in the international economy as rapidly as possible. I do not mean to suggest that small and poor countries have a viable alternative to dependence, but rather that there are differing degrees and qualities of dependence and that strategies that encourage premature integration need to be reconsidered.[5] This will be especially true if resources rise in cost, as competition for scarce resources with the developed countries is not likely to be productive.

Will the Group of 77 remain unified and will it continue to rely on a negotiating strategy that encourages demands for massive and immediate global restructuring? These are crucial questions, for the answers are likely to set the critical operating boundaries for the North-South policies of the developed countries. I should begin by warning of the dangers of oversimplification. A split within the Group of 77 is neither good nor bad in and of itself for either developed or developing countries; one must understand why and how it occurred and what practical effects it might have on the prospects for meaningful negotiations. And in the same sense, the continuation of the North-South Dialogue in its present form can be judged only by the results achieved (including psychological benefits and learning effects) and not as something that is intrinsically good or bad. There are too many analysts in the developed world who take it for granted that a split in the Group of 77 would somehow benefit the developed countries, and there are too many elites in the Third World who take the persistence of the Dialogue as a good, irrespective of the results achieved. It should go without saying that matters are more complex.

The Group of 77, like most international institutions, is not an autonomous structure. Its success or failure is more the result of external developments than of its own actions. The Group's leadership, however, has made strong efforts to increase solidarity, if primarily to thwart suspected "divide and conquer" tactics by the developed countries. Thus major efforts have been made to improve coordination and to establish and maintain common positions within and between the various groups of the Group of 77 and other Third World institutions. Moreover, a shared view of the world and shared problems (poverty, equity, debt, agrarian difficulties, reliance on raw materials exports, political instability, etc.) have been emphasized far more than differences on specific issues. These considerations, combined with the disarray (and limited generosity) of the developed countries and the rising importance of resource issues, have given the Group of 77 more unity and more power than a simple addition of tangible elements of power might suggest. In any case, the glue provided by shared resentments and shared fears should never be underestimated.

There can be no doubt, however, that the difficulties of maintaining unity will increase in this decade. On the one hand, differentiation among the developing countries is growing. Different starting points, different resource endowments, different degrees of commitment to development, different degrees of stability, and, of course, different records of success and failure, among other things, have come together to increase economic, social, and political differences within the Third World. Constructing a consensus in these circumstances has required great effort and some sleight of hand; conflicting and divergent interests have not been compromised, but rather obscured or simply added together. On the other hand, as I have indicated in previous chapters, trends in food, energy, trade, and debt may very well end by setting developing country against developing country. This is especially true in terms of the effort by the NICs to protect their markets in the developed countries and to open up markets in the rest of the Third World and of the ability of the more advanced developing countries to bid away food, energy, and capital imports from the poorer developing countries. In short, the pressures on unity are coming from two directions: increasing internal differentiation, which leads to divergent patterns of interests and needs, and increasing external pressures, which lead to sharp competition for necessary but scarce external resources.

Several points about these differences (actual and potential) ought to be noted. First, they provide some indication of why the demands of the developing countries frequently appear inconsistent or ambivalent. There are too many different needs and approaches to permit the construction of a completely coherent program. In this sense the developing countries pay the cost of the kind of unity they have maintained: The vast package of demands is intrinsically difficult to negotiate, not least because it is unclear how demands for more rapid growth, increased equity, and decreased dependence on the developed countries can be reconciled.[6] Second, the developing differences within the Third World are more significant than earlier differences (between, say, "Third," "Fourth," and "Fifth" Worlds). More is at stake; needs are greater, and direct conflicts over the distribution of tangible benefits are becoming more salient.

Third, in contrast to the past, the assumption that lower-level groups will gradually progress into membership in upper-level groups seems untrue. We may be passing from a class system, in which status can be changed by socioeconomic growth, to a caste system, in which inferior status is difficult to alter. This may mean the creation of a substantial group of countries more or less permanently on the dole, which implies the need to reconsider a number of liberal assumptions about North-South relations — especially the idea that concessional resource transfers will become progressively unnecessary as the developing countries achieve "self-sustaining" growth.

Fourth, despite these arguments, it should not be assumed that the Group of 77 will disintegrate. There are two major reasons why unity may persist in spite of differentiation. In the first place, Third World leaders are very conscious of the dangers of disintegration and have been very suspicious of efforts to emphasize differentiated and functionally specific policies (especially when negotiations will be moved out of global arenas like UNCTAD and the UN General Assembly). Thus the Executive Committee of the Third World Forum, one of the Third World's most influential organizations, has warned that

> the policy of differentiation among Third World countries resorted to by some rich industrialized countries . . . is increasingly used to undermine the solidarity of the Third World. [The Executive Committee] emphasized that the heterogeneity of interests among developing countries is overemphasized and inflated by the North. If it is recognized that the core of the present Third World struggle is economic decolonization, the basic convergence of interests among Third World countries become apparent. While possible areas of conflict of interest among Third World countries should be carefully analyzed, and means to deal with them should be devised, these conflicts should not overshadow the political character of the task.[7]

This might be aptly described, within the Third World context, as a staunch defense of the conventional wisdom. Whatever one chooses to make of the ideological character of this argument, differentiation is a fact, and attempts to disguise it with political rhetoric are not likely to succeed. Indeed, such attempts at disguise will make it more difficult to reform the North-South Dialogue or to establish new patterns of practical cooperation.

Second, a number of calculations of self-interest may also facilitate the maintenance of unity. The poor LDCs obviously have no place else to go. The leverage they get in the Dialogue and the support that they receive for their programs—in exchange for support of programs of interest to the more advanced—is much greater than anything they might reasonably expect if left to bargain on their own. And as I have already indicated, the NICs and the other advanced developing countries, while very dependent on access to developed-country markets, also need and want access to Third World markets. One need hardly add that the recent rise in protectionism by the developed countries and growing doubts about the wisdom and constancy of U.S. leadership among even the most conservative developing countries reinforce the desire to keep as many doors open as possible. In addition, although the point cannot be made with great confidence, the rise of extremist, anti-Western, fundamentalist movements—as in Iran and Saudi Arabia—is likely to encourage even conservative leaders to maintain something more than rhetorical support for Third World positions.

Precise predictions of how these divergent pressures will work themselves out are impossible. Nevertheless, one might venture the judgment that, if the developed countries and OPEC do not plunge the entire system into a massive crisis, and if the present emphasis on limited, coping policies persists, the forces for unity — feelings of solidarity, increasing institutionalization, the existence of some tangible benefits — are likely to be powerful enough to sustain the continuation of the North-South Dialogue. But as the forces for disunity are likely to have their first impact on governments at home, the quest for bilateral "deals" and concessions is also likely to escalate. In effect, the outcome would reinforce the two-track strategy in North-South relations: on the level of the Dialogue, continued rhetorical support for radical changes in the system's operating rules, but on the bilateral level, a potentially nasty competition among developing countries to win special favors from particular developed countries.[8] This is unity, but of the worst kind: It would be primarily ceremonial, it would prevent reforms of the Dialogue that might make it more effective, and it might also inhibit the negotiation of some sensible subregional and regional agreements with the developed countries (if such agreements were to be regarded as inimical to the grand principles ostensibly at stake in the Dialogue). The central point may be that disconnections between the two tracks could become even more salient; the possibility of effective integration of the two policy levels, which may be crucial for long-term development prospects, may diminish even further. In the circumstances, the Dialogue is not likely to do much to relieve the severe pressures that many developing-country governments are likely to face in this decade.

I have already argued in Chapter 2 that the many and varied political conflicts within and between Third World states, although not a direct concern of this study, are likely to reinforce some primary economic fault lines. Existing political conflicts may well be sharply exacerbated by a deteriorating economic environment, and existing political and ideological friendships may well become less consequential as a unifying force if all available resources must be expended on immediate national needs and attention must be diverted to pursuing special arrangements with the developed countries. One must emphasize that the presumed dominance of economic pressures, which is implied by these comments, is hardly absolute. In some cases the political conflicts may be so severe and disabling that economic considerations are largely ignored (if only for relatively brief periods of time, economic needs being what they are). But perhaps one ought to add another qualification. If the present two-track approach to North-South relations persists, if in a worsened and even less effective form, the economic fault lines may still appear, but in a less clear and more ambiguous fashion. The uncertainties may be so great and the pressures — both internal and external — so powerful that persisting relationships may be very difficult to establish and maintain. In short, even the fault lines may be unstable as states shift rapidly in pursuit of quick gains.

The developed countries confront the same external pressures and the same need for solidarity and institutional creativity in their own relationships. The latter may be difficult to achieve, however, for much the same reasons that the developing countries may find it difficult to maintain unity. In a period of slow growth, trade with the developing countries may become increasingly important to many developed countries, but cooperative agreements will be difficult to achieve because the costs and benefits of that trade fall very asymmetrically. In this sense, the unity of the developed countries and the creation of common policies toward the South may also become increasingly empty and ceremonial as each privately seeks special agreements with particular developing countries. Indeed, even a tacit agreement on "spheres of interest" might be undermined by the same asymmetries: For example, trade with the richer countries of Latin America might be relatively more beneficial to the United States than trade with Africa might be for the European countries. At any rate, although the problem of asymmetries may not be as difficult to deal with for the developed countries, if only because the amounts involved will be less significant, there is still a dangerous potential for an increasingly fragmented Northern response to Southern demands. This potential might be increased by the existence of different attitudes and perspectives within the Northern coalition on North-South issues.

The direction and force of major external trends and the political and economic responses of the developing countries, both individually and as a broad coalition, are likely to set the framework within which the developed countries must devise and implement their policies toward the South. But as the future is not wholly determined by trends and the responses of the developing countries are malleable, the United States—especially in conjunction with the other developed countries—can have a substantial impact on Third World developments. All the states in the international system may confront a decade of limited choices, but such choices remain meaningful. At a minimum, significant (but not decisive, because domestic choices for both groups of countries are more crucial) amounts of help can be given to a reasonably large number of developing countries; at a maximum, perhaps major steps might be taken toward the creation of a more stable and beneficial North-South order. All of this, however, rests on the presumption that the United States has set clear priorities among the varied goals it pursues in and toward the Third World. This issue is the last that I want to examine in this section.

Much has been made of the fact that the United States pursues multiple and occasionally conflicting goals in its Third World policies. Rapid growth, the reduction of poverty, increased equality, the improvement of human rights, integration into the international system, democratic and stable political systems, and support in the East-West conflict have all, at one time or another, seemed to receive the highest priority. This is neither surprising nor necessarily contradictory, as all are reasonable goals, and shifting interpretations of needs and possibilities of more than a hundred diverse countries mean that multiple goals are imperative. Confusion results primarily from the tendency to treat what are or should be discrete policies toward particular groups of developing countries as if they were universally applicable, from a failure to indicate the rationale for shifts in priorities, or from ambiguities about the relationship between different goals (as with basic human needs and rapid growth). Still, despite these real or potential confusions, it could well be argued that a number of more general — essentially liberal — goals have provided a large element of consistency and coherence in U.S. Third World policies.

Liberal policy toward the Third World obviously reflected U.S. history and values, but it was also closely related to Cold War considerations, that is, to a particular perception of U.S. global interests in the East-West struggle. Three underlying assumptions were critical: The United States had a general interest in an open system that protected and reflected its values and interests; the developing countries would be integrated into that system by moderate and gradualist means and by the construction of new institutions and patterns of cooperation; and Soviet aggression (direct and "indirect"), which might undermine the previous assumptions, would be resisted, not so much to collect allies and dependents, although that sometimes resulted, as to deny the Soviets any extension of territorial control.[9] Foreign aid and other forms of support were perceived as transitory, as necessary catalysts in the early stages of development, but as unnecessary once "self-sustaining" growth began. In sum, as a recent report has noted, "progress with stability has always been the basic goal of U.S. foreign policy."[10] Presumably both progress and stability would encourage, and in turn be encouraged by, the emergence of democratic political institutions.

At the height of the Cold War, East-West competition for the allegiance of the South was something of a substitute for direct East-West conflict, which was clearly too dangerous in an era of nuclear power.[11] At the same time, the developing countries were not very important to the United States in economic terms. In the long run, as liberal doctrine argued, growth and development might create major new markets in the Third World, but in the short run what happened to the developing countries was perceived primarily as a residual of the Cold War — either in the direct sense of denial to the Soviet Union or in the indirect sense of the alleged superiority of our

economic doctrines or political institutions.[12] Moreover, relatively limited
experience with the problems of development and underdevelopment
facilitated excessive optimism about the reliability of extrapolations from
Western experience, about the inevitability of economic progress, and
about the likelihood of the emergence of stable, democratic political
systems. Recent events, however, have undermined all these beliefs. The
United States may still desire stability and progress, but the world in which
they must be pursued, and the means available to do so, have changed
markedly.

The increasing salience of the North-South axis of concern does not
mean that East-West conflicts are less important, but it does mean that
events in the South can no longer be perceived as a residual of the "relationship of major tension." Events in the South now intersect directly and
immediately with Northern interests, not only in the traditional domain of
foreign policy (both political and economic) but also in domestic policy.
One hardly needs to rehearse the growing importance of trade with the
South and its implications for many domestic industries, the importance of
agricultural exports in the balance of payments, the dangers and opportunities of increased lending by commercial banks to a number of developing countries, the significance of the control of potentially scarce resources
by the South, or the effects of conditions in the South on OPEC's production and pricing policies—among other things.

All of these developments have the potential of increasing North-South
(not to say North-North and South-South) conflict, but they can also
sharply increase domestic difficulties in the North if they generate rising
protectionism, the development of unnecessary domestic capacity, or the use
of more costly domestic resources. Furthermore, a growing concern for
economic security, perhaps inevitable in so uncertain an environment, has
made questions of access to resources and the protection of foreign investment increasingly relevant. Even the apparent revival of Cold War competition in the South cannot merely repeat earlier patterns of engagement:
The stakes are different, the potential for disunity within the Western coalition is much higher, the reactions of the South are much more consequential, and the time horizons are very different. In short, if the Cold War is
revived in the South, U.S. objectives will no longer be merely denial to the
East and indication of the superiority of our institutions.

What this means is that there has been a major shift in the structure of
the goals that the United States pursues in the South. It is still concerned
with what Arnold Wolfers called "milieu" goals—the creation of a systemic
environment that protects and encourages its values and interests—but it is
now also concerned with "possession" goals—the achievement of specific,
tangible national interests.[13] This raises a very crucial strategic question

about whether or how the United States can achieve these specific goals. Put differently, how important will the North-South focus be if specific U.S. goals relate primarily to individual developing countries or small groups of developing countries? And can the United States achieve its specific goals if it does not also cooperate in the pursuit of broader systemic goals?

There are no simple answers to such questions, but, as we shall see in the discussion of policy options, some clear choices will nonetheless be imperative. These choices may require some adjustment of the liberal canon, not so much in goals (which are hardly more than com-monplaces—stability and progress in an open system), as in assumptions about how to pursue such goals in an environment that may encourage in-wardly oriented policies, that may make gradual change both difficult and insufficient, and that may require massive and continuing resource transfers to stabilize.[14] As it is improbable that a domestic consensus on these matters is likely to emerge quickly, if at all, one conclusion is that the United States will be required to deal with North-South issues in the 1980s without the doctrinal support and elite consensus that prevailed throughout most of the (pre-Vietnam) Cold War years.[15]

None of the issues that I have been discussing provide much ground for optimism about the future of North-South relations. At the same time, it would be a mistake to be completely pessimistic, not only because all of the judgments made are eminently challengeable, but also because there are policy alternatives open to the United States and the other developed coun-tries that might avert some of the worst outcomes or at least diminish their effects. The preceding discussion has not been designed to produce one or several forecasts of the future of North-South relations, but rather to discuss a number of separate issues that should play some role in all forecasts. Therefore, before discussing specific policy alternatives, I should like in the next section to discuss several scenarios that relate the preceding analysis to other factors that will be important in the North-South arena. I should emphasize that my scenarios are not meant to provide a complete picture of different worlds, but rather to be suggestive of the spectrum of policy choices.

Scenarios: A Range of Possibilities

A simple extrapolation of existing trends and prevailing patterns of behavior generates very discouraging, if not disastrous, outcomes. Presumably at some point along the way governments will be sufficiently energized to take action to avert a major crisis or diminish its effects. But such actions in a deteriorating environment might be narrowly self-interested and protective, thus exacerbating the outcomes or even guaranteeing the worst results. However, awareness of the possibility, perhaps as a result of historical memories of the 1930s, might induce a search for more cooperative actions, either regional or global. This formulation of the alternatives seems inherently plausible, but the obvious point that all scenarios are not more than oversimplified analytical constructs should be emphasized. Thus in practice the most likely outcome might well be a confused and incoherent mixture of elements from all the scenarios. In this sense, one major purpose of designing scenarios that indicate some of the costs and consequences of particular patterns of action is to attempt to avert or diminish the dangers of drift and of "choosing by not choosing."

All of the scenarios that I shall discuss have an inherently pessimistic bias. They take seriously the judgments that emerged from Chapters 3, 4, and 5: Import growth rates for food and energy will continue to increase in most developing countries, debt problems wi'' mount, and available finance will be used primarily to stay afloat and not for long-term investment needs. More generally, the scenarios presume that we shall have to deal with the consequences of generally slower growth rates of both GNP and world trade. At best, growth rates might more or less match the rates achieved from 1960 to 1973, but the more likely general pattern would see a minority of developing countries doing well (matching or even exceeding historic rates) and the rest doing very badly.

One might justify concentration on slow-growth scenarios by noting that the few (short-term) forecasts of a return to rapid growth are entirely normative or are based on assumptions about the cyclical or aberrational origins of present difficulties that seem incorrect or oversimplified.[16] Alternatively, one might argue that high-growth scenarios, if they were feasible, do not require extended comment: More rapid growth might diminish problems sufficiently so that traditional patterns of behavior (ad hoc incrementalism) would suffice. But this, too, oversimplifies. A return to rapid growth by the developing countries, in the absence of serious efforts at income distribution, would probably lead to unmanageable balance of payments deficits. From this perspective, basic human needs, redistribution, and slower growth might be a more manageable development strategy, reducing capital and resource intensities, *if* accepted by ruling elites.[17] Nevertheless, although the developing countries have adjustment problems with either rapid or slow growth rates, external support is much more likely if growth resumes. But at this time, what seems most probable is slower growth *plus* inappropriate development strategies—and thus pessimism.

Scenario 1: Permanent Low-Level Crisis

The notion that a continuation of present trends will lead to a systemic crisis is probably correct, but it is not sufficiently differentiated. All will suffer, but some will suffer much less than others. This fact will make cooperation difficult, as doubts about the possibility of agreement and divergent calculations of self-interest will sharply limit what can be achieved. Slow growth, an incremental policy style in the North, and un-negotiable demands for massive and rapid change by the South suggest a policy stalemate, growing conflict as needs continue to rise, and intermittent and perhaps partially successful efforts to prevent a total systemic breakdown.

Slower growth in the world economy will be especially costly to countries that are heavily dependent on trade. Particularly hard-hit will be Japan, some of the smaller European countries, OPEC, and the NICs. The attempt to maintain existing markets and to acquire new ones may cause especially bitter conflict between Japan and Europe, probably generating increased restrictions on market access and accelerating Japan's movement toward the Third World. OPEC and the NICs will be caught between two worlds, but will probably resist efforts to split away from the rest of the Third World, unless they (especially the NICs) are also gradually excluded from some key Third World markets. The rest of the South will be forced to retrench, cutting back long-term investment and concentrating on meeting short-term consumption needs. This implies a distorted form of a basic needs strategy, in which the emphasis is on immediate relief of poverty, not on increasing equality and the redistribution of wealth. The latter would require more rapid growth and more generosity by the developed countries. Collective self-reliance will remain essentially rhetorical, if primarily because so much effort must be expended on paying for food, energy, and capital imports from the developed countries and OPEC. Instability as a result of rising domestic discontent will be very prevalent.

Policy measures at the international level will be designed primarily to limit and contain the existing crisis and a number of potential emergencies (especially in the banking system). These measures are likely to be at least partially successful, particularly in terms of dealing with deficits induced by the oil price explosion. Joint interests in averting a massive debt crisis are sufficiently clear to induce an important degree of cooperation. This will require more involvement by the IMF, because of the growing strains on the private banking system, and a struggle over the terms of conditionality (the measures governments must take to gain access to the fund's resources) is likely to remain a basic theme of the decade. But efforts to diminish the long-term problems of the developing countries—to prevent the short-term crisis from becoming permanent—will remain fragmentary and incomplete. This crisis of things not done, which has already begun, may be the most important North-South issue, but it may also be lost to sight amid intense efforts to deal with the immediate crisis. Coherent development policies will become even more difficult to devise, as many developing countries will lack the resources either to carry out existing strategies or to invest in new strategies. Attempts to ameliorate this problem in a deteriorating environment are not likely to be facilitated by the continued propensity of the developing countries to demand massive, automatic, and unsupervised transfers of resources.

On trading issues, agreement not to move backward may be the most that can be achieved. "Standstill" agreements and "fair weather" rules may become the norm, but resorts to "selectivity", "organized free trade," and liberalized safeguard clauses may become more common. Adjustment mechanisms may be improved enough to prevent a full retreat from an open trading system, but continuing conflicts over whether to adjust domestic economies to the growing interdependence of the world economy or to adjust the international economy (by nationally determined restrictions) to domestic pressures will persist. Clear resolution of this conflict is unlikely in a period of slow growth, and the growing need for international coordination of national policy targets is likely to generate only loose forms of consultation. A partially closed system with selective protectionism is also likely to accelerate the trend toward increased government involvement in the determination of trading patterns.

What will emerge is a system much like the present system, but with more frequent crises and a more rapid movement toward the dominance of short-term, narrowly nationalist responses. With luck, ad hoc and partial responses may succeed in warding off total breakdown. There is so much awareness of the dangers of present tendencies and of the costs of breakdown that the willingness to improvise stopgap measures will be widely prevalent in each crisis, but the inability to sacrifice short-term gains and the belief that wider agreements are improbable (or unstable) will mean that the stopgap measure reflects the limits of the possible. Coalitions on both sides will probably remain together, but more formalistically than substantively: The cracks within will barely be papered over. The poorest developing countries will continue to be subsistence states, perhaps receiving emergency aid as necessary, but with the prospects of growth and development set back for decades. The North-South Dialogue may become increasingly bitter and increasingly inconsequential. But the question of fairness implicit in the disappearance of the growth "bonus" will arise in acute form.

In short, this is a system that may stumble along, praying for a *deus ex machina*, avoiding a massive crisis for the rich, but assuring one for the poor.[18] Mending and managing will be the basic themes: mending small tears as they occur and managing the crises that develop. This has a familiar, but not a reassuring, sound. Business as usual may neither resolve nor even diminish problems that are unique, profound, and interdependent.[19] The key question is whether fear of breakdown is sufficiently strong to overcome the obstacles to wider agreement or whether the obstacles are sufficiently strong so that even maintaining the status quo becomes problematic.

Scenario 2: Disintegration and Disorder

A complete breakdown of the international economic system is possible, but not probable. The same is true for a full breakdown of the North-South relationship. Nevertheless, the prospects for the latter are not as impossible or improbable as the prospects for the former. The fail-safe mechanisms, the insurance schemes, and the margins of error that the developed countries (individually and jointly) have devised or possess may suffice to maintain a precarious stability; they may be insufficient for poor countries that are already on the edge of disaster and that are only residual concerns of existing safety nets. But the alternatives to seeking increased support from the North are either so impractical or so long-range that the developing countries may not have much choice in the 1980s except to gamble on the (revived) generosity of the North. The tactics that the developing countries have adopted in the North-South Dialogue do not, however, suggest that they have a realistic sense of what can be gotten or how to do it.

There are many ways that the North-South framework could disintegrate. For purposes of illustration, I will briefly note two possibilities. If economic conditions continue to deteriorate and the levels of external aid continue to stagnate, a debt crisis will become increasingly likely. At some point, probably when inward flows sink below outward flows, default will look more and more reasonable. Inhibitions created by the notion that default will end the prospect of future resource transfers or foreign investment will be less convincing if aid and investment levels have already fallen (or have not risen). The major debtors are, of course, the advanced developing countries, which is to say, the countries likely to lose most from a North-South breakdown.

But at the same time, if the developed countries cut aid and investment and the developing countries make an effort to establish their own trading system (via a preference arrangement), the advanced developing countries might be induced to turn away from the North. They might be especially receptive because they would earn by far the largest share of an increasing amount of South-South trade—not enough to compensate for lost trading opportunities with the developed countries, but perhaps enough to induce separation if the wider trading opportunities are being denied. One should also note that, as the non-OPEC developing countries are forced to retrench and to cut back imports, and indeed to adopt more inwardly oriented development strategies, the attractiveness of trade with other developing countries will rise (if a payments scheme that avoids dependence on hard currencies can be devised). There will be no other alternatives, and much of what the South will need—except food—can be supplied by other Southern countries, if at some loss in efficiency, variety, and style.[20]

This is a picture of drifting apart, with perhaps a final crisis providing the occasion for formal separation. There are reasons, however, to question the plausibility of this scenario. This is not merely because of the obvious fact that income and production would fall in both North and South, thus presumably generating resistance to a split. More crucially, there would be a transition period of perhaps a decade in which the South would first have to establish the conditions for a viable separation by becoming more dependent on the North for infrastructure, technology, food, and other necessities. This period has not really even begun, except in a few countries, for the South continues to develop an economic structure that presupposes ultimate integration with the international economy, not one that would facilitate increasing degrees of self-reliance. In addition, while OPEC is caught between North and South, and dependent on both in different ways, it is unlikely that more than a few of its members would support separation—and without OPEC support, separation is even more illusory. OPEC would also have to revise rather radically its own notions of optimum development strategies; rapid industrialization and an emphasis on energy-intensive petrochemical exports might not make much sense if Western markets were closed. Finally, the inevitable asymmetries between winners and losers within the Third World that would emerge if the South created its own system might be even more unfair and more difficult to compromise than such asymmetries with the North, because the winners would have relatively fewer resources to buy off the losers and relatively less guilt about earlier patterns of exploitation. In sum, increasingly desperate conditions in the South are more likely to lead to massive pressure on the North than to separation from the North, at least through this decade.

A North-South breakdown might also come from a more dramatic event: invasion of one or more OPEC countries to assure a supply of oil. If such military action resulted from a prior invasion by the Soviet Union (or any other external power), and if the existing government asked for military support, reactions to military intervention would be muted, although the consequences would still be incalculable. But if invasion came simply because oil prices were raised too high and/or domestic conservation and exploitation of indigenous fuels failed to be seriously implemented, disastrous outcomes are highly probable. The other OPEC countries would probably cut supply to balance the short-term gains from invasion (obviously there may be none, if the oil fields are sabotaged), a "sacrifice" made increasingly easy by the levels to which oil prices have already risen. Fear of being the next victim—hardly irrational if current energy policies prevail—would probably generate solidarity not only within OPEC, but also with the rest of the Third World.

Thus invasion, although ostensibly designed to gain time, may not increase oil supplies and will certainly lead to widespread terrorism (oil fields, refineries, tankers, storage depots, etc.). It may also mean the definitive end of the existing world order, either from war or from the creation of bitterly hostile coalitions of the poor and (formerly) rich. Of course, these are speculations, and other outcomes are surely possible, but the record of U.S. military intervention hardly implies that pessimism is out of place. One has the feeling that military action may be tried sooner or later not because anyone (except a few armchair strategists) believes it will accomplish its stated ends, but out of frustration and desperation—domestic failure generating, in an argument usually applied to autocracies, external adventure.

In the last analysis, I do not really believe that either of these possibilities (or others that can be foreseen) is very probable. Nevertheless, the potential for a North-South split is surely there. It has some advocates in both camps, and it will remain at least a minor but persistent theme of this decade. What seems likely to me in these circumstances is not a complete North-South breakdown, but rather a number of partial breakdowns and perhaps a number of individual withdrawals from the existing system by very poor countries (like Burma's attempt, at great cost, in the 1960s).

Scenario 3: The Quest for a Global Bargain

The first two scenarios have concentrated on the consequences of continued commitment to existing policies and patterns of behavior, the first envisaging the maintenance of a very precarious stability, the second envisaging the possible destruction of that stability. The danger of persisting in present patterns is self-evident, for even the "winners" manage only to lose less. Indeed, the primary struggle in both of these scenarios will probably center on attempts, overt and disguised, to shift adjustment costs outside national boundaries. There is thus increasing interest, both in and out of governments, in devising policies that might generate more palatable outcomes. I shall discuss two scenarios that might result from such shifts in policies and patterns of behavior. But I shall do so only very briefly, as I will deal with the problems and prospects of these new approaches in much greater detail in the next section.

The attempt to establish a comprehensive agreement between North and South has been a persistent theme for at least two decades. But the attempt has taken on much more urgency since the oil crisis began in 1973, not only because of the growing desperation of much of the non-OPEC South, but also because of the growing importance of North-South trade. One should also note the potential impact of North-South relationships on the policies of OPEC; even if that impact has been minimal, the potential for greater effect has been widely perceived. In general, the many suggestions for a "global bargain" rest on very similar assumptions: that North and South have many common or mutual interests; that the North will ultimately benefit from greater prosperity in the South; and that the North should transfer sharply increased resources to the South now in order to share in the long-term benefits. Morality and self-interest thus seem to come together to justify a major attempt to restructure the North-South arena.

This formulation of the problem has always foundered on its impracticality. There is no great difficulty in imagining the outlines of a more beneficent future, but the details of how to get there from the present — how to strike a bargain between a large number of countries with many divergent or conflicting interests and different visions of the world in an environment of slow growth — are usually ignored. Or they are dismissed with the ritual incantation that "only the absence of political will prevents agreement." Is there no possibility, then, that the quest for a comprehensive agreement will ever be much more than a harmless intellectual game?

I shall discuss one possibility (or perhaps one variation on a theme) later: the attempt to work up to a different kind of agreement from existing circumstances. But the attempt to move quickly toward the kind of global agreement recently advocated by the Brandt Commission seems possible only under very special conditions (especially if the global reformers continue to ignore the need for a *strategy* of persuasion). If the international system confronts a massive crisis, and if all the alternatives are sufficiently bleak, perhaps all the major actors would be willing to set aside short-run interests (and ideologies) and negotiate a fundamentally restructured system. More than a conventional North-South agreement would be necessary: The Soviet Union and China would probably have to participate. I should emphasize that this presupposes that the crisis has not *already* destroyed the system; if it has, the system may be reconstituted, but not by a comprehensive agreement between North and South.

One must be careful not to dismiss a comprehensive global agreement simply because it seems impracticable. In the best of circumstances, it would take many years to negotiate, but an explicit agreement to set out on this path would have great symbolic significance. Moreover, although the complexities are staggering, the agreement on long-term goals might actually facilitate movement toward immediate, practical agreements among more limited groups of states (which would not have to promise equal benefits to states not involved in the negotiations, if the latter were pursuing their own interests in other negotiations). In effect, one might diminish the hold of the increasingly misleading notion of a North-South dichotomy by reaching broad agreement on goals, but leaving details to be settled by the parties with an interest in the issue. Unfortunately, this kind of agreement may be impossible just because the terms of the North-South debate and the proferred solutions by groups like the Brandt Commission are too biased and oversimplified. Indeed, they may do actual harm by diverting attention from less exciting, but more feasible, alternatives. I shall return to this issue.

Scenario 4: Differentiation, Selectivity, and the "New Influentials"

The Brandt Commission has forecast a disastrous future if present policies are not changed, and it advocates leaping into a first-best world in which all obstacles to progress have been eliminated. But if one believes that the obstacles are far too formidable to be removed by "political will," manifested at a summit of the world's leaders (as the Brandt Commission suggests), then the quest for second-best solutions may not be inappropriate. This is especially true if the quest for a first-best solution to the deficiencies of a second-best world seems likely to fail — and perhaps to lead to a third-best world (the disintegration of the system). Nevertheless, it is worth reemphasizing that the second-best is second-best: It has costs and dangers of its own that need to be calculated. I shall briefly examine a few second-best options in this scenario, but it should be noted that the underlying theme is differentiation, which can take many forms — regional, subregional, or cross-regional. The choice must be made on empirical grounds — what works. What is important in this approach is the intention to concentrate resources and attention on a selected group of developing countries. I should note that differentiation can take relatively benign or relatively malign forms, depending on origins or intentions. I shall return to this issue in the next chapter.

Regionalism, which is a classic second-best option, is not a self-explanatory term.[21] The range of behavior subsumed within it can extend from informal cooperation on particular projects to economic union. One can also envisage regionalism in the Third World with or without the support of the developed countries, dominance by a regional "great power," or continued unity within the Group of 77, among other things. In the present context, however, I mean to refer only to one variation: something roughly corresponding to traditional spheres of interest. This presupposes that tensions within both coalitions have risen, although both continue to function, and that there is movement on both sides to establish or improve special relationships. In addition, these relationships may be more likely and more extensive at the subregional level or with one or more particularly important regional powers, not only because the economic and strategic importance of different countries varies greatly but also because some countries will reject association for a variety of reasons (ideology, other opportunities, etc.).

Regional spheres of interest may become increasingly attractive as conditions deteriorate. As questions of political and economic security become more salient, the effort to cement ties with particular regions may take greater and greater priority. This might also be justified by a simple calculation of economic and political interests as well as by the conviction that resources, power, and knowledge are limited and thus ought to be expended where they can do the most good and not dissipated across a wide canvas. But there are many problems, as we shall see, with a regional approach.

An alternative to the regional approach, or perhaps a variation on it, would combine some elements of regionalism (with Mexico and the Caribbean) with primary concentration on a small number of particularly large or influential developing countries—the "new influentials," as they were called early in the Carter administration. The two approaches, while differing geographically, share an emphasis on selectivity. With resources very scarce, not all developing countries can be helped, and the primary criterion for selection would be self-interest. Only a few developing countries can take action that inflicts great harm on the United States or that has some potential to destabilize the international system. Consequently their needs should take priority in our policies. In this scenario the North-South Dialogue would be sharply downgraded, perhaps kept going primarily for the sake of appearances or for small amounts of help to the least developed countries. And in sharp contrast with the regional focus, concentration on the influentials would clearly work better if all of the major developed countries provided collaborative and cooperative support.

Movement in this direction seems to me already well under way. It may well accelerate in the future, although some amount of ambiguity is inevitable. Even the most important developing countries would be extremely reluctant, if not fearful, to be perceived as abandoning the other developing countries. But there are reasons to doubt that this approach is as realistic as its proponents believe. Still, with some adjustments, it may be the least costly choice, which is not to say that it will not be costly.

These scenarios are useful only if they suggest some consequences of persisting in present patterns of behavior and if they raise questions about the choices before the United States now. The present situation is characterized by drift, uncertainty, and great danger. Insofar as these scenarios have any credibility, the United States might respond by trying to improve the means by which the existing degree of stability is buttressed, it might seek to achieve wide agreement on the fundamentals of a new order, or it might try to construct a partial order with a selected group of particularly important developing countries. Or, as we shall see, it might seek an innovative compromise between different approaches. I turn to these matters in the final chapter.

Notes

1. There is a good, brief discussion of these tactics in Paul Diesing, *Reason in Society: Five Types of Decisions and Their Social Conditions* (Urbana: University of Illinois Press, 1962), pp. 105ff.

2. One interesting discussion of the consequences of a failure of leadership during the world crisis of 1929–1939 can be found in Charles P. Kindleberger, *The World in Depression, 1929–1939* (London: Allen Lane, 1973).

3. The quoted phrase is from Richard Rosecrance, ed., *America as an Ordinary Country — U.S. Foreign Policy and the Future* (Ithaca, N.Y.: Cornell University Press, 1976).

4. For a moderate statement, see Carlos F. Diaz-Alejandro, "Delinking North and South: Unshackled or Unhinged?" in Albert Fishlow et al., *Rich and Poor Nations in the World Economy* (New York: McGraw-Hill, 1978), pp. 87–162.

5. For a broad discussion of this issue, see Robert L. Rothstein, *The Weak in the World of the Strong: The Developing Countries in the International System* (New York: Columbia University Press, 1977).

6. The rapid industrialization policies still favored by many, if not most, developing countries are threatened by rising energy costs, slower growth of the world economy, and increased competition within the South. In any case, this strategy increases inequities within and between developing countries and between North and South. The alternative of collective self-reliance may decrease dependence, but if it leads to technological backwardness and a loss of the potential gains from trade, the cost may be much slower growth and, ultimately, less equity and more dependence. Perhaps incompatible goals are maintained because it is too costly politically (and psychologically) to admit that some desired goals cannot be achieved. But the North-South Dialogue might be improved if it dealt with rather than ignored these issues.

7. *Third World Forum Newsletter,* no. 3 (November 1978):4.

8. As I noted in Chapter 5, the competition might also be quite sharp with the socialist countries — East and South competing for the same access to Northern

markets, credit, and food exports.

9. For one discussion of these assumptions, see Lincoln P. Bloomfield, *In Search of American Foreign Policy — The Humane Use of Power* (New York: Oxford University Press, 1974), pp. 130ff.

10. *Preliminary Report of the Presidential Commission on World Hunger* (Washington, D.C.: Presidential Commission on World Hunger, 1979), p. I-3.

11. For discussion of this issue, see Rothstein, *Weak in the World of the Strong,* pp. 112–130.

12. I do not mean to deny that many companies had a great stake in various developing countries, but rather that — in the aggregate — this was not greatly important to U.S. prosperity.

13. See Arnold Wolfers, *Discord and Collaboration — Essays on International Politics* (Baltimore, Md.: Johns Hopkins University Press, 1962), pp. 67–80.

14. The last point will require adjustment in the view that aid would be necessary only for a reasonably brief period — until growth "takes off." There would also probably be some need to adjust the notion that democratic political regimes will gradually emerge, as instability and rising pressures will probably ensure the dominance of authoritarian regimes. Population pressures alone, in some areas, may create massive problems: The flood of young adults — uneducated, unskilled, unemployed — will crest in the 1980s (reaching 25–33 percent of total world population) and may generate a great deal of revolutionary violence and discontent. For the figures, see Phyllis T. Piotrow, "Population Policies for the 1980s: Meeting the Crest of the Demographic Wave," in George Tapinos and Phyllis T. Piotrow, *Six Billion People — Demographic Dilemmas and World Politics* (New York: McGraw-Hill, 1978), p. 144.

15. Dealing with these issues will be much easier if liberal analysts make a greater effort to deal with the real problems that impede progress instead of imagining a variety of "global bargains" to be achieved by an act of will. Efforts of the latter kind, apparently much admired by the Carter administration in its first six months, are responsible for the conservative critique of liberal policy as "sentimental." The critique seems to me largely justified, which is not to say that the alternative policies of the conservatives are more likely to be effective. In effect, virtually all of the attempts to fit U.S. policy toward the Third World into a single mold seem essentially simplistic; whether it be the radical commitment to socioeconomic revolution, the liberal commitment to food (as the Presidential Commission on World Hunger argues), the liberal-conservative commitment to human rights, or the conservative commitments to the free market and/or anticommunism.

16. There is a sharp critique of the McCracken Report, which was done for the OECD, from this perspective in Robert O. Keohane, "Economics, Inflation, and the Role of the State: Political Implications of the McCracken Report," *World Politics,* Vol. 31, no. 1 (October 1978):108–128.

17. There is a good discussion of the balance of payments issue and the need for new strategies in Joseph J. Stern, "Growth, Redistribution and Resource Use," in Nake M. Kamrany, ed., *International Economic Reform: Issues and Policies* (Washington, D.C.: University Press of America, 1977), pp. 197–244.

18. One analyst has described this state of affairs as "semiorganized anarchy." See Assar Lindbeck, "Economic Dependence and Interdependence in the Industrialized World," in *From Marshall Plan to Global Interdependence: New Challenges for the Industrialized Nations* (Paris: Organisation of Economic Co-operation and Development, 1978), pp. 59–86.

19. In Robert L. Rothstein, *Global Bargaining: UNCTAD and the Quest for a New International Economic Order* (Princeton, N.J.: Princeton University Press, 1979), pp. 14–16, I discussed some of these issues in terms of a "failed incremental system."

20. Obviously a North-South split could take many forms, not all of them implying that the South would band together. For example, one might imagine new alignments emerging around regional "great powers" (Nigeria, Brazil, etc.) or, conversely, the absence of alignments and continuous low-level conflict over resources and territories. Much would also depend on whether the North remained (relatively) united or whether some countries chose to realign with all or parts of the South.

21. This is also true in a technical sense, as the most extensive application of the theory of the second-best has been in relation to customs unions. The elimination of trading restrictions among members of a union may decrease global welfare, primarily by trade diversion; if so (and it is not always so), it is a second-best step justified only by the argument that distortions in the wider trading system cannot be removed.

7
The United States and the Third World in the 1980s: Policy and Choice

Choosing Without Clear Choices

The United States needs a consistent policy toward the Third World that protects its short- and long-term interests within an international environment that may be characterized by instability, the fragmentation of traditional coalitions, and rapid and unpredictable change. Multiple and shifting goals make the establishment of priorities exceptionally difficult. Moreover, a shift in the structure of goals, in that the United States now has major economic interests (petroleum, raw materials, access to markets) in the Third World, and not merely traditional Cold War interests of denial of territory and illustrations of institutional superiority, further complicates the problem of choice. And, of course, so does the reputed or actual decline in U.S. power and influence.[1] Finally, the likelihood of slower growth in the world economy, a difficult struggle with the forces of protectionism, and the continuation of an unstable oil market create additional problems, not only in terms of their immediate effects but also in altering perceptions and expectations about what can or must be done.

These conditions seem inevitably to suggest that stability should be the primary aim of U.S. policy, as only a stable order permits the pursuit of our other goals. Stability cannot be the only goal, and its achievement in a rapidly changing system can never be absolute and unquestioned—a "more or less," not an "either/or" goal—but it cannot be dismissed simply because it has so frequently been used as a disguise for support of right-wing repression. Stability also does not imply the absence or prohibition of change, even major change; rather it implies change that is bound by mutually agreed rules.

The key to stability in any system, but especially a system dominated by uncertainty and fears of instability, must lie in expectations of dependability—keeping arrangements, fulfilling promises, honoring obligations, justifying exceptions by resort to agreed procedures, and applying sanctions against malfeasance. It does not seem possible, however, to establish such expectations among states divided by conflicting interests and divergent views of what should and can be done.² Still, over time a careful series of negotiations that set out new and widely accepted operating rules might permit a degree of progress, as it did with the Soviet Union, even at the height of the Cold War. But within this decade the prospects for movement in this direction are grim. Indeed, although theory and knowledge about stability and instability are in a very rudimentary state, hardly permitting any very confident generalizations in particular cases, one can at least suggest that the variables usually associated with instability seem likely to become increasingly influential in the years ahead.

Stability is thus a very problematic goal. In the circumstances, it seems sensible to begin by emphasizing a few commonplaces that tend to be forgotten in many discussions about the dangers and uncertainties of instability. There are obviously many forms and varieties of instability, but perhaps the key point in terms of U.S. interests is that instability is not always a negative factor, in terms of either U.S. interests or the interests of the affected country. Too many other variables intervene to permit the simple generalization that instability is always deleterious or that it must or can be resisted. The United States needs to recognize that it is rarely stability or instability per se that is of concern to it, but rather whether the degree of change that is occurring (or not occurring) seems likely to work against perceived U.S. policy interests in particular countries. And to come to some judgments about this issue the United States needs to ask a prior question about the goals it is seeking to pursue. And here, of course, the shift in U.S. goals in much of the Third World—away from simple anti-communism and toward increased concern with economic performance—adds a significant complication to any assessment of the importance of, and the reaction to, likely degrees of instability. A few of these complications are worth noting, even if they cannot be resolved.

One major complication is illustrated by a familiar question: Is stability impossible without development or is development impossible without stability? Obviously stability by itself does not guarantee development; it may be and has been used in some cases as an excuse for a repressive defense of the status quo. As development itself can be a very destabilizing process, the fear of moving beyond stability to a genuine development program may be very strong among governing elites who lack great power, who cannot become a "loyal opposition" if defeated, and who have (or may be able to manufacture) significant internal and external enemies. By the same token, of course, the failure to seek development may be equally destabilizing, as well as leading to a degree of international ostracism, although perhaps not a sufficient degree (as with the reluctance to condemn Idi Amin or the "Emperor" Bokassa).

Unfortunately, the stability-development relationship is too complex and too much affected by the play of situational factors to permit any simple generalization, except perhaps for the commonplace that each case will have to be judged on its merits. Still, if we set aside the conceptual debate on which must come first and how we can know, and if for practical purposes we begin with things as they are, it seems clear that an important degree of stability must be achieved by any regime—left, right, or center—if development is to proceed. This is necessary but not sufficient; subsequent judgments must be made about a regime's commitment to development and perhaps about how to balance movements toward progress and maintenance of stability.

Put another way, the issue is not merely stability, but stability for whose benefit? In the best of all possible worlds the United States might hope for a reasonably clear choice between "good" stability (a regime that offers political support and also seeks genuinely equitable development for its citizens) and "bad" stability (a regime that is hostile or that is anti-communist but also corrupt and/or indifferent to equitable development). Unfortunately, the United States may not have the luxury of such clear choices; rising internal and external pressures may mean that repression combined with a fitful and erratic commitment to development could become the norm. And, of course, the same conditions may very well undermine any stability at all. This might appear to suggest that the United States ought to limit its commitments to any regime or at least restrict its commitments to those regimes that are genuinely important to U.S. interests and seem to have some prospect of survival. But in practical terms these judgments will be very difficult to make and implement, not only because of the impact of earlier commitments (and present needs) but also because they cannot be made with any degree of confidence (as policymakers will be forced to act on partial insights and rough and ready rules of thumb). These difficulties are only part of the problem; one must also raise questions about the relationship between systemic stability and the stability of particular countries.

The achievement of stability, as a prerequisite for the pursuit of other goals, may be undermined by adverse external developments; but even if stability can be maintained, this does not guarantee the achievement of other U.S. goals in the Third World or in individual developing countries. On the one hand, the United States does not have the power to impose stability (except perhaps in a limited number of individual cases), at least not at a cost that seems bearable or appropriate in economic, political, and moral terms. And in many cases, the developing countries themselves lack the power or resources to defeat opponents decisively or to buy them off; arms spending may go up, sometimes at great cost to development programs, but the result may be no more than stalemate, a transitory truce, and continually festering disputes. On the other hand, where stability exists in particular countries, ensuring effective performance and a friendly response by weak, poor, and sometimes hostile governments may be beyond the means of the United States. It may be able to bolster a threatened government in some cases, and it may be able to help governments genuinely committed to development, but there is no single policy or combination of policies that can be automatically applied across the board to assure both stability and effective performance. The United States simply cannot control—although it may be able to influence—the internal decisions and the external trends that are likely to affect the capacity and the willingness of developing-country governments to cooperate in pursuit of goals that parallel its own.

This does not mean that a coherent policy is impossible or that none of the goals of the United States can be achieved, but it does mean at the least that expectations of instability and unreliability must be built into policy calculations. Perhaps one should begin by recognizing a distinction between fostering stability in particular countries and in the international system at large. The former requires a sense of priorities in two areas, the first requiring a short-run distinction between countries whose instability might directly threaten U.S. interests and those that do not (Saudi Arabia and Mexico, say, versus Chad and Sri Lanka), and the second requiring more effort to develop an integrated policy toward the crucial countries (so that, say, arms policy, human rights policy, trade policy, and the development policy are not treated as isolated fragments). Still, while U.S. short-run interests (political, strategic, economic) in the stability of a few developing countries are substantial, there is no sure guidance for effective policy: Which policy or combination of policies is most likely to succeed is unclear.

Systemic stability is a broader, looser, and more long-range goal, but it must be sought. Not only will it affect the behavior of the more important developing countries, it will also have a decisive impact on the ability of the United States to achieve its other foreign policy goals toward the Third World and toward the international order itself. This will probably require a much more favorable response to many Third World demands, although it cannot be argued that more generous policies in particular areas (trade, aid, debt, institutional reform, etc.) will necessarily have a beneficial impact on short-term stability or perhaps even long-term stability, as too many factors are at work to permit more generous policies to be decisive by themselves. One can only argue that in the long run it is at least plausible to work on the assumption that more generous policies might strengthen systemic stability and that this in turn might strengthen stability in particular countries. But the ambiguities and uncertainties are unavoidable. This suggests at least the need to give a fair hearing to policies that insist either that much more needs to be done to foster systemic stability or that concentration on stability in the key countries is all that needs to or can be done.

Another point about the relationship between stability in particular countries and systemic stability may be worth noting at this time, if only because it intersects so forcefully with domestic discussions of Third World policy in the United States. I should emphasize that instability and revolution in the Cuban or Chinese style are hardly equivalent. A great deal of instability in the Third World seems inevitable, but it is very unlikely that this will generate a series of "Cubas," which is to say a series of revolutions that directly threaten U.S. interests and that are sufficiently contagious or exportable to begin to undermine systemic stability. Revolutionary success of the Cuban or Chinese variety seems to require a dedicated elite, the acceptance of an austere development strategy by both elites and masses, and the absence of substantial military resistance or middle-class opposition (note the safety valve provided by the emigration of Cubans to the United States and Chinese to Taiwan). At any rate, while the conditions for success can be endlessly debated, it does not seem very probable that many developing countries will fulfill the necessary conditions. Instability may be followed by revolutionary rhetoric but not by very much revolution. There is no need to panic every time a corrupt and repressive regime is overthrown by "revolutionaries." Indeed, if economic conditions continue to deteriorate, the new regime may be forced not only into austerity but also into a growing recognition of the need for whatever external support can be obtained.

A more relaxed posture toward the assertion of radical intentions by new regimes may also be justified by other factors. Most radical governments are likely to be forced into moderation by the pressures of dealing with massive internal and external problems (and perhaps by the inefficiency of some "radical" solutions), and U.S. interests are not greatly implicated in the majority of Third World countries. There are undoubtedly a few exceptions to this in terms of both strategic and economic interests, but generally the case for noninvolvement in turmoil seems strong. This also suggests that the search for a "perfect" formula to deal with cases of instability—whether to support the "center," to ally with the forces of change, or to support the ostensible defenders of stability on the right—probably ought to be abandoned. No formula can effectively capture all the forces at work or overcome our ignorance about how to control the process of change. The contention that the United States ought to abandon support for regimes that seem likely to be overthrown, because it has interests in particular countries, not particular regimes, is also an inherently ambiguous formula. It is difficult to tell who and when to abandon, as the existence of particular regimes is not irrelevant to the question of whether the United States can protect its interests in particular countries, and enunciation of such a policy might in itself have certain negative effects on patterns of behavior in both the North-South and the East-West dimensions. Still, to the degree that this approach reflects U.S. inability to do much at an acceptable cost about most cases of instability and to the degree that it suggests the need to question where genuine interests really exist, it is a step in the right direction.

Given the vast uncertainties, perhaps the best formula (or rule of thumb), except in the few cases where real and immediate interests are engaged, is nonintervention (or sharply diminished support for regimes that promise, at best, "bad" stability) combined with an effort to create a systemic framework that seems likely to encourage long-term stability. And certainly, even where real interests are at stake, military commitments (especially, of course, commitments to engage U.S. forces directly) should be sharply limited to the case of direct external aggression. The very few instances in which this constraint might have to be reconsidered (for example, Saudi Arabia) hardly invalidate the general point.

The quest for stability on either or both the domestic and the international levels is never likely to be more than a partial success. At the same time, the United States and the other developed countries are becoming relatively more dependent on the developing countries for resources, for markets, and for cooperation in the creation of a particular kind of international system. There have been a variety of responses to increasing dependency, ranging from the denial of dependence to advocacy of military takeovers, the "new isolationism," and the acceptance of one or another "grand design" for a new international order. As we shall see, more sensible (or at least feasible) responses may be available. It also seems clear, however, that some short-run U.S. responses to dependence, which may be justified by the dangerous international environment and by rising insecurities, could create conflicts with long-run U.S. goals and policies. We need to consider this issue before proceeding, if only because it should have some influence on the policymaking process.

There are a number of short-term measures that can diminish the dangers of dependence. Potential suppliers can be diversified, emergency stockpiles can be created, investment can be directed to relatively safe countries, and conservation and the exploitation of domestic resources can be accelerated. Also, support can be directed primarily to the countries where U.S. economic interests lie, thus (presumably) increasing the chances for stability. These are familiar, if costly and inefficient, policies. But the greatest danger is that implementation of such protective short-term policies may erode U.S. ability to develop effective long-term policies toward the developing countries. Put differently, pursuit of such goals may reduce the ability of the United States to establish an open and progressive international economic order, which has been the country's declared aim, but it may not erode U.S. ability to establish a more closed, selective international economic order.

Long-term goals frequently seem virtually meaningless. At a sufficient level of generality, there is probably widespread agreement that the United States seeks a stable, progressive system that protects its values and interests, that integrates the developing countries into the system on terms that are fair and beneficial to both sides, and that rests on a normative consensus about principles and patterns of behavior. But it is never very clear what relationship there is between such goals and specific, short-term actions, and there is frequent cynicism that the goals are used primarily to rationalize actions taken on more narrow grounds of self-interest. Still, the positing of long-term goals is necessary, if only to prevent drift and to provide guidance for short-term decisions; the potential for dishonesty is certainly present, but no more dangerous than the potential inconsistencies implicit in a lack of agreed directions.

If we assume that long-term stability requires a progressive system (one that aims at openness, but that grants special concessions to developing countries to compensate for existing handicaps), and if we believe that this kind of system can only be created by moderate or conservative steps, we can perhaps foresee the difficulties that might be created by short-run U.S. policies. The protective policies already noted may succeed in creating some stability in one part of the system, but at the cost of exacerbating instability in other parts, thus generating an increasingly closed system and an increasing demand for radical measures of relief. If the two parts of the system can be kept isolated, this may protect short-term U.S. interests; if they cannot, the United States will face increasing difficulty in achieving either its short-term or its long-term goals. What may result is not stability in a progressive system established and maintained by incremental steps, but instability in a closed system maintained by increasingly radical means, such as military force, special deals, or the export of domestic problems.

There are no solutions for these conflicts between short-term and long-term interests—they are always present, although in shifting patterns—but there are better or worse approximations. It is useful to emphasize a truism: Short-term U.S. actions will have a significant influence on the kind of international system that emerges from the present chaos; they are actions, whether this is intended or not, that have more than one layer of significance. This remains true despite the relative decline in U.S. power and influence; the country's leadership role is now much more difficult, but not less imperative. I note these matters here primarily to indicate that in the discussion of policy options that follows I shall make some effort, where possible, to indicate not only long-run consequences, but also short-run choices that might inflict less damage on the long-run goals that the United States seeks. Put differently, in the short run it needs to take actions that protect its interests and that help to stabilize the existing system; but as these actions will not suffice in the long-run and may perpetuate and exacerbate the present crisis, the United States needs a clearer sense of the kind of international system that it wants to emerge and of the kind of short-run actions that protect its interests but do not foreclose movement toward desired goals.

Policy as a Holding Action

The current policy orientation of the United States toward the Third World can be sharply criticized, but the difficulty of devising viable alternatives and a clearer understanding of the obstacles to reform suggest that merely continuing and sustaining existing policy responses should not be summarily dismissed. The emphasis of U.S. policy has been on short-run measures to stabilize the system and to contain or limit the effects of a number of potential breakdowns. The "standstill" agreement within the OECD to prevent backsliding into a trade war is illustrative; so too are a number of agreements about behavior in the event of a financial crisis.

In more direct relation to Third World demands and needs, responses have been limited and incremental: promises of more aid (which have not been fulfilled), marginal concessions in the multilateral trade negotiations (MTNs), some movement on some kind of common fund, and mostly cosmetics elsewhere (for example, the science and technology issue, shipping, and institutional reform). There has also been extensive discussion of various means of assuring the financing of oil deficits, although the outcome (and the role of the IMF) remains uncertain. Within the North-South Dialogue itself, the emphasis has been primarily reactive and defensive. In effect, the main focus of Third World policies, apart from the Middle East and Southern Africa, has been on OPEC and a number of key bilateral relationships.[3] There has been no coherent effort to develop an effective policy toward the long-term problems of the developing countries; at best, the United States has sought means to manage crises if they emerge but has only vaguely and intermittently discussed measures to avert crises. Taken together, these measures may limit damage in the short run, but they seem to rest on prayer (for an imminent return to economic health and to the growth rates of the 1960s) for the long run. What more can be done? This is not an unreasonable response. Public and congressional support for foreign aid is hardly likely to increase suddenly or substantially. There is also, as I have argued in Chapters 1 and 6, great uncertainty about the best policy choices in a number of areas, thus suggesting the apparent wisdom of incremental and limited policy steps. And what the United States can do by itself is sharply limited, not only by the need to reach agreement with its allies, but also by the difficulty of negotiating with the Group of 77. In the latter case, although there has finally been some recognition by the Group of 77 leadership that demands for immediate global restructuring and massive transfers of resources are unrealistic, the need to maintain unity and to adjust inflated expectations to reality have still impeded the negotiating process. The disastrous UNIDO Conference in New Delhi is illustrative; it ended in failure because the Group of 77 would not budge from a demand for a $300 billion fund entirely under the control of the recipients. Thus the limited gains that might be possible if both sides negotiated pragmatically have been spurned, at least by the leadership of the Group of 77 (as distinct from a number of governments, who are more concerned about real benefits).

There are, however, two major problems with this policy orientation. In the first place, U.S. rhetoric frequently promises more than it can deliver. The United States contributes to one of the cardinal sins in this system: the dangerous inflation of expectations that it can neither satisfy nor control. This is far from a trivial concern because it encourages the tendency among the developing countries to rely on external salvation and to delay difficult but necessary domestic adjustments. If the United States is to continue to pursue an essentially incremental policy, it needs to be much more modest in what it promises and what it expects. Periodic outbursts of enthusiasm ("This is the year of the Third World," as one official intoned to me a few weeks before the Shah fell) need to be restrained, and the United States must instead emphasize that external support is not likely to be greatly increased and that development will be largely a function of self-help.

The other problem with an incremental, ad hoc approach to policy is that it is likely to work well through this decade only with great good luck. Problems tend to accumulate in an incremental system, especially for the poor who lack the resources to be effective participants in the game. This is especially true if growth slows, for then the system falters; there are no funds to buy off the poor or to raise their income levels. In the present context, the key point is that most of the non-OPEC developing countries lack the resources to deal with anything but survival matters, which means that their difficulties will grow over time and their demands on the system will escalate. The conjunction of rising food and energy imports, insufficient investment to increase domestic agricultural productivity and the exploitation of indigenous energy resources, stagnant aid commitments, and diminishing opportunities for trade will generate frequent crises that strain managerial capabilities. In addition, patterns of behavior and expectations of breakdown that make the process of adjustment progressively more difficult will be encouraged. The United States may be able to protect some of its short-term interests reasonably well, even in this kind of system, but the desire to establish a stable, open international system that reflects its values will be a major casualty. A drift to closed and hostile blocs may accelerate. In sum, policy as a holding action does not suffice: Not enough holds when the environment of decision is in flux.

The dangers of relying on an ad hoc, incremental policy approach and on crisis management should be apparent, especially in a period of slow growth, increased insecurity, and rapidly declining confidence in the ability of conventional doctrines to produce anticipated or acceptable outcomes. External critics, seeing the "whole problem" and free to put sufficient weight on long-term consequences, have an easy target to attack. But U.S. policymakers, even if they agree with the diagnosis of the problem, must play with the cards in their hands—a public demanding quick results, a recalcitrant and divided Congress, allies pursuing their own interests, and developing countries intent on establishing "developmental responsiveness" as the primary decision rule for the international system. Taking what can be gotten, on the assumption that something is better than nothing—that is, incrementalism—seems the only feasible alternative.

This *may* underestimate the willingness to change, to accept bolder initiatives, that may now be *somewhat* more prevalent. But if we assume for the moment that incrementalism reflects the limits of the possible, are there policy measures that at least keep open the possibility of more cooperative outcomes, or that foreclose the least number of options? Incrementalism within the context of systemic deterioration can lead much too easily to a systemic breakdown; measures that attempt to avert this by indicating delay, not disavowal, of long-term goals and that emphasize joint (and prior) attempts to contain crises may thus be useful both practically and symbolically. One could also argue that the goal in this context is to prevent slipping from the first scenario (permanent, low-level crisis) to the second (disintegration and disorder) by emphasizing measures that are relatively more concerned with systemic issues and relatively less concerned with immediate national interests.

There is great difficulty in finding such measures in an incremental system. Incremental decisions are by their very nature transitory and experimental. If they do not work or if the configuration of forces supporting a particular decision alters, a new incremental decision supersedes the old. This pattern, which has a sophisticated justification in a universe of limited knowledge and capacities, nevertheless means that each decision is attended with an additional element of uncertainty. The significance of this in the present context is that it is difficult to make concessions to the developing countries (in addition to those implicit in simply maintaining existing policies) that are certain, that can be taken for granted in their own policymaking decisions. This is one reason why the developing countries have been so insistent on automatic resource transfers.

Some marginal improvements in present trade policies might be possible. The panoply of measures by which the developed countries seek to protect their own industries—safeguards, selectivity, "voluntary export restraints"—probably cannot be eliminated. But they are distortions of the principles that the developed countries ostensibly seek to implement, and thus they undermine expectations (and the reality) of fair treatment. Perhaps the most that can be achieved would be an agreement to limit the effect of such measures by setting more rigorous conditions for their use and more specific time limits on their existence. In addition, as the danger of backsliding is evident, perhaps a "standstill" agreement with the developing countries might be considered. These actions would not be very costly to the developed countries, and they may—barely—be politically negotiable; they also provide a critical piece of evidence to the developing countries that the developed countries do not intend to turn completely away.

A second area in which a degree of progress might be possible concerns the system's emergency relief mechanisms. These are necessary on both humanitarian and practical grounds, as a scramble for supplies (and plans) during a crisis is costly and inefficient. Because the United States is usually least affected by such crises, the sense of urgency in negotiating emergency systems is limited and the dominance of short-run political considerations (e.g., the voting power of wheat growers) is strong. But it makes sense to treat these matters more seriously, particularly as the insecurities of developing-country governments need to be allayed as much as possible. The United States should put pressure on its allies and on the developing countries to reach agreement on a viable food emergency stock, and it might begin to think about an agreement with OPEC to guarantee a fair share of available oil supplies to the non-oil LDCs if another supply shortfall occurs.

The United States should also reconsider its policies in the North-South Dialogue. The incremental policy approach implies a low profile and subdued rhetoric in the Dialogue, but this does not mean that the Dialogue should or can be treated cynically or indifferently. The United States needs to think of the Dialogue as a potential communications network that has gone awry. But if the Dialogue could be improved, an outcome that is not entirely in U.S. hands, its role in affecting the tone and climate of the system in a joint learning process, and in setting the system's norms, could be important. Whether the United States can achieve or approximate these ends in current circumstances is unclear.

The United States has tried to treat proposals on their merits in the past and it should continue to do so, even though merit is not the only issue at stake. But it needs to go beyond this, for merely reacting to proposals developed by others is insufficient. The United States needs a much larger and much earlier research effort to prepare proposals reflecting mutual interests. It also needs to make a better effort to play the game more effectively in terms of staffing, of consultations with allies, the Group of 77, and the international bureaucracy, and of understanding what can and cannot be reformed.[4] It should also establish more coherence in its own interpretations of proper development strategies. The Carter administration's basic human needs fiasco might have been considerably diminished if it had been aware beforehand of the probable reactions of developing-country elites and if it had thought through the relationship between basic human needs and the demands for a New International Economic Order.

The practical aim of the measures that I have discussed would be to maintain and extend, where possible, the principle of preferential treatment for the developing countries and to provide an additional degree of security by prior planning for emergencies. These are not large or profound measures, which would, in any case, be a contradiction in terms in an incremental system. But they may diminish uncertainty, instability, and fragmentation, they will certainly help some countries to deal with escalating pressures, and they might make it easier to develop a new policy approach if the opportunity (or the necessity) arises. In the last analysis, however, the effort to devise such measures may be more important than the practical effects; evidence of tangible commitment in a difficult environment may alter patterns of expectation about what can and must be done to maintain a viable North-South relationship. Excessive optimism would clearly be out of place, but the risks are great enough to make the effort worthwhile.

Global Restructuring

The most popular and the most enticing alternative to incrementalism is its polar opposite, global restructuring. Efforts to restructure the international order established after World War II, particularly the North-South component of that order, stretch back almost twenty years. These efforts never received much support before the oil crisis of 1973 and its aftermath, perhaps because the assumption that the developing countries would benefit sufficiently from the continuation of rapid growth rates in the world economy still prevailed and because the North-South dimension itself was perceived primarily as a residual of the East-West dimension. In any case, public support for helping the South was never very wide or very deep and tended to trail well behind elite support. Events since 1973, however, have altered the calculus rather fundamentally. There are few fervent apostles of the status quo left; even the great majority of conservative spokesmen accept the need for some kind of structural change. Conflict instead centers on the principles to guide restructuring, the extent and pace of necessary changes, and the means by which such changes can be implemented.

There are differences in detail between the various proposals for restructuring, but there are also important similarities in intent and principles.[5] All seek major changes in the operating rules and the major institutions of the existing system. The proposals emanating from the Third World, such as the disparate demands packaged into the New International Economic Order, generally take "developmental responsiveness" as the primary (or sole) guiding principle for change, but some of the more balanced proposals (such as the Brandt Commission Report) usually combine "developmental responsiveness" and an emphasis on the *long-term* exchange of mutual benefits. In any case, in the short run all seek to alter the order of beneficiaries in the international system by quick implementation of a variety of familiar policies: massively increased resource transfers, development taxes that provide automatic transfers, restructuring of commodity trade (with development support, not efficiency, as the first principle), increased access for Third World exports, controls on multinational corporations, a reordering of the process of technology transfer, and new patterns of voting and access to resources in international institutions. In what follows, my comments will be directed at the general effort to institute a fundamental restructuring of the global system, rather than at any one of the specific proposals or programs, such as the NIEO or the Brandt Commission Report.

Two preliminary points must be made, if only to avoid misunderstandings. Many of the specific proposals within the broader programs or blueprints for global reform are already being actively negotiated (for example, in commodities, trade, and transfer of technology). Controversy relates primarily to details or timing, not to the need for such changes. These negotiations, as I have already argued in Chapters 3, 4, and 5, are of great potential importance, irrespective of what happens with the more extreme and more controversial proposals for global restructuring. But I shall concentrate here on the latter—on demands for global development funds, international development taxes, or for a new range of authority and power and financing for international institutions and central planning mechanisms — because it is these proposals that create controversy and that differentiate the ongoing North-South Dialogue from efforts to transform the international order itself. The second point is that criticism of some of the more extreme proposals for restructuring is in no sense meant as a denial of the need for global reform or for a more significant effort to help the developing countries. What is at issue here is whether the means proposed are likely to be effective and how the process of global reform can or must be pursued in an environment characterized by slow growth, an increasing concern for security, a declining willingness to support foreign aid, and the prevalence of weak governments.

Apart from moral justifications, which are very powerful but have a tendency to diminish in force when most needed, the most persuasive argument for acceptance by the developed countries of demands for global restructuring seems to be self-interest. Short-term sacrifices, from this perspective, would be more than compensated by increased long-term benefits, much as the Marshall Plan more than repaid U.S. resource transfers — although this calculation, of course, was only one part of the Marshall Plan's rationale. Moreover, just as early domestic social welfare programs were primarily designed to ward off dangerous actions by the poor rather than to institute a welfare system based on need or long-term community interests, support for global restructuring might be justified as an attempt to avert or diminish the need for extreme or irrational actions by increasingly desperate countries. The "whole problem" perspective, so familiar in discussions of scientific method, might also lend some support to the very broad focus of most of the restructuring proposals. Dealing with interconnected structural problems by bits and pieces and without a vision of shared ends seems bound to fail; only an approach that is broad enough and deep enough to incorporate all the critical factors will suffice. Finally, what Paul Streeten has called the "William Tell" approach must be noted.[6] Only by aiming high, as William Tell presumably did, would we be assured of a margin of safety and a degree of achievement that at least approximates what needs to be done. These are not irrelevant arguments, even if they are not completely persuasive, but they also avoid or obscure a number of difficulties that any serious argument for global restructuring must confront.

We can begin to understand the difficulties if we ask what conditions must prevail to make the negotiation of global restructuring possible *before* a crisis.?[7] Previous "constitutional" settlements have generally followed a major war and have indeed been victors' settlements: The dominant position of one or two states permitted the establishment of an international order in which maintenance and improvement of the existing status quo and protection against a recurrence of the last war were the essential principles. The problem now is not merely the absence—yet—of an event shocking enough to overcome parochial concerns or even the absence of a powerful and determined leader, but also the need to institute vast changes across a much wider range of activities. Helping the great majority of developing countries will require much more than regulatory rules and a greater degree of surveillance of international economic activity. It will require, at least if we are to take the demands of the developing countries as a rough guide, central direction of much of the international economy, very close coordination of national economic policy targets, and great foresight about future trends in international comparative advantage. One would also need agreement on the principles by which decisions would be made.

Two other conditions might facilitate movement toward a global agreement. The first is a return to rapid growth and to confidence that it will persist. Slow growth creates problems that presumably generate a willingness to contemplate more than normal degrees of change, but slow growth also creates perhaps even more severe obstacles to effectuating change. Rapid growth reverses the balance: It reduces obstacles, but it diminishes the willingness (and perhaps the need) to contemplate change. Still, overcoming obstacles must take precedence in this context, not least because the inevitable asymmetries that emerge between winners and losers from any global agreement require a growth "bonus" to pay off the losers (and to increase the generosity of the winners). I should also note that slower growth in the developed countries makes the gains that might be earned in Third World markets appear increasingly important, perhaps to the extent that efforts to tie up or close off those markets might be encouraged. This obviously diminishes whatever potential there is for global agreements (and facilitates a policy of differentiation, as we shall see in the next section).

A second condition is an agreement on oil production and pricing, as the insecurities and uncertainties generated by an unstable oil market make any wider agreement improbable. The oil agreement might be made part of the wider agreement, as the Brandt Commission suggested, but without it the only kind of restructuring that is possible may emerge from the ruins of a mismanaged crisis. Neither a return to rapid growth nor an oil agreement seems imminent, but these are situational factors that might be altered, however improbable it seems now, during the decade. But other difficulties with the idea of global restructuring may be equally severe, if more controversial.

Agreement on ordering principles is not always necessary to implement major programs of change. For example, the European Economic Community was established without prior agreement on a number of crucial issues of principle: conflicts between Christian Democrats and socialists,

between free-marketeers and planners, and between federalists and con-
federationalists were simply set aside for later resolution. But these were
countries with a shared history and culture, with common problems and a
common enemy. And, of course, they had the strong support of the international system's leading superpower and the beneficial impact of system-
wide rapid economic growth. In effect, they had enough in common and a
sufficiently favorable international environment to gamble that conflict
over principles could be successfully compromised at a later date. None of
these conditions hold in the North-South arena.

Slow growth is particularly important, because it means that conflicts
over who benefits would arise more quickly and would be more difficult to
settle. The commitment of the developing countries to "developmental
responsiveness" as the first principle of a new order would probably become
more insistent as the pressures from stagnant or declining growth rose.
Simultaneously, however, that principle would become even less acceptable
to the developed countries as they would confront the need to fulfill prior
responsibilities to their own citizens and to the stability of the international
system itself. Questions of justice and fairness would arise very quickly, but
it is unlikely that they could be settled, with so many divergent statements
of faith, or bypassed, with so much distrust of ultimate intentions. Moreover, given the continued commitment of the Third World to unified
negotiating positions, possibilities of avoiding conflicts over principles
would become even slimmer. Unity could be maintained only by agreement
on very broad and general principles and by delaying conflicts over detail.

Implementation of many of the developing countries' demands would
also appear to require a vast and unprecedented increase in central direction of the international economy. There is no single term that adequately
describes the degree or kind of centralization that would emerge; each proposal or demand has its own variety (from central guidance or surveillance
to central planning, management, or control). The key point in all cases is a
movement toward increased power and authority for existing or new international institutions to intervene in the international economy and to exercise an increased effect on national decision making. New institutions
would be created with an extraordinary range of powers — to collect international taxes, to intervene in domestic economic decisions, to supervise
industrial redeployment, to control the transfer of technology, to impose
sanctions on violators of legally binding codes of conduct, and to carry out
other tasks to insure the establishment of a new order. Indeed, the demands
in toto are astounding not only in the powers granted to a large number of
new institutions in many areas, but also in the assumption that the governments of the developed countries can or will alter existing laws and
socioeconomic patterns to accommodate the demands of the developing

countries.[8] Nevertheless, from the point of view of the developing countries, central direction or control seems necessary because merely reforming the existing system will not transfer resources quickly enough or
massively enough, will distribute benefits unfairly even within the Third
World, and will only increase opportunities to earn benefits, without
guaranteeing that the benefits will in fact be earned.

These demands have been dismissed by most Western governments as
ventures into fantasy. There is obviously some justification for the
criticisms, but they are not all that needs to be said about the matter. There
is, after all, a growing trend toward increased governmental involvement in
both domestic and international economic activity; what the developing
countries want is novel only in the extent, not the direction, of their
demands and in the narrowness of purpose — their own development. In
any case, negotiations to establish new institutions and new operating rules
would take many, many years; the changes would be steady, but not
necessarily precipitous. These negotiations would obviously be easier if
prior agreement on an ordering principle had been established (in effect, to
create a centrally managed international welfare system), but perhaps some
initial steps could be undertaken in areas of common interest (e.g., the
oceans, the environment) even without such an agreement. There has also
been at least partial movement toward the idea of a voluntary (i.e., state-
determined, not automatic) welfare system and the legitimacy of a "tilt"
toward the needs of the developing countries. From this perspective, then,
the struggle seems to be about degrees of difference, not differences in kind.

This would seem to imply that both sides are actually moving toward
each other, if at a fitful and erratic pace, and that only the absence of
"political will" by the leadership of the developed countries prevents a
meaningful compromise. Unfortunately, this greatly oversimplifies, not
merely in ignoring obstacles and perceiving more movement than may
have occurred, but also in taking for granted that we are wise enough and
farsighted enough to operate a centrally controlled or centrally guided
international system efficiently and equitably.

I do not mean to appear to be defending some notional idea of the "free
market" or to be ideologically opposed to the idea of increased international
governance. Indeed, I would accept the proposition that we need more
central guidance and coordination of national policy decisions and that the
force of events will make this increasingly apparent in the next two decades.
And I do not mean to suggest that there are no short-term benefits for the
United States in some of the restructuring proposals (for example, commodity price stabilization) or that all the proposals necessarily lead to a
degree of international intervention that is either unwise or inappropriate.
At the same time, I should note that what we seem to need and what we can

accomplish are not necessarily congruent and that even if it were to prove politically feasible to implement some of the suggested policies, it is not always clear that the result would be beneficial.

The failures and disabilities of the existing order are apparent, but they do not necessarily justify the assumption that central guidance or international intervention in large parts of the international economy will produce superior outcomes, even for the developing countries alone. The grounded theory, the reliable forecasting models, and the evidence of experience that might justify (or make a reasonable risk of) such a leap of faith does not exist. This seems especially true because the design of many of the Third World's restructuring proposals (for example, in commodities, in debt, and in the transfer of technology) have been sharply criticized not only by developed-country economists but also by some of the Third World's leading economists. In any case, very few of the proposals have won widespread support on their technical merits, even among analysts whose support for the Third World cannot be questioned. This is not inconsequential; such proposals, even if well drafted, are hardly likely to receive strong support from the developed countries, which is an obvious prerequisite for success, unless they seem likely to be able to achieve their intended effects.

Moreover, the record achieved by central management or central planning of the economy does not generate much optimism about future prospects, especially in a system in which the appeals of sovereignty and national willfulness are not diminishing and the costs of maintaining an everincreasing international bureaucracy are not trivial. The market (free or otherwise) has not worked very well for most of the developing countries, which need more than equality of opportunities; but the failures of national planning and the increased complexity of decision making in an interdependent and quickly changing environment hardly suggest that the solution is a very rapid increase in the power and authority of central institutions — especially when these central institutions must establish common goals for countries with different values, interests, and levels of development. Consequently, even apart from the issue of political feasibility, a good case can be made for a moderate approach to central direction or for seeking other approaches to global reform.

It might be argued that these criticisms are justified for some of the functional proposals that have been made but not for the proposals that simply provide for increased and automatic resource transfers (for example, via the doubling of aid in real terms, the establishment of a development tax of some sort, or the creation of a world development fund). This may well be true, although the bureaucracy that might become necessary to devise, collect, and implement a development tax — should one ever become politically feasible — could be substantial (especially if it were to have a role in administering grants or evaluating results).

There are, however, at least two major problems with the demand for automatic resource transfers. In the first place, although the Brandt Commission Report clearly emphasized the fact that money collected by means of a development tax should not simply be disbursed automatically, but rather should be disbursed in response to internationally agreed criteria of performance and need, the fact remains that the developing countries want the aid without such limitations — "without strings", as the phrase goes. Their representatives within the Brandt Commission, according to several reports, fought very hard for automaticity or for only nominal controls on recipients. Moreover, the demands of the developing countries themselves (as distinct from a mixed group like the Brandt Commission) have frequently emphasized the automatic transfer of resources. In addition, even if reasonably strong criteria of disbursement were established, there is a strong possibility that they would be gradually eroded. The institution charged with the task of collecting and disbursing the taxes would be under pressure to expend available resources and to respond to the pressing needs of the developing countries, even if this required a diminished concern for performance.

This brings us to the second problem implicit in the idea of automatic resource transfers. There is an assumption in many of the taxing proposals that merely transferring resources will suffice; that is, that recipients will use the resources equally well, that substantial degrees of external intervention to assure that resources will not be wasted will not be necessary, and that the process of resource transfer will gradually come to an end and will not become too onerous. Some countries will certainly grasp the opportunities created by the new tax system, but many may not do so (for a variety of reasons, such as incapacity, domestic turmoil, corruption, or external "shocks") and may become virtually permanent welfare recipients. Indeed, unless the developing countries adopt new development strategies (taking account of food and energy pressures) and unless the oil price explosion is contained in some manner, merely transferring more resources will help only those already able to help themselves and will not do very much to create genuine progress in the South. Effective performance in some cases may require a degree of external intervention that is unacceptable to either donor or recipient. And the viability of the external aid system is closely connected to the domestic performance of the recipients. Unless it can be safely assumed that the level of performance will be acceptable, the donors are bound to become increasingly disenchanted with a taxing system that seems to waste increasing amounts of scarce resources, and the central system itself may be seriously weakened by its escalating claims for resources that may not be used productively.[9]

In a large sense, the point of these arguments is that the acceptance of a progressive development tax, an apparently simple and clear idea that has great resonance in development circles, has profound implications about the kind of international system that one is seeking to establish and about the degrees of responsibility toward each other that nations are willing to accept. It would be dangerous to act as if these broader and deeper values are more widely shared than they appear to be, for the result might well be increased cynicism and desperation. In a narrower sense, then, the point is that the dangers of a backlash by the developed countries are great, and the likelihood that merely transferring much larger amounts of resources will solve the problems of enough developing countries (that is, doing more than helping more countries to stay afloat during the present crisis) is debatable. Hence, a new and progressive system—if it is to become at all possible—must be phased in very carefully and must be sharply controlled in terms of how and why resources are expended. This sacrifices some short-term gains in the hope of establishing a more stable and effective long-term system. It also permits public support in the developing countries to be gradually developed for a system that in fact seems to be producing genuine *mutual* benefits. And again, the point is not about whether the developing countries should be helped, but about how to do it in the most effective fashion.

The implications of this argument can be quickly summarized. There is little political support in most developed countries for global restructuring that is designed primarily to benefit the developing countries. Even if such support gradually materializes, it would be a good many years before restructuring proposals could be successfully negotiated and implemented. This suggests the danger that attention will be diverted from more practicable short-term reforms that are equally imperative, that are more feasible, and that do not necessarily require the support of over 150 countries. Moreover, it is not clear that all of the restructuring proposals *should* be implemented; some are badly drafted, and there is uncertainty about whether they will produce superior benefits for either the developed or developing countries. Also, restructuring would help some countries much more than others—and would perhaps harm those who used it as an excuse to avoid difficult domestic reforms.

Finally, if restructuring were accepted and the transferred resources were used primarily for immediate consumption and not for long-term investment needs or to facilitate a shift in development strategies, an ostensible effort to create a more stable and more just international system might be transformed into an ineffective, but very costly, venture into patchwork. And if large amounts of time and money were invested in establishing a new order that is less efficient (and *perhaps* less equitable in some cases) than its predecessor and that insures that all crises will be systemic and that all issues must be dealt with in an increasingly dubious and difficult North-South framework, the consequences, especially for the developing countries, could be disastrous.

This is not all that needs to be said, however, for some amount of global restructuring is imperative. The key issue, which is obscured by manifestos and the rhetoric of joint salvation, is how to proceed in a very complex and uncertain environment. What has been absent from the appeals for global restructuring is a political strategy that indicates how support for significant change can be built and how the many obstacles — political, economic, psychological — can be overcome. At any rate, in practical terms, until greater support has been generated in the developed countries, prudence dictates that increased central coordination of national policies must be developed very slowly and carefully, that intellectual and conceptual disagreements must be clarified before risking massive change, and that this venture into global policymaking must rest on a more cooperative and less confrontational approach to the negotiating arena. With so much at stake, movement toward international governance must be cautiously phased in, risks must be moderated, results must be evaluated before additional movement, and political and intellectual support must be actively sought and cultivated.

In short, potentially beneficial but also potentially controversial and uncertain liberal goals must be pursued by essentially conservative tactics — if not because this is a sensible policymaking response to a complex environment, then because it may be (or may become) the only politically feasible strategy of change. But the developing countries (or rather, their leaders in the North-South Dialogue) have rejected this approach as too little and too late. This is certainly true in the short run, but it must also be noted that restructuring would take many years to implement. And in the long run, this more moderate approach may be the only hope of progress. I shall return to it in the discussion of the final policy alternative.

The issue of how to proceed cannot be dismissed simply by asserting that many of the restructuring proposals are in the long-term interest of the developed countries. This may well be true, but it tends to sharply over-value the weight developed-country governments are likely to put on putative long-term gains and to undervalue the weight they are likely to put on the need to protect and enhance short-term gains. And I should emphasize that any attempt to satisfy the full range of developing countries demands would involve substantial short-run costs and difficulties for the developed countries. This would be especially true if the necessary changes were implemented quickly, as political conflicts would be severe, adjustment costs would be high, and the potential for (and the consequences of) mistakes would surely rise. This is not to deny that there are also some important short-term gains for the developed countries from some proposals (for example, commodity price stabilization or increased access for developing countries exports). But these gains are not large enough to justify—politically—a risky venture into global transformation, and they may not persist for very long if developing countries demands continue to escalate, which seems likely to be the case if initial reforms fail to solve all of the problems of the developing countries and if domestic reform fails to be undertaken.

One must also note that the idea of another Marshall Plan, which seems the implicit inspiration for many restructuring schemes, may not be a very reliable analogy. Apart from other considerations, the Europeans possessed all the basic skills to operate an advanced, highly developed economy; they lacked only catalytic resources and a functioning infrastructure. Foreign aid could thus be legitimately perceived as a transitory phenomenon. For the developing countries, the needs are greater, they will persist for decades, and they might require a degree of intervention that neither donor nor recipient would find acceptable. This is not, of course, an argument against external support, but rather an argument for recognition of realities. The failure of developing-country governments and of advocates of global restructuring to think contextually about these issues not only diminishes the chances of getting what can be gotten now but also exacerbates the tendency to act as if the politics of persuasion and compromise were not important in the North-South arena.

It should be clear that the obstacles to global restructuring are currently very powerful. Slow growth, the absence of strong leadership, disagreement about the first principles, the dangers and uncertainties attendant on centralized control and guidance of the international economy, and the tendency to ignore the politics of policymaking in the North-South arena hardly suggest that we are about to witness a new constitutional convention—a North-South Bretton Woods, so to speak. Analysts who advocate one or another form of global bargain, but who fail to indicate how these obstacles should or can be dealt with, are thus essentially irrelevant (if not actively harmful, to the extent that they distract attention from real difficulties). At the same time, I should strongly emphasize that the concerns that generated demands for global restructuring are very real and very important. They cannot be ignored, which is what the previous policy approach does; but they also cannot be dealt with merely by asserting the need for a New International Economic Order or even—as with the Brandt Commission—by appealing to long-term self-interest. The question that remains is whether global restructuring can be rescued by another approach to ends and means. I shall discuss this issue shortly, but I want first to discuss the third policy option open to the United States.

Selectivity and Differentiation

A third approach to Third World policy has already been foreshadowed in the Carter administration's early concentration on the new influentials—the very large or economically powerful developing countries, most of whom are either members of OPEC or among the newly industrializing countries (NICs). In a sense such a focus is inevitable, but the key question concerns the relationship between a differentiated concern with a small group of particularly important countries and a more global concern with all of the Third World and the North-South Dialogue. Elements of both the global and the differentiated focus will always be present, but a decided "tilt" toward one could have serious implications for relations with the other. This is especially true because the pattern of concerns varies greatly within the two relationships. In this context I shall assume the growing dominance of the differentiated focus, with the global focus downgraded or treated primarily as a residual area of concern.

A number of forces are propelling the United States and the other developed countries toward an increasingly selective concern with a relatively small number of developing countries. Resources are very scarce, and dissipating them across a very wide spectrum of countries, some of whom may be hostile or may squander resources, may seem unwise. Concentration on a small number of countries may thus increase the effectiveness with which available resources are used—especially if resource transfers must attain a certain threshold of significance before they can have a major impact on performance. This policy also reflects the conclusion reached at the end of Chapter 2: None of the arguments that might seem to justify a fundamental shift in U.S. policy toward all of the Third World (as distinct from some parts of it) are completely persuasive or conclusive. I do not mean to suggest that some analysts and some political figures do not find some or all of these arguments decisive, but rather that neither the U.S. government nor the U.S. public is likely to do so—and without a broad consensus, any attempt to establish a new policy approach is bound to fail (or to take much time to implement).

Consequently the initial question for a policy of concentration and differentiation concerns the criterion or criteria of selection. Who should be selected and who ignored? During the Cold War, military allies and ideological supporters of the United States received the great bulk of support, but during the 1960s there was also some movement toward the idea that support should be given to those who needed help or who merited it on the basis of successful development performance. But circumstances have changed, and Cold War liberalism does not provide a completely reliable guide to present problems of choice. Cold War concerns have obviously not disappeared, but the United States also has a new and additional pattern of interests in at least some parts of the Third World. The criteria that establish relative degrees of importance have had to be changed.

A serious attempt to deal with the question of criteria of choice would have to begin with a discussion of the U.S. role in world order and the changing perceptions of East-West conflict. Many countries, for example, might not seem of great significance to the United States in terms of economic interests, but they might qualify as important for political, strategic, or ideological reasons. Indeed, in a sense virtually all countries were considered important in the Cold War years, insofar as denial to the Soviets was considered important and insofar as conversion to socialist dogmas could somehow seem a blow to the presumed superiority of Western ideas and institutions. Moreover, this area of concern could once again become important if the economic problems that the Soviet Union seems likely to confront in this decade generate efforts to acquire access to oil and other resources or lead to efforts to guarantee stable and friendly neighbors (as in Afghanistan). In addition, a serious analysis of this issue would also have to deal with the domestic impact of developments in various Third World countries, not only in terms of Arab-Israeli and African issues, but also increasingly in terms of a growing Hispanic minority group in the United States. But my intention here is only illustrative. Consequently I shall deal with criteria of importance primarily in relation to more narrowly defined North-South concerns.

The shifting and ambiguous meaning of "importance" adds another layer of difficulty to the process of determining which countries to support. During the Cold War, judgments could be made implicitly or explicitly in terms of a few simple ideas like anticommunism, "falling dominoes," or commitment to free-market orientations. But now the addition of economic goals requires a degree of economic and political performance from the developing countries (including, for example, maintaining sufficient investment in resources, enlarging the domestic market, stability — and thus perhaps increased equity) that cannot easily or effectively be guaranteed by external policy actions of the developed countries. Moreover, it is difficult to make a very strong case that more than a few developing countries (far fewer than on the list that follows) are of major significance to the United States on narrow economic grounds. Perhaps this merely reaffirms the artificiality of discussing the importance of the developing countries without reference to broader foreign policy goals: The interest of the United States is not merely in access and trade, but also in political security and systemic stability. This does not mean that a differentiated approach is wholly illusory; some developing countries are more important to the United States than others, whatever the criteria of selection—even if systemic stability is the only criterion.

But while a combination of criteria is imperative (except for a few countries that are important only because of a single factor—say, Oman's strategic location), I shall concentrate in what follows primarily on economic importance—not exclusively but in the sense of *primus inter pares*. This is not completely unrealistic even in terms of traditional East-West conflicts, as the rationale for that conflict in the Third World may increasingly come to focus on control of resources and economic performance. Indeed, pressures from the Third World on both blocs may accelerate this movement, although neither ideological nor security concerns are likely to disappear altogether.

What would a representative list of Third World countries crucial to the United States look like?[10] In Latin America, one obviously begins with Mexico, Brazil, Argentina, and Venezuela. Chile, Peru, and Bolivia must be added (in large part because of possession of key resources), perhaps Colombia (for a variety of reasons, including a functioning democratic political system) and Jamaica (because of its bauxite and its influence in the Third World), and certainly Cuba. In sub-Saharan Africa, Nigeria is crucial, followed perhaps by Kenya, the Ivory Coast, and Zaire (all three because of a combination of economic performance and resource possession), less clearly Zambia and Ghana, and finally Tanzania (for its political and moral influence) and Zimbabwe (because of its resources and political significance). In North Africa, Algeria is an obvious choice, but Morocco (political ties and resources) and Libya (oil and its political-ideological role) might also qualify. In the Middle East, Egypt, Saudi Arabia, Iran, and Iraq would be the prime candidates for inclusion. In South and Southeast Asia, one begins with India, Indonesia, Malaysia (raw materials and economic performance), the Philippines, Pakistan (primarily strategic reasons), and South Korea and Taiwan (economic performance and political and strategic interests). In short, we end with a list of thirty-two countries, ten in Latin America, eight in Africa, three in North Africa, four in the Middle East, and seven in South and Southeast Asia.

One could rightly quibble with this list on a variety of grounds. For example, one might well argue that events in several Central American or Caribbean countries are of major significance to the United States only if they threaten to affect the entire region and that in the broader context of North-South relations they would probably have less resonance than developments in a country like Malaysia (unless the United States returned to gunboat diplomacy).[11] In any case, ambiguities are inevitable in a world in which the structure of power and influence is shifting so rapidly, and my list is meant only illustratively. But more significantly, whatever the exact list of countries or the criteria of choice, there are other problems with this approach that need to be emphasized.

These problems may become more apparent if I first note some of the elements of policy implicit in concentration on particularly important developing countries. The central purpose of a policy of differentiation is to protect crucial short-run interests in a deteriorating international environment. Doing so would require major shifts in the focus of U.S. development policy. The North-South Dialogue and the quest for general goals and policies would have to be sharply and deliberately deemphasized (more so than in the first policy discussed above), and selective measures to increase growth rates (and equity), to protect foreign investment, to insure access to markets and resources, and to encourage and maintain stability in the key countries would have to be sharply and deliberately emphasized. Special preferential arrangements, perhaps guaranteed shares of developed-country markets, a shift in aid strategy (at least partially away from basic human needs and the poorest developing countries), and increased technical and military assistance perhaps illustrate the thrust of this approach. Also, to avoid misunderstandings or unnecessary conflicts and to provide ceremonial support for policy commitments, joint consultative and planning groups might be established to hold regular meetings (as with Saudi Arabia and ASEAN).

In a loose sense, there is something of the OECD idea here: a subsystem of friends and "like-minded" states, sharing some interests, seeking to settle all conflicts by agreed rules and procedures, and treating members of the "club" differently from outsiders. This is at least in intent a *relatively* benign form of differentiation, as it would be implemented before a major crisis and before a desperate scramble to protect narrow interests. I shall not discuss more malign forms of differentiation, which might emerge during a crisis and which might involve military and other hostile actions, at least in part because the criticisms of the benign form hold to an even greater degree for the less benign forms.

In geographic terms, this policy approach is not completely regional in focus, nor does it revive traditional spheres of interest. It is, rather, more subregional and transregional, if primarily because the most important countries from this perspective are widely scattered. This is true whether we define importance in terms of trading ties, access to raw materials, strategic position, or even the potential impact of events in particular countries on systemic stability. Elements of a regional bias will certainly remain (particularly *after* the policy needs of the key countries have been met), if only because of geographic and historical relationships, but an attempt to

TABLE 7.1 1977 Trade Figures: U.S. Trade with non-OPEC
Developing Countries (billions of dollars)

Trading Partners	Exports to U.S.	Imports from U.S.
Mexico	$ 4.7	$ 4.8
Korea	2.9	2.4
Brazil	2.2	2.5
Taiwan	3.7	1.8
Hong Kong	2.9	1.3
Israel	0.6	1.4
Malaysia	1.3	1.3
All others	10.8	11.3
Total	29.1	26.8

Source: World Bank data.

reestablish spheres of interest in narrowly geographical terms seems unlikely to succeed. This reflects the fact that, although strong trading ties between the United States and Latin America, Europe and Africa, and Japan
and the rest of Asia will surely persist, these ties have been declining in
relative importance, in part because of the developing countries' desire to
diversify and in part because of the developed countries' desire to open new
markets. As an illustration, the United States now has more trade with Asia
than it has with Europe, and Japan is increasing its trade with other
developing-country regions faster than it is increasing trade with Southeast
Asia. And the United States now faces sharp competition in Latin America
from both Japan and some European countries.

It would be impossible to discuss the issue here, but I should also note
that the many factors that have impeded regional cooperation in the past
(especially the absence of economic complementarities) have not diminished in force.[12] As a result of these considerations, the most likely model
for a policy of differentiation is the subregional "club," perhaps clustered
around a regional great power.

One criticism of this approach is not very persuasive. Many analysts
have pointed out the growing importance of trade with the developing
countries to the prosperity of the developed countries.[13] But aggregate
figures are very misleading in this case. Table 7.1 illustrates why: Trade
with the non-OPEC developing countries was highly concentrated among a
small number of countries (seven countries provided 63 percent of the
exports and took about 58 percent of the imports). Taken by themselves,
then, the trade figures seem to justify differentiation and selectivity.

An argument has also been made that the opportunities for more profitable investments in the future may fall largely in the developing countries. Thus, presumably, the returns on capital will diminish if investments must be generally limited to the "mature" economies. This may well be true, but one should also note (as with the argument about trade) that it is likely to be true only for a limited number of already wealthy and stable developing countries and that it may also require a degree of openness to foreign capital that is not likely to be present in a large number of cases. In short, although the opportunities for investment may be there, they may not be as attractive or as widespread as is generally assumed. At any rate, proponents of this argument and of the argument about the growing importance of North-South trade also fail to recognize that there is very little evidence that bilateral opportunities for trade and investment are very much affected by what happens in the global North-South Dialogue.

The argument is also frequently made that the United States and the other developed countries are becoming increasingly dependent on Third World suppliers of a number of crucial mineral resources. This is certainly true, but again it seems to provide more support for a policy of differentiation than for a policy of radical restructuring. At any rate, there is very little evidence (as with OPEC) that the mineral producers are motivated by much beyond calculations of individual self-interest. They do not appear to have either the capability or the intention of cooperating politically to pursue broad North-South goals. And, of course, the developed countries could pursue a variety of options — diversification of suppliers, stockpiling, development of substitutes — to thwart any effort to withhold supplies. Indeed, the key problem may not be withholding supplies, but rather the unavailability of sufficient supplies because of a failure to invest in new capacity. And here the best tactic might be a concentration on helping particular suppliers joined to a long-term effort to create a more stable international climate for investment.

I do not wish these criticisms to be misunderstood. Arguments about the growing importance of trade with the Third World, the beneficial returns on investment in the Third World, and growing resource dependency on the Third World are all true and important. But the key political point is that *in the short run* they are not very persuasive arguments about the need for a radically new approach to North-South relations because the benefits and dangers are only gradually becoming salient and because there is so little evidence that individual Third World countries will alter their policies either positively or negatively because of the general state of the North-South Dialogue. Over the long term, however, these arguments are (or should be) very persuasive because potential benefits and dangers could be sharply rising. Moreover, insofar as there is a strong rationale for a more forthcoming posture in the short run, it lies in the fact that although existing benefits can be achieved by concentrating on a limited number of countries and existing dangers can probably be inhibited in the same fashion, the continuation of a negative posture on the more general issues that divide North and South may well generate patterns of thought and behavior on both sides (hostile, protectionist, self-centered, and so on) that make the acquisition of genuinely important mutual long-term benefits progressively more difficult. Unfortunately, these kinds of connections between present and future are generally ignored or dismissed as academic irrelevancies.

Other criticisms of this approach may be more persuasive. One concerns the reactions of the targeted countries. It is not self-evident that they will willingly accept inclusion in a "special relationship" with one or more developed countries if it impedes efforts to diversify ties with both developed and developing countries and if it creates a great deal of domestic discontent. The latter point may be especially important because weak and unstable governments, while desperately in need of external support to diminish rising domestic pressures, may still be reluctant to accept what will inevitably be described as a revived form of neocolonialism if that activates domestic radicals (of both the left and right) and if it engenders hostility from the rest of the Third World. Consequently, this policy approach may be acceptable only as a last, desperate resort; in that case it may be too late to be effective.

Another problem or set of problems concerns the interests and attitudes of the United States itself (and, presumably, the other developed countries, if they followed the same course). The degree of obligation implicit in this policy approach may actually be greater than a strict reading of U.S. interests would suggest, except in the limiting cases, say Mexico and Saudi Arabia. After all, the commitment is very great: not merely to help them to manage their problems and to provide additional aid and support, but also to assure an important degree of stability. The latter may be beyond U.S. power or, put differently, it may take a much greater degree of direct involvement than the United States (or the developing countries) may be willing to contemplate. Iran may provide an object lesson in the limits and costs of this kind of relationship. And the difficulty of devising a policy package that is politically, economically, and psychologically acceptable to both the United States and Mexico may also be indicative. The "bargains" are easy to imagine in the abstract, but they may start to unravel when they are put through the domestic political processes of countries that do not share a common view of the world or an untroubled history. In addition, the United States would have to change a number of laws, all of which were initially passed only with great difficulty (e.g., the shift in aid to the poorest countries or the general system of preferences), before differentiation and selectivity could be effectively implemented. In short, the United States obviously has much greater interests in some developing countries than others, but it is not clear that those interests are sufficient to justify the degree of commitment that may become necessary, that the policy itself will work, or that differentiation can succeed without a simultaneous effort to deal with broader North-South issues. In response, however, it is only fair to note that alternative policies cannot guarantee any greater degree of success.

There is another way of looking at this issue. In one sense, differentiation is a policy of selective linkage; in another sense, it is of course a policy of selective delinking with countries that seem of lesser importance. But both the linking and delinking may be problematic, the former for reasons already noted and the latter because of potentially rapidly shifting criteria of importance, important cross-cutting ties between the "linked" and the "delinked," the need to pursue some milieu goals that require more general patterns of cooperation, and the dangers of destabilizing and/or irrational actions by the delinked. These considerations tend to suggest that, at best, differentiation will be an unstable, inconsistent, and potentially contradictory policy choice — unless the international system has already deteriorated so radically that essentially simplistic choices are virtually imposed by the force of events.

One last point needs to be made. The countries excluded by this approach are the poorest countries — the countries that most need help, even if they are not always able to use it well. This raises a severe moral question: Does the United States really want to turn away from these countries simply because they can have little direct effect on its prosperity or security? One doubts that it will be acceptable, at any rate without significant domestic conflict. In effect, this approach to policy may suffice as a stopgap measure during a period of crisis, but it does not provide a moral, a political, or an economic basis for a viable long-term North-South policy.[14]

Primary concentration on the developing countries that are of most importance to the United States is a policy with many deficiencies, but the force of events — a deteriorating international environment, diminishing resource transfers, increasing hostility from many developing countries — may gradually compel its adoption. With no other attractive options, it might be justified as a political form of the second-best: the creation of new distortions in and new obstacles to an open international system in order to overcome or bypass existing distortions and obstacles. If such a policy is indeed adopted only as a last resort, it will be very difficult to diminish its negative effects or to implement it in a relatively less costly manner. Nevertheless, the attempt to minimize its worst consequences and to keep open the possibility of movement toward a more cooperative system should remain an important policy consideration.

The means of doing this are probably impossible to detail in advance. Still, some indications of direction may be possible. The North-South Dialogue and the global dimension of North-South relations will lose some salience if differentiation and selectivity become the policy focus, but a major effort should still be made to treat these broader issues seriously and without cynicism. It must be remembered that, as I argued in Chapter 2, a major rupture in the Dialogue would have negative effects on bilateral relations with *all* the developing countries. This does not mean that it will be impossible to deal effectively with individual developing countries, as many will be seeking the best deal for themselves irrespective of the state of the Dialogue, but it does mean — given the probable continuation of a commitment to Third World unity — that bilateral or subregional negotiations will be more difficult if the Dialogue deteriorates even further.

But beyond this, there are some issues that can be ultimately resolved only in very broad global forums, and there are other issues that might continue to be sensibly treated there. For example, continued support for a basic human needs policy orientation might be more effectively implemented through the international institutional system where it is less likely to elicit suspicion about intentions. In addition, support for efforts at collective self-reliance should be actively encouraged, as they may provide the poorest countries a degree of protection against a dangerous environment. And in an effort to prevent the creation of permanent fissures between the advanced developing countries and the poorer developing countries, the benefits given to the former should be limited in duration and an attempt should be made to ensure that the advanced countries do not take advantage of their poorer neighbors. As far as possible, the difficult balancing act between a global and a differentiated posture should not be wholly abandoned in favor of the immediate needs of the countries that seem most important to us. However, it will be even more difficult to accomplish this end than it is within the context of the first policy approach, not only because of deteriorating economic conditions but also because concentration on the most important countries will antagonize the other developing countries and increase strains on Third World unity.

Policy Options: Problems and Prospects

None of the three policy alternatives that I have been discussing is very appealing. This clearly suggests that policy as a holding action is likely to remain the dominant focus, at least until external conditions virtually compel a search for new directions. As neither global restructuring, whatever form it takes, nor concentration on a small number of developing countries, however they are defined, seems likely to work very well, a period of vacillation between different choices might ensue. This will probably guarantee prolonged instability. At any rate, it is difficult to see how the United States can achieve its major goals in a consistent fashion by pursuing any of these choices. At best, some short-term stability goals and some short-term economic goals might be achieved or protected, but medium- and long-term goals might become increasingly problematic. Advocates of global restructuring would undoubtedly contest these views, but it must be emphasized that they ignore the difficulties of seeking a major breakthrough in present circumstances and underrate the significance of underlying conflicts of interest, perspective, and value.

The obvious question that arises is whether an alternative, or combination of alternatives, exists: Is there something better than drift, narrow self-interest, and postulations of long-term harmony? An affirmative answer is impossible, but I shall conclude with a few speculations about altering the range of choice within a very dangerous international environment. To avoid unnecessarily raising expectations about the quest for an alternative approach to policy, one point needs *very* strong emphasis: The outcome cannot be a clear and elegant and original set of policies that resolves all the dilemmas and ambiguities that exist in the North-South relationship. These will persist whatever the policy choice, and there is neither new knowledge nor a new interpretation of the environment of choice on which to build a new approach. What the United States can seek within these constraints is greater clarity about the consequences and costs of each choice and a better sense of how the different policy pieces can be brought together to reflect both short-term and long-term goals and interests. Critics who contend that this approach is insufficiently "heroic"—not a "grand design," not without ambiguities, not resonant—must at least explain why or how their alternatives are more likely to produce genuine results.

I asked earlier whether cooperation with some developing countries was possible (or likely to be effective) if simultaneous efforts were not made to improve prospects for developing countries by means of major international reforms. It might be useful, before turning to the last policy approach, to summarize very briefly the answers to this question that are implicit in the three alternatives already discussed. The first approach,which concentrates on short-run holding actions, essentially ignores the question or at least fails to take a clear position on it; the pressures of coping with immediate needs and crises tend to overwhelm the need to think also about a very complex and difficult issue. Advocates of global restructuring, of course, would insist that major international reforms are imperative, for otherwise efforts to help individual countries are bound to be futile. In an interdependent system, all will be implicated in the problems of some. But global reformers have been very weak in attempting to indicate how obstacles to reform can be overcome; they have also failed to make a completely persuasive case for some of their proposals.

Advocates of selectivity and differentiation, however, implicitly maintain that the international process is primarily rhetorical and that there is much evidence to suggest that the developing countries will accept (if not actively seek) special arrangements at the expense of their neighbors and peers. This seems largely true, especially if economic conditions deteriorate, but it is a doubtful basis for an effective long-term North-South policy. In the last policy, I shall seek to accept both the reality of short-term needs and pressures and the imperative of working more rapidly toward some forms of restructuring. The short-term perspective needs to be carefully and progressively extended, but the key question, so often ignored or undervalued by advocates of global reform, will be how to proceed in an exceptionally unfavorable domestic and international environment.

Eclecticism: Viable Strategy of Change or Euphemism for Inaction?

Both North and South are preoccupied with their own short-term problems. Unfortunately, the short-term problems are not identical. The United States and most of the other developed countries, conscious of the constraints imposed by domestic political and economic circumstances and fearful that a retreat into nationalist postures will gradually undermine the stability of the international system, have emphasized measures to cope with the existing crisis and to maintain existing gains. This perspective is narrow, but nonetheless critically important; failure to solve these short-term problems only guarantees that there will be no acceptable solutions for the long-term problems of both North and South. The developing countries, conscious of rising demands on desperately scarce resources and convinced that incremental reforms are a badly disguised means of maintaining an unfair international system, have emphasized measures to transfer massive amounts of resources quickly and to establish a new order deliberately biased toward their needs. This is also a narrow but crucially important perspective; failure to respond to it may be bearable in the short-run, but virtually guarantees the emergence of an unstable and unjust international system. But the riddle of how to progress in the face of divergent, but firmly held and apparently well grounded, interpretations of what can and must be done remains unresolved.

The need to broaden perspectives is readily apparent, as is the difficulty of doing so under current circumstances. It may be useful to begin, therefore, by emphasizing a simple point. Any attempt to overcome existing problems by ignoring *either* side's short-run interests is not only doomed to failure, but also likely to diminish the possibility of devising mutually acceptable agreements. The trade-off between short-run sacrifices and long-term gains for the developed countries must be reconsidered: Short-term gains for both groups of countries need *not* be equivalent, but much more concern for mutual benefits and for some tangible returns to the developed countries is imperative. This may be criticized as unfair or unwise, but we are operating in an international system in which mutual long-term gains are likely to emerge only from a process that encourages mutual short-term gains. The emphasis on long-term U.S. interests is perfectly legitimate and may become a powerful justification for action if present difficulties are resolved, but to offer very abstract long-term benefits as compensation for some very real short-term losses in an environment of slow growth and rising insecurities is naive and futile. Indeed, proponents of such an exchange open themselves to the charge that they are more interested in ingratiating themselves with some of the ideologues on the international development circuit than in generating real benefits—benefits that are insufficient, but surely better than no benefits at all—for desperately needy countries.

An international policy process that responds to these considerations *but also* seeks to provide a foundation for the creation of a restructured international system (which does not necessarily imply acceptance of existing "blueprints") cannot be established if current bargaining patterns in the North-South Dialogue persist. The Dialogue as a dialogue—in the sense of conversing and reasoning together—has performed some useful functions, but as a means of negotiating meaningful substantive agreements it has been less than successful. One might go even further and argue that the Dialogue has produced few agreements and has also focused attention on a North-South dichotomy that is too simplified for the pattern of relations that exists in the world and that can only produce agreements that, with too few exceptions, yield primarily rhetorical benefits. This issue—the effectiveness of the policy process through which decisions are reached—is persistently ignored or undervalued by analysts in both North and South, especially those who offer "will" as the missing link between demands and policies. Unless genuine reforms are possible in the way North and South settle their conflicts, a steady shift away from the Dialogue by both sides seems very likely, except perhaps by those who have no alternative.

I have already discussed the various obstacles that impede North-South bargaining: intellectual and conceptual disagreements, the emphasis on unity and on patchwork group bargaining postures, the interests and biases of the institutions that provide the setting for negotiations, and the decision to demand immediate commitment to new and untested principles of order.[15] And, of course, the prospect of slow growth, the uncertainties generated by the oil crisis, and the absence of strong leadership on both sides have added more layers of difficulty.[16] What has emerged from the interaction of these factors is a bargaining process dominated by the demands of a single-issue constituency — the impact of such groups is roughly similar to that of single-issue constituencies in the U.S. political context — that perceives all issues in terms of its own immediate needs and that is reluctant or fearful to accept compromises that appear to guarantee too little or that threaten to unravel unity.

Moreover, the demands for more central management or control of many sectors of the international economy in order to insure favorable outcomes for the developing countries would also, if implemented to the degree demanded, severely strain the capacity of an already weakened institutional structure. It is not self-evident that the increasing overload on national governments, which results in part from the growing complexity and the growing number of problems that must be resolved by the political process, can be sensibly diminished by thrusting more and more national failures on an international structure that lacks power, authority, and legitimacy. At a minimum, the justification for central direction needs to be more carefully considered. In any case, the impasse that results from these conflicting demands and perspectives succeeds in blocking much more than rhetorical progress at the North-South level, while encouraging the quest for private deals and the expression of private contempt for a process increasingly perceived as meaningless, if not actually harmful, by a growing number of participants on both sides.

The United States and most of the other developed countries would obviously prefer a different kind of international policy process. There is no single decision-making strategy that is always correct; the question of how to proceed cannot be answered without knowledge of the context of decision and the factors in play in particular situations. In terms of the North-South arena, one key determinant of context is that the economic issues that are primarily at stake in the Dialogue are far more affected by the domestic political process in the developed countries than are (or were) more traditional security concerns. A foreign policy consensus may sustain a U.S. security commitment to a number of developing countries, but a commitment on trade or commodities or foreign aid cannot be made without a close calculus of degrees of support or opposition in Congress and the public. Consequently the decision-making style that seems most appropriate for the majority of North-South issues would seem to require the kind of compromise mentality, mutual benefits, and trade-offs across issues that dominate pluralist political systems. The analogy between the domestic and the international policy process has to be made with great caution, as domestic community and international society are hardly identical, but the continued erosion of the boundary between the two arenas suggests that it is not entirely inappropriate.

The essentially incremental policy process that the United States has advocated seems to be a prudent response to the complexities and uncertainties of the international environment, but it clashes with the approach of the developing countries in the Dialogue. Instead of the development of cross-cutting coalitions and the forming and reforming of different coalitions on issues that activate different patterns of interest, the Dialogue has encouraged the creation of rigid and at least partially artificial coalitions of principle. Reform cannot be achieved by merely reemphasizing the futility of present patterns of interaction, because neither the United States nor the other developed countries offer enough to make the dissolution of unity or the sacrifice of some potential gains from it seem attractive. From the perspective of the South, the rejection of incrementalism is fully justified: Its conservatism and the dominance of the powerful in constructing winning coalitions within it hardly guarantee the developing countries enough benefits to make it an attractive alternative. In short, if the developed countries want to establish a new pattern of North-South relations, they must make a sufficiently strong *initial* commitment to the South, which would not only generate real benefits but also establish expectations of continued fair (i.e., preferential) treatment. It is not clear that this can be done, but it does suggest that the crucial question—if we want to create an effective Dialogue—is whether a politically feasible bargain can be struck somewhere between the inadequacies of incrementalism and the impossibility of global restructuring on the principles of the developing countries. A detailed answer to this question is obviously impossible, but for purposes of illustration only I shall very briefly indicate the general outline of one intermediate bargain, as well as its problems and prospects.

The United States and the other developed countries have generally accepted the need for structural change in the international system, but they have done little to articulate the form of such changes or to provide evidence that something more than mild reform of the existing system is intended. But an explicit commitment to structural change and to a set of mutually acceptable guiding principles is probably the minimum offer that might attract sufficient support within the Third World. The guiding principles would reflect a commitment to institute some elements of a modified international social welfare system. One might consider, for example, an automatic development tax, but with some important qualifications: Total amounts collected would have a fixed ceiling that could be altered only by joint agreement, and the process of disbursement would *not* be automatic, but rather would be governed by jointly agreed criteria of need and merit. But even with these qualifications, a development tax is probably politically infeasible — not to mention some of its technical problems. This suggests that the most likely basis for an agreement might be a commitment to allocate to the developing countries most of the revenue (beyond operating costs) collected from a variety of licenses and user's fees for sea-bed mining, fishing, the use of radio frequencies, and other such activities. This has the virtue of concentrating on new sources of revenue, thus avoiding conflict with vested interests, but it also has a major deficiency: Potential revenues from such activities are probably not substantial enough to satisfy the developing countries. Perhaps a firm commitment to increase resource transfers to reach targeted figures (0.7 percent of GNP in official development assistance, a figure with symbolic, if not technical, significance) within a designated period might suffice: the two sums together would increase aid levels significantly, but would not be massively expensive or more-than-usually controversial for the developed countries.

Other concessions might also be necessary in the trading arena, as the potential for conflict is great. Patterns of special treatment for the developing countries might be extended for at least another decade, and the restraints and controls available to the developed countries might be more severely limited. These measures might not be sufficient, however, which implies the need to consider guaranteed markets and a form of managed trade for some products of particular interest to the developing countries. This is obviously a move away from the ideal of an open trading system, but there seems little doubt that the great majority of developing countries (other than the NICs and a few near-NICs) will need such help to become effective participants in the trading system. In any case, the movement toward increased state control of international trade is already well under way, and the effort here would concentrate on exposing the process to a degree of international accountability and insuring that the developing countries received a fair share of the benefits. Finally, an intergovernmental committee could be established immediately to work out the details of this agreement and to prepare the ground for a negotiating conference that could establish and legitimize agreed principles and necessary institutions.

There is an implicit exchange underlying this agreement. The United States, by making a fundamental commitment of this nature, would hope to arrest the drift and uncertainty of an incremental approach to policy and to end the immobility of the North-South Dialogue. In exchange for an explicit commitment to principles that would guarantee the developing countries increased and continuing external support for their needs, the United States (and the other developed countries) would hope to receive a commitment from the developing countries to carry on the agreed negotiating process on individual issues in a moderate, pragmatic, perhaps conservative fashion. The hope would be that the provision of additional resources to the developing countries would reduce the need to treat each negotiation of a specific issue as a disguised effort to transfer resources.

There would need to be a shift away from the South's tendency to create vast packages of demands that are designed to promise something to *all* members of the Group of 77, a practice that generates interminable delays in establishing a Group position and that makes subsequent negotiations something of a charade, as compromise threatens to unravel the entire package.[17] Perhaps gradually a competition between shifting and transitory coalitions of interest could supersede the rigid and permanent coalitions of principle that now hinder progress. In turn, the developing countries would have to conclude that a general commitment to structural change, even a degree of structural change that still seems insufficient, would yield more real benefits than the insistent demand that prior commitment to more radical principles of change must precede or be incorporated in each negotiation. In sum, the bargain implies acceptance of a relatively liberal order approached by relatively cautious or conservative steps instead of a revolutionary order approached by radical steps. The improbability of the latter might make the seeming inadequacy of the former less disabling.

Would the developing countries accept such an exchange? If external conditions continue to deteriorate, this kind of agreement might come to seem increasingly attractive, but the delay may make it less effective and more difficult to negotiate. Apart from this possibility, one can only be very pessimistic. There are formidable obstacles to the quest for an interim agreement—the absence of strong leadership, the enormous pressure of immediate needs on all governments, and perhaps even the hopes raised by the Brandt Commission and others that only the absence of will and the inability to perceive real interests stand in the way of massive change. Moreover, the negotiation of such an agreement would probably require several years, it still might not provide the developing countries with the degree of support they need, and disagreements about the principles of disbursement might be irresolvable. And in the prevailing atmosphere of suspicion and distrust of intentions, the developed countries themselves might well fear that acceptance of the proferred concessions would be soon followed by a new set of demands. In any case, the immediate reaction of the developing countries (as a group, if not individually) to this proposal is probably predictable. It would be denounced as too little and too late, an attempt to restore an old order that has failed, and a disguised effort to divide the Third World against itself.

From a short-term, "unsentimental" perspective, these judgments might be dismissed as unimportant. Whatever crisis develops, the United States will probably be able to protect its interests and to recover more quickly than any other countries. Moreover, the developing countries that are important to the United States may also have the resources to survive some difficult years, especially if the United States directs most of its aid and support to these countries. And, as some of the self-styled realists also maintain, the analogy with domestic bargaining and the assumption that we are or should be heading toward an international social welfare system may be excessively optimistic. Differences between domestic and international politics are more important than apparent similarities, and states will only act to protect their own perceived interests, occasional acts of charity not withstanding. There is something to all of these views, but not enough to provide sensible policy guidance.

There is no need to reemphasize at this point the reasons why the failure of the North-South Dialogue is a profoundly serious matter, in terms of systemic stability as well as the inability of the developing countries to carry out successful domestic development policies without additional complementary support from the international system. But there seems to be very little that the United States can do by itself to alter the prevailing state of affairs, except in the sense of simply playing the existing game better.[18] What this seems to imply, then, is the need for a three-track strategy, a point that I have emphasized in Chapters 3, 4, and 5. Rather than choosing clearly between any of the policy alternatives discussed above, the approach must be essentially eclectic: some elements from the incremental approach, some from the concentration on key developing countries, but also an additional and longer-term effort to prepare the ground for the kind of systemic restructuring that appears increasingly imperative. As I have already noted, eclecticism is an easy target for critics (especially those who criticize but do not feel the need to devise or offer practicable alternatives of their own), but it is worth emphasizing that I am not advocating ad hoc or random eclecticism. What I seek is a balance between real but divergent needs and pressures, and what is involved is a conscious effort to choose the least costly short-run options and to move toward the most beneficial long-run options. In short, there is a difference between a deliberate strategy of eclecticism and the random eclecticism that usually prevails in an incremental system.

The emphasis on coping measures within the incremental approach, which has been the focus of much of U.S. policy, needs very strong—perhaps additional—support. Stabilizing the existing system only seems like a minimal policy approach, but failure will destroy any opportunity to move to more cooperative systemic patterns. The conventional measures that the United States has pursued, such as standstill agreements, new rules on nontariff barriers, "safety nets" of various kinds, emergency food reserves, and cooperative agreements in the event of a monetary crisis, are thus very crucial. The United States should also take much more seriously the need to strengthen the disaster relief system. Insofar as possible, it should encourage subregional cooperative efforts among the developing countries, as such efforts might provide a degree of support if the international environment deteriorates and they might be easier to implement quickly. The United States should also make a much greater effort to moderate the Dialogue and to reduce some of its rhetorical excesses by making sure that home governments understand its position (and their interests) on specific issues in the Dialogue, perhaps thereby reducing the power of the diplomats and international staffs in Geneva and elsewhere. This is one aspect of playing the game better, to which others can be added. The United States must also alter its rhetorical approach so that it does not promise more than it can deliver and so that it begins to emphasize the genuine dangers facing the developing countries in this decade and how much of those dangers they will have to confront with their own resources and skills.

Concentration on the countries that are most important to the United States in political, economic, and strategic terms is likely to become increasingly prominent during this decade. This is justified not only by U.S. national interests, but also by the fact that several of these countries (e.g., India and Nigeria) could have a serious impact on systemic and subsystemic stability if their problems become unmanageable. But the United States should avoid formally signifying that the new influentials are now the primary focus of its Third World policies and instead should offer support without calling great attention to it. The low profile is justified by the need to avoid arousing domestic discontent within these countries, by the desire to limit adverse reactions by the rest of the developing countries (against the United States and against the countries accepting its support), and by the need of the United States to avoid excessive entanglement with countries that may still be unstable, no matter how great an effort it makes. At the same time, it needs to narrow the list of critically important countries to many fewer than the thirty-two noted earlier so that major commitments are made only where major interests are involved. This means, for the most part, a few OPEC countries, the regional superpowers, near neighbors, and a few strategically located countries. Thus, some resources are left for other developing countries, and the United States does not foreclose the opportunity of developing a wider coalition of "like-minded" countries in the developing world.[19] The last point provides a link with more long-term U.S. needs.

Long-term considerations justify an increased concern with the issue of global restructuring, but on terms that are broader and more politically feasible than any suggested thus far. The United States needs to begin thinking about what this means now, not only to determine the content of a mutually acceptable agreement, but also to begin to build political support for it. It seems to me useful for the U.S. government to begin this process by establishing a highly qualified work-group to study the issue seriously and by bringing into the process from a reasonably early stage Congress and other influential groups, our allies in the OECD, and key intellectual and political figures from the Third World. The form and content of this agreement probably cannot be specified beforehand, but an exchange that approximates the interim bargain that I have just described may be generally indicative: a promise of additional, continuing, and guaranteed help in exchange for abandonment of premature global blueprints and acceptance of a more moderate approach to ultimate ends.[20] There will also be some need, especially if conditions in the world economy do not improve, to emphasize programs that promise short-term benefits for both sides (although the benefits need not be equivalent). And there will be a strong need to seek more coherence in the discussion of appropriate development strategies. The present tendency to ignore this issue or to simply add together a hodgepodge of disparate—if not conflicting—demands merely ensures confusion and the need for even more difficult adjustments at a later date.

While the United States seeks an exchange of substantive concessions for a commitment to a more manageable negotiating process, it will also need to recognize explicitly the need for some degree of international planning and coordination, for despite their familiar limitations only planning and coordination seem able to avert chaos and help enough developing countries. Central control may be too ambitious for a complex and rapidly changing international system, but some forms of central guidance and some effort to provide more information about intentions and opportunities—some effort to fill the gap between central control and complete autonomy—seem both necessary and feasible. The United States needs to be less ideological and more open in response to such efforts to move beyond a market approach that has not worked either well or fairly, especially in areas of direct concern to the developing countries. Consultations and negotiations at the global level may not be able to move much beyond setting very general guidelines and goals, but it might be feasible at the regional and subregional levels to increase substantive consultations (which might serve as an early warning mechanism) and to establish codes of behavior that reduce uncertainty and help to create convergent patterns of expectations.[21] These regional and subregional efforts might become a network of building blocks for the larger system, especially if such efforts were limited and guided by the more general rules and norms established at the global level. Thus one needs to seek an appropriate balance of global, regional, and national tasks, not the dominance of a single level of concern.

Indication of U.S. seriousness about the quest for agreement could in itself have a beneficial impact on the climate of the North-South Dialogue, but more importantly, some convergence of views might gradually become apparent. I should also emphasize that the United States need not be hostage in this effort to the quest for unanimity: Rather than seeking complete agreement with all of the developing countries, it could seek to build up from agreement with particular developing countries (or groups like ASEAN and the Caribbean countries) that are willing to accept the outcome of this quest for a more acceptable restructuring process. The focus would be broader than simply the countries most important to us, but narrower than the whole Group of 77. If the U.S. offer was generous enough, and if its seriousness was apparent, the intermediate group might include most of the developing countries that are making a serious commitment to development and that are willing to seek integration within this system of relations. We do not really need "global" agreement if enough countries are willing to establish new principles and operating rules among themselves, with future accession left open to any country willing to accept the principles and rules (a "coalition of the willing").

The quest for a meaningful restructuring process within the North-South dichotomy seems doomed to failure, whether we start from the global perspective of the Brandt Commission or my own suggestion of an intermediate perspective. This is of course especially true if there is no oil agreement, the absence of which makes the quest for a long-term settlement very academic. Nevertheless, given the importance of restructuring and of signifying a commitment to seek a more stable and a more equitable international order, the effort to set the process going now, *officially,* and to work upward from "like-minded" countries might be useful in both the short-term and the long-term.[22]

The process of reform will be difficult and will undoubtedly confront setbacks along the way, and there will be a need for constant experimentation and evaluation. Hence three final points are worth emphasizing. The first is that the official effort to get the process under way should not be begun under the auspices of institutions like UNCTAD and the UN General Assembly; public bargaining by large groups does not facilitate compromise or substantive agreement. Second, as the positions that emerge must reflect not only mutual interests but also the likelihood of implementation, an effort must be made from the start to devise policies that reflect the constraints under which LDC governments operate—in effect, policies that this, the practical point may be that these arguments about responsibility further delay an effective response to the needs of the non-OPEC countries.

4. These issues are discussed in greater detail in Rothstein, *Global Bargaining,* pp. 229–233.

5. One major difference concerns the oil crisis, which is discussed in most Western or joint North-South proposals such as the Brandt Commission report, but is generally ignored in Southern proposals. The latter tend, of course, to be more ideological and more radical. Southern proposals also usually cover a wider front, as they appear in different contexts and meetings on almost all issues on which North and South confront each other. For the Brandt Commission proposals, see *North-South: A Programme for Survival* (Cambridge, Mass.: M.I.T. Press, 1980).

6. See Paul B. Streeten, "Summary of S.I.D. Conference," (draft report on the 1979 Conference of the Society for International Development).

7. Even if only a crisis makes global restructuring possible, discussion of the content of such changes is still useful. It would mean that negotiations after the crisis would not have to begin from scratch; also, demands for restructuring have the virtue of raising consciousness about Southern problems and perhaps providing some evidence that Southern needs have not been completely forgotten.

8. I do not think it necessary to provide details of these demands, which have been made in the New International Economic Order proposals and also more recently in the meetings of various international institutions such as UNCTAD, UNIDO, and the United Nations Educational, Scientific and Cultural Organization (UNESCO), not to mention the Nonaligned Conference in Havana. As I have already indicated, these demands are more extensive than the Brandt Commission proposals. At any rate, my comments refer primarily to the specific demands of the developing countries, because these seem to me to provide a more complete picture of what is being sought.

9. This argument looks different from each side of the "great divide": The developed countries, having much to lose, are very risk averse; the developing countries, having less to lose, are more willing to take great risks (i.e., changing prevailing patterns even without complete certainty that the results will improve on present performance).

10. The list is based on what might be called "casual empiricism"—that is, I have looked at trade figures, resource needs, and a few other variables to make some rough judgments. It does not seem necessary to discuss these judgments at great length or to provide bits of evidence, as the list of chosen countries is neither surprising nor incontestable (which may be part of the point). I have been told by someone with access to such information that my list is close to, but not identical with, a similar list produced by the CIA, but I cannot vouch for this information. It would be interesting to know the purpose behind such an official list, if it in fact exists.

11. It would be possible to devise broader or narrower lists virtually ad infinitum, and this particular list could also be broken down further—perhaps in terms of concentric circles that (presumably) distinguish degrees of importance. For example, Saudi Arabia and Mexico might be in the innermost circle, thus receiving the greatest support and commitment; Brazil, Venezuela, Nigeria, Iran, Egypt, India, and the Philippines in the next; and so on. All such judgments contain large

the governments see as in their interests, not merely policies that seem the "best" bargain from the perspective of negotiators in the North-South Dialogue. Finally, as the mere enunciation of agreement will not insure instant acceptance by public and official audiences in the developed countries, a deliberate effort must be made to devise a strategy of persuasion—in effect, a campaign strategy—that will indicate just how support for global reform can and should be built.

The international system of the 1980s may become an operator's paradise and a conceptualizer's nightmare. Patchwork is likely to be the order—and an absolutely crucial order—of the day, but if nothing more is done, forecasts that now seem "too bad to be true" may soon seem excessively optimistic. What the United States can do is limited, but it is more than anyone else can do. Perhaps the greatest mistake in these circumstances would be not to choose at all, to drift along; but choosing naively, without consideration of both long-term and short-term U.S. interests, may be just as dangerous. But the difficulty of balancing these interests in a period of great uncertainty and rising insecurity seems to me finally to justify or indeed to necessitate the choice of an eclectic interim policy approach, combining elements from the other approaches but seeking always to keep in focus the need to choose short-run policies that contribute to the achievement of the long-run goals that the United States *must* pursue simultaneously.

A point about this eclectic strategy needs to be better understood by the developing countries. The latter complain bitterly about the failure of the developed countries to accept initiatives like the Brandt Commission Report, and they attribute responsibility for the failure to the recession or to bad timing (the report should have come earlier or later or whatever). But such efforts to restructure the international system will always encounter resistance, if not because conditions are bad, then because they are good and thus apparently eliminate the need for major changes. Acceptance of such large changes is likely to come only after political support has been carefully and deliberately created and nurtured. In an interdependent world, in which the issues at stake directly affect strong domestic interests in the developed countries, this implies an effort to take more account of developed-country concerns. *Immediate* developed-country interests should be emphasized, something of importance (especially reflecting the increased concern of the developed countries for economic security) should be offered in return, and programs that can resist technical assaults by friend and foe alike should be devised. In short, the Brandt Commission Report will be accepted not because it (or any other grand design) is an idea whose time has come, but because support for it has been built by means of a conscious political strategy. The developing countries cannot afford to ignore the need for such a strategy or to assume that a rhetoric of desperation and gloom will suffice.

In addition, the developing countries will need to assess for themselves the wisdom of relying on unity and solidarity, bolstered by promises of gains to all on each issue, when such a negotiating strategy virtually guarantees immobility. Put differently, they may need to recognize that it is not only the stubbornness and shortsightedness of the developed countries that prevents progress, but that the negotiating system engendered by unified group bargaining shares some of the responsibility for the lack of major substantive agreements. One might also add that the need for a political strategy of persuasion is also imperative for the developed countries; merely resisting developing-country demands only guarantees immobility and crises.

The argument that I have made might appear to bear some kinship with what might be called moderate or pragmatic liberalism. This is certainly true in some senses: My argument also rests on the need and the desire to help the developing countries as much as possible, and I have attempted throughout to recognize and take account of difficulties and uncertainties and to avoid the easy descent into the rhetoric of gloom or of ultimate harmony. But I should also emphasize that my argument differs in at least one fundamental way from the "moderation-plus" arguments of pragmatic liberals. The latter arguments, I believe, tend to be content with the injunction to "do more," but they are much weaker substantively in indicating just what and just why the more ought to be. Consequently such arguments are likely to fall prey to some major weaknesses of incrementalism: drifting without clear direction and the accumulation of small problems into large crises. By contrast, I have at least attempted to provide specific suggestions for the short term as well as the long term. Moreover, these suggestions deliberately seek to establish a bridge between what the United States must do now and where it would like to arrive some years hence. Implicitly, then, there has been both a goal and a strategy in these pages.

It may be useful to conclude by recapitulating the basic theme of this discussion.[23] The primary (but not the only) goal of the United States in North-South relations at this juncture must be stability, which is a prerequisite for the achievement of other goals. But stability, even if achievable, is necessary but not sufficient for the pursuit of other goals, not only the protection of tangible economic interests but also cooperation in establishing a particular kind of international system. The latter goals require much more liberal and progressive policies toward the Third World (which implies greater support and a guarantee of continuous support, but not a commitment to some of the more grandiose proposals for change), for only this will permit sufficient progress or at least inhibit destructive reac-

tions. Such policies hardly guarantee either stability or the effective p[er]formance of development tasks within the Third World, but it is plausi[ble to] argue that they are more likely to succeed than any other alternative[.]

But liberal and progressive policies must overcome many pol[itical] obstacles in the developed countries, especially in current political [and] economic circumstances, and the United States and other developed c[oun]tries need to proceed carefully in implementing such policies because o[f the] limitations of our knowledge and foresight. Successful implementation [of a] new order will also require the cooperation of the developing countries [and] important changes in both their domestic and international policies. [For] these reasons, the approach to a liberal order must come by means—[by] policy steps—that are prudent and moderate (conservative, but *not* in [the] free-market sense). This also necessarily implies a long and difficult tra[nsi]tional period in which the effort to construct a more stable and equitable [in]ternational system will be threatened by the need to deal with immedi[ate] pressures that are complex and powerful. But both short-term and lon[g-] term interests and needs can be achieved or more nearly approximated [by] the United States—and, of course, all other crucial participants—explici[tly] recognizes the legitimacy of both present and future needs, if it explicit[ly] seeks the least harmful short-term responses, and if it has a clear sense [of] the kind of international system that it hopes to encourage and establish[.]

Notes

1. In development terms U.S. power and influence has probably always been les[s] than the United States perceived. Once the naive notion that foreign aid, filling a foreign exchange or savings "gap," would serve as a necessary catalyst for development was largely discredited, it became clear that much more was involved—and most of the much more related to domestic commitments and policies. Over these areas, the United States had much less power—and in current circumstances U.S. power in these areas is even further diminished. This is one of the key facts that must be dealt with in determining policy.

2. For a more extensive discussion of dependability, see Robert L. Rothstein, *Global Bargaining: UNCTAD and the Quest for a New International Economic Order* (Princeton, N.J.: Princeton University Press, 1979), pp. 265–271.

3. There has also been much fencing with OPEC about who is more responsible for the difficulties faced by the non-OPEC developing countries and about who should do what to help these countries. OPEC is obviously not responsible for all of the problems that the non-OPEC LDCs confront, but OPEC's policies have massively increased these problems and sharply diminished the likelihood that much external support will be made available—and OPEC's much-touted aid commitments hardly provide more than a very small degree of compensation. Despite

elements of subjectivity and ambiguity, but they may be made anyway if this policy approach is adopted.

12. The background papers prepared for the Interfutures project at the OECD were almost uniformly pessimistic about the prospects for regional cooperation. The papers were not for attribution and cannot be quoted — nor is it really necessary, as most were very impressionistic *tours d'horizon* — but the views expressed, which reflected shared judgments of various groups of experts, tended to be very pessimistic not only about economic complementarities, but also about instabilities generated by volatile political systems, unreformed social institutions, and the failure to create and expand domestic markets.

13. See, for example, John W. Sewell, "Can the North Prosper without Growth and Progress in the South?" in Martin M. McLaughlin, ed., *The United States and World Development: Agenda 1979* (New York: Praeger Publishers, 1979), pp. 43–76.

14. One should also note another potential cost: the difficulty of reaching agreement in those areas that do require global cooperation. As I assume that the differentiated approach will be implemented in a determined and consistent fashion only if world conditions become increasingly desperate, this is, however, only a minor issue here; global agreement will not be possible in any case. Still, there is a kind of dialectic at work between the global and the differentiated response. The latter might work (or be attempted) when the former functions badly, but differentiation would work much better (and might not be necessary) if the global response was more effective. Put differently, the two levels are likely to share a linked fate, but differentiation may be the most difficult bilateral policy in terms of constructing effective global agreements.

15. These issues are discussed in Chapters 1 and 2 and in greater detail in Rothstein, *Global Bargaining*.

16. The latter difficulties may also, of course, have a beneficial impact if they intensify the desire to search for new approaches to present difficulties. This is already happening to some extent, as more and more studies call for some kind of North-South breakthrough — although none that I have read has a clear idea of how to deal with the obstacles in the way.

17. The Secretary-General of UNCTAD has recently complained about the time lost at meetings as each group attempts to create a common position, thus limiting the time available for group-versus-group negotiations. He wants to diminish these difficulties by allowing the UNCTAD staff to play a greater role in preconference consultations and by having ministerial-level participation at the beginning of conferences, not merely at the end. This mistakes the real problems, which are the home governments' indifference to the substance (as distinct from their symbolic significance) of many Dialogue issues and the need for the Group of 77 to agree on a proposal that promises something to everybody (see the comments on this in Chapter 2). As long as these problems persist, the suggested reforms will be ineffectual. For a report on the Secretary-General's views, see UNCTAD, *Monthly Bulletin No. 159* (March 1980).

18. These issues are discussed in Chapters 1 and 2 and in greater detail in Rothstein, *Global Bargaining*.

19. The smaller list of key countries might include India, Mexico, Brazil, Saudi

Arabia, Nigeria, and Indonesia. Perhaps the Philippines, South Korea, Iraq, Iran, Venezuela, and the Caribbean countries (as a group) should be added.

20. The primary battleground in this debate, at least for the next few years, is likely to be the trading system. In part, this may reflect an underlying philosophical conflict between support for a free-market system that gives unequal rewards to participants and an international system that is becoming normatively a degree more democratic and that seeks to reduce the risks to the developing countries and to provide them with unequal rewards as compensation for past exploitation and present deficiencies. In practical terms, however, the main battle may be fought out within the developed countries on the issue of "industrial policy." The key in that complex (and as yet essentially rhetorical) debate may be whether there is a decision to move toward "reindustrialization" (which seems to mean reviving dying industries, thus creating great difficulties for developing countries that should be moving into such industries) or toward more rapid movement out of old industries and toward more advanced industries (which might be beneficial to many LDCs), or whether there is no clear decision at all. Within the international system itself, one key will be whether some mutually acceptable meaning can be given to the idea of "organized free trade" (and its many variations). As yet, it seems a euphemism for national willfulness, but it is not impossible to negotiate rules that limit the range and duration of particular distortions, that expose these distortions to some degree of mutual accountability, and that provide special exemptions for the developing countries. The difficulties of negotiating such complex agreements might suggest the advisability of having separate sets of rules for differently situated states, perhaps interlocking with a more general set of guidance rules and methodological norms (i.e., how to go about things), rather than attempting to establish a single set of rules and norms. I have argued this point at greater length in Rothstein, *Global Bargaining,* pp. 269–272.

21. I have been favorably impressed by Japan's effort to adjust to new developments, not only nationally but also regionally. At the latter level, increased consultations and serious efforts to establish codes of conduct in a variety of areas, as well as the use of long-term contracts, with Australia and other Pacific countries provide an indication of direction for other countries and areas. See especially Sir John Crawford and Saburo Okita, eds., *Raw Materials and Pacific Economic Integration* (London: Croom Helm, 1978).

22. Movement in this direction would at first be resisted by the leadership of the Group of 77, who fear any attempt to differentiate or to bypass the Dialogue (wherein lies their power). This suggests the need for careful preparation and private initiatives until more of the content of a final agreement can be determined. It should also be noted that other individuals and groups within the Third World have begun speculating about alternatives to a Group of 77 that includes a fair number of reactionary or repulsive regimes. For example, a spokesman for the International Foundation for Development Alternatives has argued that "a smaller group of like-minded governments would be better able to resist pressure and divisive tactics than a larger group whose ideological cracks are thinly papered over." He advocated a coalition across bloc lines, primarily committed to basic human needs and self-reliance, joining together the "progressive" countries in both

groups. While we need not accept his definition of a progressive coalition, we should note the key point in this context, that efforts to move out of the North-South framework will not be denounced everywhere in the Third World, as distinct from everywhere in the Dialogue. For the quote, see Michael Zammit Cutajar, "Notes on a Political Preamble for Another Development Strategy," *IFDA Dossier 4* (February 1979), p. 6.

23. I have not directly discussed the policies of the developing countries themselves in this study, as my central concern is with U.S. policy. Nevertheless, there is at least an implicit judgment throughout these pages about what policies most of the developing countries are likely to adopt (or maintain) during the first part of the 1980s: Most are likely to persist in present policies (which aim at rapid growth and industrialization); very few are likely to make a genuine commitment to implementing basic needs or redistribution policies (especially if they require diverting funds from other goals). If economic conditions deteriorate, the latter policies may become even more imperative for many countries, but even more difficult to implement effectively with so many competing demands for scarce resources. At any rate, the failure to alter conventional development strategies—a theme that appeared in Chapters 3, 4, and 5—may be understandable in light of the risks involved (both political and economic), but the risks of not altering strategies may soon prove to be even greater. One can only hope that this judgment is too pessimistic and that many of the poorest countries will somehow be able to "muddle through" current and emerging difficulties; but there is so little discussion of this issue in official circles, perhaps because so little can be done, because of sensitivities about intervention, or because of fears of seeming too pessimistic, that pessimism seems amply warranted.

Index

Abolfathi, Farid, 140 n54, 141 n59
Ahmed, Abdelkader Sid, 140 n52
Aid. *See* Foreign aid
Allen, Edward L., 136 n9
Anthony, Kenneth R. M., 84 n38
Anticipatory adjustment, 159-161
Aronson, Jonathan David, 186 n77
Atter, Steven, 83 n29
Aziz, Sartaj, 82 n23, 83 n29, 86 n58

Balassa, Bela, 180 n8, 181 n20
Barnett, A. Doak, 86 n55
Basic human needs strategy, 10-11,
    138 n29, 245
Beek, David C., 186 n80
Bell, Daniel, 15 n1, 80 n2
Billerbeck, K., 182 n25
Blitzer, Charles, 140 n45
Bloomfield, Lincoln P., 212 n9
Bogue, Donald J., 83 n82
Brandt Commission, 41 n21, 78-79,
    139 n37, 208, 227-234
Braun, Ferdnand, 184 n48
Braun, H. G., 87 n68
Brodman, John R., 136 n11
Burki, Shakud Javed, 82 n19, 83 n35
Byer, T. A., 137 n23, 138 n26

Caribbean countries, 83 n35, 239
Carter administration, 138 n29, 212
    n15
"Center" versus "periphery"
    argument, 144-145
Central management or guidance, 6,
    230-232, 249, 255

Chenery, Hollis B., 180 n11, 181
    n15
Chernick, Sidney E., 84 n35
China, 86 n55, 167-168, 219
    trade with developing countries,
    167-168
Chou, Marylin, 83 n27
Choucri, Nazli, 80 n1, 80 n5
Cline, William R., 39 n5, 186 n79
Cold War, 199-201, 238
Collective self-reliance, 78, 162-168,
    184 n53, 211 n6
Concepts, validity of, 12-14, 18 n21
Connection between domestic and
    external policies, 31-33,
    178-179, 233-235, 259
Crawford, Sir John, 262 n21
Cummings, Ralph W., 81 n15, 83
    n27, 83 n31
Curry, Robert L., 86 n59

Debt problem, 171-177
    connection to export prospects, 174
Delinking strategy, 163, 193, 244
Developed countries, 32-33, 36-38,
    57, 79-80, 140 n53, 150-151,
    154, 169-170, 198
    importance of South for, 32-33,
    36-38, 143-145, 200, 208,
    220-221, 253
    pressures on unity, 150-151, 154,
    170, 198
    See also North-South Dialogue;
    OECD
Developing countries, 11-12, 45-46,

77, 162, 193–194, 251–252, 258
goals in North-South Dialogue,
    11–12, 251–252
growing dependence on North,
    45–46, 193–194
need for new negotiating strategy,
    162, 251–252, 258
See also Food problems of
    developing countries; Group of
    77; North-South Dialogue;
    Oil problems of developing
    countries; OPEC; Third World
Development strategies, 74, 79–80,
    89, 97, 100–101, 113, 141 n60
    157, 263 n23
Diaz-Alejandro, Carlos F., 211 n4
Diebold, William, Jr., 180 n5, 183
    n47
Diesing, Paul, 211 n1
Disaster relief system. *See* Emergency
    relief system
Diwan, Romesh, 82 n20
Drobnick, Richard, 83 n29

East-South trade. *See* Trade with
    socialist countries
Eckbo, Paul Leo, 140 n48
Economic cooperation among
    developing countries. *See*
    Collective self-reliance
EEC. *See* European Economic
    Community
Effects of slower economic growth
    rates, 146–147, 169–170,
    202–203, 215, 229–230
Eibenschutz, Juan, 136 n9
Einhorn, Jessica P., 186 n79
Emergency relief system, 79, 87 n70,
    225
Energy, 89–142
    differences from food problem,
        89–90
    and increasing agricultural
        productivity, 65
    and industrial strategy, 100–101

See also Oil problems of
    developing countries; OPEC
Enzer, Selwyn, 83 n29
European Economic Community
    (EEC), 160, 229
External trends, influence of, 3–4,
    8, 19, 178–179. *See also* Debt
    problem; Energy; Food
    problems of developing
    countries; Oil problems of
    developing countries
Ezzati, Ali, 140 n48

Fallen-Bailey, D. G., 137 n23, 138
    n26
Fogarty, Carol, 185 n71
Food problems of developing
    countries, 48–87
    and developed countries, 56–57,
        59, 65, 66
    and domestic policies, 60–63
    and financial needs, 64–65, 76–77
    and foreign policy, 66–72
    and global food system, 50, 56,
        71–72, 75
    implementation of policies, 57–60,
        63
    investment in agriculture, 59,
        76–77
    policy prescriptions, 53–56
    prospects for different countries,
        69–71
    and regional agreements, 72, 75
    supply and demand projections,
        50–52, 57
    and U.S. policy, 69–80
Forecasting, 1–2, 43–44, 47,
    91–92
    implications of pessimism, 6–9, 16
        n10
    implications for policy, 2
Foreign aid, 75, 77–79, 87 n65,
    175, 201, 212 n14, 232–234
Foreign trade. *See* International
    trade

Galtung, Johan, 16 n14
Giersch, Herbert, 182 n26
Global oil agreement, 122-130,
132, 135
elements, 126-129
and OPEC, 122-130
tripartite approach, need for,
125-126
and U.S. policy, 130-135
See also OPEC
Global restructuring, 226-237
and need for political strategy,
235, 257-258
problems with, 229-236
rationale for, 228
Goering, T. J., 82 n19, 83 n35
Graduation, principle of, 143,
153-154
Green, Robert T., 183 n33
Green, Stephen, 87 n70
Griffin, Keith, 61, 84 n39, 84 n42
Group of 77, 21, 25, 194-198, 223,
251-252, 262 n22
desire for unity, 21, 194-195
efforts to maintain unity, 21,
194-198
negotiating strategy, 11, 223, 252
potential splits and fault lines,
25-31, 194-198
See also North-South Dialogue;
Third World
Group system, 21-24
consequences of, 21-24
package proposals, 21-22
Growing gaps within Third World.
See Group of 77; Third World

Hamilton, Richard E., 136 n9
Haq, Khadija, 182 n28
Helleiner, Gerald K., 182 n27, 186
n74
Herman, Bohuslav, 184 n52
Hirsch, Seev, 182 n26
Hopkins, J. Wallace, Jr., 136 n9
Hopkins, Raymond F., 56, 81 n14

Huddleston, Barbara, 85 n52, 86
n53
Hughes, Helen, 184 n48

IMF (International Monetary Fund),
132, 176-177, 187 n83
and conditionality, 176
Implementation, 5-6, 73-75, 112,
256-257
Incentives, 73-75
Industrial countries. *See* Developed
countries; OECD
Influence of international staffs,
22-23, 254
Instability. *See* Stability as policy goal
Interdependence, 6-7, 67
International caste system, 46, 195
International Monetary Fund. *See*
IMF
International planning, 255-256
International social welfare system,
68, 175, 234
International system, 34, 44, 46,
68-69, 218-219, 234, 259
International trade, 36, 46-47,
143-187, 225
beneficiaries within Third World,
147-152
benefits of, 143-145, 150-151
and manufactured exports,
145-146, 148, 152
and "new protectionism," 143, 145,
153
and NICs, 147-152, 154
and North-South Dialogue, 36
prospects for southern exports,
151-152, 162-168
and shifts in comparative
advantage, 149, 158-160,
168-170
and stages of comparative
advantage, 146, 153
and U.S. policy, 160-161,
166-167
See also Redeployment of

industries; Restructuring of
world industrial order;
South-South trade

Jabber, Paul, 140 n47
Japan, 57, 150–151, 262 n21
Johnston, Bruce F., 84 n38
Josling, Tim, 85 n48

Kahn, Herman, 15 n8
Kamrany, Nake M., 212 n17
Karlik, John R., 181 n22
Keesing, Donald B., 180 n11, 181
    n15, 181 n19, 182 n27, 182
    n28, 183 n34
Keohane, Robert O., 212 n16
Kindleberger, Charles P., 211 n2
Knorr, Klaus, 15 n8, 80 n2
Krause, Lawrence B., 182 n25
Krauss, Melvyn B., 17 n15
Kravis, Irving, 179 n1
Krueger, Anne O., 180 n8, 185 n62

Lambertini, Adrian, 138 n27, 138
    n31, 140 n51
Leontief, Wassily, 81 n10, 83 n28,
    183 n37
Levy, Walter J., 141 n58
Liberal interpretation of
    North-South policies, 199–200,
    212 n15
  in Cold War, 199–200
Lindbeck, Assar, 213 n18
Lipton, Michael, 84 n39, 84 n44
Lovins, Avery, 138 n30
Lovins, Hunter, 138 n30
Lutz, James M., 183 n33

Makhijani, Arjun, 137 n14
Marshall Plan (for the Third
    World), 78–79, 236
Marstrand, Pauline K., 82 n21
Mathieson, John A., 179 n2
Milieu goals, 167, 200–201
Mishan, Eugene, 15 n7
Moran, Theodore, 140 n49

Morgan, Dan, 85 n50
Morgenstern, Oskar, 80 n2
Morton, Kathryn, 180 n6
Mossavar-Rahmani, Bijan, 139 n41,
    141 n63
Mugno, John F., 139 n44, 140 n47
Mukharjee, Santosh, 183 n45
Multinational corporations, 111–112,
    165, 182 n27
Myrdal, Gunnar, 84 n38

Nayyar, Deepak, 185 n67
Negotiating system, 12, 14, 21–24,
    248–252. *See also* Group of 77;
    North-south Dialogue
New influentials, 209–210, 237–245
New International Economic Order
    (NIEO), 35–36, 114–115, 177,
    236, 260 n8
Newly industrializing countries
    (NICs), 40 n10, 147–152, 165
NICs. *See* Newly industrializing
    countries
NIEC. *See* New International
    Economic Order
NOLDCs. *See* Nonoil developing
    countries
Nonoil developing countries
    (NOLDCs), 89–142
  and global oil agreement, 122–130,
    132
  and OPEC, 122–130, 132
  See also Oil problems of developing
    countries; OPEC
Non-OPEC oil exporters, 103, 136
    n13
Noreng, Oystein, 141 n60
North-South Dialogue, 10–15, 19–42,
    194–198, 248–252
  conflicts of vision, 10–15
  importance to U.S., 32–33, 36–38
  negotiating process, 21–24
  possible reforms of, 248–252
  relationship to home governments,
    24–33
  and unity of Group of 77, 20–21,

194–198
and U.S. policy, 31–38, 225–226,
248–252
See also Group of 77
Nove, Alec, 83 n30
Nugent, Jeffrey B., 17 n20
Nye, Joseph S., Jr., 142 n68
Nyerere, Julius, 20, 38 n4

Odell, Peter R., 141 n55
OECD (Organization for Economic
Cooperation and Development),
119, 127, 148, 150, 154, 179 n4.
See also Developed countries
Oil companies, 111–112
Oil problems of developing
countries, 89–142
and conservation, 92, 98
exploitation of indigenous
resources, 96–98, 109
and financial needs, 102, 109–111
and foreign policy, 130–135
and gap within Third World,
104–108
policy prescriptions, 92–97
projections of supply and demand,
90–92, 103
relationship to traditional and new
development strategies, 92–93,
100–101, 131
and U.S. policy, 111–112, 130–135
See also Global oil agreement;
Nonoil developing countries;
Non-OPEC oil exporters; OPEC
Okita, Saburo, 262 n21
OPEC (Organization of Petroleum
Exporting Countries), 27,
35–36, 102, 114–132, 172,
206, 259 n3
desire to help NOLDCs, 115–116,
123
future policies, 120–122
and global oil agreement, 122–130,
132, 135
and NIEO, 35–36, 114, 132
price and production policies,

116–120
and Saudi policy, 116–119
unity of, 116–120
See also Oil problems of
developing countries
Organization for Economic
Cooperation and Development.
See OECD
Organization of Petroleum Exporting
Countries. *See* OPEC

Palmedo, Philip F., 137 n21, 138
n28
Pena, Felix, 185 n65
Penrose, Edith, 140 n46, 141 n55
Pindyck, Robert S., 136 n7, 137
n18, 140 n45, 141 n56, 183 n40
Piotrow, Phyllis T., 212 n14
Poleman, Thomas T., 84 n42
Political conflicts within Third
World, 28–30, 197–198,
relation to economic fault lines,
29–30, 197–198
Population pressures, 58, 82 n25,
212 n14
Portes, Richard, 185 n66, 185 n68
Puchala, Donald J., 56, 81 n14

Recycling, 172–173, 176
Redeployment of industries, 155–162.
See also International trade;
Restructuring of world
industrial order
Reform policies, 60–63, 73, 76,
79–80, 179
Reform versus revolution debate,
60–63, 73
Regionalism, 28, 72, 86 n55, 154,
209–210, 240–241, 261 n12
Resource dependence, 242–243
Restructuring. *See* Global
restructuring; Restructuring of
world industrial order
Restructuring of world industrial
order, 155–162
and adjustment policies, 158–160

and development strategies,
157–158
and energy, 157
and shifts in comparative
advantage, 159–160
Reutlinger, Shlomo, 86 n56, 86 n57
Revolution, 60–63, 219–220
Revolution versus reform. *See*
Reform versus revolution
debate
Robertson, D. H., 179 n1
Robinson, Thomas W., 80 n1, 80 n5
Roper, Burns W., 87 n65
Rosecrance, Richard, 211 n3
Rothchild, Donald, 86 n59
Rothstein, Robert L., 15 n1, 16 n14,
18 n22, 38 n3, 41 n15, 80 n6,
81 n9, 182 n29, 211 n5, 213
n19, 259 n2, 262 n20
Rush, Howard, 82 n21
Rustow, Dankwart A., 139 n44, 140
n47

Sanderson, Fred H., 81 n16, 83
n27, 83 n30
Saudi Arabia, 101, 116–118,
128–129, 133–134, 260 n11
and OPEC, 116–118
spare capacity, 101, 133–134
Scenarios of the 1980s, 201–211
differentiation and selectivity,
209–210
disintegration and disorder,
205–207
permanent low-level crisis,
203–205
quest for global bargain, 207–209
Second-best theory and policies,
6–7, 170–171, 209, 213 n21
Security, economic aspects, 7,
143–144, 150
Sekiguchi, Sueo, 182 n25
Sewell, John W., 41 n18, 261 n13
Singh, Agit, 16 n13, 183 n41
Smith, Gordon W., 186 n79
South-South trade, 152, 162–168

composition of, 163–165
and multinational corporations,
165
prospects for, 165–166
regional patterns, 164–165
Stability as policy goal, 215–222
and other goals, 215, 217–218
and revolutionary instability,
219–220
systemic and sub-systemic,
218–219
Stern, Joseph J., 212 n17
Stewart, Frances, 87 n60
Strange, Susan, 186 n77
Streeten, Paul B., 43, 80 n3, 260 n6
Stryker, Richard E., 85 n46, 137 n16
Sub-regional agreements, 72, 86 n55,
210, 240–241

Tapinos, George, 212 n14
Taylor, Lance, 62, 84 n41
Third World, 21, 25–31, 33, 77–78,
162–168, 184 n53, 197–199
and collective self-reliance,
162–168
fault lines within, 28–30, 175,
193–196
quest for unity, 21, 77–78,
193–197
See also Group of 77
Tinbergen, Jan, 15 n6
Trade with socialist countries,
167–168
Tsui, Amy Ong, 83 n32
Tulloch, Peter, 180 n6

Uchendu, Victor C., 84 n38
Uddin, Fasih, 185 n65
Uncertainty, 7–9, 190–192
effect on developing countries,
190–191
implications for U.S., 191–192
new scope of, 190
UNCTAD (United Nations
Conference on Trade and
Development), 32, 167, 171,

256, 261 n17
UNIDO (United Nations Industrial
    Development Organization), 39
    n6, 145, 158, 171
United States' policy, 2-3, 5,
    31-38, 189-263
    and Cold War, 199-201
    and different policy choices,
        222-259
    and diminishing U.S. power,
        192-193
    eclectic strategy, 247-259
    and global restructuring, 226-237,
        254-259
    and incrementalism, 222-226,
        253-254
    and multiple goals, 198-201
    and policy of differentiation,
        237-245, 254
    and quest for stability, 215-222
    toward North-South Dialogue,
        31-38, 225-226
    See also Food problems of
        developing countries;
        International trade; Oil
        problems of developing countries

Valdes, Alberto, 85 n52, 86 n53
Vallenilla, Luis, 141 n55

Walters, Harry, 82 n21
Waterbury, John, 40 n12
Watkins, Stephen B., 181 n22
Weckstein, R. S., 86 n57
Wilson, Carroll L., 136 n12
Winfrey, Carey, 139 n43
Wionczek, Miguel S., 186 n76,
    186 n78
Wolf, Martin, 182 n23
Wolfers, Arnold, 167, 212 n13
World Bank, 111-112, 132, 137
    n14, 177, 186 n82
    changing role, 177
    energy program, 111-112
    investment in agriculture, 59
World industrial order, restructuring
    of. *See* Restructuring of world
    industrial order
Wortman, Sterling, 81 n15, 83 n27,
    83 n31

Yasugi, Y., 182 n25
Yeats, Alexander J., 180 n6
Yotopoulos, Pan A., 17 n20

Zammit-Cutajar, Michael, 263 n22

The Third World and U.S. Foreign Policy

Also of Interest

U.S. Foreign Policy and the New International Economic Order: Negotiating Global Patterns, Robert K. Olson

New Directions in Development: A Study of U.S. AID, Donald R. Mickelwait, Charles F. Sweet, and Elliott R. Morss

† *U.S. Policy in International Institutions: Defining Reasonable Options in an Unreasonable World,* Revised Edition, edited by Seymour Maxwell Fingar and Joseph R. Harbert

Global Human Rights: Public Policies, Comparative Measures, and NGO Strategies, edited by Ved P. Nanda, James R. Scarritt, and George W. Shepherd, Jr.

† *The Soviet Union in the Third World: Successes and Failures,* edited by Robert H. Donaldson

† *Change in the International System,* edited by Ole R. Holsti, Randolph M. Siverson, and Alexander L. George

† *The Challenge of the New International Economic Order,* edited by Edwin P. Reubens

The New Economics of the Less Developed Countries: Changing Perceptions in the North-South Dialogue, edited by Nake Kamrany

† *From Dependency to Development: Strategies to Overcome Underdevelopment and Inequality,* edited by Heraldo Muñoz

Latin America, the United States, and the Inter-American System, edited by John D. Martz and Lars Schoultz

†Available in hardcover and paperback.

the governments see as in their interests, not merely policies that seem the "best" bargain from the perspective of negotiators in the North-South Dialogue. Finally, as the mere enunciation of agreement will not insure instant acceptance by public and official audiences in the developed countries, a deliberate effort must be made to devise a strategy of persuasion — in effect, a campaign strategy — that will indicate just how support for global reform can and should be built.

The international system of the 1980s may become an operator's paradise and a conceptualizer's nightmare. Patchwork is likely to be the order — and an absolutely crucial order — of the day, but if nothing more is done, forecasts that now seem "too bad to be true" may soon seem excessively optimistic. What the United States can do is limited, but it is more than anyone else can do. Perhaps the greatest mistake in these circumstances would be not to choose at all, to drift along; but choosing naively, without consideration of both long-term and short-term U.S. interests, may be just as dangerous. But the difficulty of balancing these interests in a period of great uncertainty and rising insecurity seems to me finally to justify or indeed to necessitate the choice of an eclectic interim policy approach, combining elements from the other approaches but seeking always to keep in focus the need to choose short-run policies that contribute to the achievement of the long-run goals that the United States *must* pursue simultaneously.

A point about this eclectic strategy needs to be better understood by the developing countries. The latter complain bitterly about the failure of the developed countries to accept initiatives like the Brandt Commission Report, and they attribute responsibility for the failure to the recession or to bad timing (the report should have come earlier or later or whatever). But such efforts to restructure the international system will always encounter resistance, if not because conditions are bad, then because they are good and thus apparently eliminate the need for major changes. Acceptance of such large changes is likely to come only after political support has been carefully and deliberately created and nurtured. In an interdependent world, in which the issues at stake directly affect strong domestic interests in the developed countries, this implies an effort to take more account of developed-country concerns. *Immediate* developed-country interests should be emphasized, something of importance (especially reflecting the increased concern of the developed countries for economic security) should be offered in return, and programs that can resist technical assaults by friend and foe alike should be devised. In short, the Brandt Commission Report will be accepted not because it (or any other grand design) is an idea whose time has come, but because support for it has been built by means of a conscious political strategy. The developing countries cannot afford to ignore the need for such a strategy or to assume that a rhetoric of desperation and gloom will suffice.

In addition, the developing countries will need to assess for themselves the wisdom of relying on unity and solidarity, bolstered by promises of gains to all on each issue, when such a negotiating strategy virtually guarantees immobility. Put differently, they may need to recognize that it is not only the stubbornness and shortsightedness of the developed countries that prevents progress, but that the negotiating system engendered by unified group bargaining shares some of the responsibility for the lack of major substantive agreements. One might also add that the need for a political strategy of persuasion is also imperative for the developed countries; merely resisting developing-country demands only guarantees immobility and crises.

The argument that I have made might appear to bear some kinship with what might be called moderate or pragmatic liberalism. This is certainly true in some senses: My argument also rests on the need and the desire to help the developing countries as much as possible, and I have attempted throughout to recognize and take account of difficulties and uncertainties and to avoid the easy descent into the rhetoric of gloom or of ultimate harmony. But I should also emphasize that my argument differs in at least one fundamental way from the "moderation-plus" arguments of pragmatic liberals. The latter arguments, I believe, tend to be content with the injunction to "do more," but they are much weaker substantively in indicating just what and just why the more ought to be. Consequently such arguments are likely to fall prey to some major weaknesses of incrementalism: drifting without clear direction and the accumulation of small problems into large crises. By contrast, I have at least attempted to provide specific suggestions for the short term as well as the long term. Moreover, these suggestions deliberately seek to establish a bridge between what the United States must do now and where it would like to arrive some years hence. Implicitly, then, there has been both a goal and a strategy in these pages.

It may be useful to conclude by recapitulating the basic theme of this discussion.[23] The primary (but not the only) goal of the United States in North-South relations at this juncture must be stability, which is a prerequisite for the achievement of other goals. But stability, even if achievable, is necessary but not sufficient for the pursuit of other goals, not only the protection of tangible economic interests but also cooperation in establishing a particular kind of international system. The latter goals require much more liberal and progressive policies toward the Third World (which implies greater support and a guarantee of continuous support, but not a commitment to some of the more grandiose proposals for change), for only this will permit sufficient progress or at least inhibit destructive reac-

tions. Such policies hardly guarantee either stability or the effective performance of development tasks within the Third World, but it is plausible to
argue that they are more likely to succeed than any other alternative.

But liberal and progressive policies must overcome many political
obstacles in the developed countries, especially in current political and
economic circumstances, and the United States and other developed countries need to proceed carefully in implementing such policies because of the
limitations of our knowledge and foresight. Successful implementation of a
new order will also require the cooperation of the developing countries and
important changes in both their domestic and international policies. For
these reasons, the approach to a liberal order must come by means—by
policy steps—that are prudent and moderate (conservative, but *not* in the
free-market sense). This also necessarily implies a long and difficult transitional period in which the effort to construct a more stable and equitable international system will be threatened by the need to deal with immediate
pressures that are complex and powerful. But both short-term and long-
term interests and needs can be achieved or more nearly approximated if
the United States—and, of course, all other crucial participants—explicitly
recognizes the legitimacy of both present and future needs, if it explicitly
seeks the least harmful short-term responses, and if it has a clear sense of
the kind of international system that it hopes to encourage and establish.

Notes

1. In development terms U.S. power and influence has probably always been less
than the United States perceived. Once the naive notion that foreign aid, filling a
foreign exchange or savings "gap," would serve as a necessary catalyst for development was largely discredited, it became clear that much more was involved—and
most of the much more related to domestic commitments and policies. Over these
areas, the United States had much less power—and in current circumstances U.S.
power in these areas is even further diminished. This is one of the key facts that
must be dealt with in determining policy.

2. For a more extensive discussion of dependability, see Robert L. Rothstein,
Global Bargaining: UNCTAD and the Quest for a New International Economic Order
(Princeton, N.J.: Princeton University Press, 1979), pp. 265–271.

3. There has also been much fencing with OPEC about who is more responsible
for the difficulties faced by the non-OPEC developing countries and about who
should do what to help these countries. OPEC is obviously not responsible for all of
the problems that the non-OPEC LDCs confront, but OPEC's policies have
massively increased these problems and sharply diminished the likelihood that much
external support will be made available—and OPEC's much-touted aid commitments hardly provide more than a very small degree of compensation. Despite

this, the practical point may be that these arguments about responsibility further delay an effective response to the needs of the non-OPEC countries.

4. These issues are discussed in greater detail in Rothstein, *Global Bargaining,* pp. 229–233.

5. One major difference concerns the oil crisis, which is discussed in most Western or joint North-South proposals such as the Brandt Commission report, but is generally ignored in Southern proposals. The latter tend, of course, to be more ideological and more radical. Southern proposals also usually cover a wider front, as they appear in different contexts and meetings on almost all issues on which North and South confront each other. For the Brandt Commission proposals, see *North-South: A Programme for Survival* (Cambridge, Mass.: M.I.T. Press, 1980).

6. See Paul B. Streeten, "Summary of S.I.D. Conference," (draft report on the 1979 Conference of the Society for International Development).

7. Even if only a crisis makes global restructuring possible, discussion of the content of such changes is still useful. It would mean that negotiations after the crisis would not have to begin from scratch; also, demands for restructuring have the virtue of raising consciousness about Southern problems and perhaps providing some evidence that Southern needs have not been completely forgotten.

8. I do not think it necessary to provide details of these demands, which have been made in the New International Economic Order proposals and also more recently in the meetings of various international institutions such as UNCTAD, UNIDO, and the United Nations Educational, Scientific and Cultural Organization (UNESCO), not to mention the Nonaligned Conference in Havana. As I have already indicated, these demands are more extensive than the Brandt Commission proposals. At any rate, my comments refer primarily to the specific demands of the developing countries, because these seem to me to provide a more complete picture of what is being sought.

9. This argument looks different from each side of the "great divide": The developed countries, having much to lose, are very risk averse; the developing countries, having less to lose, are more willing to take great risks (i.e., changing prevailing patterns even without complete certainty that the results will improve on present performance).

10. The list is based on what might be called "casual empiricism" — that is, I have looked at trade figures, resource needs, and a few other variables to make some rough judgments. It does not seem necessary to discuss these judgments at great length or to provide bits of evidence, as the list of chosen countries is neither surprising nor incontestable (which may be part of the point). I have been told by someone with access to such information that my list is close to, but not identical with, a similar list produced by the CIA, but I cannot vouch for this information. It would be interesting to know the purpose behind such an official list, if it in fact exists.

11. It would be possible to devise broader or narrower lists virtually ad infinitum, and this particular list could also be broken down further — perhaps in terms of concentric circles that (presumably) distinguish degrees of importance. For example, Saudi Arabia and Mexico might be in the innermost circle, thus receiving the greatest support and commitment; Brazil, Venezuela, Nigeria, Iran, Egypt, India, and the Philippines in the next; and so on. All such judgments contain large